THE NEW COMMONWEALTH

THE NEW AMERICAN NATION SERIES

Edited by HENRY STEELE COMMAGER and
RICHARD B. MORRIS

* *In preparation*

THE NEW COMMONWEALTH

1877 ★ 1890

By JOHN A. GARRATY

ILLUSTRATED

HARPER TORCHBOOKS
Harper & Row, Publishers
New York, Hagerstown, San Francisco, London

First HARPER TORCHBOOK edition published 1968 by Harper & Row, Publishers,
Incorporated, New York, N.Y. 10022.

Library of Congress Catalog Card Number: 68-28198.

87 88 89 90   20 19 18 17 16 15 14

Contents

Illustrations

Editors' Introduction

THE years from the close of political Reconstruction to the nineties are, in a sense, the lost years of modern United States history, for they are almost invariably interpreted either retrospectively or prospectively—interpreted, that is, not for their own sake, but as the aftermath of Reconstruction or the prolegomena to Populism and Progressivism. It is perhaps for this reason that they have been mislabeled with such glib names as the Gilded Age, or the Brown Decades, and that their sovereignty has been uncritically conceded to Robber Barons.

It is one of John A. Garraty's signal contributions that he is prepared to accept the decades of the seventies and the eighties on their own terms and to interpret them in their own light. He does not take them to task for their failure to solve those intractable problems of Reconstruction and race relations which we have still not solved, a century later; he does not demand that they embrace the radicalisms of the nineties with which we ourselves have barely caught up; he does not present titans of industry and masters of finance as if they were villains in a morality play written especially for the edification of later generations.

Mr. Garraty interprets this volcanic era not merely as one of transition—and what era is not that?—but as one whose striking achievement was the institutionalization of those turbulent forces that were already transforming the isolated, rural, agrarian, and nativist America of the ante-bellum years into the urban, industrialized, heterogeneous world power of the twentieth century. He describes, and analyzes, the new institutions of agriculture, industry, corporations, labor unions and bureaucracy with a wealth of detail, much of it excavated from the almost inexhaustible quarries of Congressional Reports. Ready enough to concede that politics did not play a consequential role in the development of the American economy in these years, he has nevertheless done justice to the large place which parties and politics did fill in the thought and imagination of ordinary men and women, and he has made clear, too, what we are tempted to forget, that the absence of genuine choices between parties and candidates by no means moderated the fervor with which the choices were made.

For though we stress the transitional character of these years, those who lived through them did not think of themselves merely as transitional figures, nor of their time as a transmission belt from an interesting past to a challenging future, but assumed that their own interests were important and their accomplishments significant. They were confident—and this rather than the next generation was the true Age of Confidence—that they had solved many of the great problems that confronted them and were safely on the track of Progress. In their youth they had put down the great rebellion, saved the Union and freed the slave. Now, in the fullness of their powers, they wound up the troublesome business of Reconstruction and restored American politics to normalcy. In a burst of energy unprecedented in history—so they thought—they broke through frontiers everywhere, opened up a vast new West, flung railroads across a forbidding continent, dug gold and silver, mined iron ore and drilled for oil, and outstripped Britain herself in industrial production. They almost doubled the agricultural domain, brought into brief but glorious existence a cattle kingdom larger than France or Spain, welcomed millions of immigrants from every nation of Europe, confident that they could assimilate them all, built teeming cities that bid fair to outstrip the ancient towns of the Old World, doubled the wealth of the nation, and of its people. What other generation in history, they asked, had accomplished so much?

Mark Twain called it a Gilded Age, and the name caught on, and like most such names became a veneer which overlaid and hid the truth. For these decades were in fact rich not merely in material things, but in contributions to the mind and the spirit. As New England's Golden Day faded into a Genteel Tradition, a new generation infused American letters with renewed vigor: Walt Whitman, whose genius burned ever more brightly in these postwar years, Mark Twain, William Dean Howells, and Henry James, all of whom reached maturity in the eighties. This was the Golden Age, too, of American painting: Inness had reached the fullness of his genius, and younger artists like Winslow Homer, Thomas Eakins, James McNeill Whistler, and Mary Cassatt assured America a place in the history of art. In the neglected areas of science and education, this generation made even more substantial contributions, both to theory and to practice, and an era that opened with the founding of the Johns Hopkins University and closed with the creation of the University of Chicago, has some claim to a special chapter in the history of education. In the realm of social thought, too, as Professor Garraty makes clear, these years were both critical and creative. They saw the beginning of the Darwinian revolution in religion and philosophy, functionalism in economics, and pragmatism in law, the birth of sociology, and the beginnings of the welfare state in politics. Nor should we forget that along with the materialism, turbulence, and rapacity of these two decades, went an open-handed generosity and a humane concern for the fate of the dangerous and perishing, the neglected and disparaged classes of society: the Freedmen, the Indian, the immigrant, and the victims of the industrial revolution. If this was the Age of Rockefeller, Carnegie, Vanderbilt, and J. P. Morgan it was, too, the Age of Jane Addams, Lester Ward, Josiah Gibbs and Charles William Eliot.

The New Commonwealth is a volume in *The New American Nation Series,* a comprehensive cooperative survey of the history of the area now embraced in the United States from the days of discovery to our own time. Constitutional developments, cultural history, and the special histories of the South and the West as distinctive sections, will be dealt with more fully in other volumes in this series.

HENRY STEELE COMMAGER
RICHARD B. MORRIS

Preface

THIS book attempts to describe and analyze the social, economic, and political situation in the United States between the end of Reconstruction and the onset of the great depression of the 1890's. It is concerned with the structure of institutions and how they evolved. It is narrative and biographical history only in the sense that all history, to be intelligible, must respect chronology (the essence of narrative) and that institutions are created by and function through the efforts of individuals, whose particular qualities need to be considered if one is to understand the institutions.

My thesis is that between 1877 and 1890 the character of American civilization underwent a basic transformation, a change so pervasive as to justify the word "new" in my title. This change took the form of a greatly expanded reliance by individuals upon group activities. Industrialization with its accompanying effects—speedy transportation and communication, specialization, urbanization—compelled men to depend far more than in earlier times on organizations in managing their affairs, to deal with problems collectively rather than as individuals. Hence my stress on "commonwealth" in describing the new order. In the following pages I shall try to show how this process operated upon farmers, manufacturers, industrial workers, and city dwellers, and how it altered the character of politics and government. In conclusion I shall discuss its impact on social thought in America, describing how the creative minds of the era, practically without exception, reached the conclusion that laissez faire no longer provided a viable rationale in economics, in politics, or in life generally.

To argue that this transformation began and ended within the brief period 1877–90 would be absurd. From the time of the first settlements in the seventeenth century, Americans accomplished their purposes largely by working together, and the trend toward greater dependence upon organizations has continued to the present day. The choice of these dates results from the restrictions imposed by the shape of the larger co-operative scholarly undertaking of which this volume is a part. Furthermore, any periodization of the history of a complex subject implies a historical uniformity that does violence to the facts. It would be a remarkable coincidence indeed if all the evidence relevant to a proper understanding of the many facets of American development discussed in my book had originated within the same span.

However, periodization serves a useful purpose even if it necessarily oversimplifies and distorts reality. The camera's lens is not the eye, yet its sharper, less flexible focus may improve both the sight and the insight of observers. In his study *The American Mind,* Henry Steele Commager, one of the distinguished editors of the New American Nation Series, portrays the last fifteen years of the nineteenth century as a watershed in the evolution of American "thought, character, and conduct," a time during which the values and attitudes typical of the twentieth-century American were formed.[1] I believe that the underlying social, economic, and political institutions which altered American thought, character, and conduct matured between 1877 and 1890.

Many persons have helped me to formulate my ideas and clarify their expression. These include—in addition to my editors, Richard B. Morris and Henry Steele Commager—Stuart Bruchey, Joseph Dorfman, Robert M. Fogelson, William Greenleaf, Herbert G. Gutman, William E. Leuchtenburg, and David J. Rothman. I am grateful to all these friends and colleagues for their aid and, of course, absolve them from responsibility for the inadequacies of my work. I wish also to thank Ene Sirvet and Albro Martin, who helped prepare the manuscript for the printer, and Robert Cherny, who

---

[1] H. S. Commager, *The American Mind: An Interpretation of American Thought and Character Since the 1880's* (New Haven, 1950), pp. vii–viii.

patiently checked quotations and citations, and performed many other valuable services with intelligence and skill. A year's leave of absence, made possible by a fellowship granted by the John Simon Guggenheim Foundation, greatly speeded the completion of my labors.

JOHN A. GARRATY

Columbia University

CHAPTER 1

The Glitter and the Gold

THE term Gilded Age, coined by Mark Twain and Charles Dudley Warner in the novel of that name, applied originally to the early years of the General Grant era. The book was conceived on the spur of the moment at a dinner party, when the authors' wives, responding to jocular criticism of the novels they were currently reading, challenged their husbands to do better. The two men dashed it off between January and April, 1873, and published it the following December.

As Twain explained in the preface of the London edition, *The Gilded Age* sought to satirize two aspects of contemporary American life, the "all-pervading speculativeness" of the times, which pushed men to direct their energies toward material gain, and "the shameful corruption," which, Twain noted, had "lately crept into our politics." As a novel, *The Gilded Age* was at best uneven, partly because of its joint authorship, partly because of the haste with which it was written. But, particularly in the character of Colonel Beriah Sellers, he of the gilded cane, grandiose dreams, easygoing optimism, and flexible ethical standards, the book caricatured brilliantly those aspects of the American character that irritated and bemused Twain and Warner. An instantaneous popular success—40,000 copies were sold in eight weeks—it stamped its title, and thus its particular emphasis, both on the Grant era and on the whole of the following generation.[1]

[1] Charles Neider, *The Adventures of Colonel Sellers* (Garden City, 1965), pp. xii–xvii.

To emphasize either the superficiality of *The Gilded Age* or its insights, the one suggesting its inadequacy, the other its appropriateness as an evaluation of the era, would be unwise. Twain and Warner caught certain aspects of the times, yet their view was restricted and myopic, as must be any simplistic evaluation of a whole nation in a period of rapid change and growth. They were describing what, after all, was fairly obvious. Their portrayal did not differ substantially from that of many of their contemporaries. Henry Adams, far different from either Twain or Warner, characterized the typical American in words that could serve as a perfect description of Colonel Sellers: "The American thought of himself as a restless, pushing, energetic, ingenious person, always awake and trying to get ahead of his neighbors." All his energies "were oriented in one direction," the making of money. The United States, Adams said, was "a banker's Olympus." It was not so much that the American revered the almighty dollar too highly, but that he "had been deflected by its pursuit till [he] could turn in no other direction." Adams also echoed *The Gilded Age* in his attack on American politics. "The progress of evolution from President Washington to President Grant," he wrote, "was alone evidence enough to upset Darwin." Indeed, "one might search the whole list of Congress, Judiciary, and Executive during the twenty-five years 1870 to 1895, and find little but damaged reputation."[2]

Adams certainly arrived at his opinions after more deliberation than the authors of *The Gilded Age*, and as a social critic he perhaps deserves greater attention, but like them his vision was limited, his objectivity questionable. Other men evaluated their generation in different terms. To many the age was truly golden, not gilded; its materialism productive, not exploitive; its hectic, sometimes confused political style (democratic in spirit, not merely in form) an expression of the people's enthusiastic commitment to equality, compromise, and tolerance.

That the millionaire iron manufacturer Andrew Carnegie should admire the Gilded Age is not very difficult to understand, but, as his effusive volume *Triumphant Democracy* (1886) reveals, his admiration of America did not derive entirely from his appreciation of the

---

2 Henry Adams, *The Education of Henry Adams* (Boston, 1918), pp. 266, 294, 297–298, 321, 328.

money-making opportunities that it offered. He devoted much space to praising the nation's educational system, religious freedom, humane treatment of criminals, pacific attitude toward foreign powers —even its literary and artistic achievements. With patent and touching sincerity, he dedicated *Triumphant Democracy* "to the beloved Republic under whose equal laws I am made the peer of any man, although denied political equality by my native land." The reminiscences of the physicist Michael Pupin, who came to the United States in 1874, a penniless Serbian immigrant of sixteen, are full of examples of the idealism, democracy, and humanitarianism of Americans—the young farm girl who helped him learn English; her parents, who insisted on treating him as a social equal; the compassionate householders of New York City who gave him small jobs, despite the bad times, when he was down on his luck; the uneducated boiler-room fireman who "stood in awe in the presence of books," and who told him proudly: "This country, my lad, is a monument to the lives of the men of brains and character and action who made it." The historical record contains hundreds of equally favorable descriptions of American society.[3]

When twentieth-century historians began to study the era closely, however, most adopted the interpretation of Mark Twain and Henry Adams. None argued the case more persuasively than Vernon L. Parrington in the third volume of his *Main Currents in American Thought,* written in the 1920's. "Exploitation was the business of the times," Parrington wrote. "Freedom had become individualism, and individualism had become the inalienable right to preempt, to exploit, to squander." The politicians of the period made of government "a huge barbecue . . . to which all presumably were invited" except "inconspicuous persons" such as industrial workers and small farmers. Society had become "only too plainly mired . . . in a bog of bad taste," producing a "triumphant and unabashed vulgarity without its like in our history." Parrington mentioned the fictional Colonel Sellers as epitomizing certain aspects of the times, but as the "very embodiment" of the period he selected the real-life mountebank P. T. Barnum, "grow-

[3] Andrew Carnegie, *Triumphant Democracy: Or Fifty Years' March of the Republic* (New York, 1886) , Chaps. 6–8, 14, 15, 17, *passim;* Michael Pupin, *From Immigrant to Inventor* (New York, 1929) , pp. 48–56, 65, 75, 79.

ing rich on the profession of humbuggery, a vulgar greasy genius, pure brass without any gilding."[4]

Yet when the materialism, corruption, and vulgarity of the times have been described, even when the roots of these unlovely characteristics have been dug out and untangled (and this, too, is not a particularly demanding assignment), we will still not understand very much. For this interpretation implies that human nature is more variable and more mercurial than experience suggests, and that men's views of their obligations to society can be altered radically in a generation and can then revert in the next generation substantially to what they had been before. The very Americans who dominated the Gilded Age had endured a bloody Civil War rather than abandon their image of what their society should be. Many of their sons proved equally willing to subject their individual interests to the common good, first by becoming progressives, then by fighting another war, however misguidedly and fruitlessly, for equally idealistic reasons. Historians who are satisfied to examine only those aspects of post–Civil War life that dismayed men like Twain and Adams must either ignore much of what came before and after or make unsupportable assumptions about both human nature and social evolution.

It seems useful to assume that the qualities of American civilization that troubled contemporary critics were more in evidence in the 1870's and 1880's than they had been in earlier decades, and that, beginning in the 1890's and with increasing velocity in the early years of the twentieth century, these aspects of the American character again became less noticeable. The task then is to explain the shifts in emphasis and to call attention to other facets of the history of those times which throw light on the continuity, rather than the aberrations, of American development.

First, however, the qualities which gave the age its unsavory reputation require elaboration. Callous selfishness characterized the treatment afforded most minority groups. The Indians, for example, ruthlessly exploited at every stage in American history, were destroyed as a people during these years, broken in spirit, culturally

4 V. L. Parrington, *Main Currents in American Thought* (3 vols., New York, 1927–30), III, 10–23.

emasculated, finally herded onto sterile reservations. The United States government repeatedly broke solemn treaties in order to make Indian lands available to miners and farmers, while greedy placemen in the Indian Bureau systematically cheated the tribes of the supplies and subsidies due them under these treaties. In 1881 Secretary of the Interior Carl Schurz aptly dubbed these bureaucrats, who were nominally under his control, "sharks," but neither he nor his successors were able to stop their depredations. General William Tecumseh Sherman, commander of American troops in the Indian country, claimed that but for political pressures he and his men could settle Indian troubles "in an hour." Sherman and other soldiers, such as General Philip Sheridan, expressed a good deal of sympathy for the tribesmen along with genuine admiration of their fighting abilities. Nevertheless, they destroyed them heartlessly. "We must act with vindictive earnestness against the Sioux," Sherman declared, "even to their extermination, men, women, and children."[5]

The welfare of the Indians was, however, more ignored than consciously undermined; the crushing of the native culture was in large part unintentional. No one was responsible for the heavy toll taken by smallpox and other "white men's" diseases. White hunters butchered countless millions of buffalo, mainstay of the economy of the plains tribes, simply for sport, because of the fad that developed in the 1870's for buffalo robes, and because the flesh of these great beasts provided cheap and handy nourishment for the gangs of construction workers employed in building the transcontinental railroads. Governmental inertia, inefficiency, and indifference rather than deliberate greed and aggression destroyed the Indians, but this did not alter the result.[6]

The fate of Negroes in the Gilded Age was almost equally unfortunate. Their limited political and social gains of the Reconstruction period were steadily eroded away. In the South, after the last

---

[5] L. D. White, *The Republican Era: 1865–1901* (New York, 1958), p. 180; H. E. Fritz, *The Movement for Indian Assimilation, 1860–1890* (Philadelphia, 1963), pp. 18–33, 124–127; E. B. Andrews, *The History of the Last Quarter-Century in the United States* (New York, 1896), I, 171; R. G. Athearn, *William T. Sherman and the Settlement of the West* (Norman, Okla., 1956), p. 99.

[6] Wayne Gard, *The Chisholm Trail* (Norman, Okla., 1954), p. 233; E. S. Osgood, *The Day of the Cattleman* (Chicago, 1957), p. 147.

federal restraints were removed by President Hayes in 1877, Negroes were not legally deprived of the right to vote, but they were either intimidated into voting the way the dominant whites desired or kept from the polls by terrorism, trickery, and fraud. What C. Vann Woodward has called "the Negro's psychological and economic dependence upon the white man" reduced him to the status of a political pawn.

In the nation as a whole, Negro rights were repeatedly restricted by the Supreme Court, most lamentably in the Civil Rights Cases (1883), which, by declaring the Civil Rights Act of 1875 unconstitutional, enabled restaurants, hotels, theaters, and other places of public accommodation to bar or segregate members of the race, and in *Plessy* v. *Ferguson* (1896), which established the notorious "separate but equal" doctrine, legalizing segregation on railroads and in schools and other public facilities. "If one race be inferior to the other socially," Justice Henry B. Brown declared in the *Plessy* case, "the Constitution of the United States cannot put them upon the same plane." The general contempt of Negroes during this period is reflected in the treatment of racial questions in the nation's leading newspapers and magazines. The most respected "organs of opinion" repeatedly applauded restrictive and discriminatory legislation, and held the poor Negro up to ridicule and scorn, cruelly stereotyping him as "lazy, improvident, child-like, irresponsible, chicken-stealing, crap-shooting, policy-playing, razor-toting, immoral and criminal."[7]

Other minority groups fared little better. Mexicans who labored in the grazing areas of the West were typically referred to as "dirty, greasy . . . with unintelligible jargon," and scorned for their easygoing ways and "indifference" to material values. They found it difficult to rise above the status of common hands.[8] The Chinese who came to the Far West to find work in the mines and on railroad construction crews added a mere trickle in the stream of immigrants

---

[7] C. V. Woodward, *Origins of the New South: 1877–1914* (Baton Rouge, 1951), pp. 55–58; T. D. Clark and A. D. Kirwan, *The South Since Appomatox: A Century of Regional Change* (New York, 1967), pp. 62–63; U.S. *v.* Singleton, etc., 109 U.S. 3; Plessy *v.* Ferguson, 163 U.S. 537; R. W. Logan, *The Negro in American Life and Thought: The Nadir, 1877–1901* (New York, 1954), pp. 159–190, 239–274.

[8] Gard, *Chisholm Trail*, pp. 163, 187; Lewis Atherton, *The Cattle Kings* (Bloomington, Ill., 1962), p. 123.

entering the country. They were first discriminated against and exploited; then, when their numbers suddenly increased in 1882, Congress cut off the flow completely with the Chinese Exclusion Act. Even after the passage of this law, local feeling in many far-western cities flared repeatedly against what one newspaper in Washington Territory variously characterized as "the treacherous almond-eyed sons of Confucius," "those yellow rascals," and "rat-eating Chinamen." In Seattle, for example, during the winter of 1885–86, mobs attacked Chinese residents, wrecked their homes, and unceremoniously "deported" several hundred of them to San Francisco. When leaders of the rioters were brought to trial, juries promptly acquitted them.[9]

No important federal restrictions were placed on other immigrants, but, beginning in the late eighties, several states barred noncitizens from employment on public-works projects. That workingmen and even many employers attacked "cheap" and "unstable" foreign-born labor as antithetical to their interests was understandable, if selfish; but especially during bad times, large numbers of citizens exhibited a hysterical xenophobia, denouncing foreigners, Catholics, and other uninfluential minorities on totally irrational grounds. The tendency, clearly, was to make scapegoats of the strange, the weak, and the dissatisfied whenever the social fabric of the country threatened, under the pressure of rapid industrialization and urbanization, to weaken or give way.[10]

---

[9] Gunther Barth, *Bitter Strength: A History of the Chinese in the United States, 1850–1870* (Cambridge, 1964), pp. 131–134, 143–144, 155–156; John Higham, *Strangers in the Land: Patterns of American Nativism, 1860–1925* (New Brunswick, 1955), p. 25; Oscar Lewis, *The Big Four* (New York, 1938), pp. 70–75; J. D. Hill, "The Early Mining Camp in American Life," *Pacific Historical Review*, I (1932), 298; W. J. Trimble, *The Mining Advance into the Inland Empire* (Madison, Wis., 1914), pp. 145–146; J. A. Karlin, "The Anti-Chinese Outbreaks in Seattle, 1885–1886," *Pacific Northwest Quarterly*, XXXIX (1948), 103–129.

[10] Higham, *Strangers in the Land*, pp. 35–63. This aspect of the era can be observed, for example, in advertising copy designed to appeal to the middle-class majority. An expert on "trade cards," small color lithographs distributed by producers of consumer goods and avidly collected by late-nineteenth-century Americans, writes: "The public that the typical trade card aimed at was middle class, with . . . middle-class prejudices. . . . [In the illustrations] 'foreigners' . . . were thought of as legitimate targets for ridicule, not necessarily bad-tempered but often unkind just the same. The German was fat and stupid, and would never learn to talk without an absurd accent; the Chinese were all laundrymen

The exploitation of human beings was paralleled by the exploitation of the natural resources of the nation. Of course, earlier generations of Americans had tended to gobble up these resources as though they were inexhaustible. The immensity of the supply in comparison with the number of the exploiters explains, if it does not justify, the general attitude. But after the Civil War the pace at which the resources were expropriated increased, despite the fact that the limits of the supply were becoming ever more apparent. Government policies permitted, even encouraged, heedless waste and private gain at the expense of the national interest.

The nation's most valuable asset was its unoccupied lands. In the early days of the republic, the sale of public land had provided essential income for the government; but as other sources of revenue became more readily available, Congress had evolved a land policy aimed primarily at encouraging the settlement and development of new areas. While the selling of land at public auction continued, the federal government granted large tracts to the states and to corporations in support of education and internal improvements. It also made it easier for poor settlers to obtain homesteads without large outlays of cash. Besides reducing the minimum cost of land, it allowed pioneers to buy farms without competing with speculators in the open market, and to postpone paying for their lands until they had established themselves. Finally, in 1862, Congress passed the Homestead Act, which authorized the granting of 160 acres free to settlers who would live on and cultivate the land for five years.[11]

The Homestead Act implied a fundamental change, not merely a further liberalization, of federal land policy. As Paul W. Gates has shown, it was "incongruous" with the system of selling land to individuals, and also with the policy of granting land to the states

---

who had barely missed Mongolian idiocy; the Irish were ever ready for a shillelagh free-for-all. As for the Negro, he was a home-grown alien who was amusingly inferior but always good natured." W. G. McLoughlin, "Trade Cards," *American Heritage*, XVIII, No. 2 (February, 1967), 48–63, esp. 62. In discussing the popularity of Currier and Ives prints, Russell Lynes makes the same point: "Irishmen and Negroes are the butts of most of the jokes in the comic prints." *The Tastemakers* (New York, 1949), p. 69.

11 P. W. Gates, *Fifty Million Acres: Conflicts Over Kansas Land Policy, 1845–1890* (Ithaca, 1954), pp. 4–5, 13; B. H. Hibbard, *A History of the Public Land Policies* (Madison, Wis., 1965), pp. 56–115, 136–170, 228–268, 347–385; R. M. Robbins, *Our Landed Heritage: The Public Domain, 1776–1936* (Lincoln, 1962), pp. 3–116, 203–211.

and to corporations to encourage the building of schools, railroads, and other public facilities, since that policy presupposed the eventual sale of the land to accomplish its objective. Obviously, if any bona fide settler could obtain free public land on the frontier, the whole basis of selling such land would collapse.

These earlier policies were not abandoned, however, and in the post–Civil War decades, the noble principle of the Homestead Act, not the materialistic principle of treating the public domain as a source of revenue, was repeatedly compromised. Of some one billion acres of available government land in 1862 (much of it mountain and desert unfit for agriculture), about half was disposed of over the remainder of the century. But only 10 or 12 per cent of this was obtained free under the Homestead Act. As late as 1890, homesteaders had perfected their claims to only about 48 million acres. The government sold roughly 100 million acres to private citizens and corporations in this period, granted (between 1862 and 1871) another 128 million acres to railroads, and gave huge additional tracts to the states, which sold most of them to the highest bidder.

The Homestead Act itself had serious inadequacies. Few poor men could take advantage of the law, because the cost of building a house, fencing the property, and purchasing tools and seed exceeded their means. A "commutation clause" in the act, which allowed homesteaders to purchase their claims outright for $1.25 an acre after a few months' residence, proved a powerful temptation to speculators. Much of the area opened to homesteaders was of poor quality, or far removed from available transportation, or in arid regions where 160 acres was inadequate to support a family. Homesteading was not permitted in areas adjacent to railroad lands, lest the availability of free land depress the value of the railroads' grants. In Kansas, for example, a potential homesteader of the early 1880's could file on some 10 million acres, but most of this lay in the arid western part of the state where farming was hazardous. If he was willing to *purchase* undeveloped land, however, he could obtain former Indian holdings, state-owned land, or railroad property, all suited for agriculture, at prices averaging from $1.25 to $3.50 an acre.[12]

[12] P. W. Gates, "The Homestead Law in an Incongruous Land System," *American Historical Review*, XLI (1936), 652–681; F. A. Shannon, "The Homestead Act and the Labor Surplus," *ibid.*, p. 638; F. A. Shannon, *The Farmer's Last*

Other federal policies also favored exploitation of the public domain by speculators and large commercial interests. Vast areas of Indian land ceded to the United States by treaty were sold directly to railroads and other influential private interests instead of being placed in the public domain where homesteaders might obtain a share. Allegedly useless "swamp lands" were turned over to the states, only to end up in private hands, their boggy character mysteriously having disappeared. The Desert Land Act of 1877 and the Timber and Stone Act of 1878, measures nominally designed to help small operators obtain holdings larger than 160 acres in regions where farms of that size were impractical, were so loosely drawn that speculators, cattlemen, and lumber companies could use them to engross huge tracts. These interests hired "dummy entrymen" to file claims, then transferred title to themselves.[13]

Thus materialism and corruption combined to make a mockery of the homestead ideal. Upon taking charge of the General Land Office in 1885, William A. J. Sparks found to his horror that the "public lands had been to a wide extent wasted under defective and improvident laws and through a laxity of public administration astonishing in a business sense if not culpable in recklessness of official responsibility."[14]

Ruthless and venal men seized upon the other resources of the West with similar avidity. The western mining camps were sleazy monuments to the materialism, individualism, coarseness, and immorality of the times, full of vulgar, cruel, combative, and shortsighted characters who devoted enormous energies to the pursuit of treasure, pleasure, and the main chance. Speculators, confidence men, and outright thieves flourished, while law-abiding persons, absorbed in money getting, were seldom willing to make the

---

Frontier: Agriculture, 1860–1897 (New York, 1945), pp. 51–71; Gates, Fifty Million Acres, p. 238.

[13] Gates "Homestead Law," pp. 660–661, and Fifty Million Acres, pp. 106–229; Shannon, Farmer's Last Frontier, pp. 58–62, 68–69; R. A. Billington, Westward Expansion (New York, 1960), pp. 699–700. Under the Desert Land Act, grazing land could be had for $1.25 an acre; under the Timber and Stone Act, forest land for $2.50 an acre. The former law required that the land be irrigated before final title was granted, but this provision was easily circumvented. The latter act required claimants to swear that they had not agreed in advance to transfer title, but did not prevent them from disposing of timber rights to the property.

[14] Gates, "Homestead Law," pp. 655–656.

slightest sacrifice to advance the public good. In the post–Civil War silver-mining camps at Treasure Hill, in eastern Nevada, the diggers engaged in an "indiscriminate scramble to gouge out the richest ore" and displayed great reluctance to pay taxes to support community services. Lawlessness (ranging from murder and housebreaking to cattle rustling and claim jumping) and vulgarity characterized life at Treasure Hill. "Society, properly speaking, there is none, and the community is in a wild, seething, chaotic transition state," a visitor noted.[15]

Mining districts were by their nature difficult to govern, but rough frontier conditions cannot entirely account for this state of affairs. The territorial policy of the federal government, at once arbitrary and inept, added greatly to the confusion. Most territorial officials were third-rate hacks who got their posts in payment for political debts and without regard for their ability to perform the duties required. Turnover among them was enormous; of the 428 top territorial administrators appointed between 1869 and 1890, only sixty served for more than four years. Between 1876 and 1889, Congress did not allow a single territory to become a state. It refused to permit the Westerners to govern themselves, yet failed either to adapt territorial law codes to the special needs of the mining frontier or to enforce existing law efficiently. The disgraceful conditions that existed appear even worse when compared to the orderly and circumspect character of mining camps in British Canada, where an effective government kept vice and corruption to a minimum and provided adequate security for life and property.

In the cattle country of the high plains, the average cowboy was as crude and licentious as the typical miner, although probably less avid for wealth. Many of them used their trade as a cover for cattle-rustling operations. In the seventies the cow town of Abilene,

15 Billington, *Westward Expansion,* pp. 617–634; J. D. Hill, "Early Mining Camps," *Pacific Historical Review,* I, 309–310; E. S. Pomeroy, *The Territories and the United States, 1861–1890: Studies in Colonial Administration* (Philadelphia, 1947) , pp. 52–55, 62, 106–107; H. R. Lamar, *Dakota Territory, 1861–1889: A Study of Frontier Politics* (New Haven, 1956) , pp. 17–20; R. W. Paul, *Mining Frontiers of the Far West: 1848–1880* (New York, 1963) , pp. 8, 164–168; Trimble, *Mining Advance,* pp. 139–247; W. T. Jackson, *Treasure Hill: Portrait of a Silver Mining Camp* (Tucson, 1963) , pp. 11, 60–61, 67, 69, 94, 101, 111; D. A. Smith; *Rocky Mountain Mining Camps: The Urban Frontier* (Bloomington, 1967) , pp. 80–82, 221–241.

Kansas, with its bars, gambling joints, dance halls, and 100-foot-long whorehouses, was a "seething, roaring hell" where "civilizing influences" were almost nonexistent. When the town fathers put up signs banning the carrying of arms, toughs shot them to bits contemptuously.[16]

The ranchers who employed the cowboys, many of them substantial men of affairs, although less superficially lawless and coarse, did not differ basically in their social attitudes. Most were highly individualistic and materialistic. Paying lip service to the importance of domestic peace and the civilized virtues, they seldom hesitated to break the law when it suited their interests to do so. Perhaps as much as 95 per cent of the federal land occupied by ranchers under the Desert Land Act was obtained through fraud. The Homestead Act was also abused, ranchers frequently encouraging their hands to file claims in order to sell them to their employers. At the time of his death in 1878, the Colorado cattleman John F. Iliff owned 105 small parcels of land, a total of about 15,500 acres. But by locating his holdings around strategically placed sources of water, he had engrossed a vast domain on the semiarid plains, extending over an area roughly one hundred miles by sixty. Men like Iliff viewed the territory they dominated as their private possession, and seldom hesitated to use either fraud or force to keep others off it or to protect their livestock.[17]

Stories of the ranchers' disregard for the property of others, such

16 Atherton, *Cattle Kings*, p. 107; Osgood, *Day of the Cattleman*, pp. 148–149; Gard, *Chisholm Trail*, pp. 162–179. The classic account of cow-town highjinks is J. G. McCoy, *Historic Sketches of the Cattle Trade of the West and Southwest* (1874), R. P. Bieber, ed. (Glendale, 1940), pp. 204–210. Of the "general character" of cowboys, McCoy wrote: "They are, as a class, not public spirited. . . . They are prodigal to a fault with their money when opportunity offers to gratify their appetites or passions. . . . Their consciences are fully as pliant as are those of any other section . . . nor are they any more brave, or more fond of facing death's cold pellets on an equal footing with their adversaries, than are men in general." But McCoy added: "Sanguine and speculative in temperament, impulsively generous in free sentiment, with a strong innate sense of right and wrong, with a keen sense for the ridiculous and a general intention to do that that is right and honorable in their dealings, they are, as would naturally be supposed when the manner of their life is considered, a hardy, self-reliant, free, and independent class, acknowledging no superior or master in the wide universe." *Ibid.*, pp. 212–214.

17 Atherton, *Cattle Kings*, pp. 111–112, 173; Shannon, *Farmer's Last Frontier*, p. 61; Osgood, *Day of the Cattleman*, pp. 143, 203–208.

as the fable of the widow who claimed she would as soon eat one of her children as stoop to killing her own cattle for meat, were standard jests in the range country. Frontier conditions, especially the inadequacy of local law-enforcement agencies, sometimes justified the tendency of cattlemen to take the law into their own hands, but arrogance and selfishness account for far too many instances of privately administered "justice." Even a respectable, sophisticated rancher like George W. Kendall of Texas could write a friend coolly: "Lynch law, in a new country, is better than any law formed by the wisdom of man since the Mosaic—has fewer flaws and quibbles, and metes out more even justice."[18]

This catalogue of post–Civil War selfishness and materialism could be expanded almost indefinitely. Among American businessmen, there developed in these years the "Robber Baron," an unscrupulous, greedy industrial and financial type who competed ruthlessly with his fellows, exploited his labor force callously, bilked investors, and corrupted legislators and other public officials without conscience, all the while masquerading behind a façade of unctuous respectability. Ever since 1871, when Charles Francis Adams, Jr., described the unsavory practices of Jay Gould and Cornelius Vanderbilt in their battle to control the New York Central Railroad, historians have been uncovering fresh evidence of the antisocial actions and attitudes of these piratical characters. Vanderbilt may never have actually uttered the famous remark: "Law! What do I care about the law? Hain't I got the power?" but he expressed that basic philosophy many times, and under oath. Gould's career encompassed almost every known variety of chicanery, from stock watering and industrial blackmail to bribery, market manipulation, and union busting. Even his most sympathetic biographer, in a study designed to stress his positive accomplishments, admits that the little tycoon broke his word and violated both business contracts and the law of the land whenever it served his interests to do so. Gould "possessed a cold-blooded unscrupulousness which enabled him . . . to adapt to his purposes the low state of political morals prevailing at the time."[19]

[18] Atherton, *Cattle Kings*, p. 33; H. J. Brown (ed.), *Letters from a Texas Sheep Ranch* (Urbana, 1959), p. 100.

[19] Matthew Josephson, *The Robber Barons: The Great American Capitalists, 1861–1901* (New York, 1934), pp. 195–210, *passim;* John Tipple, "The Robber

Many other supposedly respectable businessmen were only slightly less unprincipled than Gould. John D. Rockefeller of Standard Oil extracted secret rebates from railroads, sold petroleum products at a loss in local areas to ruin small competitors, engaged in industrial espionage, and paid bribes to legislators.[20] Dozens of railroad men plundered their companies by setting up dummy construction corporations to lay track at exorbitant prices; they cheated investors by issuing false prospectuses and by watering stock, blackmailed local communities by threatening to by-pass them when new lines were being built, overcharged customers by organizing pools, and corrupted legislators in a variety of ways.[21] When the inventor Thomas A. Edison got involved with bankers and businessmen in the course of his efforts to develop the electric lighting business, he became swiftly disillusioned. In 1883 he promised a plant manager a bonus for achieving a certain degree of efficiency. But the directors of the company would not authorize the expenditure because Edison had neglected to obtain their approval in advance. Edison felt obliged to pay the money—$10,000—out of his own pocket. "They said they 'were sorry'—that is, 'Wall Street sorry,' " he noted. "This shows what a nice, genial, generous lot of people they have over in Wall Street." After a few more years of experience with businessmen, the inventor concluded sadly that taking out a patent was "simply an invitation to a lawsuit." Yet such was the moral climate of the times that Edison himself engaged in attempts to get around the patents of others, and even in the bribing of legislators, promising certain New Jersey representatives

Baron in the Gilded Age," in H. W. Morgan (ed.), *The Gilded Age: A Reappraisal* (Syracuse, 1963), p. 36; Julius Grodinsky, *Jay Gould: His Business Career, 1867–1892* (Philadelphia, 1957), pp. 595–596, *passim*.

20 Allan Nevins, *John D. Rockefeller: The Heroic Age of American Enterprise* (2 vols., New York, 1940), I, 515–516; II, 38, 87–89, 106–111; H. F. Williamson and A. R. Daum, *The American Petroleum Industry: The Age of Illumination, 1859–1899* (Evanston, 1959), pp. 426–428.

21 See, for example, James McCague, *Moguls and Iron Men: The Story of the First Transcontinental Railroad* (New York, 1964), pp. 357–360; Lewis, *Big Four*, pp. 44–45; T. C. Cochran, *Railroad Leaders: 1845–1890* (Cambridge, 1953), pp. 99–100, 112–115, 169–170, 195, *passim*; J. F. Stover, *The Railroads of the South, 1865–1900: A Study of Finance and Control* (Chapel Hill, 1955), pp. 63–98, 150–152, 222; R. E. Riegel, *The Story of the Western Railroads* (New York, 1926), *passim*.

a thousand dollars each "payable after the passing" of a law he was interested in.[22]

Other "gilded" aspects of the age, such as the political corruption (amply illustrated by what has already been said) and the ostentatious vulgarity of the new-rich tycoons, are equally easy to document. From New York to Chicago to San Francisco, from Newport, Rhode Island, to Virginia City, Nevada, tasteless ornate mansions, built without style (in some instances, apparently, without plan), dotted the urban landscape. On Nob Hill, in San Francisco, the builders of the Central Pacific Railroad led the way, Charles Crocker's four-story, $1.25-million monstrosity, "a delirium of the wood carver," challenging in ugliness Mark Hopkins' maze of towers, turrets, and gables, which spread itself out over half a city block.[23] On New York's Fifth Avenue, the railroad king William H. Vanderbilt built a $3-million brownstone, and department store magnates, steel barons, and other millionaires raised similar palaces, monuments to unvarnished materialism and in some cases to the colossal egotism of their owners, many of whom ruthlessly altered or cast aside the plans of the architects they had hired to design their mansions in order to gratify their passion for ostentatious display.[24]

The aesthetic standards of the less affluent were equally materialistic and pretentious, if perforce expressed on a more modest scale. Middle-class taste in furniture tended toward the massive and the overstuffed; rooms were cluttered with a bewildering variety of useless (and generally ugly) objects, totally unrelated one to another. "Beauty," as Lewis Mumford has said, "was defined in terms of visible possessions." In art, sentimentality and banality reigned

[22] Matthew Josephson, *Edison: A Biography* (New York, 1959), pp. 148–150, 296, 355.

[23] Lewis, *Big Four*, pp. 112, 136–137. The Hopkins dining room seated sixty; the master bedroom was finished in ebony inlaid with ivory and semiprecious gems. "The level of architecture was low in the country, [but] it touched the bottom of the abyss in the city." Lewis Mumford, *Sticks and Stones: A Study of American Architecture and Civilization* (New York, 1955), p. 109.

[24] Wayne Andrews, *Architecture, Ambition, and Americans* (New York, 1955), pp. 156–157; Lynes, *Tastemakers*, pp. 98–99, 121–131; E. C. Kirkland, *Dream and Thought in the Business Community, 1860–1900* (Ithaca, 1956), pp. 29–49; A. M. Schlesinger, *The Rise of the City* (New York, 1933), 83–84, 280. Schlesinger suggests that by the late 1870's the nation "had run architecturally amuck."

supreme, as seen, for example, in the enormous popularity of Currier and Ives prints and the sculptures of John Rogers, whose little plaster "groups" adorned a hundred thousand American parlors. The Currier and Ives company issued over 6,800 prints covering an enormous variety of subjects, all pictorially literal, but utterly unrealistic as social commentary. Noble Indians, happy children, sturdy, self-reliant farmers, rakish clipper ships, clean, brightly painted trains, cute puppies and kittens, prize fighters posing "like undressed statesmen." As the proprietors boasted, they provided "subjects best adapted to suit the popular taste, and to meet the wants of all sections."[25]

The public's literary tastes were in the main equally crude. Middle-class readers devoured the sugary, moralistic romances of Mary J. Holmes, Mrs. E. D. E. N. Southworth, and other "scribbling women" in wholesale lots, while the masses reveled in the blood-and-thunder dime novels ground out for publishers like Erastus Beadle by a horde of hacks, in the lurid sensationalism of the *Police Gazette*, and in the rags-to-riches tales of Horatio Alger, monuments to unalloyed materialism. The popular worship of worldly success is also observable in the rash of literature explaining how to get rich, ranging from Congressman James A. Garfield's pamphlet, *Elements of Success* (1869), and the Reverend Russell Conwell's *Acres of Diamonds,* a lecture he delivered more than 6,000 times, to more substantial treatises, such as P. T. Barnum's *The Art of Money-Getting* (1882). "If any youth of the Gilded Age failed to achieve a position of wealth and eminence," a modern historian has remarked, "it was not for lack of printed advice."[26]

This, then, is the conventional picture of post–Civil War America. Plausible explanations of its gilded character are not difficult to come by. The tremendous economic opportunities generated by

[25] Lewis Mumford, *The Brown Decades: A Study of the Arts in America, 1865–1895* (New York, 1955), p. 110; Lynes, *Tastemakers,* pp. 68–71; Morton Cronin, "Currier and Ives: A Content Analysis," *American Quarterly,* IV (1952), 317–330.
[26] F. L. Mott, *Golden Multitudes: The Story of Best Sellers in the United States* (New York, 1947), pp. 136–151, 158–159; J. D. Hart, *The Popular Book: A History of America's Literary Taste* (New York, 1950), pp. 153–156, 160–162; Dee Brown, *The Year of the Century: 1876* (New York, 1966), pp. 42–72; I. G. Wyllie, *The Self-Made Man in America: The Myth of Rags to Riches* (New Brunswick, 1954), pp. 116–132.

new industrial technology and the undeveloped resources of the Great West, the argument runs, encouraged materialism and made it easy to assume that the available wealth of the nation was so enormous that no degree of selfish individual accumulation could deprive other deserving persons, or society as a whole, of anything essential. The successful "achievers" who gathered this bonanza, like the *nouveaux riches* of every age, lacked educated tastes and a tradition of *noblesse oblige,* hence their "triumphant and unabashed vulgarity" and their lack of any sense of social responsibility.

The breakdown of idealism following the Civil War offers a further insight into the times. The failure of that great conflict, after the sacrifice of so much blood and treasure, to solve the problems of sectionalism and race relations produced a general disillusionment which led men to mistrust their better instincts, reject idealism, live for present profit and personal advantage alone. To wealth and cynicism add the bewildering effects of the increasing size, complexity, and impersonality of American civilization—the growth of large cities, of big industrial organizations, of other massive institutions that, by reducing men to anonymous cyphers, weakened the individual's sense of identity with his fellows, and thus his sense of any obligation to deal with them fairly according to the golden rule.

Ideas are sometimes mere expressions of a prevailing point of view, sometimes its cause. In either case the intellectual climate of the times also helps explain the so-called Gilded Age. The laissez-faire doctrines of Adam Smith and the classical economists, devised to meet the needs of a simpler economy and a less complicated form of government than those prevailing in the post–Civil War United States, nevertheless retained a persistent influence, one that appeared to justify competitive individualism. Charles Darwin's new theory of the evolution of species, with its stress on struggle and the destruction of the weak, offered, when applied to human society, an additional temptation for successful individuals to believe that their own achievements were both inevitable and socially desirable, and to harden their hearts against the "unfit" who failed to "survive" in the Darwinian world of tooth and claw.[27]

[27] Morgan, *Gilded Age,* pp. 1–4; Parrington, *Main Currents,* III, 7–43, 48–50; C. A. and M. R. Beard, *The Rise of American Civilization* (2 vols., New York,

To describe the conditions which brought out the selfish, vulgar, and materialistic elements in Americans after the Civil War is not to prove, however, that their behavior cannot be explained on other grounds, or that the conditions were uniquely American, or that all Americans allowed these qualities to dominate their lives. Criticism of the Indian policy of the United States, for example, tends to ignore the difficulties that stood in the way of attempts to reconcile white and Indian interests. The enormous impact of the white man's civilization on the Stone Age culture of the tribes was little understood by contemporaries. In earlier times, direct confrontations between the two civilizations were seldom decisive—the Indians could fall back and preserve their cultural integrity farther west.[28] By the 1870's this was no longer possible, yet it is hard to imagine how, given the inadequacy of anthropological knowledge, an intelligent solution to the Indian problem could have been devised.

Important American anthropologists, most notably Lewis Henry Morgan, whose influential *Ancient Society* was published in 1877, insisted that all cultures evolved through stages—from savagery to barbarism to "civilization." They therefore believed in solving the "Indian problem" by converting the tribesmen to white ways. Another careful scientist, Major John Wesley Powell, an intelligent and reform-minded man thoroughly familiar with Indian culture, proposed (1874) that the Indians be encouraged to give up their nomadic existence, settle down as farmers, learn English, and adopt the values of the white man. "A reservation should be a school of industry," he argued. "There is no good reason why the Indians should remain Indians," Richard Henry Pratt, founder of the well-known Carlisle Indian School, explained. "I have little hope of much success in elevating the Indians, until the Indian is made an

---

1941), II, 383-399; Josephson, *Robber Barons*, pp. 28-31, and *The Politicos: 1865-1896* (New York, 1938), pp. 78-140; R. H. Wiebe, *The Search for Order: 1877-1920* (New York, 1967), pp. xiii-xiv, 11-43; G. W. Frederickson, *The Inner Civil War: Northern Intellectuals and the Crisis of the Union* (New York, 1965), pp. 183-198; Richard Hofstadter, *Social Darwinism in American Thought: 1860-1915* (Philadelphia, 1945), pp. 30-32.

28 Some tribes, of course, were shattered by contact with the Europeans even in colonial times, but many survived by retreating, and others had relatively few contacts with white men before 1865.

individual, and worked upon as such, with a view toward incorporating him on our side."

Influenced by the weight of such arguments, some of the most humane men of the era advocated policies that involved destruction of the Indians' ways. President Julius H. Seelye of Amherst College, a man widely praised for his liberality and magnanimity, demanded in 1880 that the government base its Indian policy on the principles of honesty, kindness, and patience. Yet he also said: "It will be admitted now on every hand that the only solution of the Indian problem involves the entire change of these people from a savage to a civilized life," and this "solution" was little better suited to the needs and interests of the tribes than that advocated by the tough frontier characters who claimed that the only good Indian was a dead one.[29]

Focusing upon the cruelties and selfishness of Indian policy also obscures the efforts to improve the treatment of the tribes made by thousands of citizens—Catholic and Protestant missionaries; officials of the Indian Bureau, such as George W. Manypenny, author of *Our Indian Wards* (1880), and Alfred B. Meacham, founder of the magazine *Council Fire;* scientists such as Major Powell and the Yale paleontologist Othniel C. Marsh; individual reformers, including such well-known figures as Wendell Phillips, Harriet Beecher Stowe, and Helen Hunt Jackson, whose criticism of government policy, *A Century of Dishonor* (1881), created a sensation. The appearance of organizations like the Women's National Indian Association (1879), the Indian Rights Association (1882), and the National Indian Defense Association (1885), and the foundation of many privately and publicly supported schools for Indians, reflect the genuine and increasing desire of many persons to deal fairly with the Indian problem. More might have been accomplished if these reformers had not taken, in the main, an unrealistically romantic view of the Indians, which was a further product of the general ignorance of anthropology. As men who had dealt with the Indians

---

[29] L. A. White (ed.), *Lewis Henry Morgan: The Indian Journals, 1859–62* (Ann Arbor, 1959), pp. 10–11; W. H. Goetzmann, *Exploration and Empire* (New York, 1966), pp. 570–571; W. G. Sumner, "The Indians in 1887," *Forum*, III (1887), 262; Fritz, *Assimilation Movement*, p. 19; "Julius Hawley Seelye," *Dictionary of American Biography*, XVI, pp. 555–556; H. H. Jackson, *A Century of Dishonor* (London, 1881), pp. 2–3.

first hand repeatedly pointed out, the noble savage described by the reformers had never existed. And as Indian culture crumbled under the impact of white civilization, the differences between the reformers' picture of the tribesmen and reality increased steadily.[30]

Although the cruel treatment afforded the Chinese in the Far West was partly based on racial prejudice, it, too, was not entirely mean and irrational. Most of the Chinese were "sojourners" rather than immigrants; bound to Chinese masters by contracts of indenture and mysterious sociocultural influences, they had no intention of remaining in America or of making any effort to adjust to the way of life of the majority. Their motive was to save money in order to return to China; they imported more than half their food and clothing from the old country, and sent back about half the money they earned. Apparently by choice, they lived in densely packed hovels, creating hazards of fire and disease, and their addiction to opium and to gambling caused social problems. So did the fact that over 90 per cent of them were men; nearly all the Chinese women who came to America were prostitutes, "purchased, kidnapped, or lured by panderers in China, brought to America under contract, and sold to Chinese men, either as concubines or for professional prostitution."

A San Franciscan explained the Chinese problem this way to a congressional committee: "The burden of our accusation against them is that they came in conflict with our labor interests; that they can never assimilate with us . . . that their civilization is demoralizing and degrading to our people . . . and that an alien, degraded labor class, without desire of citizenship, without education, and without interest in the country it inhabits, is an element both demoralizing and dangerous to the community within which it exists." While the behavior of the Chinese in the United States never justified the violent attacks that were made upon them, the

---

30 Fritz, *Assimilation Movement,* pp. 198–211; P. J. Rahill, *The Catholic Indian Missions and Grant's Peace Policy: 1870–1884* (Washington, 1953), *passim;* Charles Schuchert and C. M. Le Vene, *Othniel C. Marsh: Pioneer in Paleontology* (New Haven, 1940), pp. 143–166; Goetzmann, *Exploration and Empire,* pp. 428–429; L. B. Priest, *Uncle Sam's Stepchildren: The Reformation of United States Indian Policy, 1865–1887* (New Brunswick, 1942), pp. 58–65, 81–86, 137–144, 148–154. For criticism of the sentimental defenders of the Indians, see Herman Hagedorn (ed.), *The Works of Theodore Roosevelt* (20 vols., New York, 1926), VIII, pp. 81–82, and Allan Nevins, "Helen Hunt Jackson: Sentimentalist vs. Realist," *American Scholar,* X (1941), 276–284.

desire to stop further immigration was certainly understandable. It is true that many of the problems created by Chinese immigration did not differ fundamentally from those created by the influx of Europeans, who also worked for "substandard" wages and appeared to resist acculturation. But with the Chinese, these difficulties were so much greater in degree that they became differences in kind. It is worth noting, too, that many Americans, including many in the areas of heavy Chinese immigration, consistently opposed violence and defended the rights of the local Chinese to live as they chose.[31]

Even the shabby treatment afforded American Negroes after the end of Reconstruction was not entirely a product of prejudice and selfishness. The best-intentioned white citizen, trying to evaluate the potential of Negroes in the climate of those times, found it hard to avoid the conclusion that they were inherently inferior to Caucasians. Interpreting lack of achievement as lack of ability, confusing effect with cause, he saw in their poverty, ignorance, and degradation evidence of inherent stupidity and moral laxity. If he turned to authority for enlightenment, his conclusions were only reinforced. The superficial knowledge of African history available to an anthropologically naïve generation suggested that Negroes, when left to their own devices, would remain in a state of savagery. Highly regarded "scientific experts" insisted that the Negro and Caucasian races were of separate origin, the former inferior in native ability to the latter. Professor Louis Agassiz of Harvard, for example, although opposed to slavery and to legal discriminations against the freed Negroes, stated flatly that the race was "indolent" and "submissive" and "imitative" by nature. He considered it "mock philanthropy" to treat them as equal to whites. Agassiz was the leading American critic of Darwin's theory of evolution, but in the 1870's and 1880's many Darwinians also believed that the Negroes were an inferior race.[32]

31 Barth, *Bitter Strength,* pp. 1-8, 55-68, 109, 126-127, 137, *passim;* E. C. Sandmeyer, *The Anti-Chinese Movement in California* (Urbana, 1939), pp. 12-39, 109; Karlin, "Anti-Chinese Outbreaks," pp. 103-129.

32 J. M. McPherson, *The Struggle for Equality: Abolitionists and the Negro in the Civil War and Reconstruction* (Princeton, 1964), pp. 134-153; J. M. McPherson, *The Negro's Civil War* (New York, 1965), pp. 99, 100-110; Edward Lurie, *Louis Agassiz: A Life in Science* (Chicago, 1960), pp. 256-262; W. R. Stanton, *The Leopard's Spots: Scientific Attitudes toward Race in America, 1815-1859* (Chicago, 1960), *passim;* Hofstadter, *Social Darwinism,* pp. 147-148.

Defenders of the Negro could point to outstanding examples of talented Negroes, and they claimed (correctly of course) that environmental conditions were responsible for the average Negro's failure to advance himself economically and culturally. But theirs was essentially an argument of the heart rather than of reason; they did not have the psychological and sociological tools to prove their case.

Furthermore, many Americans made substantial efforts to help Negroes improve their lot in this period. The American Missionary Association, which founded a number of important educational institutions for Negroes during the 1860's, including the Hampton Institute, Howard University, and Fisk University, spent large sums over the following decades. The Methodist Church contributed some $2 million to Negro education between the end of the war and the late eighties through its Freedmen's Aid Society. Charitable foundations, most notably the Peabody Fund and the Slater Fund, were created by wealthy men interested in aiding the Negro. After 1881, Booker T. Washington was conspicuously successful in collecting money for his newly founded Tuskegee Institute in Alabama. While white philanthropy was generally dispensed to Negroes with the tacit understanding that the beneficiaries would accept segregation and other aspects of second-class citizenship (which suggests that the donors did not believe in Negro equality), its extent indicates that many persons were sensitive to the Negroes' needs and willing to do something to help them.[33]

The chaotic and materialistic character of western development can also be overstated. Federal land laws, despite their inadequacies, did foster economic growth, which was certainly in the national interest. They enabled large numbers of men of modest means to obtain farms, either free or at relatively low cost. The "incongruities" of the system may well be viewed as the result of honest compromise rather than nefarious special pleading by powerful interests. Since free land did not really provide a "safety

[33] Merle Curti and Roderick Nash, *Philanthropy in the Shaping of American Higher Education* (New Brunswick, 1965), pp. 168–176; J. H. Franklin, *From Slavery to Freedom* (New York, 1947), pp. 377–379; Clark and Kirwan, *South Since Appomatox*, pp. 170–171, 189–190.

valve" for the truly poor because of the other costs of establishing a farm, the Homestead Act itself would have worked to the advantage of the relatively well-off segment of the population if applied to all public land. It would also, of course, have favored firstcomers, since the land varied enormously in fertility, workability, and accessibility. It should also be noted that both speculative land companies and land-grant railroads performed useful functions in return for the profits they made by selling property. They advertised their holdings, surveyed and subdivided them, and established transportation facilities and community services for their customers.

Furthermore, especially on the semiarid high plains, the engrossment of large areas by extralegal means reflected the inability of men quickly to adjust their institutions to radically different conditions at least as much as it reflected greed and dishonesty. Under existing law it was impossible for cattlemen to acquire title to sufficient land to graze their herds, nor could they lease grazing land from the government. Hence their tendency to employ extralegal tactics, such as the purchase of strategic water holes and the fencing of the public domain, to control land they did not own. Yet Major Powell's brilliant *Report on the Arid Regions of the United States* (1879), which suggested that the rigid system of rectangular survey and sale of government land in small units be abandoned, and that grazing land be made available to stockmen in 2,560-acre units, with the owners encouraged to develop and use scarce water sources co-operatively, raised a storm of opposition.

Powell's critics, however, were not the representatives of selfish entrenched interests. Most, indeed, were liberal and democratic in point of view. It was not the big cattlemen who fought reform (although many of them had their doubts about the Powell *Report*), but the agriculturally oriented small settler. The plan "would place large tracts . . . under the control of monopolists and speculators," the Montana legislature warned Congress. A federal commission, investigating the situation, came to the conclusion that "a system which . . . permits the aggregation of very large tracts of land into the ownership of a single person is unjust," and Congress, therefore, refused to act. The decision was shortsighted but well-intentioned. The real difficulty stemmed not from the selfishness of the cattlemen or the unwillingness of the government to discharge its obligations but from the lack of an adequate grasp of the kind of land laws that were needed in the arid West.[34]

To focus too sharply upon the disorganization and immorality of western society also distorts reality and thus limits understanding. Most cattlemen and miners probably preferred law and order to violence and vigilante justice. In the worst of the mining camps and cow towns there was always a substantial and growing element bent on curbing lawlessness and improving the moral tone of life. Excessive gambling, drunkenness, and violence marked only the early stages in the evolution of most of these communities. The history of nearly every western settlement is, in part, a chronicle of decent men and women struggling against odds to bring schools, churches, and the other amenities of civilized life to their towns. Few miners or cowboys were gunmen; the number of dedicated troublemakers among them was probably no larger than in most groups of similar size. The tendency of these men to engage in wild sprees can be explained in large measure by the loneliness and drudgery of their work, which led them to cut loose from time to time. In 1914 the historian William J. Trimble reached a judgment on this subject that no later student has improved upon:

In truth, for the observer wishing to be impartial, a great deal depends upon one's point of view. If he undertakes to apply . . . the conventional standards of conduct which ruled in . . . the East, he will find sufficient transgressions to shock him. . . . On the other hand, the impartial student . . . will remember that most of the . . . populace were young men, far from the restraints of home . . . that their excesses were often reactions against the monotony of their toil; and that many of them earned large sums of money quickly and, feeling certain that they could replace them easily . . . spend their treasure prodigally. Above all, he who seeks a just estimate . . . will make general statements cautiously.[35]

34 Shannon, "Labor Surplus," pp. 637–651; D. C. North, *Growth and Welfare in the American Past* (Englewood Cliffs, N.J., 1966), pp. 131–136; Goetzmann, *Exploration and Empire*, pp. 572–575; Osgood, *Day of the Cattleman*, pp. 196–199, 215.

35 Atherton, *Cattle Kings*, pp. 43, 46, 78–101; McCoy, *Sketches*, pp. 61–63; Jackson, *Treasure Hill*, pp. 77–80, 86–91; J. B. Frantz and J. E. Choate, Jr., *The American Cowboy: The Myth & the Reality* (Norman, Okla., 1955), pp. 88–94; Trimble, *Mining Advance*, pp. 153–154, 288; Smith, *Rocky Mountain Mining Camps, passim*.

A similar set of qualifications needs to be made to the generalization that post-Civil War American businessmen were overly selfish and materialistic. Their positive accomplishments—the construction of great industrial and financial enterprises and the development of efficient new forms of business organization—of course prove only that they were intelligent, energetic, and creative, characteristics also possessed by many outright rogues. The line of reasoning first advanced by the historian Allan Nevins that the "Robber Barons" should be accounted public benefactors, because without their success in developing the industrial might of the nation in the late nineteenth century the United States would have lost the two great wars of the twentieth century,[36] is a reflection on their historical significance, but not a judgment about their characters or motives.

It may seem absurd to suggest that men who accumulated fortunes ranging into the hundreds of millions of dollars were not especially materialistic, yet many of the tycoons insisted that this was the case. "I know of nothing more despicable and pathetic than a man who devotes all the waking hours of the day to making money for money's sake," John D. Rockefeller, the most successful of them all, claimed in his *Random Reminiscences.* "What people most seek cannot be bought with money." Rockefeller admitted that if he had his life to live over again he would not have followed a different course, but the reason, he insisted, was "for the association with interesting and quick-minded men," not for money alone. Andrew Carnegie took a similar position, boasting of the fact that many of his "clever partners" in the steel business had been his friends since boyhood, and stressing the joy he found in "manufacturing something and giving employment to many men." Even Jay Gould spoke disparagingly of "the mere making of money" and claimed that his purpose was "more to show that I could make a combination and make it a success."[37] It would be foolish to take

[36] Allan Nevins, "Should American History Be Rewritten?" *Saturday Review,* XXXVII, No. 2 (February 6, 1954), 7–9, 47–49.

[37] J. D. Rockefeller, *Random Reminiscences of Men and Events* (New York, 1909), pp. 20, 140; Andrew Carnegie, *Autobiography* (Boston, 1920), pp. 41–44; E. C. Kirkland (ed.), *Andrew Carnegie, The Gospel of Wealth and Other Timely Essays* (Cambridge, Mass., 1962), pp. 12–13; Josephson, *Robber Barons,* p. 194.

such statements *too* seriously, but equally foolish to discount them entirely.

The large gifts of businessmen to religious and charitable organizations and to colleges, libraries, and other educational institutions also suggest that they were not wholly selfish and materialistic. Rockefeller and Carnegie were no doubt outstanding in this respect,[38] but they were far from being unique. In the area of higher education alone, rich businessmen contributed money on an unprecedented scale. The names of many important universities created in this period—Cornell, Stanford, Johns Hopkins, Clark, Vanderbilt, Duke, Tulane—reflect the extent to which men of wealth were concerned with education and learning. Some founded colleges merely to perpetuate these names, or for some other noncharitable motive. The testy Commodore Vanderbilt gave half a million to Central University, an impoverished Methodist seminary, chiefly to please his beautiful young second wife, and another gift of equal size when the grateful trustees renamed the school Vanderbilt. Others contributed out of dissatisfaction with the then-current state of higher education, which they considered effete and impractical. Many, however, were motivated by pure public spirit. "I have about half a million dollars more than my family will need," Ezra Cornell, one of the founders of the Western Union Telegraph Company, told his friend Andrew D. White. "What is the best thing I can do with it for the State?"[39]

All the benefactors of colleges and universities were not multimillionaires. Columbia University increased its endowment from a mere $93,000 in 1865 to over $1.2 million in 1900 as a result of many separate gifts. When the fledgling Johns Hopkins University was stricken by a shortage of funds in the late eighties because the Baltimore and Ohio Railroad, in which most of its endowment was

[38] When the future oil king was still in his teens, he was already giving a tenth of his income to charity. "He did not wait to become rich before he became generous," his biographer explains. Allan Nevins, *Study in Power: John D. Rockefeller, Industrialist and Philanthropist* (2 vols., New York, 1953), I, pp. 16–18.

[39] Curti and Nash, *Philanthropy in Higher Education*, pp. 111, 124; Kirkland, *Dream and Thought*, pp. 85–88, and *Men, Cities, and Transportation: A Study in New England History, 1820–1900* (Cambridge, Mass., 1948), II, pp. 471–472; Philip Dorf, *The Builder: A Biography of Ezra Cornell* (New York, 1952), p. 285.

invested, passed a series of dividends, local businessmen in Baltimore quickly raised over $108,000 to see it through the crisis. Andrew Carnegie's famous "Gospel of Wealth" argument, that the rich man should devote the bulk of his resources to socially useful projects, "thus becoming the mere agent and trustee for his poorer brethren, bringing to their service his superior wisdom, experience, and ability to administer, doing for them better than they would or could do for themselves," seems insufferably patronizing to modern readers, but it was not a selfish doctrine.[40]

Nor were all industrialists and financiers antisocial individualists in their business affairs. Most of them undoubtedly opposed regulatory legislation. But in many cases their opposition derived from genuine misgivings both about the efficiency and honesty of government and about the availability of the techniques and knowledge necessary to manipulate the economy intelligently. Since a majority of the so-called "new" economists, who by the eighties were mounting sharp attacks on the theory of laissez faire, did not think their science had yet achieved enough certainty to justify large-scale public regulation, it is not surprising that businessmen felt as they did. At least in part, their argument that the economy was controlled by immutable natural laws reflected their fears and uncertainties; unable to check or even to predict the fluctuations of the business cycle, they found it reassuring to believe that some impersonal force like the law of supply and demand made regulation impossible. Moreover, this conviction that the economy was self-adjusting and that its mainspring was free competition was shared by a majority of Americans, without regard for occupation or socioeconomic status. In addition, many businessmen actively encouraged efforts to find ways of directing the economy intelligently in the public interest, through such devices as the establishment of regulatory commissions made up of nonpartisan experts. When Richard T. Ely, the most aggressive academic critic of laissez faire, founded the American Economic Association in 1885, he was able to persuade a number of wealthy businessmen to purchase life memberships in this organization, which was dedicated to the proposi-

---

[40] Curti and Nash, *Philanthropy in Higher Education*, p. 111, 118; Kirkland, *Dream and Thought*, pp. 83–84, 96, 103–113; Hugh Hawkins, *Pioneer: A History of the Johns Hopkins University, 1874–1889* (Ithaca, 1960), pp. 317–321; Andrew Carnegie, "Wealth," *North American Review*, CXLVIII (1889), 653–664.

tion that government regulation of the economy was one of the "indispensable conditions of human progress."[41]

It would be unwise to carry the defense of late-nineteenth-century entrepreneurs too far. Clearly, they were tough, selfish, aggressive characters in the main, committed by the very nature of their calling to making as much money as possible. The term Robber Baron was invented not by liberal twentieth-century historians but by contemporary observers; as early as 1869 the editor E. L. Godkin (no radical) called Cornelius Vanderbilt of the New York Central "a lineal successor of the medieval baron that we read about, who . . . had the heart and hand to levy contributions on all who passed his way." In a sense, however, the businessmen, convenient symbols of corporate power, were scapegoats rather than real villains. Critics blamed them for all the woes and social failings that industrialization and industrial giantism were unloading upon an unprepared nation with astounding swiftness.[42]

A good deal may also be said in defense of the intellectual and aesthetic standards of the era. It had its full share of P. T. Barnums, bathetic lady novelists, posturing ham actors, vacuous prophets, and materialistic cracker-barrel philosophers, yet no more, proportionately, than earlier or later periods. A recent student of its popular culture has remarked on the "degree of continuity between the Gilded Age and the pre-Civil War years" (Barnum, Mrs. E. D. E. N. Southworth, the Beadle dime novel, and the Currier and Ives print were all immensely popular before 1860), and has argued that tastes in the 1880's were no worse than in the 1960's. This was the age of the trashy adventure story, the sentimental romance, and the burlesque, of Horatio Alger and *Ben Hur* and *East Lynne;* but a large audience also existed for serious literature and music, for Shakespeare—indeed, for all the highest forms of art. It is true that some of the nation's finest creative talents, the writer Henry James

41 B. G. Rader, *The Academic Mind and Reform: The Influence of Richard T. Ely in American Life* (Lexington, 1966), pp. 37–39; T. C. Cochran, "The Legend of the Robber Barons," *Pennsylvania Magazine of History and Biography,* LXXIV (1950), 307–321; Kirkland, *Dream and Thought,* pp. 19–26, 115–143; Sidney Fine, *Laissez Faire and the General-Welfare State: A Study of Conflict in American Thought, 1865–1901* (Ann Arbor, 1956), p. 103.

42 Sigmund Diamond, *The Reputation of the American Businessman* (Cambridge, Mass., 1955), pp. 56, 178–180; Tipple, "Robber Baron," in Morgan, *Gilded Age,* p. 18.

and the artist James Whistler, for example, found the atmosphere of their native land uncongenial and spent most of their lives in Europe, and that Mark Twain's literary achievement was limited by the extent to which he was infected by the very materialism and speculative fever he excoriated in *The Gilded Age*. But other important writers and artists enjoyed successful and rewarding careers without experiencing any serious sense of alienation from their surroundings. William Dean Howells managed to be at once a sharp critic of his era and an active participator in its cultural life, both as an influential editor and as a widely read novelist and essayist. Painters like Thomas Eakins and Winslow Homer were not as highly esteemed by their contemporaries as by later generations; the realism in their work offended many persons accustomed to sugary sentimentality and stiff formality in art. Yet both earned decent livings, proof that a substantial percentage of the public appreciated them, and both lived reasonably happy lives. Nathaniel Hawthorne, who, in the 1850's, had bewailed the low state of American literary taste, was one of the most widely read novelists of the seventies and eighties. Well-known writers and intellectuals enjoyed great prestige, both in the world of the rich and socially prominent and among the politicians.[43]

In arriving at a final judgment about American taste in architecture, one must place beside the ugly mansions of the rich the work of Henry Hobson Richardson, that of the Chicago designers who developed the skyscraper, and, by the late 1880's, that of Louis Sullivan, one of the finest architects of any age. Before condemning too vigorously the aesthetic values of the typical tycoon, one must consider the numbers of wealthy industrialists and bankers who put together discriminating art collections and imposing private libraries, and the many more who contributed large sums to the establishment and support of museums, libraries, symphony orchestras, and other cultural institutions.

The period saw unprecedented advances in mass education, which had an appreciable effect on public taste, and in every field of learning and scholarship, from philosophy to physics. It would be absurd to describe the typical American as a sophisticated aesthete,

[43] R. R. Roberts, "Gilt, Gingerbread, and Realism," in Morgan, *Gilded Age*, pp. 169–95; Brown, *Year of the Century*, pp. 46–56.

but equally foolish to suggest that he was a boor. In a nation of big cities and tiny villages, of factory workers and farmers, of college graduates and illiterates, of families that traced their roots back to pre-Revolutionary days and recent immigrants from every corner of Europe, generalizations of this sort are not possible. If any trend could be discerned in the average level of taste and culture, it was probably toward improvement; the vulgar and antisocial aspects of American life, if not the materialistic ones, were distinctly less noticeable in 1890 than they had been when the *Gilded Age* was published.[44]

Social attitudes respond to changing situations only reluctantly, and often at great psychic cost to the individual members of society. The Americans of the 1860's and 1870's were particularly unfortunate in this respect. Their world had been shaken simultaneously by two great convulsions—the Industrial Revolution and the Civil War. The first put a premium on co-operation by making their civilization vastly more complex; the second, although it strengthened their sense of national identity, exacted such a heavy toll in life, property, and dashed hopes that it weakened fellow feeling, caused them to reject self-sacrifice for a supposed common good, and encouraged the pursuit of individual gain. Had there been no war, Americans would no doubt have had difficulty enough subjecting their ingrained individualism, product of two centuries of development on a sparsely settled continent rich in opportunity, to the discipline that the imperatives of industrialization imposed upon them. As it was, disillusionment with the conflict and its aftermath added to the problems of adjustment. Men clung too tightly to an outdated individualism and disregarded their newly enlarged civic responsibilities.

But the war, once ended, existed only in memory; its influence persisted, but gradually declined. Industrialization, on the other hand, exerted a steadily increasing power upon the minds of the American people. If it did nothing to inhibit their materialism, it certainly discouraged unrestricted individualism and, at least indirectly, revived their sense of social responsibility, and thus their

44 Mumford, *Brown Decades, passim;* Schlesinger, *Rise of the City,* pp. 160–319.

humanitarianism, idealism, and reform spirit. Unwillingly but inevitably, Americans adjusted their thinking to the new reality.

The conditions that made the postwar period appear "gilded" were produced by the reluctance of Americans to accept the new reality; focusing upon these conditions can contribute relatively little to an understanding of the dynamics of the times. What was most significant about the age—as nearly every contemporary sensed —was the extent to which American civilization was becoming more integrated, its various elements more interdependent.

The symbol of the emerging order (in the words of Charles Francis Adams, Jr., "the most developing force and largest field of the day")[45] was the railroad network: its rails, tying section to section, were the bone and sinew, its locomotives and cars the pumping heart and life-bearing blood of the nation. The railroad, however, like any symbol, merely epitomized something more complex: a civilization at once diverse and unified. Men could not prosper in such a civilization without paying increasing attention to one another. In economic affairs, in politics, in every aspect of day-to-day living, Americans were becoming more social-minded, in the literal if not always in the humanitarian and liberal senses of the term. Many, probably most, found the new imperatives distasteful, even frightening. Hence their continuing veneration of individualism, self-reliance, and laissez-faire economics, hence their almost universal horror of words like socialism and communism, hence the alarm that necessary new types of co-operative activity—industrial combinations, labor unions, farm organizations, governm.-nt bureaus—produced in many minds. But imperatives can be neither avoided nor denied. And so, like small boys off reluctantly to September school, squalling, protesting, mourning already the simple joys of the departing summer yet eager, too, for the mysterious adult power the future promised, the American people accepted their fate.

Revolutions only appear swift and relentless when observed from a distance; human institutions and social attitudes seem to alter imperceptibly and fitfully when the process of change is examined

[45] C. F. Adams, Jr., *Autobiography* (Boston, 1916), p. 170.

in detail. The integration of American life began long before the Civil War and has not yet ended. What follows is an account of only part of the process, but a particularly important part. Between the end of the era of Reconstruction and the last decade of the nineteenth century, the American people increased rapidly in number, added enormously to their wealth, and developed new institutions which worked in myriad ways to concentrate their individual wealth and energies, and thus to enable them to function more effectively as a social entity. In these years the United States became a modern nation.

CHAPTER 2

Agriculture

THE changing character of life in the United States in the last quarter of the nineteenth century produced many paradoxical situations, few more startling than those relating to agriculture. At the end of the Civil War, America was still primarily a nation of farmers, and as late as 1870 about 53 per cent of all gainfully employed persons in the country followed agricultural pursuits. Only about 20 per cent were engaged in manufacturing. In that year there were 2.6 million farms in the United States, valued at more than $9 billion. American farmers produced 254 million bushels of wheat, over a billion bushels of corn, some 4 million bales of cotton, and 21 million tons of hay, and they owned more than 110 million head of cattle, hogs, sheep, horses, and other livestock.

During the next two decades, the agricultural sector of the economy expanded rapidly. By 1877, when the last federal troops were removed from the South, there were nearly four million farms in the country. The production of all kinds of crops had risen sharply from the levels of 1870, wheat, for example, by almost half, corn and hay by a third, cotton by some 400,000 bales. By 1890 the nation contained over 4.5 million farms, valued at $16.4 billion, and in 1891[1] wheat production amounted to 677 million bushels, corn to 2.3 billion bushels, cotton to 9 million bales, hay to more than 51 million tons, the livestock total to 170 million head. And

---

[1] Because of widespread crop failures in 1890, statistics for that year obscure the broad trends of agricultural production.

the output of most other farm products had increased in similarly spectacular fashion.

Nevertheless, during this period American agriculture suffered a sharp decline relative to the other elements in the economy. In 1890 only 42 per cent of the gainfully employed population were farmers. Although the income and the standard of living of the average farm family had increased, the portion of the national income earned by farmers had fallen, and so had their share of the national wealth.[2]

This downward trend reflects principally the remarkable expansion of industry and commerce in the United States; if the statistical evidence suggests that farmers were alarmed by the trend, as they certainly were, it does not indicate that as a class they were actually being impoverished or that even in eastern sections farming was a dying occupation. In addition to its increasing productivity, the vitality of American agriculture was reflected in the tremendous influence it exerted on the nation's manufacturing and foreign commerce. Aside from iron and steel, all the leading industries, measured in value of product, depended directly upon the bounty of the farms and forests for their basic raw materials. This was as true in 1890 as in 1870.[3]

Besides supplying raw materials for industry, American farmers fed the new millions of workers who were producing manufactured goods and the other millions engaged in all the tasks of distribution, selling, and record-keeping that were essential to industrial development. The urban population expanded enormously in the seventies and eighties, and of course the hordes of new city dwellers, many of them émigrés from the farms, relied upon the countryside for sustenance.

Relative decline also obscured the important role played by

---

[2] *Historical Statistics of the United States: Colonial Times to 1957* (Washington, 1960), pp. 140, 278, 288–301; F. A. Shannon, *The Farmer's Last Frontier: Agriculture, 1860–1897* (New York, 1945), pp. 351, 353–354.

[3] Both the flour-milling and meat-packing industries produced more than half a billion dollars worth of goods in 1890, lumbering over $400 million, clothing over $300 million. Cotton, wool, and liquor manufacturers each turned out over a quarter of a billion dollars worth of goods in that year. The iron and steel industry, while expanding faster than any other in these decades, still ranked only third; it produced less than half a billion dollars worth of goods in 1890. U.S. Bureau of the Census, *Statistical Atlas* (Washington, 1903), Plate 193; *Hist. Stat.*, p. 350.

agriculture in foreign commerce. Although American exports nearly doubled in value between 1870 and 1890, farm products continued to account for about three-fourths of the total.[4] Most of the food exported, together with about two-thirds of the nation's huge cotton production, was sold in Europe, and again the rise reflected an ever-closer relationship between the farm and the factory. The Industrial Revolution had begun in Great Britain, but until the nineteenth century British farmers had been able to fill most of the country's food needs. By the time of the American Civil War this was no longer true, and American grain (and later meat) poured into Britain in increasing volume. By the eighties industry was sweeping across southern and central Europe, disrupting the economy of the region and propelling millions of peasants from the land into the cities or across the Atlantic to the United States and South America, thus creating a much larger demand on the Continent for American agricultural produce.

From these facts and figures, one overriding conclusion emerges. The Industrial Revolution was transforming agriculture, along with every other aspect of the economy, both in America and in Europe. Economic relationships were becoming more complex. Individuals and even whole classes might suffer in the short run from the speed with which changes were taking place; but, at least so far as the United States was concerned, if some elements were expanding faster than others, all were nonetheless dynamic and basically healthy. An integrated national economy meant that agriculture was becoming almost completely commercialized and much more specialized, the farmer dependent upon but also benefiting from a potent industrial-financial complex that took in the whole United States and much of the rest of the world as well. If farmers found this dependence psychologically disturbing, they also accepted cheerfully the conveniences that the new order made available.

One obvious illustration of the impact of industry on the farmer was the rapid increase in the use of farm machinery. The "first agricultural revolution," characterized by mechanization and the expansion of market areas resulting from the development of the

---

[4] *Hist. Stat.*, pp. 544–545, 546–547; U.S. Department of Agriculture, *Yearbook, 1891*, p. 322. Between 1870 and 1890, food imports increased from $150 million to $261 million, manufactured goods from $230 million to $348 million. *Hist. Stat.*, p. 544–545.

railroad network, occurred between 1850 and 1870, but during the next two decades the new system was consolidated and refined. As one proud agricultural historian put it at the end of the century, "invention followed invention and improvement followed improvement."

It is no longer necessary for the farmer to cut his wheat with sickle or cradle, nor to rake it and bind it by hand; to cut his cornstalks with a knife and shock the stalks by hand; to thresh his grain with a flail. . . . It is no longer necessary for him to dig potatoes, nor to cut his grass with a scythe and to spread it with a pitchfork . . . and so on with numerous operations throughout the whole range of agricultural work.

Farmers purchased agricultural machinery in steadily mounting volume, their annual expenditures quadrupling in the last thirty years of the century. In 1890 over 900 American corporations were manufacturing agricultural machinery. In that year their output was valued at over $92 million and the farmers of the country were using farm implements worth about half a billion dollars.

The new farm equipment ranged from James Oliver's chilled-iron plow, perfected in 1877, to complicated harvesting machinery. By 1880 efficient twine binders were coming into general use in the grain-raising regions of the West and machines were soon in operation capable of threshing and bagging 450 pounds of grain per minute. While the harvesting of cereal crops provided the most spectacular examples of increased agricultural efficiency, the trend toward the use of machinery pervaded most branches of farming in nearly every part of the country. The records of the Patent Office reveal the number and variety of the new inventions, which affected everything from bee culture and flower raising to the care of livestock, the fencing of fields, and the planting of trees.[5]

During the last quarter of the nineteenth century, for instance, according to one expert, "the development of dairying . . . was

---

5 G. K. Holmes, "Progress in Agriculture in the United States," Department of Agriculture, *Yearbook, 1899*, pp. 316, 319–320; P. H. Johnstone, "Old Ideals Versus New Ideas in Farm Life," *ibid., 1940*, p. 155; Shannon, *Farmer's Last Frontier*, p. 135; M. W. Towne and W. D. Rasmussen, "Farm Gross Product and Gross Investment in the Nineteenth Century," National Bureau of Economic Research, *Trends in the American Economy in the Nineteenth Century* (Princeton, 1960), pp. 260–263; Leo Rogin, *The Introduction of Farm Machinery in its Relation to the Productivity of Labor* (Berkeley, 1931), pp. 95, 113–124.

marked by events of the greatest consequence in its entire history." The dairy centrifuge, a device for separating cream from skim milk, which came into use around 1880, markedly increased the cream yield of whole milk, lowering the cost and raising the quality of butter and many other dairy products. The invention by the chemist Stephen M. Babcock of a machine for measuring the fat content of milk (1890) changed every aspect of dairying from the breeding of cows to the inspection of milk products by municipal governments, and had, one wit remarked, "more influence than the Bible in making dairymen honest." While much of the nation's cream and butter continued to be processed on individual farms, these machines created a flourishing new industry. During the eighties, commercial creameries sprang up almost like mushrooms overnight. In the northern Vermont town of St. Albans, for example, the first creamery went into operation in 1880. Ten years later there were fifteen in the town, and soon a single plant, the Franklin County Creamery, was handling the yield of over 30,000 cows and producing from ten to twelve tons of butter a day. Equally significant changes were effected in meat production by the development of mechanical refrigeration, by the introduction of assembly-line slaughtering methods, and by the more efficient utilization of a variety of by-products. Fruit and vegetable growers profited from new spraying equipment, such as the knapsack pump, and from the construction of commercial greenhouses, several thousand of which were in operation by 1890. The expanded use of agricultural machinery was one of the major causes of the growth of agricultural output.[6]

Science also played a role in the advance of agriculture. Drawing upon the discoveries of the great German pioneer Justus von Liebig, who established the relationship between minerals in the soil and plant growth, American agricultural chemists made many new discoveries in the seventies and eighties. Samuel Johnson of

[6] H. E. Alvord, "Dairy Development in the United States," Department of Agriculture, *Yearbook, 1899*, pp. 393, 398; T. R. Pirtle, *History of the Diary Industry* (Chicago, 1926), pp. 78–80; Vernon Carstensen, "The Genesis of an Agricultural Experiment Station," *Agricultural History*, XXXIV (1960), 20; B. T. Galloway, "Progress in the Treatment of Plant Diseases in the United States," and "Progress of Commercial Growing of Plants under Glass," Department of Agriculture, *Yearbook, 1899*, pp. 196, 583.

Yale, who had studied under Liebig in Germany before the Civil War, wrote two classic books, *How Crops Grow* (1868) and *How Crops Feed* (1870), as well as a large number of articles on soil chemistry, fertilizers, and plant nutrition. Even more notable work was done by one of Johnson's students, William O. Atwater of Wesleyan University, whose paper "On the Acquisition of Atmospheric Nitrogen by Plants" (1885) described how leguminous plants transfer nitrogen in the air to the soil. Eugene W. Hilgard, originally a geologist, pioneered in soil analysis, first at the University of Mississippi, then at Michigan, and finally at the University of California. Francis Storer of Harvard's Bussey Institution carried out extensive research in every area of agricultural chemistry, summed up in his massive *Agriculture in Some of Its Relations with Chemistry,* first published in 1887.[7]

The plant pathologist William G. Farlow, trained by Asa Gray at Harvard and by the German botanist Heinrich De Bary at the University of Strasbourg, did pioneering work in mycology, the study of funguses. J. C. Arthur, after 1884 director of the New York State agricultural experiment station at Geneva, conducted a series of investigations of the fungus diseases of pears, grapes, and other fruits. The mid-eighties opened up what one expert called "the epoch-making period" of plant pathology in America. In 1885 the Department of Agriculture established a mycology section. Aided by the discovery in France at about this time of the effectiveness of Bordeaux mixture (a combination of copper sulphate and lime) as a fungicide, American scientists undertook "one of the most remarkable series of investigations and experiments ever witnessed in this or any other country," leading to the control of potato funguses, peach-leaf curl, black rot of the grape, which had threatened to wipe out viniculture in America, and other plant diseases.[8]

Other scientists attacked the problem of insect pests. As late as 1877, only four states, Massachusetts, New York, Illinois, and Mis-

7 *Dictionary of American Biography,* "Samuel W. Johnson," X, 120–121; "William O. Atwater," I, 417–418; "Eugene W. Hilgard," IX, 22; "Francis H. Storer," XVIII, 94–95; H. W. Wiley, "The Relation of Chemistry to the Progress of Agriculture," Department of Agriculture, *Yearbook, 1899,* pp. 218–220, 226–228.

8 *Dictionary of American Biography,* "William G. Farlow," VI, 274–275; A. H. Dupree, *Asa Gray* (Cambridge, Mass., 1959), p. 351; Galloway, "Treatment of Plant Diseases," pp. 193–195.

souri, supported work in entomology. The federal government maintained an official entomologist, Townend Glover, but Glover was more an artist than a scientist and devoted most of his efforts to preparing engravings of various American insects and stocking an agricultural museum in Washington. In 1877, however, Congress, alarmed by the ravages of grasshoppers in a number of western states, appointed a commission headed by Charles V. Riley, generally regarded as the founder of the science of economic entomology, to study the grasshopper problem, and the next year Riley succeeded Glover as the Department of Agriculture's entomologist. A man of wide interests and enormous energy—during a rather short life he published over 2,000 reports and papers—Riley greatly increased the scope of government work in his field. In 1889, while studying the devastating effects of a scale insect on California citrus orchards, he learned that in Australia, where the insect was also present, citrus plants were unaffected by the pest. Deducing that there must be some natural enemy of the scale native to Australia, he persuaded the government to send a field worker to investigate, with the result that the ladybug *Novius cardinalis* was brought to the United States and the citrus groves saved. His studies of the resistance of American grapevines to the ravages of the insect *Phylloxera*, which was rapidly destroying the French wine industry, led to the importation into France of American rootstock and won for Riley a French decoration.

During the 1870's and 1880's, the chief insecticides used by agriculturalists were Paris green, an arsenic compound, and kerosene emulsified in soapsuds. These substances were lethal against gnawing and sucking insects like the cotton caterpillar and the larva of the coddling moth, but it required careful experimentation by large numbers of scientists to determine the proper concentrations necessary for dealing with each insect and the optimum time to use them in differing climates and for different plants. Riley was only one among many men engaged in this research, which by the end of the century had raised the United States to a position of world leadership in economic entomology.[9]

[9] L. O. Howard, "A History of Applied Entomology," *Smithsonian Institution, Miscellaneous Publications*, LXXXIV (1930) : 53–57, 99, 213–214, and "Progress in Economic Entomology in the United States," Department of Agriculture, *Yearbook, 1899*, pp. 138–156; *Dictionary of American Biography*, "Charles V. Riley,"

All this scientific progress had great long-range importance for American agriculture, but it had relatively little impact on the practices of farmers at that time. Although the consumption of commercial fertilizers almost doubled during the eighties, from 753 million tons to 1.39 billion, the amount was insufficient to raise the over-all yields per acre of most crops significantly. Yields varied from year to year without pattern, weather conditions being the chief determinant. Between 1877 and 1890, corn harvests ranged from 18.6 bushels per acre to 29.2, but revealed no trend. The best year was 1879, the worst 1881. For wheat the range was from 10.2 bushels per acre to 13.8, the extremes being reached again in 1879 and 1881. These years also marked the high and low points for crops as varied in nature and habitat as potatoes and cotton. The lack of progress is perhaps best illustrated by oat production: the best oat year was 1877, the worst 1890.[10]

The changes convulsing the American economy in these years caused some extraordinary shifts in the agricultural activities of the various sections of the country. Speaking generally, the centers of production of all the major crops moved westward,[11] but this statement both exaggerates and obscures what was happening. In the states north and east of Maryland, where industry was most concentrated and which supposedly felt the force of western competition most strongly, agriculture, even the raising of the staple crops, did not actually decline. Corn production went up; wheat held its own, as did potatoes. The raising of dairy cattle increased substantially; that of other cattle and of sheep remained stable.[12] At

XV, 609–610; "Townend Glover," VII, 333–334; A. C. True, *A History of Agricultural Experimentation and Research in the United States, 1607–1925* (Washington, 1937), pp. 48, 54–55, 64.

10 *Hist. Stat.*, p. 285; Department of Agriculture, *Yearbook, 1899*, pp. 759–765. See also C. W. Davis, "The Probabilities of Agriculture," *Forum*, X (1890), 293–294.

11 L. B. Schmidt, "The Internal Grain Trade of the United States, 1860–1890," *Iowa Journal of History and Politics*, XIX (1921), 196–245, and "The Westward Movement of the Corn Growing Industry in the United States," *ibid.*, XXI (1923), 112–141.

12 The serious decline of northeastern agriculture came in the 1890's, and then chiefly in New England. Between 1891 and 1899, corn production in New England fell from 9.3 million bushels to 6.6 million, wheat from 1.2 million bushels to 137,000. In New York in this period, corn production fell from 22 million bushels to 15.6 million, wheat from 10.6 million bushels to 7 million.

the same time the region greatly increased its production of perishable foods in response to the growing demands of its cities. As early as 1879 the northeastern states raised fruits and vegetables worth over $33 million. Growth thereafter was very rapid, until by 1899 the total had more than doubled. In addition, the output of milk, cheese, and butter rose rapidly. New York, far and away the nation's leading industrial state, maintained a flourishing agriculture throughout the period. In the decade of the 1880's the number of farms declined by only 6 per cent; in 1890 Manhattan Island still had a dozen farms, Kings County (Brooklyn) over 300. The state produced more butter and potatoes than any other; the decline of wheat, according to an official report, was "surprisingly small"; while truck farming, fruit growing, and certain other types of agriculture "developed to an enormous extent."[13]

Farmers in the northeastern states could not compete in distant markets with those of the newer areas. Land was more expensive and much of it was held in small units that reduced the efficiency of agricultural machinery. But these farmers did not have to look outside their own region for markets. So great was the increase in urban demand that they could not have filled it even if the entire area beyond the Appalachians had been a desert. Although the price of staples declined, partly in response to greater western (and foreign) production, low transportation costs enabled local farmers to sell their wheat, corn, and cattle profitably in most years. Moreover, northeastern farmers responded rationally to changing conditions; they switched to perishables, and abandoned their least fertile acres and cultivated the remainder more intensively. Despite supposedly inferior soils, yields per acre of the northeastern states were the highest in the nation for most crops. In 1891 the average acre of corn in "stony" Massachusetts produced 39.5 bushels; in Iowa yields averaged 36.7 bushels. Vermont wheat growers har-

---

The output of these crops declined much less noticeably in Pennsylvania: wheat yields remained steady at about 20 million bushels a year; corn slipped only from 46.5 million bushels in 1891 to 40.2 million in 1899. Department of Agriculture, *Report, 1891*, pp. 288–291; *Yearbook, 1899*, pp. 765–766.

[13] This production is stated in money terms rather than in volume because of the great variety of products involved. Shannon, *Farmer's Last Frontier*, pp. 260–261; New York Bureau of Statistics of Labor, *Report, 1892* (Albany, 1893), I, 207–211.

vested 17.5 bushels of wheat for every acre cultivated in 1891, well above the national average of 15.3 bushels and roughly equal to yields in Minnesota (17.6 bushels) and Illinois (18 bushels) .[14]

The southern states, including all the area south of Pennsylvania and the Ohio River, together with the trans-Mississippi states of Arkansas, Louisiana, and Texas, remained overwhelmingly agricultural. Cotton and to a lesser extent sugar, tobacco, and rice were the distinctive crops of the region, but, as in earlier times, it harvested large crops of corn, wheat, and other cereals as well. The Upper South (Maryland, Virginia, North Carolina, Kentucky, and Tennessee) , which raised over 160 million bushels of corn and nearly 39 million bushels of wheat in 1877, produced more than 270 million bushels of corn and 46 million bushels of wheat in 1891. And even in the Deep South, corn and wheat production increased during the period.[15] Southern livestock production also rose. Texas makes a special case, being better considered as a part of the West in this connection, for its output of cattle and sheep, dwarfing that of every other southern state throughout the period, nearly doubled. In the rest of the region dairy cattle and hog production expanded considerably. The raising of beef cattle and sheep declined slightly.

As for the distinctively southern crops, except for sugar, by the end of Reconstruction all had recovered from the destruction and dislocations of the Civil War to a point where output roughly equalled that of the last prewar years. The cotton crop of 1875 broke the 1859 record of 4.5 million bales and in 1878 production exceeded 5 million bales. Thereafter output rose gradually throughout the 1880's, ranging from 5.4 million bales to 7.3 million. As with other crops, the greatest expansion resulted from the opening up of new lands in the West, but the whole area substantially increased its cotton acreage. Heavy applications of fertilizer, both Peruvian guano and various chemical combinations, made expansion possible in the older sections of the cotton belt; for besides increasing yields, fertilizers shortened the growth cycle of cotton, enabling farmers to produce it in higher and more northerly

---

[14] Department of Agriculture, *Yearbook, 1899*, pp. 783–784.

[15] Except for Florida, every southern state raised over 11 million bushels of corn in 1877 and over 18 million bushels in 1891. Wheat was less important in the southern tier, but only Florida, South Carolina, Mississippi, and Louisiana failed to produce at least a million bushels in 1877 or 2 million in 1891.

districts without fear of frost damage in the spring and fall. In 1883 a North Carolina agricultural expert noted that fertilizers had caused cotton to spread "forty or fifty miles up the slopes of the Blue Ridge and northward across the Virginia line."[16]

Because of expanding demand, increased cotton production had relatively little effect on prices; although the years of thirty-cent and even of fifteen-cent cotton that had followed the war had ended, the price of the staple held remarkably steady throughout the eighties, ranging between eight and ten cents per pound, though tending toward the lower figure.

Tobacco production was also approaching prewar levels by the end of Reconstruction. In the following years, however, total output grew only slowly, and in Virginia and Maryland it declined. Tobacco was not an exclusively southern crop; significant quantities were raised in Missouri, Pennsylvania, Connecticut, and even in Massachusetts, which produced 4 million pounds in 1878. The heart of the tobacco region was in Kentucky, where production doubled in a decade. The most significant trend affecting producers in the eighties was the growth in the demand for cigarettes. Although the market for cigars and chewing tobacco remained large, cigarette consumption nearly quintupled in that decade, soaring from 533 million to over 2.5 billion. Cigarettes were made chiefly from the "bright yellow" variety that flourished in North Carolina. This helps explain why North Carolina, escaping the decline that affected Maryland and Virginia, tripled its output between 1878 and 1890.[17]

Rice cultivation, particularly hard hit by the dislocations attending the Civil War, also revived during the eighties. The major

16 Department of Agriculture, *Report, 1877,* pp. 165, 171–172; *1878,* p. 268; *1888,* p. 430; *1891,* pp. 288–291, 314–315; M. B. Hammond, "Cotton Production in the South," in J. C. Ballaugh (ed.), *The South in the Building of the Nation* (Richmond, 1909), VI, 91–92; R. H. Taylor, "The Sale and Application of Commercial Fertilizers in the South Atlantic States to 1900," *Agric. Hist.,* XXI (1947), 52. South Carolina, for example, devoted 944,000 acres to the crop in 1878 and over 1.6 million in 1887, while Mississippi's acreage jumped from about 2 million to over 2.5 million in the same period.

17 Shannon, *Farmer's Last Frontier,* p. 113; Department of Agriculture, *Report, 1878,* p. 268; *Hist. Stat.,* p. 415; Meyer Jacobstein, "The Conditions of Tobacco Culture in the South," *South in the Building of the Nation,* VI, p. 67. Between 1878 and 1890, Kentucky's tobacco crop increased from 123 million pounds to 222 million, North Carolina's from 13 million to 36 million.

development was a shift from the coastal areas of Georgia and South Carolina to the delta region of Louisiana.[18] Farmers discovered that the rich, alluvial delta soils were more easily cultivated and harvested by machines than the Carolina and Georgia lands, which helps explain the shift. Louisiana sugar producers, however, were less successful. The prewar record of over 235,000 tons was not surpassed until 1893.[19]

Thus it is clear that southern agriculture experienced considerable growth during the post-Reconstruction era. Growth, however, did not mean prosperity. Much has been written, usually in pejorative terms, about the fate of the mass of poor southern farmers, most of whom were tenants and sharecroppers. That these groups, white as well as Negro, were exploited by their more powerful neighbors is undeniable, yet their poverty was more a product of economic conditions than of human selfishness and prejudice. Both the poor whites and the former slaves aspired to become independent landowners; lacking land and capital, they had of necessity to borrow. Unfortunately capital was very scarce in the South and interest rates high; furthermore, the country was experiencing a long-range deflationary trend that put a special burden on borrowers. The farmer who owned land free of debt could do fairly well with cotton selling at eight or nine cents a pound, but such men were rare in the post-Reconstruction South.

In any case, most poor Southerners lacked access to ordinary forms of credit, for they had no assets but their labor to pledge against loans. For them, tenant farming and sharecropping offered

[18] Between 1880 and 1894, Louisiana's production jumped from 23 million pounds to 76 million, while South Carolina's declined from 52 million pounds to about 22 million. Department of Agriculture, *Yearbook, 1899*, p. 782; P. H. Mell, "The Conditions of Rice Culture in the South Since 1865," *South in the Building of the Nation*, VI, p. 75; and Shannon, *Farmer's Last Frontier*, pp. 120–121, exaggerate the expansion in Louisiana by citing Louisiana's bumper crop of 1895—127.6 million pounds. The state raised only 56 million pounds in 1896 and 75.6 million in 1897.

[19] Mell, "Rice Culture," p. 74; W. C. Stubbs, "Sugar Products in the South," *South in the Building of the Nation*, VI, 80; Shannon, *Farmer's Last Frontier*, p. 121. Since consumption far exceeded domestic cane production, extensive efforts were made to raise sugar beets, sorghum, and other sugar-yielding crops. Results, however, were negligible in this period. Because the nation imported so much sugar, Louisiana congressmen, almost alone among Southerners, were vigorous advocates of protective tariffs. Throughout the period, the tariff on sugar was 2.5 cents per pound.

at least a means of earning a living. Renting land was common in
every section of the country; indeed, as the cost of farming went up
in an era of mechanization, the proportion of tenants in the agricultural population increased steadily—from 8 per cent in 1880 to
10 per cent in 1890 and to over 13 per cent in 1900.[20] Sharecropping also existed in every state, but it was especially common in
the South. Instead of paying a fixed rent, the sharecropper turned
over part of his crop to the owner of the land, who also supplied
him with housing and sometimes with tools, seed, and even food.
Arrangements varied enormously: if the cropper contributed only
his labor, he usually gave the owner three-quarters of the harvest; if
he provided his own food as well, he kept half; if he paid also for
his tools, seed, and supplies, his share was proportionately larger.
The system was not inherently unfair and in some ways involved
less risk than tenantry, since if the harvest was meager or prices low,
owner and worker shared the resultant losses. It also gave the poor
an opportunity to rise. In the South after Reconstruction the odds
against sharecroppers were long, but some did succeed in winning
their way to independent land ownership.

Most southern landowners also lacked ready cash. To finance
their operations, they had to borrow themselves. In effect, they
pledged each year's crop in advance to obtain the money needed for
raising it. Moneylenders, besides charging interest rates ranging as
high as 20 to 30 per cent, insisted that the borrowers concentrate on
raising the staple crops, especially cotton, that could readily be
turned into cash, which compelled the landowners to insist that
their tenants and croppers do likewise. By increasing the production of a few staple crops, this situation aggravated the soil-exhaus-
tion problem, and made it more difficult for small farmers to raise
all their own food, a further drain on their resources. Experts
agreed that southern farmers should diversify their operations, both
to check the overproduction of staples and to conserve soil fertility,
and they advanced a number of simple plans for rotating crops.
Their advice was seldom followed. Beginning in the middle
eighties, truck farming and fruit growing began to assume some
importance in the region; the first rail shipments of green vegetables from Norfolk, Virginia, to northern cities was made in 1885,

20 Shannon, *Farmer's Last Frontier*, p. 418.

of Florida oranges in 1888. By the end of the century this business amounted to well over $100 million annually, but most of the growth came after 1890 and even then very little land formerly devoted to the raising of staples was involved. Whether owner or cropper, most cultivators of the staples simply could not get far enough ahead of the game to undertake long-range plans for soil improvement; current needs and pressures forced them to concentrate on crops with the largest and surest immediate return. To increase yields they depended upon commercial fertilizers, which, of course, added to their need for money.[21]

To buy food, clothing, fertilizer, and other supplies, tenants and sharecroppers relied upon credit obtained from the local storekeeper—who was as often as not also the landowner—which they secured by giving him a lien, or chattel mortgage, on their growing crops. This crop-lien system worked to the disadvantage of the farmer in several ways. Usually the storekeeper himself operated on credit, his interest payments adding to his costs of doing business and thus to his prices. Since the crop might fail or be inadequate to cover the farmer's bills, the storekeeper was assuming heavy risks; he protected himself by raising prices still higher. He was also a petty monopolist—his customers, lacking cash, had no one else to turn to for their needs. Finally, the system encouraged improvidence among ignorant, long-suffering people on whom store credit exercised a massive temptation. Often they dribbled away the fruits of their labor on liquor, small luxuries, and gaudy trinkets, so that when accounts were settled at harvest time their obligations exceeded their returns, committing them to another year in the clutches of their creditors.[22]

With the passage of time the crop-lien system became more oppressive. In South Carolina, for example, in the mid-eighties the

[21] T. F. Hunt, "Cereal Farming in the South," *South in the Building of the Nation*, VI, 111; A. M. Soule, "Vegetables, Fruit, and Nursery Products and Truck Farming in the South," *ibid.*, VI, 129, 132–133; Taylor, "Commercial Fertilizers," p. 49.

[22] Shannon, *Farmer's Last Frontier*, pp. 90–92; Theodore Saloutos, *Farmer Movements in the South, 1865–1933* (Lincoln, 1964), pp. 21–24; V. L. Wharton, *The Negro in Mississippi, 1865–1900* (New York, 1965), p. 72; G. B. Tindall, *South Carolina Negroes, 1877–1900* (Columbia, S.C., 1952), pp. 105–108; C. V. Woodward, *Origins of the New South, 1877–1913* (Baton Rouge, 1951), pp. 181–184.

legislature strengthened the power of landowners and merchants in enforcing their claims and made verbal contracts binding, an open invitation for them to take advantage of illiterate tenants and croppers. "In my State," South Carolina's lone Negro congressman declared in 1891, "if the employer states verbally that the unpaid laborer of his plantation contracted to work for the year no other farmer dares employ the man if he attempts to break the contract rather than work for nothing." Yet the sharecropping and crop-lien arrangement represented the poor man's only hope, and gave him at least a minimum opportunity to rise in the world. Wage workers were often paid in scrip and credit slips, no improvement over the lien system, and sometimes their employers cheated them outrageously. By the eighties, landless farmers preferred sharecropping to all other labor systems. A few, even among the Negroes, gradually achieved independence. In 1880 between one and five Negroes in a hundred owned their own farms. In Georgia, Negroes constituted almost half of the population, but owned less than 2 per cent of the state's landed wealth. By 1890 a larger percentage had become landowners; over 11 per cent of Mississippi's Negro farmers, for example, owned at least their own homes.[23]

Viewed in broad perspective, southern agriculture made considerable progress between 1877 and 1890. Although the region remained the poorest in the nation, although ignorance, racial prejudice, the paucity of local urban markets, the lack of capital, and other problems hindered development, conditions were improving, at least until late in the eighties. The explosion of farm discontent that shook the South in the next decade resulted as much from the reversal of this trend as from the actual problems of these years. The drastic agricultural price decline of 1890–96, product of broad national and international rather than distinctly southern events, hit southern farmers especially hard because they were so poor, and because they were debtors, but also because it wiped out the laboriously achieved advances of the years after the end of the Civil War.

The upper half of the great basin drained by the Mississippi and

---

[23] Tindall, *South Carolina Negroes,* pp. 100, 104, 111–112; Wharton, *Negro in Mississippi,* pp. 61, 67–68; Woodward, *New South,* pp. 205–206; C. A. Bacote, "Some Aspects of Negro Life in Georgia: 1880–1908," *Journal of Negro History,* XLIII (1958), 188.

its tributaries, the area from Ohio to the Rockies, from the states of the former Confederacy to Canada, was the agricultural heart of the nation. Parts of this region were rapidly industrializing, but all of it produced immense amounts of farm crops. Most of the region was remarkably fertile, parts of it incredibly so. In 1891 Illinois agricultural researchers reported with a mixture of awe and dismay that they were able to raise good crops of corn on an experimental plot where corn had been grown for fifteen consecutive years without the use of any fertilizer. A similar experiment, conducted with wheat at Kansas Agricultural College throughout the eighties, produced the same result.[24] In 1877, every state in the area except Minnesota and Colorado produced at least 20 million bushes of corn, only Colorado and Nebraska less than 14 million bushels of wheat. In 1891, the seven leading corn states and ten of the eleven leading wheat states of the nation could be found there. The dominant position of the area in cereal production, and also in the raising of cattle and hogs, was unchallenged. In addition, large amounts of other grains, together with dairy products, vegetables, and a variety of other crops, were raised in the region.[25]

Important shifts in emphasis occurred within this upper Mississippi basin during the period. Corn production in the Old Northwest (Ohio, Indiana, Illinois, Michigan, and Wisconsin) remained relatively stable, but more than doubled in Iowa and Missouri. Wheat production increased somewhat in all these states, but soared in Minnesota, Kansas, and the Dakotas. Immense "bonanza" farms, some extending over tens of thousands of acres, appeared in the late seventies and early eighties in the northern plains; in North Dakota alone, there were about 90 of them, each over 3,000 acres in area. Utilizing heavy machinery and small armies of migratory

[24] A. G. Bogue, *From Prairie to Corn Belt* (Chicago, 1963), p. 146; Davis, "Probabilities of Agriculture," pp. 293–294.

[25] Department of Agriculture, *Report, 1877*, pp. 165–167, 171–172; *1891*, pp. 288–289, 291, 314–316. In 1891 Iowa raised 351 million bushels of corn, Illinois 235 million, four other states in the region over 123 million. Kentucky, leader of the rest of the country, raised less than 83 million bushels. Minnesota, Kansas, North Dakota, and Indiana each produced more than 52 million bushels of wheat. No state outside the basin except California produced as much as 21 million bushels of wheat, and, aside from Texas and the mountain states of Wyoming, New Mexico, and Montana, in 1891 no state outside it had more than 835,000 head of cattle. Seven states in the region had over a million. The seven leading hog-producing states in the nation, topped by Iowa with 7.1 million, also lay within the area.

workers, these farms, most of them owned by corporations and run by professional managers, yielded enormous harvests in good years. The best-known bonanza, the Oliver Dalrymple "farm" in Cass County, North Dakota, produced 600,000 bushels of wheat in 1881. Dalrymple, who managed the property for two directors of the Northern Pacific Railroad, used 200 pairs of harrows and 125 seeders to get his crop in the ground, 155 binders and 26 steam threshers to harvest it. At peak seasons he employed over 600 men.

During the boom years of the early eighties, the bonanzas prospered mightily, partly because of high yields and good wheat prices, partly because their lands soared in value. Dalrymple's personal holdings, which he began accumulating in 1876 at prices ranging from 40 cents to $5 an acre, were worth $20 to $25 an acre by 1884. The assets of another bonanza, the Amenia and Sharon Land Company, owned by forty eastern investors, rose from $99,000 to $514,000 between 1876 and 1885. Farms of this type were not typical, even on the plains, but they demonstrated on a grand scale the agricultural methods that were revolutionizing cereal production everywhere.[26]

The raising of livestock increased very rapidly in all sections; the abundant grasslands of the western plains provided forage for cattle and sheep, while the relatively low price of corn encouraged farmers to fatten cattle and especially hogs in enormous numbers. Kansas was pre-eminently a wheat and cattle state, yet between 1877 and 1891 its output of hogs rose from 432,000 to 3.2 million. There were 1.7 million beef cattle in Illinois in 1891, 1.3 million dairy cattle in Iowa, 4.5 million sheep in Ohio.[27]

Agriculture was also important in the mountain states and especially along the Pacific coast. Although still sparsely settled, this huge region was growing fast.[28] Corn was not an important crop

[26] Shannon, *Farmer's Last Frontier*, pp. 154–160; H. M. Drache, *The Day of the Bonanza: A History of Bonanza Farming in the Red River Valley of the North* (Fargo, 1964), pp. 10, 43, 72–73, 92–96, 187. For a good contemporary description of the appearance of bonanza farms and the economics of their operation, based on personal observation, see W. G. Moody, *Land and Labor in the United States* (New York, 1883), pp. 31–73.

[27] Department of Agriculture, *Report, 1877*, pp. 171–172; *1891*, pp. 314–316.

[28] By 1890 California had over 1.2 million inhabitants, Washington over 357,000 (up from only 75,000 in 1880), Oregon over 313,000. Montana and Wyoming tripled during the decade, Arizona and Idaho more than doubled. Department of Agriculture, *Report, 1891*, p. 291.

except in California, but by 1891 both wheat and livestock were being raised in substantial volume in many of these states. California ranked fifth in the nation in wheat production, for example, with 36.6 million bushels, its farmers pioneering in the use of steam-driven combines capable of threshing and bagging as much as 450 pounds of grain a minute.[29] California, and to a lesser extent Oregon and Washington, also raised important quantities of fruits and vegetables. The renowned plant breeder Luther Burbank, who settled in California in 1875, was only the most famous of a number of practical nurserymen who flourished there. Burbank's new plums, peaches, apples, and vegetables, together with new types of oranges developed by other experimenters, greatly enriched the agriculture of all the Pacific states. In California grapes were the most important fruit crop; as early as 1877 the state produced 12 million gallons of wine and brandy. Early in the eighties, far-western perishables began to move over the new transcontinental railroads in refrigerated cars to eastern markets: oranges from southern California, peaches, apples, cherries, and many other fruits together with a trickle of vegetables from the region farther north.[30]

This survey of agricultural trends after 1877 reveals both the expansion of farming and its ever-increasing dependence upon the larger commerical society for its prosperity, The railroads improved in scope and efficiency with each passing year. By the mid-1880's, Allan G. Bogue has written with only slight exaggeration, scarcely a farmer in the prairie states lived "beyond earshot of the locomotive's whistle."[31] By the early nineties the railroad networks of

[29] Oregon and Washington together raised over 25 million bushels of wheat in 1891, Utah nearly 2.4 million, New Mexico, Montana, and Idaho over 1 million each. In that year New Mexico, Colorado, Wyoming, and Montana each had over a million head of beef cattle, California and Oregon well over half a million. California ranked third in the country with 4 million sheep; New Mexico had almost 3 million; Oregon, Utah, and Montana over 2 million each and Colorado and Wyoming over 1 million. Department of Agriculture, *Report, 1891,* pp. 315–31.

[30] Shannon, *Farmer's Last Frontier,* pp. 135, 264–266; H. S. Reed, "Major Trends in California Agriculture," *Agricultural History,* XX (1946), 252–255; *Dictionary of American Biography,* "Luther Burbank," III, 265–270.

[31] Bogue, *Prairie to Corn Belt,* p. 281. A writer in 1890 estimated that nine out of every ten Illinois farmhouses were situated within five miles of a railroad station. Rodney Welch, "The Farmer's Changed Condition," *Forum,* X (1890), 693.

the plains states and of the South were only slightly less complete, and four transcontinental lines had reached the Pacific coast. Most farmers were making heavy use of agricultural machinery. They depended upon banks and loan companies for credit, and on large aggregations of merchants and other middlemen to grade, store, and sell their crops. Thus they experienced both the benefits of commercial agriculture and its drawbacks to an extraordinary degree.

Whether the individual farmer profited or lost from being part of this intricate economic structure depended on climatic conditions, soil fertility, his skill both as a husbandman and as a businessman, his access to competing means of transportation, and many other things. Probably the single most important determinant was whether or not he possessed sufficient capital. To operate efficiently he had to make substantial investments in land, buildings, fencing, and machinery. He was disadvantaged if he had to borrow to obtain these essentials, because the general price level was declining. More specifically, prices fell steadily from 1865 to 1879, revived somewhat between 1879 and 1883, then fell again for the remainder of the eighties. Farmers did not suffer *as farmers* from this deflation. The data indicate that although changing crop yields caused the value of particular farm products to fluctuate quite erratically, on the average, agricultural prices followed those of other goods closely.[32] But as debtors, farmers' fixed monetary obligations represented a mounting burden when prices fell and the value of the dollar increased.

Many farmers believed that the manufacturers and middlemen with whom they did business were cruelly exploiting them. They complained that railroad freight rates and warehouse storage charges were exorbitant, that bankers demanded unreasonable rates of interest for mortgage loans, that too many middlemen extracted profits from the marketing system, and that industrial monopolists

---

[32] Corn sold at 78 cents a bushel in 1867, at 31 cents in 1878, at 63 cents in 1881, and at 28 cents in 1889. Wheat was worth about $2 a bushel in 1867, about 75 cents in 1878, nearly $1.20 in 1881, and 70 cents a bushel in 1889. The wholesale price indexes for these years (1910–14 = 100) were: 1867—162, 1878—91, 1881—103, 1889—81. Shannon, *Farmer's Last Frontier*, pp. 167, 192, 294; *Hist. Stat.*, pp. 115, 297. See also D. C. North, *Growth and Welfare in the American Past* (Englewood Cliffs, N.J., 1966), pp. 138–139. North points out that since the *quality* of manufactured goods was improving, "the farmer . . . was really getting more for his money."

set unfairly high prices on the machinery and other goods that farmers purchased. There was much truth, along with considerable exaggeration, in many of these complaints, but the cries of the farmers always became more shrill during periods of deflation, and for this tendency most of their accusations provide no logical explanation. So long as agricultural prices remained, as they did, in balance with those of other goods and services, deflation *per se* did not injure farmers or any other producers. After all, the entire economy expanded during the long postwar deflationary cycle.

The importance of debts in determining the fate of the farmer can be demonstrated by looking at the history of certain agricultural clubs and organizations. In 1867 Oliver H. Kelley, a postal employee, founded the Patrons of Husbandry, primarily in an effort to broaden the intellectual horizons and brighten the social life of rural citizens. After a slow start, the organization grew rapidly in the early seventies: between 1872 and 1874 no less than 14,000 local "granges" were established. The Grangers, as members were popularly called, inevitably became involved in attacking the problems of farmers. They established co-operatives to market their own crops and to buy farm machinery and other manufactured goods, and agitated in behalf of agricultural research, better schools, and more equitable tax laws. They became a powerful political force overnight, obtaining the passage of state laws regulating railroads and grain elevators and otherwise restricting the practices of businessmen engaged in marketing and transporting farm products. Various inflationary schemes won Granger backing as well, but it is clear that the organization considered deflation merely one among many grievances; the movement began to decline about 1875 for reasons unconnected with the deflation of values. Nevertheless, when prices rose again after 1879, the organization became practically moribund. In 1880 it still claimed 150,000 members, but it collected only $6,000 in dues in the entire country.[33]

When the price level began to slump again in the middle

---

[33] S. J. Buck, *The Granger Movement* (Cambridge, Mass., 1933), pp. 40–70, 102–114. The Patrons of Husbandry experienced a revival in the late eighties and played some part in the protest movement of the following years, but the center of its influence moved eastward and it tended increasingly to become the kind of social, nonpolitical organization that its founder had originally envisioned. R. V. Scott, *The Agrarian Movement in Illinois, 1880–1896* (Urbana, 1962), p. 2.

eighties, agricultural protest movements once more became important. In 1885, small-farm groups such as the Southern Alliance,
which had struggled merely to maintain its existence for over a
decade; the Northern Alliance, which as late as 1884 could not
muster enough interest to hold a national convention; and the
Agricultural Wheel and the Brothers of Freedom, which had barely
remained alive since their founding in 1882, suddenly began to
attract recruits by the thousands. Once again, societies that had
been set up for social and essentially local purposes began to undertake large-scale economic programs (including co-operative marketing and purchasing ventures), engage in political activity, and
advocate broad social reforms. By 1892 they had all combined in a
great national political organization, the People's, or Populist,
party. Like the earlier Grangers, the Populists sought stricter public
control of transportation and marketing corporations, tax reform,
and inflation of the currency. By the middle nineties inflation,
through the free coinage of silver, had become their major objective. Then, when the situation changed after 1896 and prices began
to rise, the Populist movement rapidly disintegrated.[34]

This congruence of deflation and agricultural unrest does not,
however, prove that the former led inevitably to the latter. In the
seventies and again in the late eighties and early nineties, agricultural radicalism was most intense in regions where farmers were
most deeply in debt. In general this meant in newly settled areas
close to the frontier, where men had not had time to build up their
resources and finish paying for their land and machinery.[35] Declining prices hit purchasers hard. The Grangers of the seventies were
particularly militant in Iowa, Illinois, and Wisconsin, less so in
Ohio, and relatively docile east of the Appalachians. The Populists
of the next decade were almost nonexistent in the Northeast, vocal
yet not politically effective in the centers of the old Granger unrest,

[34] J. D. Hicks, *The Populist Revolt* (Minneapolis, 1931), *passim;* Saloutos,
Farmer Movements in the South, pp. 69–152.

[35] In Iowa, for example, the Burlington Railroad began to sell off large
sections of its federal land grant in 1870, stimulating a rapid expansion in the
southern part of the state. Much of this land was sold on credit, "no part of the
principal due for two years, and afterwards only one-ninth annually." Declining
prices hit purchasers hard. Mildred Throne, "Southern Iowa Agriculture,
1833–1890," *Agric. Hist.,* XXIII (1949), 129.

but strong in the South, and in frontier states like Kansas, Nebraska, and the Dakotas, a potent force.

In the seventies, when farmers in Iowa and Illinois were heavily in debt, the value of their property was declining. The average farm in Iowa was worth $3,377 in 1870, only $3,061 in 1880. Illinois farm properties suffered a similar decline. In Story County, Iowa, twenty-six farmers lost their land through foreclosure proceedings in 1871; during the period 1870–74, over 5 per cent of all the mortgaged farms in the country were foreclosed. On the other hand, during the period of Populist agitation, farm values in Iowa and Illinois were rising and the percentage of land mortgaged was much lower. During that decade, the average farm in Illinois rose in value by almost one-half and in Iowa almost doubled. Less than 2 per cent of the mortgages in Story County went into foreclosure proceedings between 1890 and 1896. Farmers in these states did not stop complaining about low agricultural prices and the inequities of the transportation and marketing systems, but they failed to carry their protests to the level of political action. In 1892 the Populist presidential candidate, James B. Weaver, won only 2 per cent of the Illinois popular vote; in Iowa, his native state, he got less than 5 per cent.[36]

In the plains states farther west, however, farmers entered the deflationary period of the late eighties heavily in debt. Thousands of new settlers were pouring into the area—between 1880 and 1890 the population of Kansas increased from 996,000 to 1.42 million, that of Nebraska from 450,000 to over a million, that of the Dakotas from 135,000 to almost 540,000. These settlers had borrowed to buy land, machinery, and supplies, to build homes and barns, even, sometimes, to pay their taxes. In Kansas and Nebraska alone there were at least 200 companies engaged in financing mortgages at this time, most of them merely middlemen who obtained money for

36 Bogue, *Prairie to Corn Belt,* pp. 284, 286; Scott, *Agrarian Movement,* pp. 5, 133; Hicks, *Populist Revolt,* p. 269. See also R. F. Severson, Jr., *et al.,* "Mortgage Borrowing as a Frontier Developed: A Study of Mortgages in Champaign County, Illinois," *Journal of Economic History,* XXVI (1966), 150–155, which shows that in Champaign County, Illinois, the total mortagage debt in 1876 was over $1.5 million, borrowed at rates close to 10 per cent; whereas in 1890 it was only $785,000, borrowed at rates of about 6 per cent. See also North, *Growth and Welfare,* pp. 141–142, which minimizes the importance of farm mortgages but admits that they were a problem in the North Central region.

lending from eastern banks, insurance companies, and private individuals. Debts in this region were especially high because the boom conditions which prevailed in the mid-eighties encouraged speculation and inflated values. Above-average rainfall was producing a series of bumper crops. Arriving by wagon in tiny Beaver City, Nebraska, in September, 1885, a young lawyer named George W. Norris, later a famous congressman and United States senator, was amazed by the lushness of the countryside. "I had been raised on a farm," he recalled in his autobiography, "and . . . I had never seen better corn grow out of the ground. . . . God was smiling upon this country with its abundant crops." Norris was so impressed that he seriously considered abandoning his budding legal career and becoming a farmer. Even in eastern sections of Nebraska, long settled, farm land doubled in value between 1881 and 1887, while in central Kansas, one local historian recorded, the "microbe" of speculation infected everyone. "In one week [newcomers] became as wild as their fellows and joined the maddening crowd." Farm land near Abilene that had sold for $6.25 an acre in 1867 changed hands in 1887 for $270 an acre. In Wichita, during the first five months of 1887, $35 million dollars worth of land changed hands; so many men rich with speculative profits inhabited the city that a young life insurance salesman from Ohio, passing through on a vacation trip, sold policies worth a quarter of a million dollars in less than a month.[37]

This boom ended disastrously in 1887. A severe drought, first of a series, sharply reduced harvests. Kansas, which had raised over 20 million bushels of wheat as early as 1880 and over 31 million bushels in 1882, produced only 7.6 million bushels in that year. The yield per acre of wheat in Kansas in 1887 was only 9.6 bushels; in Illinois it was 15.2 bushels.

Local crop failures and declining world prices over the next ten years dealt the debt-ridden farmers of the western plains a series of shattering blows. In 1890 over 60 per cent of the agricultural land of Kansas was mortgaged, double the percentage in Illinois. The

37 W. F. Mappin, "Farm Mortgages and the Small Farmer," *Political Science Quarterly*, IV (1889), 435; G. W. Norris, *Fighting Liberal* (New York, 1945), p. 55; Hicks, *Populist Revolt*, pp. 24–26; O. H. Bentley (ed.), *History of Wichita and Sedgwick County, Kansas* (2 vols., Chicago, 1910), I, 433; J. A. Garraty, *Right-Hand Man: The Life of George W. Perkins* (New York, 1960), pp. 18–19.

average Nebraska farm carried a debt of over $1,500 in that year, about a third of its value. George Norris, who had developed a thriving business as a loan agent to supplement his law practice, now saw this business practically disappear as interest rates soared to 10 per cent. "Men and women who had been carefree and light-hearted were turning bitter, and there was a sudden, unheralded, spontaneous outburst of resentment over the hardships resulting from crop failures, or from low prices," Norris later recalled. Hectic expansion suddenly became stagnation, to be followed shortly by actual decline. In the western regions of the plains states, thousands of new settlers were wiped out. At least half the population of western Kansas abandoned the region between 1888 and 1892. Farther east the depression was less serious but still drastic: in 1889 and 1890 alone, Leavenworth lost 15,000 inhabitants, Wichita 13,000. Nebraska and the Dakotas suffered a similar fate. Even the efficient, well-established bonanza companies took a heavy beating. The Amenia and Sharon Land Company of North Dakota, for example, had cleared $42,000 in 1886. In 1888 it lost over $74,000. The Dakotas were "dryer than Prohibition," James B. Power, a prominent landowner, complained in 1890. "If rain does not come soon good bye to wheat again."[38]

Drought exacerbated the discontent of plains farmers, but did not provide a rationale for political rebellion; no one could blame the weather on the government or the "interests." In any case, farmers could survive even a succession of poor harvests if they did not have to contend with heavy interest charges and mortgage repayments. Debts, rather than the weather, explain the sudden growth of political insurgency on the plains and in the South in the late eighties. In Kansas, the Farmers' Alliance recruited most of its members among mortgagees and tenants. A survey conducted by the

---

[38] For crop statistics, see Department of Agriculture, *Report, 1880*, p. 192; *1883*, p. 261; *1888*, pp. 428, 430; and J. C. Malin, *Winter Wheat in the Golden Belt of Kansas* (Lawrence, 1944), p. 157. Malin offers interesting discussions of weather conditions on the plains and of the unreliability of agricultural statistics (pp. 106–109, 141–145, 155–156). On the results of the drought, see Scott, *Agrarian Movement*, p. 5; Richard Lowitt, *George W. Norris: The Making of a Progressive, 1861–1912* (Syracuse, 1963), pp. 20–21, 282; Norris, *Fighting Liberal*, p. 60; Hicks, *Populist Revolt*, pp. 32–34; P. W. Gates, *Fifty Million Acres: Conflicts over Kansas Land Policy, 1854-1890* (Ithaca, 1954), p. 240; Drache, *Day of the Bonanza*, pp. 187, 211–212.

Topeka *Advocate* in 1890 revealed that in a sample of 2,077 members of the Alliance who owned their own land, only 350 held their property free of mortgage. In 1890, farm groups in Kansas organized a People's party, won control of the lower house of the legislature, and sent five representatives and a senator to Congress. An agrarian party also carried the Nebraska legislature and elected one independent and one "fusionist" congressman; in South Dakota and Minnesota the rebels achieved less substantial but highly significant gains. Southern farm groups, working within the Democratic party, elected several governors and won control of the legislatures of eight states. In Iowa and Illinois, by way of contrast, no statewide farmer party developed in 1890 and, as we have seen, two years later the Populist party failed to make any significant impression in these or other states of the Middle West and East.[39]

The agricultural discontent of this era was produced by a variety of problems connected in one way or another with the rapid industrialization of the nation. These affected farmers in every section. But by 1890, debt-ridden western and southern farmers were becoming conscious of the central role of deflation in causing their difficulties. They did not, however, succeed in reversing the trend of prices, for their analysis of the causes of the deflation was somewhat naïve; their preferred solution, the free coinage of silver, even more naïve.

Since agriculture loomed so important in the economy, was in such a state of flux and so beset by complex problems, pressure for government action in the agricultural realm was continuous. The land laws of the nation, the regulation of corporations that farmers did business with, and matters related to finance and foreign commerce were always surrounded by political controversy. But the government also concerned itself with agricultural research and development, and this work was largely—though not entirely—removed from the area of partisan debate. Agricultural scientists drew heavily upon the federal government and the states for support. Congress first provided funds for agricultural purposes on a continuing basis in 1839, placing the work under the Patent

39 D. R. Goodloe, "Western Farm Mortgages," *Forum,* X (1890), 352–353; Hicks, *Populist Revolt,* pp. 155–181.

Office. Only in 1862, however, the year that saw the passage of the Homestead Act and the Morrill land-grant-college law, was a Department of Agriculture created. Denied the dignity of cabinet status until 1889, the department expanded steadily after the Civil War; by the late seventies its annual budgets were averaging about $200,000. Its activities included the collection and publication of statistics; the operation of experimental farms; research in soil chemistry, entomology, and plant and animal diseases; the distribution of seeds; and the maintenance of contacts with state and private organizations concerned with farm problems.[40]

Most of the early commissioners of agriculture worked energetically to expand and improve the department. Many first-rate scientists served its bureaus in the early years, such as Charles M. Wetherill, a Liebig-trained chemist, and the botanist George Vasey. The Statistical Bureau, presided over by Jacob R. Dodge, collected masses of valuable information: by 1877 some 4,000 volunteer field correspondents were turning in monthly reports on crop conditions and prices, and the department's statistical publications were outstanding for the period.

Nevertheless, all the diseases that plagued the post–Civil War federal bureaucracy infected the new department: arguments with the politicians over patronage, internal squabbling, loss of personnel because of low salary schedules, conflicts with special-interest groups outside the government, and ill-conceived and poorly executed scientific activities. The policy of distributing seeds to the public, first ordered by Congress in 1839, was theoretically sound but ineffective in practice. Congressmen soon learned that their right to mail free seed packets to their constituents was a potent method of winning voter support; as a result, immense quantities were dispensed without thought either for their suitability to local conditions of soil and climate or for the systematic study of results obtained from planting them. Although all the commissioners tried to curb this waste, and seed dealers accused the department of running a "seed store," Congress insisted on continuing the practice.

40 True, *Agricultural Experimentation*, pp. 22–25, 40–52; Department of Agriculture, *Report, 1877*, p. 20; J. M. Gauss and L. O. Wolcott, *Public Administration and the United States Department of Agriculture* (Chicago, 1940), pp. 3–12.

There were other difficulties. Editors of farm journals claimed that the publication of departmental reports and bulletins represented unfair government competition with their enterprises. Specialists in and out of the department clashed with political administrators and with farm leaders over the relative importance of theoretical and practical research, while department scientists engaged at times in selfish and unseemly squabbling. The department also devoted too much energy to futile attempts to cultivate exotic plants. During the Civil War it began to experiment with Chinese sorghum as a substitute for cane sugar, and despite repeated failures this work was continued well into the eighties. Efforts to grow tea were pushed with equal persistence; an experimental tea farm in South Carolina was not abandoned until 1912, although it was apparent from the start that both climate and labor costs militated against success. Similarly unsuccessful attempts were made to grow silk, dates, and even coffee. Writing of the department in 1874 before his appointment as chief entomologist, Charles V. Riley complained bitterly about "the large sums it now fritters away in the gratuitous distribution of seeds" and "the character of its . . . management [which] depends on political whim or fancy."[41]

Despite its weaknesses, which should be considered in the context of the deplorable state of public administration in these years, by 1877 the department was highly regarded by both Congress and the public. A succession of able commissioners, especially Norman J. Colman (1885–89), a stock farmer and editor who had served as lieutenant governor of Missouri and president of the state Board of Agriculture, steadily expanded its activities.[42] Contemporary trends

[41] True, *Agricultural Experimentation*, pp. 42, 53–54, 57, 62; E. D. Ross, "The United States Department of Agriculture During the Commissionership," *Agricultural History*, XX (1946), 130, 140–142; Nelson Klose, "Experiments in Tea Production in the United States," *ibid.*, XXIV (1950), 156–161; Howard, "Applied Entomology," p. 79.

[42] G. F. Lemmer, *Norman J. Colman and Colman's Rural World: A Study in Agricultural Leadership* (Columbia, Mo., 1953), pp. 7–83. The other commissioners during the period were General William G. LeDuc (1877–81), a Minnesota lawyer and land promoter whose bluntness irritated some congressmen but who expanded the department's work and won a reputation as a strong administrator, and George B. Loring (1881–85), a Massachusetts physician and politician, somewhat pompous and complacent, but sincerely devoted to the organization. L. D. White, *The Republican Era, 1869–1901* (New York, 1958), pp. 233–234; True, *Agricultural Experimentation*, pp. 52–60.

aided the commissioners and others eager to step up the pace of the department's work. The increasing complexity of the marketing system, together with the general malaise caused by changes result- ing from industrialization, encouraged agriculturalists to turn to the government for help.

During the late seventies and early eighties, pressure developed for federal regulation of the livestock and meat-packing industries. On the domestic scene, the spreading railroad network facilitated the interstate movement of livestock, which caused an increase in the prevalence of contagious animal diseases, especially the so-called "Texas fever" and pleuropneumonia, deadly to cattle. As early as 1877 the Department of Agriculture stationed agents in the West to report the presence of infected animals and assigned a veterinary to examine cattle in the Chicago stockyards. In 1883, this work was co- ordinated in a new Veterinary Bureau in the department. Mean- while, a rise in the volume of American meat exports was causing political problems. Beginning in 1877, the business of shipping live cattle to Great Britain suddenly boomed.[43] Alarmed by reports that some of these beasts were suffering from pleuropneumonia, the British government, in 1879, required that all cattle imported from America be slaughtered at the point of debarkation within ten days of their arrival. By preventing stockmen from reconditioning their cattle before sale, this regulation greatly reduced the value of the animals, which tended to arrive in poor shape after the long sea voyage. Exporters promptly demanded that the Department of Agriculture find a cure for the disease. This took time, but mean- while the department worked to determine the extent of pleuro- pneumonia in the United States, and sent a veterinary to England to trace cases of infected cattle to their source.[44]

Then, between 1879 and 1883, Germany, France, and seven other European countries banned imports of American pork on the ground that some of the meat was infected with trichinosis. The

---

[43] From 224 head in 1876, the volume rose to 5,000 in 1877 and to over 70,000 in 1879. W. D. Zimmerman, "Live Cattle Export Trade between the United States and Great Britain, 1868–1885," *Agric. Hist.*, XXXVI (1962), 50.

[44] *Ibid.*, pp. 46–52; F. W. Powell, *The Bureau of Animal Industry: Its History, Activities and Organization* (Baltimore, 1927), pp. 3–6; G. F. Thompson, "Administrative Work of the Federal Government in Relation to the Animal Industry," Department of Agriculture, *Yearbook, 1899*, p. 442.

trichinosis danger was not really very great—the restrictions resulted chiefly from the demands of European farmers for protection against cheap American pork and from European resentment of American tariffs on manufactured goods—but the failure of the United States to inspect meat exports played into the protectionists' hands. In any case, meat exporters were soon demanding "a rigid system of inspection for all meat products for foreign export."

These events led Congress, in 1884, to create a new Bureau of Animal Industry in the Department of Agriculture. The law authorized the commissioner of agriculture to establish quarantines and make other regulations aimed at checking contagious animal diseases, and barred the shipment of infected animals in interstate commerce. In 1886, additional legislation empowered the new bureau to purchase and destroy diseased livestock. Acting in conjunction with state authorities, bureau inspectors launched an all-out campaign against pleuropneumonia, quarantining herds, slaughtering infected cattle, and disinfecting stockyards and freight cars. By 1888 the disease had been checked and soon thereafter it was eradicated; the last case was reported in New Jersey in 1892.[45]

Inspection of meat exports took longer to achieve, partly because of American recognition of the political nature of the European boycotts and partly because of prejudice against government regulation of private businesses. However, the economic effects of the boycott, together with a blistering condemnation of the handling of domestic meat products made by a Senate investigating committee, resulted finally (August, 1890) in a law giving the Department of Agriculture authority to inspect all meat intended for export. After Congress had strengthened inspection procedures the following year, the European countries removed their restrictions on American pork.[46]

[45] J. L. Gignilliat, "Pigs, Politics, and Protection: The European Boycott of American Pork, 1879–1891," Agric. Hist., XXXV (1961), 3–10; D. M. Pletcher, The Awkward Years: American Foreign Relations Under Garfield and Arthur (Columbia, Mo., 1962), pp. 158–165; Powell, Bureau of Animal Industry, pp. 10–12; White, Republican Era, pp. 246–247; Department of Agriculture, Yearbook, 1899, pp. 443–447. During the campaign the bureau inspected over 1.6 million head, conducted 356,000 post-mortem examinations, and purchased over 6,000 diseased animals for slaughter.

[46] Powell, Bureau of Animal Industry, pp. 12–14; Gignilliat, "Pigs, Politics, and Protection," pp. 10–11.

Although spectacularly successful, the work of the department in combating animal diseases was less important in the long run than its program of experimentation and education. From earliest colonial times, abundant cheap land and high labor costs had conspired against attempts to reform the wasteful practices of most American farmers. Despite the urgings of countless agricultural societies and farm journals, few tillers of the soil did much to preserve the fertility of their lands, introduce improved methods of cultivation, or take advantage of the discoveries of agricultural scientists. By the seventies and eighties, however, farmers were beginning to turn to science for help. Easterners were becoming more concerned about restoring the fertility of worn-out soils. Wheat growers in the Middle West, alarmed by the competition of the bonanza farms of the plains region, sought means of improving yields. In the newly settled regions of the plains, farmers needed advice about which plants were best suited for local conditions and about the best time to plant each crop. Orchardists in the Far West demanded help against the ravages of insect pests. In every section farmers were disturbed by the tendency of bright, ambitious younger people to leave the farm for the city. They sensed their need for specialized knowledge if they were to make their way amid the complexities of commercial agriculture and take advantage of the opportunities offered by the emerging industrial society. Education, especially higher education designed specifically for their particular requirements and interests, seemed essential.

The colleges set up under the Morrill Act of 1862 "for the benefit of agriculture and the mechanic arts" had made few direct contributions to the welfare of agriculture. The tendency of dirt farmers to ridicule book learning and laboratory experimentation was dying, but the colleges, lacking a solid sense of direction and plagued by a shortage of professors trained in the agricultural sciences and even of good textbooks and laboratory facilities, were not turning out graduates with much practical knowledge of farming. The University of Wisconsin, for example, did not get around to appointing a professor of agriculture until 1868, and for years thereafter the professor, the university authorities, and local agricultural leaders were at a loss to know "what to do" for the farmers of the state. In 1870 President Andrew D. White of Cornell was reduced to advertising for a professor of agriculture; he was unable to find a properly qualified, full-time teacher until 1873. As late as 1879 Cornell had granted degrees in agriculture to only nine students. In Mississippi the legislature had not even established its agricultural college as late as 1877.

Farmers were vexed by the failure of the Morrill Act to achieve practical results. "We insist," the state convention of the Mississippi Grange resolved in 1877, "that the Legislature . . . establish an agricultural college in accordance with the act of Congress appropriating the proceeds of the sale of public land in this State for that purpose, and that no further delay or frittering away of the fund will be quietly tolerated by the agriculturalists of the State." Yet Granger groups in states which did have such institutions were seldom satisfied with their work. The Connecticut Grange accused Yale's renowned Sheffield School of paying too much attention to theoretical and experimental matters and not enough to practical instruction; in Wisconsin, the Grangers demanded that "farmers [should] teach farmers"; in New York, they passed resolutions condemning agricultural education at Cornell. Writing in 1875, an agricultural journalist characterized land-grant colleges, as "asylums for classical idiots and political professors," and ten years later another critic said that he knew fifty men "who claimed . . . to be educated as agriculturalists and not one of them was competent to feed pigs."[47]

Of course, the agricultural colleges were bringing higher education to hundreds of farm boys and girls and training many future scientists, teachers, and community leaders. They were responsible for many educational innovations later adopted by more prestigious institutions. Few persons, however, fully appreciated these truths, and as late as the mid-eighties it was beyond argument that the agricultural colleges had failed to provide "the special training contemplated in the [Morrill] act."[48]

Leaders in the agricultural colleges realized that they were not

[47] True, *Agricultural Experimentation*, p. 146; E. D. Ross, *Democracy's College: The Land-Grant Movement in the Formative Stage* (Ames, Iowa, 1942), pp. 80–81, 103–110, 119–120; Carstensen, "Experiment Station," p. 15; G. P. Coleman, "Pioneering in Agricultural Education: Cornell University, 1867–1900," *Agric. Hist.*, XXXVI (1962), 201; Theodore Saloutos, "The Agricultural Problem and Nineteenth Century Industrialism," *ibid.*, XXII (1948), 171–172.

[48] Ross, *Democracy's College*, pp. 133–135.

meeting the needs of actual farmers. Casting about for new means of carrying out the intent of the Morrill Act, they began as early as 1871 to talk of establishing experimental farms and laboratories independent of their regular teaching functions and of reaching working farmers by holding conferences, organizing short courses for adults, and publishing bulletins and reports. The Department of Agriculture, together with scientists teaching at private universities, also took an interest in proposals of this kind. After a department-sponsored conference in Washington in 1872, Professor Samuel W. Johnson of Yale, together with his former student William O. Atwater and a number of others, began agitating in Connecticut for a state agricultural experiment program, and in 1875 the Connecticut legislature authorized a station. Similar stations were soon founded in North Carolina, New York, Massachusetts, and a number of other states. In most cases these operated in close conjunction with the local land-grant colleges.[49]

From the beginning of the movement, the leaders had sought federal aid for the new stations. Conflicts between the Department of Agriculture and the academicians, however, had weakened their efforts. The department wished to control any federal program, while the professors naturally wished to retain local autonomy. This conflict ended in 1885, when Norman J. Colman became commissioner of agriculture. At a conference in Washington in July, 1885, Colman urged the creation of "a bond of union and sympathy between this department and the agricultural colleges." The stations should remain under local control, he said, but the department should co-ordinate their work and give publicity to their discoveries. Early in the next year Representative William H. Hatch of Missouri introduced a bill for federal aid to the stations, and in 1887 this measure became law. It provided annual subsidies of $15,000 to each state for the support of agricultural experiment stations, these to be controlled by the land-grant colleges. Congress carried out the rest of Colman's plan in 1888 by voting funds for the publication of the results of experiment-station studies. The first issue of the *Experiment Station Record* appeared in 1889.[50]

[49] Carstensen, "Experiment Station," p. 16; True, *Agricultural Experimentation*, pp. 70, 82–106, 118.

[50] Lemmer, *Colman*, pp. 97–101; True, *Agricultural Experimentation*, pp. 118–132; Department of Agriculture, *Report, 1888*, pp. 8–14, 537–541

By the end of 1888, forty-three experiment stations were receiving federal grants under the Hatch Act. It took many years merely to train enough scientists and technicians to man these stations adequately, and the efficient co-ordination of their activities proved almost impossible. But from the start their accomplishments were impressive. A "large and sudden expansion" of experimental work took place under their direction in such fields as agronomy, entomology, plant pathology, animal husbandry, and meteorology. Florida, for example, had no station of any kind before the passage of the act. By October, 1887, months before the first federal payments were actually on hand, a small staff was at work in the science laboratory of the Florida Agricultural College at Lake City. The college provided land for an experimental farm, and by the end of the year the experimenters were growing timothy seed imported from Michigan and bluegrass from Texas. Soon thereafter the station published reports on studies made of different varieties of strawberries, onions, and other crops, and of work aimed at the control of diseases and insects that plagued Florida's peach and citrus orchards. The Connecticut station at Storrs began a series of investigations in the area of food chemistry and human nutrition as early as 1888. S. M. Babcock invented his machine for measuring the fat content of milk while working at the Wisconsin station in 1890. By 1891, the stations were employing more than 450 persons, most of them skilled professionals, and distributing over 300 bulletins and reports to some 350,000 readers.

Although no sudden scientific revolution followed, the experiment stations eventually had a substantial impact on American agriculture. They also strengthened the ties between the Department of Agriculture and the scientific community in the universities, and exercised a salutary, possibly a crucial, influence on the land-grant colleges, enabling them to improve their faculties and build new laboratories and, by offering young people a chance to participate in matters of real significance, to attract more and better graduate and undergraduate students. At Cornell, for example, the staff of the faculty of agriculture was doubled in the single year 1889, the most notable addition being Liberty Hyde Bailey, a young graduate of Michigan Agricultural College who was to become one of the great horticulturalists of the next generation. By 1892,

Cornell's College of Agriculture was probably the best in the country.[51]

As its functions expanded, the Department of Agriculture increased in prestige and influence in rural areas. As early as 1876 the Patrons of Husbandry had demanded that the department be raised to cabinet status, and other groups of farmers had carried on the campaign throughout the eighties. The necessary legislation passed the House of Representatives in 1882, but the Senate did not fall in line until February, 1889. Norman J. Colman became the first official representative of agriculture in the cabinet, but the end of Cleveland's term a few weeks later brought a Republican, Jeremiah M. Rusk, to the post. Rusk, formerly governor of Wisconsin, made an energetic, imaginative, and aggressive secretary. He improved the efficiency of the department, held a nice balance between practical and theoretical research, and proved adept at getting along both with Congress and the rural press. He strengthened the ties between the department and the practicing farmer, sending representatives to agricultural fairs and meetings in every corner of the country, and maintaining close relations with thousands of unofficial "agents," who kept the department advised about crop conditions and yields. By 1891, Agriculture stood out as the best organized and most progressive unit in the federal bureaucracy. It was spending about 2.7 million a year and serving, in the words of one proud official, as "the most momentous single educational force in the United States."[52]

The changes that convulsed American agriculture in these years had the effect of confusing and upsetting many rural attitudes. Farmers have always been torn between two antagonistic aspects of their profession. On the one hand, farming is a business, the farmer a capitalist (and often a laborer too) engaged in producing goods

51 True, *Agricultural Experimentation*, pp. 141–164; A. C. True and R. D. Milner, "Development of the Nutritional Investigations of the Department of Agriculture," Department of Agriculture, *Yearbook, 1899*, pp. 408, 410, and *Report, 1891*, pp. 50–51, 524–525; Samuel Proctor, "The Early Years of the Florida Experiment Station, 1888–1906," *Agric. Hist.*, XXXVI (1962), 213–214; Coleman, "Agricultural Education," pp. 205–206; Ross, *Democracy's College*, pp. 141–144.

52 True, *Agricultural Experimentation*, pp. 172–177; Dept. of Agriculture, *Report, 1891*, pp. 67–68; White, *Republican Era*, pp. 240–242, 256; Henry Casson, *"Uncle Jerry": The Life of General Jeremiah M. Rusk* (Madison, 1895), pp. 235–314.

for sale. His ultimate objective as a businessman is to make money. On the other hand, agriculture is a way of life. The farmer co-operates with and fights against the mysterious, elemental forces of the natural world; daily he supervises and controls the miracle of creation, extracting life from the inanimate soil; his work provides satisfactions akin to those of religion and art. This aspect of agriculture is nonmaterial, or at least noncommercial.

Until well into the nineteenth century, American conditions tended to emphasize the noncommercial side of farming. The rudest frontiersman was never entirely self-sufficient, and certainly never so by choice. He was an avid speculator, a ruthless destroyer of nature's bounty, and eager for material profit. But his environment kept these aspects of his character in check. His isolation forced him to live close to nature and to know nature's ways, and to supply a large share of his own needs. He *wanted* to accumulate riches and enjoy the pleasures of a more sophisticated society, but he had to live with things as they were. Being human, he made the best of necessity and compensated for his lack of creature comforts by crediting himself with virtues that, in fact, he could not escape.

Of course, the politicians and others concerned with winning and holding the good opinion of large segments of the population eagerly exploited the farmers' willingness to glorify the agricultural way of life. Praise of the noble yeoman, like most praise, was cheap enough and relieved the speaker of any need to demonstrate his usefulness to his audience in more practical ways. Seizing upon a line of argument developed in ancient times, they expatiated endlessly on what Richard Hofstadter has called "the agrarian myth."[53] Jefferson's claim that "those who labor in the earth are the chosen people of God" is only the most famous of hundreds of similar enunciations of the agrarian myth by prominent Americans. Others range from the probably cynical pronouncement of Benja-

[53] "Its hero was the yeoman farmer. . . . Unstinted praise of the special virtues of the farmer and the special values of rural life was coupled with the assertion that agriculture, as a calling uniquely productive and uniquely important to society, had a special right to the concern and protection of government. . . . Because he lived in close communion with beneficent nature, [the farmer's] life was believed to have a wholesomeness and integrity impossible for the depraved populations of cities. His well-being was not merely physical, it was moral; it was not merely personal, it was the central source of civil virtue; it was not merely secular but religious, for God had made the land and called man to cultivate it." Richard Hofstadter, *The Age of Reform: From Bryan to F.D.R.* (New York, 1956), pp. 24–25.

min Franklin, the most urban of eighteenth-century Americans, that farming was the "most honorable of all employments" to the obviously sincere remarks of Washington, who called "the life of a husbandman" the "most delectable" of occupations and who said that he would rather retire to his Mount Vernon acres than "be made *emperor of the world.*" Dozens of poets, novelists, and farm editors also chanted the theme.[54]

The growing commercialization of agriculture around the middle of the nineteenth century neither removed the basis for considering it a noble profession nor halted the flow of words in praise of honest yeomanry. But when new means of transportation, new agricultural machinery, new scientific knowledge, and much larger urban markets made it easier for farmers to think of themselves as businessmen, the tone of agricultural opinion-makers changed significantly. In the eighteenth century farmers' almanacs seldom dealt with the practical side of farming; in the nineteenth they did so at length. As agricultural societies and farm journals proliferated, they, too, paid a great deal of attention to material problems. Horace Greeley, the most influential journalist in midcentury America, while yielding to no one in his praise of farming as a way of life, devoted much space in his New York *Weekly Tribune*, which had a wide circulation in rural areas, to how farmers could increase their incomes, and published *What I Know of Farming* (1871), a collection of "homely expositions of practical agriculture as an art based on science." In these writings Greeley recommended that farmers rotate crops, use fertilizers freely, and invest in the latest machinery to increase output. He also suggested that they concern themselves with the business side of farm management—the keeping of detailed records, the efficient marketing of crops, and so on.[55]

Rural journalists echoed Greeley's advice. Instead of stressing independence and self-sufficiency, the *Prairie Farmer* urged in 1868,

<hr />

54 C. E. Eisinger, "The Freehold Concept in Eighteenth Century American Letters," *William and Mary Quarterly*, IV (1947), 48–58, and "The Influence of Natural Rights and Physiocratic Doctrines on American Agrarian Thought During the Revolutionary Period," *Agric. Hist.*, XXI (1947), 16, 20; S. K. Padover, "George Washington: Portrait of a True Conservative," *Social Research*, XXII (1955), 200; Marcus Cunliffe, *George Washington: Man and Monument* (New York, 1960), p. 116.

55 C. E. Eisinger, "The Farmer in the Eighteenth Century Almanac," *Agric. Hist.*, XXVIII (1954), 108; E. D. Ross, "Horace Greeley and the Beginnings of the New Agriculture," *ibid.*, VII (1933), 3–17; W. H. Hale, *Horace Greeley: Voice of the People* (New York, 1961), p. 362.

farmers should concentrate on cash crops and sell as much as possible in the market. "The old rule that a farmer should produce all that he required, and that the surplus represented his gains, is part of the past. Agriculture, like all other business, is better for its subdivisions, each one growing that which is best suited to his soil, skill, climate and market, and with its proceeds purchas[ing] his other needs."[56] "The work of farming is only half done when the crop is out of the ground," another editor reminded his readers in 1887. "Watch and study the markets, and the ways of the market-men . . . and learn the art of 'selling well.' " Others urged farmers to keep detailed accounts and learn modern methods of book-keeping. "The nearer the farmers come to a correct system of accounting, of knowing what they are doing, the better they will come out," a New York fruit grower, master of the state Grange, explained. Furthermore, they should adopt a hardheaded approach to the labor problem. "The wide-awake farmer will hire all the help he can with profit, and no more," a Massachusetts farmer of long experience explained in 1901. "When profits cease he will be the first to discharge help which he does not need."

Farmers should also modify their traditional individualism, agrarian leaders insisted. Both the Grange and the various farm alliances emphasized co-operative purchasing and marketing schemes. They established social clubs, and stressed political organization as well. In the seventies the Grangers, following their dictum "in essentials, unity," made a great effort to develop co-operative activities. In the eighties the Southern Alliance, under Dr. C. W. Macune, set out "to organize the agriculturalists of the cotton belt for business purposes." By 1889 the various state alliances were so deeply engaged in co-operative activities that they established an association to plan for co-operation among the co-operators. "We have gone as far as we can as individual agents," the secretary of this body declared.[57]

Agricultural leaders insisted that if the farmer would make these adjustments to modern conditions he could have both prosperity and the full life. Relief from drudgery and hard labor, better education, cultural opportunities equal to those available to city

[56] Quoted in Hofstadter, *Age of Reform*, p. 39.
[57] Johnstone, "Old Ideals," p. 145; Industrial Commission on Agriculture and Agricultural Labor, *Report* (Washington, 1901), X, 321, 885; Buck, *Granger Movement*, p. 53; Hicks, *Populist Revolt*, pp. 134, 138–139.

dwellers, and a rich social life would all follow. For the simple yeoman of the agrarian myth, they substituted the ideal of the successful agricultural executive, managing a complex property efficiently, harvesting the rewards of modern civilization along with his crops. They never, of course, suggested that the farmer would thereby sacrifice his antique virtue; rather they were advocating, as Paul H. Johnstone has said, a neo-Calvinistic philosophy: the true compensation for virtue is material success; by accepting commercial ideals, aspiring for the things of this world, the farmer would be doing God's work and could expect his reward here on earth as well as in heaven.[58]

Obviously, the deepening involvement of American farmers in commercial agriculture was a response to the Industrial Revolution and essentially beyond their control. However, the barrage of advice and exhortation that descended upon them from agricultural organizations and the rural press certainly heightened their expectations as to what benefits commercialization would bring. Alas, for nearly all, it brought far less than they had anticipated.

In the first place, improvements in agricultural efficiency did not match those in manufacturing and commerce. The productivity of farm labor increased, but, as a group, farmers did not improve their standard of living very dramatically. In the decades of the seventies and eighties, the farmers' share of the wealth of the nation declined from about 30 per cent to about 20 per cent. Using census data, a Department of Agriculture statistician estimated that in 1890 three million agricultural laborers in the United States received wages totaling $645.5 million, whereas two million workers in trade and transportation received $745 million and five million industrial workers nearly $2.2 billion. These statistics fail to take into account the fact that most agricultural laborers lived off the land at least to some extent. It is also true that in some sections, especially in the South, farm labor probably got less than a fair share of what it produced. Nevertheless, there can be little doubt that farm work was less productive than other types and that this condition affected all farmers, not merely hired laborers.[59]

[58] Johnstone, "Old Ideals," p. 149.
[59] Shannon, *Farmer's Last Frontier*, p. 353; Industrial Commission, *Report*, X, 153; L. F. Cox, "The American Agricultural Wage Earner, 1865–1900," *Agric. Hist.*, XXII (1948), 95–114.

Furthermore, exploitation of the possibilities opened up by modern developments demanded a degree of organization and centralization that farmers did not achieve. For industrialists and even for industrial labor, conditions favored the pooling of resources and brains in order to improve efficiency and strengthen the political, social, and economic power of special groups. Like a watch, the emerging system was very complex, but structurally integrated and capable of adjustment by human beings. Railroadmen were discovering methods—some legal, some illegal—of eliminating competition and otherwise regulating their affairs in ways profitable to themselves. In many industries, a relative handful of manufacturers could determine, or at least significantly influence, the amount and quality of goods produced according to their understanding of market conditions. By the standards of the twentieth century their efforts appear fumbling, for their view both of their own interests and of the workings of the economy was usually myopic; nevertheless, they did try, and not entirely without success.

But there were too many independent farmers, dealing with too many different kinds of problems and subject to too many unforeseeable contingencies to manipulate the national output of wheat or cotton or beef or any other product of the soil. Farmers did cooperate politically to obtain government regulation of some elements of the system that affected them tangentially, such as railroads and commodity exchanges, but they did not succeed at all in combining their intelligence to influence agricultural production, their major concern. The determination of what was grown and how much remained in the hands of millions of unco-ordinated individuals and the unpredictable elements, which is to say that there was no rational control at all. When the National Grange urged farmers to reduce production of a particular crop, the effect was actually to encourage them to raise it. The average member felt "a temptation . . . to increase the size of his own crop when he believes that the total crop is going to be decreased."[60] Obviously, this situation operated to the disadvantage of farmers.

Finally, farmers discovered that many of the material and cultural advantages that the Industrial Revolution had made available to the residents of cities would not flourish in a rural environment.

[60] Buck, *Granger Movement*, p. 296.

Testifying before the Industrial Commission in 1899, George K. Holmes, a statistician employed by the Department of Agriculture, said:

This is a new age to the farmer. He is now, more than ever before, a citizen of the world. Cheap and excellent books and periodical publications load the shelf and the table in his sitting room and parlor. He travels more than he ever did before, and he travels longer distances. His children are receiving a better education than he received himself, and they dress better than he did when he was a child. They are more frequently in contact with town and city life than he was. They have a top buggy, and a fancy whip, and a pretty lap robe, with a fast stepping horse, whereas their father had an old wagon and a less expensive horse. The farmer's table is better too; his food is more varied, and more of it is bought by him and less of it is raised on his farm.[61]

Despite its optimistic tone, this statement, generally accurate as a description of the more substantial class of agricultural landowners, is notable for the modesty of its claims. That farmers could lead a better life in the nineties than was possible in the seventies is chiefly a commentary on the meagerness of the earlier opportunities. If rural education had improved, as Holmes said, the progress was far less remarkable than that in urban regions. Between 1870 and 1890, national expenditures for public education rose from $63 million to $145 million, the number of teachers from 128,000 to 340,000.[62] But in country districts there were fewer schools, with shorter sessions, less adequate facilities, and less-well-trained teachers than in the towns and cities.

Growing up in Mitchell County, Iowa, in the 1870's, Hamlin Garland attended "a barren temple of the arts" with a single room, graceless, bare, and without "one touch of color." Although the area was growing rapidly, the school actually deteriorated with the years. "Its benches, hideously hacked and thick with grime, were as hard and uncomfortable as when I first saw them," Garland later wrote. Calvin Coolidge's first school, in rural Vermont, was similar. The future President entered it in 1877, at the age of five. There was a single, ill-paid teacher; the oldest of Calvin's twenty-two classmates

---

61 Industrial Commission, *Report*, X, 157.
62 *Hist. Stat.*, pp. 66, 315.

was eighteen. School sessions were short, held in slack periods when the children were not needed for farm work. "Few, if any, of my teachers reached the standard now required by all public schools," Coolidge recalled in later years, adding that his little sister qualified for a teaching certificate and actually taught a term of school at the age of twelve.

The future automobile manufacturer Henry Ford attended a somewhat larger rural school in Michigan at about that time. It had three sessions, but only in the winter did older farm boys find time to attend. Few of the teachers were employed on a year-round basis. "We started school off with a song or a prayer," Henry's younger sister later recalled. "There wasn't any set schedule. It depended on the mood of the teacher." Writing of his education in Nebraska during the 1880's, the educator Alvin Johnson said: "The school was in operation only three months, December through February. . . . The teachers were prevailingly those who had failed elsewhere or were just beginning. . . . We expected to learn nothing in school, and we were not disappointed."

Urban schools, especially those in the poorer sections of the great cities, were far from perfect, but they were always larger, and usually offered longer sessions and a wider choice of subjects. Even in a small town like Eldorado, Kansas, where the editor William Allen White was educated in the late seventies, the school was "well equipped, with good seats and desks and blackboards." Unlike the one-room cabins of the countryside, where six-year-olds often sat beside six-footers, the Eldorado school was graded "from the primary to the high school."[63]

Sparsity of population, not lack of public support, accounted for the lag in rural education, and also for the backwardness of rural roads and sanitation and the inadequate facilities for cultural development. Many of the most striking of the new conveniences of the era, such as the telephone and the electric light, were unavail-

[63] Hamlin Garland, *A Son of the Middle Border* (New York, 1962), pp. 80–81, 123; Calvin Coolidge, *Autobiography* (New York, 1929), p. 31; C. M. Fuess, *Calvin Coolidge: The Man from Vermont* (Boston, 1939), pp. 27–29; Allan Nevins, *Ford: The Times, the Man, the Company* (New York, 1954), p. 45; Alvin Johnson, *Pioneer's Progress* (New York, 1952), p. 40; Everett Dick, *The Sod-House Frontier: 1854–1890* (New York, 1937), pp. 319–328; W. A. White, *Autobiography* (New York, 1946), pp. 37–38.

able to farmers for the same reason. Even free rural mail delivery was not begun until the 1890's.[64]

Farmers expected machinery to lighten their labors, and to a degree it did, but the cost of machinery added to the pressures on farmers to increase the area they cultivated. The whole tendency of commercial agriculture was to make farmers work harder. When Alvin Johnson and his brothers decided to turn their father's subsistence farm into a money-maker so that they could go to college, they accomplished their purpose, but only after enormous effort and immense strain. "In the few years of our operations," Johnson wrote in his autobiography, "we did more worrying than my father did in all his life." After describing the harshness of his boyhood on the Iowa prairie, Hamlin Garland explained: "The Garlands were not so poor as all this would seem to imply, for we were now farming over three hundred acres of land and caring for a herd of cattle and many swine." When the choice lay between buying a new carpet for the parlor or a new wagon, the senior Garland chose the wagon. "Most of the duties of the farmer's life," Garland also wrote, "require the lapse of years to seem beautiful in my eyes."

Many observers commented on the hard lives of women and children on farms. One rural editor, testifying before the Industrial Commission about conditions in South Dakota, said: "I myself have seen more than one worn-out farmer's wife. . . . Many boys and girls are worked so hard on land that forever afterwards the thought of farming is distasteful to them." Endless labor, few social contacts, an almost total absence of the amenities and small comforts associated with civilized life, were the lot of most, especially in newly settled regions. When Garland published *Main Travelled Roads* in 1891, a book in which he tried to describe the "essential ugliness" of the lives of farm women, his mother wrote him: "You might have said more, but I'm glad you didn't. Farmers' wives have enough to bear as it is." Some commentators, such as the agent of the Farmers' Alliance who claimed that the isolation and drudgery of farm life drove many women insane, undoubtedly exaggerated the hardships, but the general conclusion of such critics, that "the isolation, the lack of social enjoyment and intercourse, the yearning for the

64 White, *Republican Era,* p. 259.

society of others, for excitement, for amusement" was driving ambitious individuals from the countryside to the cities, was undoubtedly true. Even Liberty Hyde Bailey, one of the most outspoken advocates of the virtues of an agricultural existence, spoke of the dearth of "opportunities for social pleasures and for physical comforts," as well as "the lack of ordinary means of sanitation" and "the hard lot of the [farm] woman."[65]

These unavoidable frustrations probably account for the reactionary elements that many students have noted in the farm protest movements of the late nineteenth century, for the paradoxical fact that behind the genuine and in so many ways forward-looking liberalism of the Grangers and Populists there lurked a mean and irrational aspect. Some agrarians did display an almost paranoid tendency to see a vicious conspiracy in every disagreement over railroad rates, every decline in the price of wheat or cotton, and a somewhat schizoid willingness to adopt the practices of commercial agriculture eagerly while idealizing the nonmaterial rewards of the rural life in a past, supposedly golden age, when every farmer had been a sturdy yeoman immune from materialist temptations. The slogan of the Grangers, "In essentials, unity; in non-essentials, liberty; in all things, clarity," contrasts strangely with many aspects of their actual behavior, which was often selfish and illogical. Solon J. Buck, historian of the Granger movement, concluded that the "hope of pecuniary profit was the motive factor in enducing large numbers of farmers to join," that "the deciding factor in determining the action of a [local] grange . . . was generally the financial interests of the individual Grangers," that Granger efforts to establish co-operatives usually foundered because the organizers placed more faith in "home-made theories" than in the experiences of other co-operative enterprises, and that most members were too self-centered even to respond to efforts made by the national organization to collect and publish crop reports.[66] When the Alliance movement blossomed into populism at the end of the eighties, it, too, took on overtones that hint at illiberal and irrational elements in the agrarian mind. Suspicion of the city and in some

[65] Johnson, *Pioneer's Progress*, p. 69; Garland, *Son of the Middle Border*, pp. 72–75, 86–87, 108–110, 116, 124, 352–353; Industrial Commission, *Report*, X, 275, 286, 936, 1014. See also Dick, *Sod-House Frontier*, pp. 232–243.

[66] Buck, *Granger Movement*, pp. 64, 117, 275–277, 295.

cases of immigrants, industrial workers, and Jews, a tendency to blame their difficulties on "international bankers" or other remote and wealthy "conspirators," a penchant for shifting responsibility for the frustration of their hopes from themselves to others, were characteristic of the mentality of a number of rural reformers. Many farmers had difficulty in grasping certain aspects of contemporary reality—the declining influence of agriculture in the United States and its relative inefficiency, the fact that no one was co-ordinating the activities of millions of farmers effectively, and the built-in provinciality and cultural poverty of rural life. They preferred to denounce their enemies rather than to face hard truths.[67]

The reactionary aspects of agricultural thinking have been most strongly emphasized by Richard Hofstadter in *The Age of Reform*. More detailed studies, inspired by Hofstadter's analysis, have tended to minimize this side of the farm protest movement. To admit that rank-and-file members of the Grange and the Farmers' Alliance were less dedicated to the common interests of all farmers than the principles of these organizations required is merely to say that they were human beings. It also seems clear that only a handful of the rural radicals were authentic anti-Semites or strongly anti-labor. Most farmers had had little experience with Jews or industrial workers and, if prejudiced at all, probably did not consider such persons to be injuring them in any significant way.[68] Rural fulminations against the evils of the city were not entirely unreasonable, nor did the fact that farmers also hankered for the advantages of urban life prove that their thinking was confused. Urban civilization was full of contrasts; one's attitude at any moment depended upon which aspect of the city one was considering. Illinois farmers might worry about the physical and moral safety of their sons and daughters in wicked Chicago; but when the city was destroyed by fire in 1871, the rural press was full of proud prophesies that the

[67] Hicks, *Populist Revolt*, p. 299.

[68] Hofstadter, *Age of Reform*, pp. 60–93. For criticisms of the Hofstadter view and other works differing with his interpretation, see W. T. K. Nugent, *The Tolerant Populists: Kansas Populism and Nativism* (Chicago, 1963); Norman Pollack, *The Populist Response to Industrial America* (Cambridge, Mass., 1962); two articles by Pollack, "Hofstadter on Populism," *Journal of Southern History* XXVI (1960), 478–500, and "The Myth of Populist Anti-Semitism," *American Historical Review*, LXVIII (1962), 76–80; C. V. Woodward, "The Populist Heritage and the Intellectual," *American Scholar*, XXIX (1959–60), 55–72.

"queen city," the "Blossom of the West," would soon "Rise Again."[69]

Farmers were undoubtedly too prone to blame their troubles on the machinations of nonexistent conspirators; there was, for example, no conspiracy of bankers to deflate the currency. But a small number of powerful financiers did exercise a great influence on banking practices and on government monetary policy. Deflation was a fact and it did hurt farmers who were in debt. There was nothing muddleheaded about their view of actual conditions. They made a false inference, but not an unreasonable one.[70] It is, of course, impossible to determine what all the ordinary farmers of the period actually believed. The evidence suggests that most of them were less radical and less irrationally ambivalent than their spokesmen. The average dirt farmer had few illusions about the virtues of subsistence agriculture, however fond he might be of listening to orators expounding upon the virtues of the noble yeoman of yesteryear. He no doubt fumed when hard work and high hopes failed to lead to much improvement in his lot; nevertheless, he was neither a potential socialist nor a protofascist, though extremists of both types flourished in the agrarian movement. When bad times and natural catastrophes buffeted him, he became indignant and listened more closely to radicals of the left and right. On balance, however, he remained what he had always been—a middle-class American capitalist, optimistic and opportunistic, a democrat and an individualist, immersed in himself, his family, and his land, but reasonably tolerant of the interests and aspirations of his fellows.

[69] M. L. Woodward, "The Northwestern Farmer, 1868–1876," *Agric. Hist.*, XXXVII (1963), 139.

[70] F. C. Jaher, *Doubters and Dissenters: Cataclysmic Thought in America, 1885–1918* (Glencoe, Ill., 1964), p. 139.

CHAPTER 3

Industry

I N the year 1889, the economist David A. Wells, attempting to summarize the trends of the past two decades, wrote: "An almost total revolution has taken place, and is yet in progress, in every branch and in every relation of the world's industrial and commercial system." Wells brought intelligence, shrewdness, and scholarly zeal to bear in an effort to explain this revolution, but without much success. He offered no confident opinion of his own to account for the extraordinary events he described. "The world wonders," he admitted, "and commissions of great states inquire, without coming to definite conclusions." His analysis was crowded with words like "curious," "unprecedented," and "abnormal."

The conditions that Wells was trying to understand were indeed both revolutionary and perplexing. A "great depression" seemed to be in progress. All over the industrial world, markets were glutted; prices had been falling almost continuously since the early seventies and no prospect of a reversal of the trend was in sight. Moreover, the pace of economic activity had been fluctuating rapidly, often without apparent cause or pattern. Wells noted that the price of pig iron had fallen from $41 a ton to $25 in a three-month period in 1880, only to rise again so sharply in 1881 that the American Iron and Steel Association could characterize that year as "the most prosperous . . . iron and steel manufacturers have ever known." He could as easily have chosen any of a hundred other illustrations of the erratic short-run course of economic activity. Consumers purchased 21.7 million pounds of copper in 1871, 42.8 million in 1873, 26.7 million in 1876, 87.1 million in 1882. The rate of business failures jumped from 6.4 per thousand firms in 1871 to 14.2 per thousand in 1876, dropped back to 6.3 per thousand in 1880, and then rose again to 12.1 per thousand in 1884. Falling prices and sudden sharp shifts in the level of industrial activity were a constant source of mystification and worry to businessmen and economists both in the United States and in Europe. Wells quoted experts from many countries in his book; these authorities differed as to the cause of the troubles, but all agreed that since 1873 the world had been passing through a prolonged period of depression.[1]

Yet from another perspective there had not been any depression at all, at least none of any great seriousness or duration. The years from 1873 to 1878 were at worst a period of stability; industrial growth was negligible, but in most fields there was no important decline in output. There followed a great boom that lasted well into 1883. Then came a brief slump, again more a leveling off than an actual downturn, and then another powerful upward thrust that continued with a few short interruptions from 1886 to the panic of 1893. The pace of industrial activity, in other words, was erratic. For short periods factories might stand idle, unemployment mount, public confidence fall. But it was, in the main, a time of rapid expansion. Wells and other students realized what was happening to production, but discounted its significance; in their minds the price depression and the chaotic fluctuations in the level of activity outweighed growth as an indicator of economic conditions. "Statistics," Wells wrote, "prove that those countries in which depression has been and is most severely felt are the very ones in which desirable commodities of every description . . . have year by year been accumulating with the greatest rapidity, and offered for use or consumption at rates unprecedented for cheapness."[2]

The price deflation and instability of the era go far to explain the

[1] D. A. Wells, *Recent Economic Changes* (New York, 1889), pp. 13, 111, *passim*; Edwin Frickey, *Production in the United States: 1866–1914* (Cambridge, Mass., 1947), p. 12; *Historical Statistics of the United States, Colonial Times to 1957* (Washington, 1960), p. 570.

[2] Rendigs Fels, *American Business Cycles: 1865–1897* (Chapel Hill, 1959), pp. 107–178; Wells, *Recent Economic Changes*, pp. 14–25.

behavior of its businessmen, but the expansion of production had a much greater effect on the history of the United States. From any perspective the prodigies achieved in the 1870's and 1880's by American industry were impressive. Using the year 1899 as a standard, the output of manufactured goods increased from an index of 25 in 1870 to 30 in 1877, 42 in 1880, 71 in 1890, and 79 in 1892, and in the same years the value of manufactured products doubled.[3]

Old and "basic" industries led the way. Pig-iron production increased from 1.8 million tons in 1870 to 10.3 million in 1890. American textile mills consumed 797,000 bales of cotton and 227 million pounds of wool in 1870, 2.6 million bales and 402 million pounds in 1891. Between 1870 and 1890, flour production rose from 47.9 million barrels to 83.3 million, tobacco products from 102 million pounds to 253 million, lumber from 12.7 million board feet to 27 million, paper from 386 million tons to 935 million. For most other important manufactures, figures exist only for value of output, but these show the same rapid growth rate. The clothing industry turned out about $230 million worth of goods in 1869 and $589 million in 1890, the shoe industry $185 million and $250 million in the same years. The value of manufactured construction

---

[3] Frickey, *Production*, p. 54. The index fell during the "depression" of the middle seventies only from 31 (1872) to 28 (1876). The downturn of 1884-85 also produced a drop of only three points, from 50 to 47. In no other year between 1865 and 1893 was there any decline. Furthermore, certain important manufactures (processed foods, tobacco goods, steel, and, with the exception of a single year, alcoholic beverages) *never* suffered an actual decline in annual output in this period. The comments of economists Milton Friedman and A. J. Schwartz are pertinent. "Contemporary observers regarded these years [1873-79] as a period of marked 'depression and disturbance of industry.' But the sharp decline in financial magnitudes, so much more obvious and so much better documented than the behavior of a host of poorly measured physical magnitudes, may well have led contemporary observers and later students to overestimate the severity of the contraction and perhaps even its length. Observers of the business scene then, no less than their modern descendants, took it for granted that sharply declining prices were incompatible with sharply rising output." *A Monetary History of the United States, 1867-1960* (Princeton, 1963), pp. 87-88. It must be pointed out, however, that the available statistics on late-nineteenth-century industry are both incomplete and inaccurate. In presenting his indexes of manufacturing production, Edwin Frickey writes: "Research workers . . . should bear in mind that for the most part these indexes are based upon sample data and indirect representation." *Ibid.*, pp. 38-43. See also the charts in A. H. Hansen, *Business Cycles and National Income* (New York, 1951), pp. 27-28.

materials soared from $325 million to over $1 billion, that of magazines, newspapers, and books from $39 million to $131 million.[4]
A number of more recently developed manufactured products
flourished still more vigorously during the period. Steel had been
made in only trivial amounts in America before the Civil War, but,
with the introduction of new techniques in the late sixties, output
soared. In 1870, 68,700 tons were manufactured; in 1890, over 4.2
million tons. Another relatively new industry was petroleum refining. In 1869, manufacturers turned out about 3.2 million barrels
of illuminating and lubricating oils; by 1890, they were averaging
about 22 million barrels. Alexander Graham Bell first exhibited his
telephone in 1876; by the mid-nineties, over 300,000 phones were in
use. Thomas A. Edison produced his first practical incandescent
lamp in 1879 and opened his first central power station three years
later; by 1890 he was manufacturing nearly a million light bulbs a
year, and various companies with which he was connected were
doing an annual business of $7 million. The electrical equipment
industry, practically nonexistent in 1870, produced goods worth
$1.9 million in 1879 and $21.8 million in 1890.[5]
The leading American industries throughout the period were
those concerned with food processing, textiles, iron and steel, other
metal products, lumber, paper and printing, alcoholic beverages,
chemicals, and leather. Ranking them presents many difficulties, for
it depends first of all on how various businesses are lumped together, and second on whether one stresses capitalization, the
number of workers employed and their wages, or value of product.

[4] *Hist Stat.*, pp. 365–366, 415, 419–422; Frickey, *Production*, pp. 8–16, 69, 89.
The figures on pig-iron production, when converted to long tons of 2,240 pounds
for the purposes of comparison with steel statistics, are 1.7 million tons and 9.2
million. Peter Temin, *Iron and Steel in Nineteenth Century America* (Cambridge, Mass., 1964), pp. 266–267. A random sampling of minor products reveals
the same tendency. The value of toys and sporting goods manufactured in 1869
was $13 million, in 1890 $23.3 million. Comparable figures for jewelry and
watches were $41.6 million and $90.2 million, for house furnishings $12.8 million
and $34.5 million, for scientific equipment $1.6 million and $3.2 million, for
tombstones $6.6 million and $17.3 million.

[5] *Hist. Stat.*, pp. 416–417, 421; H. F. Williamson and A. R. Daum, *The American Petroleum Industry: 1859–1899* (Evanston, 1959), pp. 633, 738; E. C.
Kirkland, *Industry Comes of Age: Business, Labor, and Public Policy, 1860–1897*
(New York, 1961), p. 167; Matthew Josephson, *Edison* (New York, 1959), p.
300.

By most standards, textiles, iron and steel, food processing, and lumber products were the most important, and of these the iron and steel industry was the fastest-growing. The relative position of the leaders in 1890 is shown below.

RANKING OF MAJOR INDUSTRY GROUPS, 1890[6]

Capitalization	Number of Workers	Wage Bill	Value of Product
Textiles ($1 billion)	Textiles (824,000)	Iron and steel ($285 million)	Food processing ($1.6 billion)
Iron and steel ($998 million)	Lumber (548,000)	Textiles ($278 million)	Textiles ($1.3 billion)
Lumber ($844 million)	Iron and steel (532,000)	Lumber ($202 million)	Iron and steel ($1.1 billion)
Food processing ($508 million)	Food processing (249,000)	Paper and printing ($118 million)	Lumber ($878 million)

Industry was concentrated in the northeastern quarter of the United States; slightly more than 85 per cent of the manufactured goods produced in 1890 came from the areas designated by the census as the North Atlantic and North Central divisions. But the South and West had considerable industry too; only eleven states in 1890 turned out less than $32 million worth of manufactured goods and a majority of these were located in the newly settled districts of the plains and the Rockies. New York, Pennsylvania, Illinois, Massachusetts, and Ohio led by a wide margin, but states as different in size and location as Connecticut, Missouri, and California produced over $200 million each in that year.

Furthermore, while many industries, large and small, were heavily concentrated in particular regions, a condition made possible by the improved transportation system and the general integration of the economy, the size of the country and its widely scattered resources prevented extreme localization in nearly every case. The shoe industry, for example, was relatively centralized. Throughout the period, Massachusetts produced well over half the shoes manufactured in the United States. However, thirteen other states each

6 U.S. Bureau of the Census, *Abstract of the 12th Census* (Washington, 1904), p. 324.

made over $1 million worth of shoes in 1880, and fifteen did so in 1890. The great Chicago meat packers made Illinois the leading state for livestock slaughtering, but in 1880 twenty-three states, and in 1890 twenty-two states, slaughtered over $1 million worth of livestock each. Thirty-eight states milled over $1 million worth of flour in 1880; forty did so in 1890.[7]

The dispersal of American industry can also be shown by an examination of the production of individual states. California offers an excellent example. The state accounted for $116 million worth of manufactures in 1880 and $213 million in 1890. Of the sixty-seven products listed in the 1890 census of manufactures, California produced measurable amounts of fifty-six.[8]

Certain geographical shifts occurred during the period, especially in those industries most directly involved in processing raw materials. Minnesota became the leading flour-milling state, Michigan and Wisconsin led in lumbering, Illinois, as we have seen, in meat packing. The manufacture of agricultural implements was also concentrated in Illinois, the state's output increasing from $15.4 million in 1880 to $24.6 million in 1890.[9]

Manufacturing also became more important in the South. Although the region did not expand its industrial output more rapidly than the rest of the nation, the mere fact that it could

[7] *Ibid.*, pp. 331–333; U.S. Bureau of the Census, *Report on Manufactures of the United States, 10th Census, 1880* (Washington, 1883), pp. 92, 448, 451, 465, and *11th Census, Bulletin 380* (Washington, 1894), pp. 8, 37, 19.

[8] Some of the most important are listed in the following table (*ibid., passim*), together with the total national production of each item in 1890 ($ million):

Item	California	United States
Agricultural machinery	1.6	81
Boots and shoes	3.4	221
Flour	14.2	514
Foundry products	7.8	413
Leather	5.7	138
Lumber	8.5	404
Men's clothing	2.6	251
Sugar refining	22.6	123
Tobacco products	3.1	196

[9] *Ibid.*, pp. 6, 19, 27, 37; *Rept. on Manuf.*, pp. 446–447, 451, 455, 465; R. A. Easterlin, "Interregional Differences in Per Capita Income, Population, and Total Income, 1840–1950," National Bureau of Economic Research, *Trends in the American Economy in the Nineteenth Century* (Princeton, 1960), pp. 73–140.

approach the growth rate of the North reflected a significant change of emphasis. Manufacturing grew so rapidly in some southern states that many contemporaries came to believe that industry had not really existed there before 1880. This, of course, was untrue. But, beginning about that year, a combination of undeveloped resources, abundant cheap labor, a fresh influx of northern and foreign capital, and a redirection of southern energy that took on the aspects of a crusade indeed produced wonders.

The southern textile industry had prospered modestly after 1865; nevertheless, in 1880 the entire South still produced less than the single state of Massachusetts and had a smaller share in the industry's capacity (about 5 per cent) than it had in 1860. Thereafter the pace quickened spectacularly. Using chiefly local capital, but importing machinery and skilled textile engineers and superintendents from the North, Southerners shifted the balance in the industry noticeably. The important Whitin Machine Works of Massachusetts, for example, increased its southern business more than tenfold in the early eighties, then more than doubled it again by the end of the decade, when it was selling about a third of its production in the South. Another Massachusetts textile-machinery firm, the Lowell Machine Shop, raised the proportion of its southern business from about 15 per cent in 1870 to 38 per cent in the late eighties. By 1890, southern mills were turning out one-tenth of the nation's cotton goods and increasing this percentage steadily.[10]

Southern production of iron increased enormously, especially in northern Alabama and eastern Tennessee, around Chattanooga and the new boom town of Birmingham,[11] where rich deposits of coal and iron ore favored development. By the end of the decade Alabama ranked third among the states in iron manufacturing, with nearly 10 per cent of the national total. Tobacco manufac-

[10] C. V. Woodward, *Origins of the New South, 1877–1913* (Baton Rouge, 1951), pp. 112–115; J. S. Ezell, *The South Since 1865* (New York, 1963), p. 142; Easterlin, "Interregional Differences," pp. 85–89; E. M. Coulter, *The South During Reconstruction: 1865–1877* (Baton Rouge, 1947), pp. 265–269; Broadus Mitchell, *The Rise of Cotton Mills in the South* (Baltimore, 1921), pp. 105–112; T. R. Navin, *The Whitin Machine Works Since 1831: A Textile Machinery Company in an Industrial Village* (Cambridge, Mass., 1950), pp. 209–217; G. S. Gibb, *The Saco-Lowell Shops: Textile Machine Building in New England, 1813–1949* (Cambridge, Mass., 1950), p. 243.

[11] The population of Birmingham rose from 3,000 in 1880 to 26,000 in 1890.

turers in Virginia and North Carolina also prospered, taking advantage of the sudden popularity of cigarettes, which caused a per capita increase in the national tobacco consumption of over 40 per cent during the eighties. The South also raised its output of lumber and fertilizer, and of cottonseed oil, used in the manufacture of fertilizers, soap, and cooking oils.[12]

Thus, while the South remained predominantly agricultural, cotton the mainspring of its economy, nevertheless, industrialization invaded the area with full force in the years after reconstruction. Alabama quadrupled its manufactures; Georgia, North Carolina, and South Carolina roughly doubled theirs; Kentucky and Tennessee made similar gains. Yet it must be repeated that northern industry dwarfed that of the South; as late as 1890 the industrial production of the entire region was worth only slightly more than half that of the single state of New York.[13]

Fundamental to the industrial growth of the nation was the completion of an efficient system of internal transportation; the expansion and integration of the railroad network between 1877 and 1890 was probably the most significant single reason why the economy developed so rapidly in those years. During that period the volume of railroad freight rose from 231 million tons to 691 million, passenger traffic from 180 million persons to 520 million. Robert W. Fogel, an economic historian, estimates that if western farm products had been moved to market over roads and waterways instead of railroads in 1890, the additional costs would have amounted to about $140 million, and that if all goods had been transported by these means the country would have suffered a loss of perhaps $560 million, between 4 and 5 per cent of the gross national product in 1890.[14]

[12] Woodward, *Origins of the New South,* pp. 126–131; Ethel Armes, *The Story of Coal and Iron in Alabama* (Birmingham, 1910), pp. 266–419; Temin, *Iron and Steel,* pp. 198, 280; Ezell, *South Since 1865,* pp. 145–146; N. M. Tilley, *The Bright-Tobacco Industry: 1860–1929* (Chapel Hill, 1948), pp. 568–592; V. S. Clark, *History of Manufacturers in the United States* (2 vols., New York, 1929), II. 519–523.

[13] *Abstract of 12th Census,* pp. 331–333. For an interesting discussion of southern industrialization, see C. G. Bellissary, "The Rise of Industry and the Industrial Spirit in Tennessee: 1865–1885," *Journal of Southern History,* XIX (1953), 193–215.

[14] Frickey, *Production,* p. 100; R. W. Fogel, *Railroads and Economic Growth* (Baltimore, 1964), pp. 17–110, 219–223; A. D. Chandler, Jr., "The Organization of

Besides facilitating the movement of goods, the railroads consumed immense amounts of iron and steel, coal, lumber, and other products, and provided employment for hundreds of thousands of workers. In the decade 1881–90, railroad companies purchased nearly 15 million tons of rails, buying in some years over 90 per cent of the rolled steel manufactured in the United States. In 1889 alone they bought $87.3 million worth of rolling stock, bringing the total investment in railroad equipment at that time to nearly $8.6 billion, the total number of passenger and freight cars to over a million.

The railroad mileage of the United States increased between 1877 and 1890 from 79,082 to 166,703, the latter figure amounting to roughly one-third of the world's total. In several of these years more than 10,000 miles of new track were laid. Even more important than the expansion of the system, however, was its unification. At the outbreak of the Civil War the nation already had over 30,000 miles of track, but most of this was organized in small, unco-ordinated units, serving local rather than national needs. One could travel from Boston to Albany on the Boston and Worcester and from Albany to Buffalo over the New York Central, but there was no railroad bridge across the Hudson joining these lines. Six railroads radiated from Richmond, Virginia, but the city's four terminals, all located within a mile of one another in the heart of town, remained unlinked. No railroad bridged the Mississippi, or even the Ohio. Furthermore, a bewildering variety of track gauges prevented the movement of cars from one line to another. As late as 1880 the

---

Manufacturing and Transportation," in D. T. Gilchrist and W. D. Lewis (eds.), *Economic Change in the Civil War Era* (Greenville, Del., 1965), pp. 141–151. Fogel argues that in the absence of railroads other improved means of transportation would probably have been developed sooner. He rejects the theory that railroads were "indispensable" to nineteenth-century American economic expansion. "Growth was not induced by a single technological change. . . . The fact that the condition of cheap transportation was satisfied by one innovation rather than another determined, not whether growth would take place, but which of many possible growth paths would be followed." *Railroads and Economic Growth*, pp. 236–237. However, his work does not prove that railroads were not an extremely important stimulant to the economy. For a thoughtful critique of Fogel's work, see Marc Nerlove, "Railroads and Economic Growth," *Journal of Economic History*, XXVI (1966), 107–115. See also Albert Fishlow, *American Railroads and the Transformation of the Ante-Bellum Economy* (Cambridge, Mass., 1965), which argues that the contribution of the railroads to gross national product in 1890 was "at least 15 per cent."

shipment of bulky textile machinery from Massachusetts to South Carolina required as many as eight transshipments, involving wagons, railroad cars, and ocean vessels.[15]

Wartime needs and postwar economic expansion soon convinced the country of the need for integrating the network. Vital connecting links were built and different roads began to pool their freight cars in co-operative "fast freight" organizations to speed and simplify the movement of western grain and other goods. These fast-freight groups also issued through bills of lading covering shipments from point of origin to final destination instead of separate bills for each line. Gradually the "standard" gauge of four feet eight and one-half inches became predominant. As late as 1880 over 20 per cent of the nation's track varied from this measurement, and a great deal of "narrow" gauge track was still being laid, but by 1886 only the southern lines had failed to adopt standard gauge. They finally did so on May 31–June 1, 1886, in an immense, co-ordinated effort involving over 13,000 miles of track. The smoothness and speed of the conversion symbolized the new philosophy of integration.[16]

By 1890 the physical integration of the railroad network had been substantially completed. Urban terminals had been connected, the great rivers bridged repeatedly, heavily used lines double-tracked. The roads had also made great strides toward administrative uniformity. Standard freight classifications had been adopted and the nation divided into four time zones to facilitate train scheduling. There were still well over a thousand operating companies and no truly transcontinental railroads were built, but large trunk lines had emerged in the three major sections: the New York Central, the Pennsylvania, the Erie, and the Baltimore and Ohio in the region east of the Mississippi and north of the Ohio; the Richmond and West Point Terminal Company, the Louisville and

15 Temin, *Iron and Steel*, pp. 275–276; *Hist. Stat.*, 421, 427–428; G. R. Taylor and I. D. Neu, *The American Railroad Network: 1861–1890* (Cambridge, Mass., 1956) , pp. 3–14, 16, 37, 47; Navin, *Whitin Machine Works,* p. 213.

16 Taylor and Neu, *Railroad Network*, pp. 65, 77–82; Kirkland, *Industry Comes of Age*, pp. 46–49. Actually, the southern gauge was set at four feet nine inches to conform to that of the Pennsylvania Railroad, the principal connecting line between the South and the Northeast, but this small variation did not prevent the movement of cars over standard gauge. A. T. Hadley, *Railroad Transportation: Its History and Laws* (New York, 1885) , pp. 88–90.

Nashville, and the Atlantic Coast Line in the South; and the western "transcontinentals" beyond the Mississippi.

Lines serving the same region fought fiercely for business. Competing lines sometimes organized pools—extralegal agreements to share traffic or earnings according to a prearranged formula—but the public associated pooling with extortion and, since such arrangements were unenforceable in the courts, greedy railroadmen tended to break them frequently. The famous Iowa Pool, encompassing the roads running between Chicago and Omaha, worked fairly effectively from 1870 to 1874 and less so for another decade, but most pools were short-lived. The Eastern Trunk Line Association (1877), made up of "all the principal east and west roads as far as the Mississippi," succeeded only sporadically in preventing rate wars between Chicago and the Atlantic seaboard. The czar of this association was a brilliant German-born man named Albert Fink, a former vice-president of the Louisville and Nashville Railroad. "The railroad system," he said, "has become so extended and the business relations of so many roads to each other have become so complicated that . . . there should be organized cooperation." Fink's logic was irrefutable, his prestige immense, but he could not make the pool work—"the poison of bad faith and failure," as one historian has said, "worked through the organization." Beginning in 1879, Charles Francis Adams, Jr., served as arbitrator for the association, but in 1884 he resigned. The members, he told a Senate committee, "reminded me of men in a boat in the swift water above the rapids of Niagara," and in his autobiography he wrote: "The Trunk Line Arbitration was not a success. The time for it had clearly not come."[17]

Where technical and administrative matters were concerned,

[17] U.S. Senate, *Report on . . . Labor and Capital* (Washington, 1885), II, p. 464; E. C. Kirkland, *Charles Francis Adams, Jr., 1835–1915: The Patrician at Bay* (Cambridge, Mass., 1965), pp. 59–62; C. F. Adams, Jr., *Autobiography* (Boston, 1916), p. 191. J. W. Midgley, another railroad man with experience as a pool arbitrator, told the same committee that it had been the "mortifying experience of all compacts" that few roads could resist "the blandishments of shippers" and "adhere strictly to the agreement[s]." Gabriel Kolko, *Railroads and Regulation: 1877–1916* (Princeton, 1965), p. 10. But cf. D. T. Gilchrist, "Albert Fink and the Pooling System," *Business History Review*, XXXIV (1960), 24–49, and P. W. MacAvoy, *The Economic Effects of Regulation: The Trunk-Line Railroad Cartels and the Interstate Commerce Commission before 1900* (Cambridge, Mass., 1965), pp. 50–109.

however, integration proved more practicable. Connecting roads commonly worked out methods of exchanging cars, prorating charges, and sharing terminal facilities. The American Railway Association, formed in 1891 to regulate safety standards, scheduling, and similar matters, functioned admirably and provided an institutional framework for further rationalization of the network.[18]

In one sense the improvement of American railroads reflected the technological advance that was affecting every branch of industry. The railroad system of 1890, for example, differed from that of the 1870's not merely in size and uniformity; trains were also faster and larger, equipment more durable and reliable. In 1870 the average freight car on the Pennsylvania Railroad had a capacity of about ten tons; by 1881 the average capacity had doubled. The substitution of steel rails for iron, the invention of the air brake, and improvements in safety growing out of the introduction of better signal equipment and the use of the telegraph for communication made this increase possible.[19]

Truly, American industrial technology was the wonder of the world, far in advance of Europe's in most fields, despite the fact that Europeans made most of the key scientific discoveries on which it was based. The relatively high cost of labor provides a partial explanation of American technological leadership, for it encouraged manufacturers to invest their capital and energy in mechanizing their operations to reduce labor costs. The rapidity of American expansion also stimulated technological innovation. So, in many subtle ways, did the structure of society. Americans, far less bound than most Europeans by a respect for tradition, adopted new methods more willingly. Workingmen saw the relationship between productivity and wages more clearly than their European counterparts, and manufacturers were less reluctant to share the results of increased productivity with their workers.

[18] Kirkland, *Industry Comes of Age*, 49–50, 81–88; T. C. Cochran, *Railroad Leaders: 1845–1890* (Cambridge, Mass., 1953), pp. 167–171; Julius Grodinsky, *The Iowa Pool: A Study in Railroad Competition, 1870–1894* (Chicago, 1950), *passim*; C. F. Adams, Jr., *Railroads: Their Origins and Problems* (New York, 1878), pp. 150–179; Hadley, *Railroad Transportation*, pp. 91–99; Julius Grodinsky, *Transcontinental Railway Strategy: 1869–1891* (Philadelphia, 1962), pp. 105–111, 338–364; Kolko, *Railroads and Regulation*, pp. 8–10, 17–20.

[19] J. S. Jeans, *Railway Problems* (London, 1887), p. 324. For a brief account of the deplorable railroad safety standards, see Kirkland, *Adams*, p. 51.

The strongest pressure for technological innovation was generated by the steady erosion of prices, which had the effect of wearing away the profit margins of inefficient manufacturers. Worry about "overproduction" thus paradoxically inspired industrialists to introduce techniques that enabled them to produce still more. Perhaps the major element in the success of the greatest tycoons was their willingness to expand capacity in this way in the face of presumably glutted markets. A few, such as Andrew Carnegie, correctly assumed that the potential demand for their goods was almost unlimited and adopted efficient new techniques confidently. Others, less sure of the future, did so fearfully, almost desperately, which helps account for the pessimism and the confused economic thinking so prevalent at the time.[20]

The most important technological advance of the last half of the nineteenth century was the invention of efficient methods for making steel; nothing so well illustrates American adaptability as the way the nation's ironmasters took over and improved upon these new methods. The advantages of steel over iron, its combination of strength and durability, were well known long before the nineteenth century, but until the 1860's no technique had been devised for making steel efficiently. Steel is a mixture of pure (wrought) iron and a small amount of carbon. It was originally manufactured by adding carbon to wrought iron in small charcoal furnaces. However, the quantities of heat required to keep the wrought iron, which has a very high melting point, in a liquid state made large-scale operations impossible. In 1859, however, Henry Bessemer in England and William Kelly in America independently discovered that by forcing air into molten pig iron, which contains large amounts of carbon and other impurities, the impurities could themselves be set afire, thus providing the heat needed to keep the metal liquid as the purification process raised its melting point. In the process of combustion, the impurities combined with the lining of the container. When the carbon content had been reduced to about 1 per cent, the whole mass became steel; at this point the container, called a converter, was tipped over and the steel poured into molds.

20 H. J. Habakkuk, *American and British Technology in the Nineteenth Century* (Cambridge, Eng., 1962), pp. 91–131, 189–220.

The Bessemer process reduced the amount of coal required to make a ton of steel from seven tons to less than one ton and cut the cost of labor and machinery proportionately. Bessemer production soared: from 2,000 tons in 1867 to 38,000 in 1870, to over one million in 1880, and to nearly 3.7 million in 1890. This expansion had widespread ramifications.[21] "No improvement in practical metallurgy since the time of Tubal-Cain," as one proud pioneer put it, "realized such magnificent results in increasing the quantity produced and diminishing the selling price of a metal as that which is known world-wide as the 'Bessemer process' of manufacturing steel." This process, however, was merely a transitionary stage in steel technology. As early as the sixties a British inventor, William Siemens, had devised a method of turning iron into steel by superheating the ore in regenerative furnaces fired by gas, eliminating the need for the air blast, This "open hearth" method, combined with the Thomas-Gilchrist "basic" process, which removed phosphorus from the molten metal by causing it to combine with lime in the lining of the refining vessel, enabled manufacturers to use ores unworkable by the Bessemer process and to produce a more uniformly high quality of steel. The weakness of the Bessemer process, unknown at the time, was that forcing air into the molten pig iron caused it to absorb nitrogen, which occasionally produced undetectable flaws. For rails and other forms not subject to sudden strains, Bessemer steel was adequate; but as steel began to be used in the eighties for structural purposes, machinery, and armor plate, its unpredictable tendency to break under strain led to its gradual abandonment. The proportion of steel made by the open-hearth method tripled between 1879 and 1891, although open-hearth output did not exceed Bessemer until early in the twentieth century.[22]

Although these steelmaking techniques came from abroad,

[21] At first Bessemer steel went almost entirely into rails, for steel rails outlasted iron ones ten times or more under heavy use. In 1870, the industry rolled 523,000 tons of iron rails and 30,000 of steel, in 1882, 203,000 tons of iron rails and 1.3 million tons of steel. By 1883, steel rails had become *cheaper* than iron as well and practically monopolized the market. In 1890, only 14,000 tons of iron rails were rolled, as against nearly 1.9 million tons of steel rails. Temin, *Iron and Steel*, pp. 125–126, 131, 222, 270, 283–284.

[22] T. A. Wertime, *The Coming of the Age of Steel* (Chicago, 1962), *passim*, esp. pp. 285–293; W. F. Durfee, "The Manufacture of Steel," *Popular Science Monthly*, XXXIX (1891), 743–744; Temin, *Iron and Steel*, pp. 138–152, 272–273.

American producers led the world in applying them effectively. In 1874 the best Bessemer mills in the United States were already outperforming British mills by 50 per cent; by 1880 they had doubled their capacity and increased their lead. Alexander L. Holley, for example, redesigned the basic layout of Bessemer plants and invented a converter with a removable bottom, which made it unnecessary to wait until the converter had cooled before installing a new lining after each heat. American blast-furnace and rolling-mill practices also soon outdistanced European. Andrew Carnegie's giant Lucy Furnace produced 13,000 tons of pig iron in 1872; by 1890 it was capable of turning out as much as 100,000 tons a year and a number of other furnaces were averaging over 1,000 tons weekly. George and John Fritz devised means of rolling steel ingots while still hot, sharply reducing fuel costs, and other engineers, such as Captain William Jones, invented machines that moved and manipulated the metal during the rolling process, thus effecting tremendous savings in labor.[23]

At the Midvale Steel Company plant, near Philadelphia, "a regular hive of inventive ingenuity," men like William F. Durfee, a pioneer in the application of chemical knowledge to steelmaking, and Frederick W. Taylor, a brilliant engineer, introduced a variety of significant innovations. Taylor worked out his controversial system of "scientific management" at Midvale in the eighties and invented a revolutionary steam-powered hammer and other important steel-fabricating machines. By the early nineties, as Durfee explained, the entire industry had been transformed by "wondrous changes in the construction and management of [its] furnaces, steel-works, and rolling-mills." After visiting American steel mills in 1901, a British commission reported: "The American manufacturer is not so conservative in his methods and ideas." No expense was too great if it would "make for increased economy."[24]

23 D. L. Burn, *The Economic History of Steelmaking: 1867–1939* (Cambridge, Eng., 1940), pp. 47, 183–184; Temin, *Iron and Steel*, pp. 133–136, 159, 164–165; Clark, *History of Manufactures*, II, 254–256, 265–269; Navin, *Whitin Machine Works*, pp. 120–121.

24 F. B. Copley, *Frederick W. Taylor: Father of Scientific Management* (2 vols., New York, 1923), I, 190–191, 196–201; W. P. Strassmann, *Risk and Technological Innovation: American Manufacturing Methods during the Nineteenth Century* (Ithaca, 1959), pp. 38–39, 132; Clark, *History of Manufactures*, II, pp. 258, 265–270; W. F. Durfee, "The Manufacture of Steel," *Popular Science Monthly*,

The daring, if not the skill, of these innovators should not be overestimated. Most American steelmen scrapped obsolete machinery only reluctantly, and often rejected the suggestions of engineers with new ideas. They took few large risks, proceeding usually only after the most careful scrutiny of each innovation. After studying the textile and machine-tool industries as well as iron and steel, economist Paul Strassmann concluded that the "technological revolution in manufacturing methods . . . was brought about, not by heroic gambling, but by the cautious exploitation of vast and multiplying opportunities."[25] Yet one of the marks of the most successful manufacturer was his willingness, once convinced of the practicability of a new method, to stake his future upon it.

Whether one stresses the imagination and initiative of the manufacturers or the "multiplying opportunities" of the times, the extent of technological progress was enormous. During the eighties the rate at which patents were issued nearly doubled, exceeding 25,000 a year by 1890. "America has become known the world around as the home of invention," Patent Commissioner William E. Simonds boasted in 1892.[26] In cotton textiles, better machinery made the use of lower-quality fiber possible and lightweight spindles almost doubled spinning speeds between 1870 and 1890. The Northrop automatic loom, perfected between 1888 and 1893, reduced labor costs in weaving by 25 per cent, while improvements in the production and transmission of power led to large increases in the size and efficiency of factories. Technological advances in wool manufacturing (while important) were less spectacular, but the ready-made clothing business profited from the application of electric power to sewing machines and the invention of mechanical buttonhole makers and machines for cutting cloth.[27] Further development of

---

XL (1891), 23–27, 40; David Brody, *Steelworkers in America: The Non-union Era* (Cambridge, Mass., 1960), p. 1. Taylor's scientific management was, of course, as much a part of the deflation-inspired drive to cut costs as a form of technological advance.

[25] Strassmann, *Risk and Innovation*, pp. 48–49, 63–66, 104–106, 226; Navin, *Whitin Machine Works*, pp. 114–115.

[26] L. D. White, *The Republican Era: 1869–1901* (New York, 1958), p. 222; *Hist. Stat.*, p. 607. The vast majority of patents issued were, of course, for trivial inventions.

[27] Strassmann, *Risk and Innovation*, pp. 96–98, 104–106; Gibb, *Saco-Lowell Shops*, pp. 260–266; A. H. Cole, *The American Wool Manufacture* (2 vols.,

the sewing machine in the complex operations of shoe manufacturing increased efficiency and cut labor costs in that industry. Even in the process known as lasting, which involves the fitting and sewing of the shoe upper to the sole, machines devised in the eighties greatly reduced the need for hand labor. The roller process of making flour, introduced in the seventies, reduced costs and raised the quality of the nation's bread; mechanical refrigeration, as we have seen, revolutionized meat packing and the distribution of perishables; new chemical knowledge changed the brewing of beer "as it had not been changed for millennia"; earth-moving equipment increased five to ten times in efficiency, and the quantity of labor employed in the manufacture of agricultural machines was halved.[28]

Studies of newer industries reveal similar advances. Most of the basic techniques for refining petroleum had been introduced by the early seventies, including the "cracking" process, which enabled refiners to regulate the yield of different products by rearranging the molecular structure of the crude oil. But technological progress thereafter constantly raised the quality and number of petroleum products. In the late eighties, the chemist Herman Frasch developed a method for precipitating sulphur from crude oil by the use of metallic oxides. This gave a great boost to the industry, for it opened the way to the full utilization of the sulphurous Ohio crude, which by older refining techniques had yielded a smoky, evil-smelling kerosene and lubricants that corroded machinery.[29]

Technological progress was especially rapid in the new field of electricity. By 1887 Charles F. Brush and others were building practical dynamos in America.[30] These machines for converting

---

Cambridge, Mass., 1936), II, 79, 99–101; Clark, *History of Manufactures,* II, 386–389, 422–423, 447.

[28] Clark, *History of Manufactures,* II, 468–471; G. A. Rich, "Manufacture of Boots and Shoes," *Popular Science Monthly,* XLI (1892), 510; Kirkland, *Industry Comes of Age,* pp. 171–172, 175; J. C. Malin, *Winter Wheat in the Golden Belt of Kansas* (Lawrence, 1944), pp. 188–192; T. C. Cochran, *The Pabst Brewing Company: The History of an American Business* (New York, 1948), pp. 110–123; Wells, *Recent Economic Changes,* p. 50; Illinois Bureau of Labor Statistics, *4th Report* (Springfield, 1886), p. 475.

[29] Williamson and Daum, *Petroleum Industry,* pp. 218–219, 475, 616–619; R. W. and M. E. Hidy, *Pioneering in Big Business: 1882–1911* (New York, 1955), pp. 155–168.

[30] The principle of the dynamo was discovered by the British scientist, Michael Faraday, in 1831.

mechanical energy into electricity, which impressed Henry Adams so much that he called them "a symbol of infinity," a kind of "moral force" typifying modern industrial society, led to many revolutionary advances. First came the introduction of the arc light as a means of illuminating cities. Then Thomas A. Edison, who grasped their importance instantly, plunged into the work that resulted in his invention of the incandescent lamp. In 1881, Edison began to supply current to a network of eighty-five customers in New York City, and by the late eighties electric lighting had become a big business. Developments in telephonic communication proceeded apace; in 1888 the New York metropolitan area had more telephones than the entire United Kingdom. During the eighties many improvements were also made in the design of electric motors, principally by Frank J. Sprague, an Annapolis-trained engineer. Sprague helped perfect the electric elevator for tall buildings. In 1887, he installed the first practical electric street-car system, in Richmond, Virginia. It was so successful that, within three years, fifty-one cities had adopted this method of transportation.[31]

To the public Edison was the electrical genius of the age and, while he was no theoretician, his reputation was fully deserved. Aside from his inventions, he brought to American technology the idea of organized team research. His laboratory at Menlo Park, New Jersey, opened in 1876, an unpretentious clapboard structure to all outward appearances, was actually the prototype of the great industrial research laboratories of modern times. His second research center, established at West Orange, New Jersey, in 1887, was the largest and most complete in the world, employing both scientists (such as the mathematical physicist Francis R. Upton, the electrical engineer Frank J. Sprague, and the chemist J. W. Aylsworth) and draftsmen, mechanics, and common laborers. Edison promised to turn out "a minor invention every ten days and a big thing every six months or so," and he made this boast good. Working with Upton, who supplied precise mathematical formulations for Edison's insights, he designed a series of improved dynamos, larger and

[31] Henry Adams, *The Education of Henry Adams* (Boston, 1918), p. 380; James Bryce, *The American Commonwealth* (2 vols., New York, 1895), I, 665; *Dictionary of American Biography*, "Frank J. Sprague," XXI, 669–670; A. M. Schlesinger, *The Rise of the City* (New York, 1933), p. 92; Josephson, *Edison*, p. 327.

more efficient than any in the world. Countless experiments leading to dozens of small improvements enabled him to reduce the cost of manufacturing an electric light from $1.21 in 1880 to 22 cents in 1888.[32]

As a source of industrial power, however, electricity was not much exploited until the 1890's, after George Westinghouse had demonstrated that high-voltage alternating current could be transmitted economically and safely over long distances. Earlier, some factories had replaced inefficient systems of belts and shafts with direct-current electric motors, but as late as 1888 only an estimated seven or eight thousand such motors were driving machinery in the entire United States.[33]

Water power and steam were the prime movers of American machines in the seventies and eighties, and with each passing year steam became more dominant. In 1870, water power approximately equaled steam as an energy source; by 1880, steam had forged far ahead. In 1876, the mighty Corliss engine was the cynosure of the Centennial Exposition, symbolizing the new industrial age. Yet a succession of improvements soon made it obsolete. Boiler pressures were raised, speeds increased, and wear sharply reduced. In the seventies, a steam engine could be worked continuously for no more than two weeks; before 1890, engines capable of running more than a year without stopping had been built, and they were both more powerful and cheaper to operate than earlier models. Steam turbines were also first introduced in the eighties.[34]

Industrial growth, especially in conjunction with technological changes requiring heavy expenditures for machinery, powerfully affected the size and structure of American business. Most obviously, individual enterprises tended to become larger. In 1870 there were about 252,000 companies engaged in manufacturing in the United States, in 1890 about 355,000, an increase of some 40 per

[32] Josephson, *Edison*, pp. 131–137, 198, 207–211, 246, 257–258, 299–300. Standard Oil had a fairly large laboratory as early as 1882, but in most industries research was carried on in an informal, almost haphazard manner. Hidy and Hidy, *Pioneering in Big Business*, p. 98; Navin, *Whitin Machine Works*, pp. 119–120.

[33] Kirkland, *Industry Comes of Age*, pp. 168–169; Wells, *Recent Economic Changes*, p. 66.

[34] Clark, *History of Manufactures*, II, 533–534; Kirkland, *Industry Comes of Age*, pp. 169–170.

cent. The capital invested in manufacturing concerns rose in this period more than 300 per cent, from $2.1 billion to $6.5 billion.

To most observers this was the age of the corporation. However, thousands of individual and partnership enterprises still existed, some of them very large. In 1878 only 520 of the 10,000-odd manufacturing concerns in Massachusetts were corporations and two-thirds of the manufactured goods produced in the state were turned out by nonincorporated firms. But the trend was running from the simple to the complex; between 1878 and the mid-nineties a phenomenal expansion of the number of corporations took place in all sections of the nation.[35]

Corporations first became important because of the principle of limited liability: their stockholders were responsible for corporate obligations only to the extent of their actual investments. Since the sums necessary to organize a business, while growing larger, did not yet require drawing upon the assets of thousands of small investors, the corporate device was seldom essential for the raising of capital. Most industrial concerns were closely held by a comparatively small number of persons. As late as the eighties one could construct a substantial oil refinery for $50,000,[36] and even a steel mill did not involve outlays beyond the means of a small group of wealthy men. Most of the big industrialists of the era expanded by combining with competitors and plowing back profits, not by floating new stock issues. Carnegie did not even incorporate his steel empire until late in the nineties and Rockefeller's Standard Oil Company did not offer its stock for public sale. "We never attempted . . . to sell the Standard Oil stock on the market," Rockefeller wrote in his reminiscences. "We decided to pursue the policy of relying upon our own resources." In 1896 only twenty industrial concerns listed their shares on the New York Stock Exchange.[37]

[35] *Abstract of 12th Census*, pp. 300–301; Kirkland, *Industry Comes of Age*, p. 198; G. H. Evans, Jr., *Business Incorporations in the United States: 1800–1943* (New York, 1948), pp. 31–32.

[36] After the Civil War, John D. Rockefeller paid $72,500 for his first refinery, but he bought it in competition with his former partner and later claimed that it was worth considerably less than $50,000. J. D. Rockefeller, *Random Reminiscences of Men and Events* (New York, 1909), p. 81.

[37] Kirkland, *Industry Comes of Age*, pp. 216–217, 226; J. W. Hurst, *Law and Economic Growth: The Legal History of the Lumber Industry in Wisconsin* (Cambridge, Mass., 1964), pp. 413–414; Hidy and Hidy, *Pioneering in Big Business*, p. 37; Rockefeller, *Reminiscences*, pp. 92–93.

Railroads, "the nation's first big business," did require large-scale financing. Even before the Civil War, ten American railroads were capitalized at $10 million or more, and in 1883 over 40 fell into this class, eight of these possessing assets worth more than $135 million each. A considerable proportion of the early railroad construction had been supported by public assistance in the form of loans, gifts of land, exemptions from taxation, and stock purchases, but the last federal grants were made in 1871 and state aid dried up after the onset of the panic of 1873. The great expansion of 1879–90 was financed almost entirely by private capital.[38]

That the huge sums necessary for this construction could be accumulated in an economy ravenous for capital was a tribute to the productivity of that economy and to the optimism of the investing public. Everyone recognized that the country needed railroads and that, since economic growth would increase their business over the years, railroads could be expected to earn very large profits. Yet most construction during the late seventies and the eighties involved either extending track into the unsettled West (where traffic was sure to be light for years) or pushing into regions that already had railroads (which usually resulted in fierce competition disastrous to profit-making). Railroad securities, in short, were tempting but risky investments. For this reason conservative investors preferred railroad bonds, which were secured by the land and other assets of the lines, rather than stocks, with the result that by 1890 the bonded indebtedness of American railroads had risen to

38 A. D. Chandler, Jr. (ed.), *The Railroads: The Nation's First Big Business* (New York, 1965), pp. 17, 43; E. C. Kirkland, *Men, Cities and Transportation: A Study in New England History, 1820–1900* (2 vols., Cambridge, Mass., 1948), II, pp. 313, 316–322. An important reason for the ending of government support for railroads was the controversy that developed in the 1870's and 1880's over the taxation of railroad lands. Court decisions protected the lines against local property taxes until their properties had been formally patented. Therefore, the lines sometimes deliberately delayed patenting their claims. On the other hand, the procedures of the understaffed federal land office were slow and cumbersome; delays in completing patents of as long as two years were not uncommon. Studies of a number of Nebraska and Kansas counties suggest that, in general, the land-grant railroads paid a reasonable share of local taxes, but the delays in patenting claims played an important part in the public's disenchantment with subsidization. L. E. Decker, *Railroads, Lands, and Politics: The Taxation of the Railroad Land Grants, 1864–1897* (Providence, 1964), pp. 10–86, 155–250. However, a few local communities continued to supply aid into the nineties. Hurst, *Law and Economic Growth*, p. 250; Kirkland, *Industry Comes of Age*, pp. 66–67.

over $5 billion, nearly five times the debt of the United States government.[39] This fact, however, does not really explain how the railroad men of the period raised funds. Much depended on the current condition of each company, on the fluctuations of the business cycle, and on the reputations of the individuals in charge of each line.

A great deal of what has been written about railroad finance has focused upon the chicanery whereby promoters diverted railroad assets into their private pockets by false statements, stock-market manipulations, and by the use of dummy construction corporations that overcharged the lines outrageously. These practices, although common enough, had little to do with the process of capital accumulation itself. Until the railroad companies had raised money, it was difficult to steal money from them. Of course, a promoter who released false information or rigged the price of shares on the stock market before floating new issues might inveigle investors into parting with funds they would otherwise have employed differently. When insiders purchased stock in a construction company, knowing that the company would receive the securities of a new railroad at below their true value in return for the work done, they were actually investing in the railroad. But in most cases these sharpsters were simply defrauding persons who had already put up money; they were not adding to the amount of capital invested in railroads.

Established lines in settled regions could usually finance expansion without difficulty. Some did so out of profits. James J. Hill extended the Manitoba road westward through the Red River Valley between 1879 and 1883, a period of prosperity, by largely forgoing dividends. He mollified his stockholders and raised additional cash by allowing them the privilege of buying 6 per cent bonds at ten cents on the dollar. Others floated bond issues; the Baltimore and Ohio, for example, mortgaged itself so heavily that by the late eighties interest charges were eating up a major proportion of its income. Promoters of new roads in the undeveloped West raised money in several ways. Some liquidated their holdings in established roads to pay for the building of new ones; others pledged the securities of one road in order to raise money to build

[39] *Hist. Stat.*, pp. 428, 721; Cochran, *Railroad Leaders*, p. 107.

another, or obtained short-term loans from banks on the strength of their personal credit.

Collis P. Huntington, a master of railroad finance, employed all these techniques in extending his Southern Pacific line across the Arizona wilderness from California in the late seventies and early eighties. At the start of the period, when railroad securities were depressed, Huntington depended on bank loans. After conditions improved in 1880, he raised $6.3 million by selling some of his stock in the then-prosperous Central Pacific Railroad at a high price. He also floated a $10 million bond issue by first exchanging the bonds of the new road for those of the parent Southern Pacific and then leasing the Southern Pacific to the flourishing Central Pacific. To make bonds attractive, railroad entrepreneurs sold bonds and stocks in combination, the bonds representing a supposedly secure income, the stocks the hope of speculative profits. In 1879 the Northern Pacific *gave* preferred stock with a par value of $1,000 to every purchaser of a thousand-dollar bond; two years later the Denver and Rio Grande Railroad offered a thousand-dollar bond and $500 in stock for $1,100. Personal success sometimes simplified the process of money-raising, thus breeding further success. Jay Gould, the dominant figure in many southwestern railroads, had such a reputation for financial wizardry that word of his interest in a line often made it easy for it to borrow money and sell stock. In 1881 Henry Villard, after a series of profitable speculations in the Northwest, raised $8 million in New York City merely by announcing a "secret" project that he proposed to undertake.[40]

Promoters who correctly anticipated the alternating tides of prosperity and depression often made a great deal of money; those who misjudged conditions (often the same men) lost heavily. While railroad financiers tended to issue stock certificates far in excess of the current worth of the lines and to borrow recklessly on the prospect of future earnings, their activities did result in rapid

[40] Grodinsky, *Railroad Strategy*, pp. 181–189, 198; Cochran, *Railroad Leaders*, pp. 100–103; Kirkland, *Men, Cities and Transportation*, II, pp. 317–318; W. Z. Ripley, *Railroads: Finance and Organization* (New York, 1915) , p. 107. Villard could have obtained his $8 million (which he needed in order to obtain control of the Northern Pacific) by more conventional means, but his famous "blind pool" nonetheless demonstrates the power of reputation in financial circles. See T. C. Cochran, "The Legend of the Robber Barons," *Pennsylvania Magazine of History and Biography*, LXXIV (1950) , 307–321.

growth, with large benefits to the economy. Railroad financing also affected the character of American financial institutions. Railroad securities dominated the transactions of the New York Stock Exchange, and the flood of new railroad bond issues played a major part in the emergence of the Exchange as the central market for all security transactions. Beginning in 1868, Henry Varnum Poor's annual *Manual of the Railroads of the United States,* which offered statistical data of great value to prospective investors, helped persuade railroad executives—and indirectly other industrialists—that they should make full and accurate information about their businesses available to the public. General financial periodicals, most notably the *Commercial and Financial Chronicle,* also devoted much space to railroad affairs. The evolution of these publications during the era of railroad expansion established the pattern for modern financial reporting.[41]

The complexities of railroad finance stimulated the growth of private banking houses, such as J. P. Morgan and Company and Kuhn, Loeb and Company in New York, and Lee, Higginson and Company in Boston. These firms served as underwriters for railroad securities and, through their European connections, attracted foreign capital into railroad enterprises. Directors of solvent railroads could treat bankers merely as valuable servants; those in financial trouble came to rely upon them as saviors and in such cases the bankers exacted a price: control over the lines' affairs, at least to the extent of naming the key men who managed them. In the eighties fierce competition, overexpansion, and reckless railroad management brought an increasing number of roads into the latter category. J. P. Morgan in particular became a major figure in American railroading, reorganizing bankrupt concerns and employing what a biographer called his "inexorable logic and inexorable will" to compel the lines to substitute "mutual co-operation" for cutthroat competition. The experience, wealth, and prestige gained in railroad finance enabled bankers to exert a growing influence over manufacturing corporations as well. Morgan, for example, was interested in the electrical industry from its earliest beginnings.

41 Kirkland, *Industry Comes of Age,* pp. 226, 233–234; A. D. Chandler, Jr., *Henry Varnum Poor: Business Editor, Analyst, and Reformer* (Cambridge, Mass., 1956) , pp. 224, 247–270; T. R. Navin and M. V. Sears, "The Rise of the Market for Industrial Securities," *Business History Review,* XXIX (1955) , 105–138.

The day when the "money trust" allegedly controlled industrial concerns worth many billions of dollars had not yet arrived, but the foundations of banker domination were being laid.[42]

The emerging importance of bankers in railroading illustrates a broad characteristic of industrialization in the 1880's: as businesses grew in size and complexity, managerial skills became more vital to their success. The need for manufacturing skills also expanded as production became more specialized, but production experts were seldom the real masters of American businesses. Those who knew how to manage big organizations efficiently issued the orders; the technicians merely carried them out.

In large, heavily capitalized enterprises selling goods all over the United States and sometimes in international markets, too, the coordination of many different operations taking place at widely scattered sites made management itself a specialized profession. The ability to see the structure whole, to appreciate its interrelations, became essential. What may be called the elimination of administrative friction—between individual personalities as well as between the separate parts of the industrial organism—was as necessary as the proper lubrication of the machines that actually produced the goods. Furthermore, mere production became relatively less important as the structure supporting it grew larger. Overhead, those expenses not directly related to the volume of output, occupied an ever-larger space in the cost structure of industry, making it more difficult to adjust production to current demand and to determine proper business strategy. On the other hand, as output went up, the most minute improvements in the manufacturing process could have spectacular effects on profits. A fraction of a cent saved in making a single unit meant thousands of dollars if millions of units were being produced. When John D. Rockefeller focused his attention on small details, such as the number of drops of solder required to seal an oil can, he was not being penurious, nor was he exhibiting a lack of ability to delegate authority. In 1885 his Standard Oil Company succeeded in reducing the cost of processing

[42] F. L. Allen, *The Great Pierpont Morgan* (New York, 1956), pp. 41, 43, 60; N. S. B. Gras and H. M. Larson, *Casebook of American Business History* (New York, 1939), pp. 552–555; Josephson, *Edison*, pp. 188–189, 201–202, 291–293, 351–354; H. C. Passer, *The Electrical Manufacturers: 1875–1900* (Cambridge, Mass., 1953), p. 85.

a gallon of crude oil by .082 cents. Since Standard Oil refined over 730 million gallons of crude in that year, its profits rose by about $600,000 as a result of this improvement.[43]

The railroads pioneered in devising novel forms of business management. Even before the Civil War, many lines had worked out elaborate techniques for keeping track of their far-flung operations. They set up separate departments to handle finance and bookkeeping, others to supervise the movement of trains and the procuring of business. As the trunk lines expanded in the seventies and eighties, railroad executives paid more attention to defining the lines of authority and responsibility connecting the managers in the field with the central administration. Charles E. Perkins of the Chicago, Burlington and Quincy was especially active in working out what he called the "natural laws" of railroad management, which involved the careful definition of executive functions and the delicate balancing of local autonomy and centralized control.

Because so much of the cost of running a railroad consisted of items like maintenance, wages, and interest payments, which were not directly related to the movement of goods and passengers, railroad men concentrated upon perfecting their accounting procedures. As early as the 1870's they were making the analysis of expenditures an exact science. In 1875 Albert Fink broke down the cost of operating the seven sections of the Louisville and Nashville system in detail, his figures—accurate to three decimal places—showing that actual "movement expenses" varied enormously from one branch to another.[44]

When industrial concerns began to rival the railroads in size, they too began to refine and expand their managerial structures. Carnegie applied sophisticated accounting techniques to his operations as early as 1875, hiring a railroad-trained auditor, William B. Shinn, as general manager of his company. Rockefeller organized his refineries with equal precision, and so did the McCormick family in the agricultural-machinery business. As national markets developed, manufacturers had also to give more attention to the prob-

[43] Hidy and Hidy, *Pioneering in Big Business*, pp. 107, 187.

[44] Chandler, *Railroads*, pp. 97–100, 110, 118–125; Chandler, "Manufacturing and Transportation," pp. 143–147; Cochran, *Railroad Leaders*, pp. 58–61, 80–86; Gilchrist, "Albert Fink and Pooling," *Business History Review*, XXXIV, 29; Kirkland, *Men, Cities and Transportation*, II, 328–332.

lems of distribution and sales. The proportion of the labor force engaged in distributing goods rose steadily at the rate of a little over 2 per cent per year throughout the seventies and eighties.[45] Most of the work of distribution was performed by independent middlemen. Some large producers of consumer goods, such as the meat packer Gustavus F. Swift and the cigarette manufacturer James B. Duke, began to build their own marketing organizations, but the percentage of finished goods sold in retail stores rose only slightly during the period. Retailers also did most of the advertising of goods, although the growth of national urban markets was gradually leading industrialists to push their own wares. The railroads printed their timetables in the newspapers together with notices of special excursions and new facilities. Many lines that had obtained government land grants, such as the Illinois Central, the Burlington, and the Northern Pacific, published what the New York *Tribune* called "glaring . . . advertisements and glowing descriptions of the country" to attract settlers. A number of the most characteristic aspects of modern-day advertising—exaggeration, the use of illustrated brochures, the lavish entertainment both of prospective buyers and of "opinion makers"—were introduced to the business world by Henry Villard of the Northern Pacific and other railroad men in the 1880's.[46]

During the immediate post–Civil War period, the makers of patent medicines and the book publishers were the leading advertisers among manufacturers; but while they increased their expenditures steadily, their relative importance in the field shrank rapidly. By the nineties processors of sugar, flour, and other packaged foods, together with manufacturers of sewing machines, farm implements, clothing, tobacco, soap, and petroleum, had become the

[45] Brody, *Steelworkers*, p. 18; Robert Ozanne, "Union-Management Relations: McCormick Harvesting Machine Company, 1862–1886," *Labor History*, IV (1963), 139; Harold Barger, *Distribution's Place in the American Economy Since 1869* (Princeton, 1955), pp. 4, 7. There were about 1.4 million persons directly engaged in transporting and selling goods in 1870 and 3.3 million in 1890.

[46] A. D. Chandler, Jr., "The Beginning of 'Big Business' in American History," *Business History Review*, XXXIII (1959), 1–31; Barger, *Distribution*, p. 22; P. W. Gates, *Fifty Million Acres: Conflicts Over Kansas Land Policy, 1854–1890* (Ithaca, 1954), pp. 272–273; Cochran, *Railroad Leaders*, pp. 150–151; J. B. Hedges, "The Colonization Work of the Northern Pacific Railroad," *Mississippi Valley Historical Review*, XIII (1926), 311–343; R. C. Overton, *Burlington West: A Colonization History of the Burlington Railroad* (Cambridge, Mass., 1941), *passim*.

chief national advertisers.[47] These manufacturers devised trade-marks to identify their goods[48] and, taking advantage of improvements in printing and photoengraving, produced larger, better-illustrated advertisements in order to add to the impact of their messages. As advertising became more important, manufacturers turned to experts for help in preparing copy and organizing their campaigns. The advertising agent, originally a mere peddler of newspaper space, became a skilled, almost professional specialist.[49]

However, the changes in the distribution and advertising of goods were trivial compared with those affecting the basic organization of large business enterprises. By the late seventies some concerns were carrying on many different operations, in plants scattered over broad sections of the country. For example, the petroleum empire of John D. Rockefeller and his associates included refineries and other facilities in many states. It sold a wide variety of products in every part of the United States and in many foreign countries. This sprawling, decentralized complex had grown rapidly and, except that the Rockefeller group had been bent upon winning control of the entire refining industry, without plan.

Between 1879 and 1886, the leaders of this Standard Oil group fashioned their holdings into an efficient, co-ordinated industrial machine. First they assigned the stock of the forty corporations they controlled to nine trustees, headed by Rockefeller, receiving in exchange trust certificates in proportion to their holdings. The trustees were given the power to elect the officers of all constituent companies, to create new companies, and to manage the business "in the manner they may deem most conducive to the best interests of the holders of said Trust Certificates." Although the trustees left day-to-day operations in the hands of men already in charge of the

[47] Kirkland, *Industry Comes of Age*, pp. 272–274; Frank Presbrey, *The History and Development of Advertising* (Garden City, 1929), pp. 289–301, 337–344; R. M. Hower, *The History of an Advertising Agency* (Cambridge, Mass., 1949), pp. 206–213; J. H. Young, *The Toadstool Millionaires* (Princeton, 1961), p 104; Woodward, *Origins of the New South*, p. 130; J. S. Ewing and N. P. Norton, *Broadlooms and Businessmen* (Cambridge, Mass., 1955), pp. 93–94; Hidy and Hidy, *Pioneering in Big Business*, pp. 117, 297–298. There is much colorful detail in J. P. Wood, *The Story of Advertising* (New York, 1958), pp. 181–284.

[48] The first trade-marks were registered with the Patent Office in 1870; by 1875, the office had 1,138 on file. Wood, *Advertising*, p. 191; *Hist. Stat.*, p. 608.

[49] Hower, *Advertising Agency*, pp. 13–17, 62; Presbrey, *History of Advertising*, pp. 302–318, 348.

local companies, they set up a number of advisory committees at their New York headquarters to help them determine policy. These committees specialized in such matters as purchasing, packaging, transportation, personnel, and foreign trade. The trustees also created eleven departments to deal with routine aspects of management—auditing, legal affairs, sales, and the like. A steady stream of information poured into the New York office, where it was processed into daily, monthly, quarterly, and annual reports for the edification of the trustees.[50]

This system enabled Standard Oil to adjust rapidly to changing conditions in the oil business and to make full use of the special abilities of all its executives, which helps explain why the trust excelled in introducing the latest technology and in expanding into new fields. In the eighties Standard Oil built a network of pipelines to bring crude oil directly to its refineries, and put together a comprehensive marketing organization. It reduced shipping costs 25 per cent by transporting kerosene to local distributing centers in tank cars rather than in barrels. In the early nineties it extended its bulk delivery system directly to the retailers through the use of tank wagons.[51]

The trust was a legal device created by the Standard's lawyer, Samuel C. T. Dodd, to circumvent the laws of Ohio, Pennsylvania, and other states, which restricted interstate corporations severely. This fact, together with the refining monopoly effected, led to much public criticism, but the administrative advantages of the arrangement were equally important to the Rockefeller group. In 1882, when the trust was established, Standard Oil of Ohio alone held assets scattered over thirteen states and several foreign countries. Other units in the combination were only slightly less complex. These circumstances probably made it inevitable that the leaders of Standard Oil would take steps to centralize and rationalize their business, and they help explain why, before 1890, the manufacturers of cottonseed oil, sugar, whisky, and many other products had followed their example. After a brief investigation in 1888, a

---

50 Hidy and Hidy, *Pioneering in Big Business*, pp. 32–75.

51 *Ibid.*, pp. 59, 196–197; Williamson and Daum, *Petroleum Industry*, pp. 528–538; 687–692; A. M. Johnson, *The Development of American Petroleum Pipelines: A Study in Private Enterprise and Public Policy, 1862–1906* (Ithaca, 1956), pp. 100–122.

congressional committee reported that "the number of combinations and trusts formed and forming in this country is . . . very large. . . . New ones are constantly forming and . . . old ones are constantly extending their relations." The weight of the evidence suggests that in most cases efficiency, not price control, was the major objective of the consolidators.[52]

Social reformers, and businessmen who had not achieved the kind of dominance that Rockefeller had won for himself, denounced these trusts as monopolistic monsters and predicted that they would destroy the competitive system, perhaps even democracy itself. Their concern was certainly justified, for the masters of the new combinations often took selfish advantage of the power that combination gave them. Few adequate social or political institutions existed to restrain them.

Yet the trust device, which was a sort of halfway house between the informal pool and the later holding company (a corporation established for the purpose of owning other corporations), served a valuable function. As the processes of production and distribution in an expanding national market became more diverse, pressures for both horizontal and vertical integration in business affairs mounted. The trusts were the brains designed to direct and co-ordinate the many specialized limbs of the new industrial organisms. Indeed, the combination movement in industry was part of a general late-nineteenth-century tendency toward co-operation. In many fields of human endeavor new technical knowledge and improved means of communication were leading to specialization, diffusion, and then, for purposes of co-ordination, to combination. The decade of the eighties saw—and these are but examples—the combination of labor unions into the American Federation of Labor, of agricultural groups into the northern and southern farmers' alliances, of political reformers into the Civil Service Reform League, of disaster-relief agencies into the American Red Cross Society. As John M. Glenn, a leader of the organized charity

[52] H. B. Thorelli, *The Federal Antitrust Policy: The Origination of an American Tradition* (Baltimore, 1955), p. 158; Chandler, "Beginning of 'Big Business,'" pp. 1–31. Even relatively small manufacturing corporations in fields like textiles (where the combination movement did not develop) often responded to the increasing complexity of their businesses by strengthening the control of the central management and improving their accounting methods. See, for example, Navin, *Whitin Machine Works*, pp. 137–158.

movement in Baltimore, wrote: "We live in an atmosphere of organization. . . . Men are learning the disadvantages of isolated action. Whether or not we approve of trusts and trades-unions and similar combinations, and whatever their motives, they rest on a foundation which is sound alike from the business and religious standpoint; namely, the principle of union and co-operation." Even scholars responded to these conditions. The Modern Language Association, the American Historical Association, the American Economic Association, the American Mathematical Society, the National Statistical Association, and many similar groups were all founded between 1883 and 1888.[53]

Critics insisted that the trusts would destroy competition, the basis of the free enterprise system. Their fears were exaggerated, for the economy remained intensely competitive despite the tendency toward consolidation. Prices declined even in monopolized industries like petroleum. Improved transportation facilities undermined local monopolies faster than trustifiers could create national ones, while technical advances and expanding markets brought new firms into most fields faster than established ones could smash or swallow them. "The more successful the Trust, the surer . . . offshoots are to sprout," Andrew Carnegie, no friend of the trust movement in the eighties, explained. "After a time the growth of demand enables capital to receive an unusual profit. This in turn attracts fresh capital to the manufacture, and we have a renewal of the old struggle."[54]

However, the *conditions* of competition were changing. Rockefeller's statement that "the day of individual competition in large affairs is past and gone,"[55] written after his company had engaged in ruthless price-cutting and other unscrupulous practices to drive other refiners out of business, was as untrue as it was self-serving;

53 Kirkland, *Industry Comes of Age*, pp. 199–205; J. W. Hurst, *Law and the Condition of Freedom in the Nineteenth-Century United States* (Madison, Wis., 1956) , p. 85; Roy Lubove, *The Professional Altruist: The Emergence of Social Work as a Career* (Cambridge, Mass., 1965) , pp. 6–7; Schlesinger, *Rise of the City*, p. 221.

54 Kirkland, *Industry Comes of Age*, pp. 214–215; Andrew Carnegie, *The Empire of Business* (New York, 1902) , pp. 160–161. It is interesting that Carnegie soon changed his view of the combination movement. In 1900 he wrote: "This overpowering, irresistible tendency toward aggregation of capital and increase of size in every branch of product cannot be arrested." E. C. Kirkland (ed.) , *The Gospel of Wealth and Other Timely Essays* (Cambridge, Mass., 1962) , pp. 82–83.

55 Rockefeller, *Reminiscences,* p. 65.

but in giant industries with immense resources and heavy fixed costs, competition did not function the way the theorists of an earlier day had described it. The classical economists had assumed that when manufacturers could not sell their output at a profit they would stop producing, and that the resultant decline in the volume of available goods would drive prices up until, eventually, production would again become profitable. In the late nineteenth century, most businessmen, while only sketchily acquainted with economic theory, accepted as axiomatic this "natural law" of supply and demand, and preached the virtues of a self-regulating economy as fervently as Adam Smith had in the eighteenth century and David Ricardo in the early decades of the nineteenth.

Men with experience in railroading and in heavy industry, however, quickly learned that they could not shut up shop whenever their costs exceeded their returns. As early as 1878, Charles Francis Adams, Jr., was pointing out that in the railroad business "the recognized laws of trade" worked "imperfectly at best." A few years later another railroad expert, Arthur T. Hadley, noted that although the law of supply and demand "was approximately true when Ricardo wrote," it did not apply to modern conditions in the railroad industry. And while still defending competition ardently in 1889, steelman Andrew Carnegie confessed: "Political economy says that . . . goods will not be produced at less than cost. This was true when Adam Smith wrote, but it is not quite true to-day." Overhead expenses, in other words, often forced manufacturers to produce at a loss rather than shut down their factories. In the railroad business the fact that unsuccessful competitors continued operating even after being bankrupted further complicated the problem. Simon Sterne, a New York lawyer, explained this state of affairs in 1879: "In a railroad war, when you have ruined your rival, you have put him into the hands of a receiver, and the trains are dispatched and arrive in the same manner as before, with the difference that you have exempted your rival from the obligation to pay dividends, and have thus put him in a conditon of greater and more effective rivalry than he was in at the outset of the fight!" Albert Fink put the matter bluntly. "Competition," he testified in 1883, "don't work well in the transportation business."[56]

---

[56] Adams, *Railroads*, p. 81; Hadley, *Railroad Transportation*, p. 70; Carnegie, *Empire of Business*, p. 154; Chandler, *Railroads*, p. 198; Lee Benson, *Merchants*,

Ruinous railroad rate cutting was the most common example of this nonself-limiting competition. In 1876–77 the published rate for first-class freight between Chicago and New York fell from 75 cents a hundredweight to 25 cents, that for agricultural products from 50 cents to 18 cents, and many shippers obtained still more fortunate terms through secret rebates. In 1881 the rate fell to as little as 8 cents a hundredweight. At one point the lines were carrying live cattle over this route for a dollar a carload! In 1883 a judicial decision breaking up a western pool led to a desperate battle for business between the Union Pacific and the Denver and Rio Grande. When the Union Pacific announced a 50-cent rate between Salt Lake City and the Missouri River, the Rio Grande responded by driving the price down to 25 cents, which only guaranteed that both roads would lose money. Such contests seldom lasted very long, but with the railroad network expanding throughout the eighties, competition became ever more intense. More significant than any particular rate war was the steady erosion of average rates. Country-wide, these declined from $1.23 per ton-mile in 1882 to 92.7 cents in 1890. The tendency of railroads to consolidate and of railroad men to question laissez-faire economics can only be understood against the background of this situation.[57]

If industrial developments seemed to be changing the laws of economics, they were also changing the laws of the nation and the states. Relationships between business and government were shifting rapidly; for as the industrial system became more intricate, more attention had to be paid to directing its course. As businessmen improved their ability to manage their affairs and began to substitute co-operation for competition through the instrument of trusts, the public, through the instruments of state and national government, began to exercise more control over the economy too.

Farmers, and Railroads: Railroad Regulation and New York Politics, 1850–1887 (Cambridge, Mass., 1955), pp. vii, 116; U.S. Senate, 49 Cong., 1 Sess., Select Committee on Interstate Commerce [Cullom Committee], *Report No. 46* (Washington, 1886), Part I, p. 43; U.S. Senate, *Report on . . . Labor and Capital*, II, 472.

57 Kirkland, *Industry Comes of Age*, pp. 80, 93–96; Adams, *Railroads*, pp. 152, 166; Grodinsky, *Railroad Strategy*, pp. 238–239; *Hist. Stat.*, p. 428; Kolko, *Railroads and Regulation*, p. 5; U.S. Senate, *Report on . . . Labor and Capital*, II, 474. MacAvoy, *Effects of Regulation*, pp. 64, 89, 102, 107, presents different but related figures on rate fluctuations.

Technology, by speeding communications and fostering specialization, was making every element of society more dependent on
every other and broadening the national conception of the public
interest. In 1876, at the very beginning of our period, the Supreme
Court reaffirmed an old common-law principle: "When private
property is devoted to a public use, it is subject to public regulation." In this case, *Munn* v. *Illinois,* the justices upheld the right of
Illinois to regulate the storage charges of grain elevators within its
borders. While admitting that no precedent existed for considering
warehouses public utilities, they showed that the Illinois elevators
were handling the "vast productions" of seven or eight western
grain-raising states on the way to eastern markets. The storage
business had "become a thing of public interest and use," and the
Court therefore justified extending the public-utility concept to
cover it. "The business is one of recent origin . . . its growth has
been rapid, and . . . it is already of great importance."[58]

The case for considering the grain warehouses of Illinois public
utilities seemed clear cut, but in a sense nearly every business in an
integrated economy was a public utility. It followed (although not
without argument) that the public had an interest in business
activity of every kind. Hand in hand with industrialization went an
expansion of government regulation of industrial, indeed of all,
economic affairs. As James Bryce wrote in his brilliant discussion of
laissez faire in *The American Commonwealth:* "New causes are at
work in the world tending not only to lengthen the arms of government, but to make its touch quicker and firmer."

The change was neither sudden nor revolutionary; as Bryce also
noted, "few but lawyers and economists" appreciated what was
happening. Much of the confusion of the period resulted from the
inability of people to cast off old-fashioned economic ideas when
they faced problems requiring different approaches. Throughout
the early nineteenth century the government had sought repeatedly
to stimulate economic development. Protective tariffs, public grants
to railroads and canals, and other forms of aid, all violations of
laissez-faire theory, had been justified on the ground that they stim-

---

[58] Munn *v.* Illinois, 94 U.S. 113. For the background of the Munn case, see the
essay by C. P. Magrath in J. A. Garraty (ed.) , *Quarrels That Have Shaped
the Constitution* (New York, 1964) , pp. 109–127, and Magrath's *Morrison R.
Waite: The Triumph of Character* (New York, 1963) , pp. 173–189.

ulated (as J. W. Hurst has said) "the release of individual creative energy" and thus advanced the common good.[59] In the last quarter of the century, however, as men combined to achieve their ends, as everyone's business affairs became more dependent upon everyone else's, and as competition ceased to be effectively self-regulating, government economic legislation became more restrictive in character. Without abandoning free enterprise as an objective, legislators found themselves limiting the choices of enterprisers instead of broadening them, sometimes with the concurrence, even the connivance, of the enterprisers themselves.[60]

Once again, the new conditions appeared first and most clearly in the railroad industry. Originally, governmental authority had been used almost exclusively to aid railroads. Besides various forms of financial assistance, state charters typically gave railroad builders the right to lay track along and across public rights of way, to bridge streams, to fix their own "reasonable" rates, and (especially important) to exercise the right of eminent domain in obtaining necessary land. Although the fact that roads had to obtain franchises to operate was a tacit admission that they were subject to public control, state legislatures imposed few controls upon them; most persons were so beguiled by the potential advantages of rail connections that they failed to anticipate the power which the completed lines would have over the communities they served.[61]

However, as discriminatory pricing policies and irregularities in railroad finance caused public resentment to mount, the states began to apply certain restrictions to the lines. The commercial revolution was increasing interregional competition. However well meaning, every decision by a railroad executive benefited some section or interest and hurt others. It was no mere question of

---

59 Bryce, *American Commonwealth*, II, 539, 542; Thorelli, *Antitrust Policy*, p. 165; Hurst, *Law and the Condition of Freedom*, p. 7, and *Law and Economic Growth*, pp. 409–411. See also Carter Goodrich, *Government Promotion of American Canals and Railroads: 1800–1890* (New York, 1960). Goodrich concludes: "This use of the public powers conformed to the traditions, and served the purposes, of individualistic free enterprise." Pp. 294–295.

60 Hurst, *Law and the Condition of Freedom*, pp. 71–90.

61 Hurst, *Law and Economic Growth*, pp. 274–275, 559–560; for an interesting discussion of the close relationship between railroads and local government, see H. R. Lamar, *Dakota Territory, 1861–1899: A Study of Frontier Politics* (New Haven, 1956), pp. 127–147. "The railroad promoters and builders were synonymous with the political leaders," Lamar concludes.

shippers versus railroads, of farmers versus middlemen. Merchants in Boston and Philadelphia battled for business with merchants in New York, and the railroads could determine the outcome of these conflicts apparently at will. At the same time, powerful interests in every major city could exact special favors from the railroads, thus disadvantaging brother merchants in their own communities. Inevitably the injured parties sought relief in the form of legislation. Many strange marriages of convenience resulted and many cherished ideological convictions about the role of government were cast aside, but the result was the regulation of the railroad network, first by the states, then by the federal government.

Public control, however, was difficult; it posed problems of enormous complexity. Recognizing the highly technical character of railroad regulation, many states, beginning with Rhode Island in 1839, established commissions of experts to supervise the lines within their borders. Two types of commission evolved over the years. The "advisory" type, first developed in the northeastern states, had no direct authority over railroad policies. These commissions investigated complaints, collected statistics, and published reports on the rates and practices of local roads, the idea being, as Charles Francis Adams, Jr., of the Massachusetts commission put it, to serve "as a sort of lens" to focus public attention on what the railroads were doing. When directed by strong and intelligent men, as was the case in Massachusetts during Adams' tenure and in Alabama under Walter L. Bragg in the early eighties, these advisory commissions had great influence. Political leaders consulted them about proposed legislation, railroad men were at pains to please them, and their recommendations weighed heavily with the average citizen. Many merchants and businessmen preferred this type of regulation because it did not involve direct control of private enterprises by the government.[62]

In the Middle West, however, stronger controls were developed. In the early seventies, Illinois, Iowa, and a number of other states established maximum rate schedules and outlawed the granting of rebates and other favors to particular shippers or localities. Then

---

[62] Kirkland, *Men, Cities and Transportation*, II, 232–235, 239–240, 304; Adams, *Railroads*, p. 138; Kirkland, *Adams*, pp. 41–44; Kirkland, *Industry Comes of Age*, pp. 117–119; Chandler, *Railroads*, pp. 185–186; J. F. Doster, *Railroads in Alabama Politics, 1875–1914* (University, Ala., 1957), pp. 11–26.

they created supervisory commissions and gave them authority to enforce these railroad laws and punish violators. This more stringent type of regulation grew out of the complaints of local merchants and shippers against freight charges that favored their big-city rivals in St. Louis and Chicago, who, because of the intense railroad competition at these points, were able to obtain much lower rates. Farm groups supplied highly vocal support to the antirailroad forces, but the movement antedated the rise of the Grangers and would almost surely have achieved its objectives without Granger backing.

In 1879 a committee of the New York legislature, headed by Alonzo B. Hepburn, conducted an eight-month study of the state's lines which gave the country a shocking but convincing picture of the chaotic condition of the railroads. New York City merchants in combination with upstate farm organizations precipitated this investigation because the major trunk lines were simultaneously discriminating against New York farmers in their competition with western grain raisers and against metropolitan merchants who were battling for western markets with the merchants of other eastern cities. From the books of railroads, from the reluctant testimony of railroad executives, and from the eager disclosures of merchants and farmers, the committee extracted a mass of evidence about rate discrimination and financial malpractices which greatly strengthened the demand for regulation. Simon Sterne, who, as counsel for the New York Chamber of Commerce, practically directed the investigation, scarcely exaggerated when he said that the hearings revealed "the most shameless perversion of the duties of a common carrier to private ends that has taken place in the history of the world."[63]

Out of the New York investigation came a number of relatively mild laws, including one (1882) establishing a commission of the Massachusetts type. But in New York and in most other states,

63 S. J. Buck, *The Granger Movement: A Study of Agricultural Organization and Its Political, Economic and Social Manifestations* (Cambridge, Mass., 1933), pp. 232–237; F. A. Shannon, *The Farmer's Last Frontier: Agriculture, 1860–1897* (New York, 1945), pp. 310–311; Kirkland, *Industry Comes of Age*, p. 119; G. H. Miller, "Origins of the Iowa Granger Law," *Mississippi Valley Historical Review*, XL (1954), 657–680; Benson, *Merchants, Farmers, and Railroads*, pp. 115–138; State of New York, *Proceedings of the Special* [Hepburn] *Committee on Railroads . . .* (5 vols., New York, 1879), *passim*.

regulation proved generally unsatisfactory for several reasons: the impossibility of determining rates that were both fair and uniform, the fact that most shipments crossed state lines, the ineptitude of many railroad commissioners and the careless way in which some of the laws were drafted, the discouraging effect that regulatory legislation had on investments in new railroads. In any case, the pressures on the roads to discriminate in favor of large shippers at competitive points and to compensate by raising rates in areas where they held monopolies were irresistible. Even the most well-meaning railroad executives often succumbed to these pressures and took their chances with the law. Therefore, although the desire to control the railroads remained, as early as the mid-seventies, a reaction had set in against the particular devices employed to do the job. Many of the stricter midwestern laws were repealed. In 1887 less than half the states had railroad commissions and only eight of these commissions had the power to control rates.[64]

Concurrently, however, a movement for federal railroad regulation was gathering force. Advocates of federal action sought both to lower rates generally and to outlaw discrimination in favor of individual shippers. In 1874 the House passed a bill creating a national railroad commission with power to prepare maximum-rate schedules and bring suit against violators, but this measure failed in the Senate. Over the next few years a number of bills were introduced and there was much debate in Congress, the controversy tending to center more on rate discrimination than on rate reduction, although both problems were discussed. John H. Reagan of Texas, chairman of the House Committee on Commerce, emerged as the leader of the congressional regulators; his proposal, introduced in 1878, outlawed the giving and receiving of rebates and other special favors and the charging of more for a short haul than a long one. It also forbade pooling agreements.

Various special-interest groups urged Congress to act: farm organizations, oilmen in the Pennsylvania fields who were being squeezed as a result of pressure applied to the railroads by the refiners, merchants, even some railroad men themselves. By the mid-eighties, as the *Commercial and Financial Chronicle* noted, "friend

---

[64] Benson, *Merchants, Farmers, and Railroads*, pp. 143–144, 167–173; Kirkland, *Industry Comes of Age*, pp. 120–124; Kolko, *Railroads and Regulation*, p. 16.

and opponent alike" were "pleading for redress at the hands of the Government."[65] This organized demand was widespread but sporadic and constantly shifting. Farmer interest in railroad regulation slackened in the early eighties and so, apparently, did that of merchant groups. Declining rates made regulation appear less urgent to shippers, despite their continuing resentment when they were discriminated against. But it was a general if vague understanding of the changing realities of economic conditions on the part of Congress, businessmen, and the public at large rather than the diverse and sometimes conflicting arguments of persons most directly concerned that finally produced results.[66]

Railroad men were divided, some even in their own minds, about federal regulation. When they focused on the evils of rate cutting or the confusions resulting from multiple regulation by the separate states, they tended to favor federal controls; but when they considered the question more abstractly, their distaste for government interference with their freedom as enterprisers caused them to have second thoughts. Usually, their feelings about regulation were governed by specific circumstances rather than by theoretical considerations. Certainly, no consensus existed among them, and thus they exerted no overwhelming influence on Congress. Some, such as Albert Fink of the Eastern Trunk Line Association, wanted a federal law authorizing and enforcing pooling agreements. Many favored, or were at least reconciled to, the establishment of a commission with investigatory and advisory powers. Men of this persuasion justified federal intervention by reference to such judicial landmarks as John Marshall's decision in the Dartmouth College case, believing, as an official of the Erie wrote, that a federal commission would provide "conservative protection against radical assaults" on the lines by the states. When business slumped and competition sharpened, a number of railroad men even flirted with

---

[65] L. H. Haney, *A Congressional History of Railways in the United States: 1850-1887* (Madison, Wis., 1910), pp. 282-289; G. D. Nash, "Origins of the Interstate Commerce Act of 1887," *Pennsylvania Magazine of History and Biography*, XXIV (1957), 184-187; Benson, *Merchants, Farmers, and Railroads*, pp. 117-124, 201, 204, 212; Kolko, *Railroads and Regulation*, pp. 20-29.

[66] Buck, *Granger Movement*, p. 230; Benson, *Merchants, Farmers, and Railroads*, pp. 230-231, 245; Kolko, *Railroads and Regulation*, pp. 24-25, 31-33; E. A. Purcell, Jr., "Ideas and Interests: Businessmen and the Interstate Commerce Act," *Journal of American History*, LIV (1967), 561-578.

the idea of federal rate fixing. Very few, however, were actually enthusiastic about regulation. Charles E. Perkins of the Chicago, Burlington and Quincy, for example, thought it "obvious" that the government should "leave [railroads] alone commercially" and that "*all* such legislation must fail in the end." James C. Clarke of the Illinois Central advocated "the least possible experimental legislation." John Murray Forbes, director of a dozen lines, denounced "any hasty or ill digested measures of interference with the Management of R.Roads by Congress." Jay Gould flatly opposed any government controls.[67]

Nevertheless, Congress moved steadily toward regulation. In December, 1884, another version of the Reagan bill passed the House and in February, 1885, a bill introduced by Shelby M. Cullom of Illinois passed the Senate, both by solid majorities. At first, attempts to reconcile these measures failed. A Senate committee headed by Cullom then conducted extensive hearings, taking testimony in most of the major rail centers of the nation, from Boston to Omaha and from Minneapolis to New Orleans.[68] The Cullom Committee report (January, 1886) led to a renewal of the congressional debates and in May, 1886, both houses again passed railroad bills, the major differences being that the Senate (Cullom) bill did not outlaw pools and placed only vague restrictions on the right of railroads to charge more for short hauls than for longer ones, while the House (Reagan) bill did not provide for a federal commission and applied only to freight. The two measures were tied up in conference committee for months, chiefly by Reagan's insistence that pools be declared illegal. In October the Supreme Court, in the case of *Wabash, St. Louis, and Pacific Railway* v. *Illinois,* declared an Illinois long-and-short-haul law unconstitutional on the ground that a state could not regulate commerce that extended beyond its limits. This decision added to the pressure for compromise by emphasizing the inability of the states to handle the railroad regu-

[67] Cochran, *Railroad Leaders,* pp. 189, 191, 440–442, 301, 341; Kolko, *Railroads and Regulation,* pp. 27, 38–39; Benson, *Merchants, Farmers, and Railroads,* pp. vii–viii; J. W. Neilson, *Shelby M. Cullom: Prairie State Republican* (Urbana, 1962), pp. 114–116; U.S. Senate, *Report on . . . Labor and Capital,* I, 1081.
[68] Haney, *History of Railways,* p. 290; S. M. Cullom, *Fifty Years of Public Service* (Chicago, 1911), p. 317; Cullom Committee *Report, passim;* Neilson, *Cullom,* pp. 89–92, 99–108.

lation problem. Cullom finally agreed to include an antipooling provision in the measure (the House conferees had yielded on most of the other points in dispute), and in January, 1887, the Interstate Commerce Act became law.[69]

This act prohibited the granting of rebates and other favors and made it unlawful "to charge or receive any greater compensation . . . for a shorter than a longer distance over the same line," but it also prohibited pooling agreements. Thus Congress struck at both the monopolistic and the competitive evils connected with railroading. Although the law did not presume to set actual freight and passenger tariffs, it declared that rates must be "reasonable and just," and it compelled the roads to publish their rate schedules for all to see. A five-man Interstate Commerce Commission was created to conduct investigations and enforce the law, ultimately by prosecuting violators in the federal courts.

The Interstate Commerce Act was vague in many sections; after its passage some railroad executives proposed a general conference with their best legal brains "in order to determine what the bill actually means," and the *Railway Review* complained about its "obscure and contradictory wording." Senator Nelson W. Aldrich of Rhode Island, a foe of regulation, characterized it as an "empty menace."[70]

Its lack of clarity aside, the law proved difficult to administer and enforce. The commission was immediately inundated with business —over a thousand questions and complaints poured in upon it in the first few months. The short-haul provision posed the knottiest problems. Some trunk lines insisted that if they reduced local rates to the levels of those charged for highly competitive longer hauls, they would bankrupt themselves; whereas if they made through rates proportionate to local ones, they would lose business to

[69] Haney, *History of Railways*, pp. 291–292; Cullom, *Fifty Years of Public Service*, pp. 322–327; Wabash . . . *v.* Illinois, 118 U.S. 557. The Wabash road had charged 15 cents a hundredweight for carrying freight from Peoria to New York and 25 cents for carrying the same class of goods from Gilman, which was nearly 100 miles nearer the metropolis. Such traffic, the Court held, could only be regulated by Congress.

[70] *U.S. Statutes at Large*, XXIV, 379–387; Cochran, *Railroad Leaders*, p. 198; Kolko, *Railroads and Regulation*, pp. 45–46; N. W. Stephenson, *Nelson W. Aldrich: A Leader in American Politics* (New York, 1930), p. 68.

competing water transportation and to Canadian railroads, which remained unregulated. Roads with roundabout connections between distant points could not hope to compete under this section of the act unless they slashed local rates ruinously. The commission therefore authorized the lines to ignore this regulation in special circumstances, on the ground that in some parts of the country "the immediate enforcement of an iron-clad rule would have worked changes so radical that many . . . railroads would have found it impossible to conform without suffering very serious injury."[71] Of course, this decision triggered protests from many shippers.

It also proved next to impossible to determine whether or not a rate was "reasonable and just," because any change in a tariff was sure to injure some parties and benefit others. "The question of rates," the commissioners reported, "is often quite as much a question between rival interests and localities as between the railroads." Although they insisted that the roads apply their policies impartially to all shippers, the commissioners leaned over backward to accommodate them, even accepting the argument that rate agreements between competing companies did not constitute pooling so long as freight and territories were not parceled out among them.[72] Even so, after a brief period when most of them tried honestly to obey the law, many railroad men began to evade it through such devices as downgrading freight classifications and making secret cash refunds for big shippers. By 1890 one western railroad executive was claiming that "there is not a road in the country that can

[71] Kolko, *Railroads and Regulation*, p. 49; Grodinsky, *Railroad Strategy*, pp. 322–323, 326, 342; Neilson, *Cullom*, pp. 114–115; Interstate Commerce Commission, *First Annual Report* (Washington, 1887), p. 16; Kirkland, *Industry Comes of Age*, p. 132.

[72] Kolko, *Railroads and Regulation*, pp. 52–53, 58–61; I.C.C., *First Report*, p. 41; A. T. Hadley, "The Workings of the Interstate Commerce Law," *Quarterly Journal of Economics*, II (1888), pp. 162–187. Late in 1888, at the instigation of J. P. Morgan, the heads of some of the major lines formed the Interstate Commerce Railway Assocation to maintain "reasonable, uniform, and stable rates" in co-operation with the I.C.C. A committee headed by Charles Francis Adams, Jr., then president of the Union Pacific, conferred in January, 1889, with two members of the commission and obtained their informal approval. "While we avoid the pool so-called," Chauncey Depew of the New York Central explained, "we do evidently under the sanction of the Interstate Commerce Commission." Kolko, *Railroads and Regulation*, p. 60; Kirkland, *Adams*, pp. 119–120; Grodinsky, *Railroad Strategy*, pp. 345–346.

be accused of living up to the rules of the Interstate Commerce Law."[73]

Nevertheless, the Interstate Commerce Act was of epochal significance. It created the prototype of the modern commissions of experts that now regulate communications, power, tariffs, and other important elements in the economy as well as railroads. In 1887 few persons recognized the revolution thus begun; the commission seemed to most merely a modified copy of the state regulatory bodies, more powerful than the Massachusetts type, less so than those developed in the Middle West. As Senator Cullom later wrote: "Considering the abuses that existed, the Act of 1887 was conservative legislation." Yet even at the start the law had a powerful and positive impact on the country. Although the commission proceeded cautiously and some railroad executives failed to live up to the spirit of the new regulations, the commission's rulings had an immediate stabilizing impact on the transportation industry. By conducting investigations, collecting statistical data, and disseminating its findings widely, it made large strides toward forcing sounder financial practices on the railroads and encouraging them to rationalize their rate structures. Rate differentials between competitive and noncompetitive points were reduced sharply. In some circumstances, the roads used the act as an excuse for resisting the demands of shippers for special favors. In countless subtle ways, it compelled railroad men to recognize some of their *public* responsibilities.[74]

In the mid-nineties the Supreme Court emasculated the commission, and state regulatory agencies as well, by sharply limiting their power. A resurgence of cutthroat competition followed.[75] Truly

---

[73] Grodinsky, *Railroad Strategy*, p. 354. To cite a single example of the difficulty of obtaining redress under the act, in 1890 a group of Wisconsin lumbermen asked the commission to force a rate reduction on local roads. Both the lines and rival Wisconsin lumbermen contested this action. In 1892 the commission ordered a reduction, but only one road complied and then only for a short time. The commission finally undertook an investigation in 1897, but a few months later a Supreme Court ruling deprived it of the power to act in such situations. Hurst, *Law and Economic Growth*, pp. 563–564.

[74] Cullom, *Fifty Years of Public Service*, p. 327; Chandler, *Railroads*, pp. 186–187; Kirkland, *Industry Comes of Age*, pp. 134–136; Cochran, *Railroad Leaders*, pp. 198–199, 401; MacAvoy, *Effects of Regulation*, pp. 108, 113–133, 144–146, 201.

[75] In the state field, the key cases were Chicago, Milwaukee and St. Paul Railroad Co. *v.* Minnesota (134 U.S. 418), declaring that the determination of

effective supervision of railroads did not come until the twentieth century. Congress could conceivably have prevented this judicial frustration of its efforts by a more precise wording of the act or by further legislation. But as the Cullom Committee pointed out in 1886, "in undertaking the regulation of inter-State commerce, Congress [was] entering upon a new and untried field." No one knew exactly *how* to control interstate commerce, but ignorance was no excuse for inaction. The need for federal regulation was clear. If a perfect method was not immediately forthcoming, the Act of 1887 nevertheless represented an intelligent basis for further experimentation.[76]

Whether the Sherman Antitrust Act of 1890, the other major federal attempt of the period to deal with industrial problems, was equally sound in conception has long been debated. The Interstate Commerce Act was based on the implicit assumption that in railroading, competition no longer functioned according to the model described by the classical economists. However, the fact that railroads were public utilities (natural monopolies) probably had more to do with persuading Congress to pass the act than any real grasp of the way the commercial revolution was affecting economic behavior. In dealing with the big new manufacturing combinations,

---

the reasonableness of rates was a judicial function and could not be transferred by law to railroad commissions, and Reagan *v.* Farmers' Loan and Trust Co. (154 U.S. 362) and Smyth *v.* Ames (169 U.S. 466), which established judicial review of rates even when determined by state legislatures themselves. The major cases affecting the Interstate Commerce Act were I.C.C. *v.* Cincinnati, New Orleans, and Texas Pacific Railway Co. (167 U.S. 479), definitively depriving the commission of the power to fix rates, and I.C.C. *v.* Alabama Midland Railway Co. (168 U.S. 144), gravely weakening the short-haul section of the act. However, the Court interpreted the antipooling provision of the law strictly. In U.S. *v.* Trans-Missouri Freight Association (166 U.S. 290) it forbade rate agreements even when made with the approval and under the supervision of the commission. In *Railroads and Regulation* (pp. 80–83), Gabriel Kolko argues that in these decisions the Court was adopting a rigid laissez-faire position as unpalatable to the railroads as to the commission. However, Kolko's general conclusions, that the commission was almost slavishly prorailroad and that the Interstate Commerce Act was totally ineffective, seem overstated. See also Robert W. Harbeson, "Railroads and Regulation, 1877–1916: Conspiracy or Public Interest?" *Journal of Economic History*, XXVII (1967), 230–242; A. M. Paul, *Conservative Crisis and the Rule of Law: Attitudes of Bar and Bench, 1887–1895* (Ithaca, 1960), p. 228n., and MacAvoy, *Effects of Regulation*, pp. 153–176.

[76] Cullom Committee, *Report*, p. 214; Cullom, *Fifty Years of Public Service*, pp. 323–326.

most Americans, and certainly most congressmen, continued to postulate that so long as competition existed, the economy would inevitably regulate itself in the public interest. Paradoxically, they exaggerated the extent to which "the trusts" had destroyed competition, and minimized the extent to which large-scale industry had ceased to respond in the old-fashioned way to competitive forces. Most critics interpreted the growth of large manufacturing combinations like the Standard Oil Trust as a threat to competition and therefore to a self-regulating economy, not as a response to the changing character of the economic system. Their attack on trusts—profoundly conservative in motivation and philosophy—sought to restore competition on the theory that competition still worked in the simple, automatic way that the classical economists had described. This was at least partially untrue.

Although some early state constitutions prohibited business practices that restricted competition, important state antitrust activity began only in the late 1880's. When the public became aware of the trend toward industrial combination at this time, it demanded that the trend be reversed. This demand, however, while pervasive, was not especially intense. Most people had mixed feelings about big business; they took pride in its efficiency and grandeur, even admired the wealth, energy, and ingenuity of the great industrialists. The danger of monopoly remained largely hypothetical, since prices were not going up significantly at any time during the eighties. Most Americans objected to trusts in principle, just as they revered competition in the abstract, but few were suffering noticeably or directly. They wanted action but did not know exactly what they wanted done. By 1890, as a result of this situation, twenty-one states had attempted to "restore" competition either by incorporating antitrust clauses in their constitutions or by statute. These measures ranged from vague denunciations of monopoly to detailed laws spelling out illegal practices and imposing specific penalties upon violators. The Texas antitrust act of 1889 was among the most comprehensive, a "dragnet of great sweep and close mesh" outlawing combinations designed to restrict trade, control production or prices, and prevent competition.

These laws seldom had much effect, however, first because the states which enacted them were mostly in the South and West where few large industrial concerns existed, and second because they were laxly administered and extremely difficult to enforce.[77] Since most combinations were engaged in interstate commerce, often, as in the case of Standard Oil, with facilities scattered over wide regions, state legislation could have only limited success at best.

The failure of state laws to reverse the trend toward consolidation, together with the evidence of trust malpractices uncovered by private researchers and by a number of legislative investigations, soon produced a movement for federal action. In 1884 the Republican party had ignored the trust problem and the Democrats had spoken only vaguely and without emphasis of the "prevention of monopoly" and the curbing of "corporate abuses." A national Antimonopoly party polled only 173,000 votes in the presidential election of that year. Four years later, however, the Republicans declared themselves opposed to "all combinations of capital organized in trusts" and the Democrats were equally outspoken. President Grover Cleveland claimed in 1888 that the people were being "trampled to death beneath [the] iron heel" of the trusts, and the next year his Republican successor, Benjamin Harrison, called trusts "dangerous conspiracies against the public good."[78] Of course, these modest examples of the hyperbolic political rhetoric of the eighties do not prove that the voters were clamoring for a strong federal antitrust law. Nevertheless, the sudden shift in the attitude of the major parties suggests clearly that public opinion, alarmed by the growth of giant corporations, was moving rapidly in that direction.

The first federal antitrust bill was introduced in the House of Representatives in January, 1888; the first Senate proposal was submitted in May. The House measure, and fifteen similar bills, never got out of committee. In the Senate, a bill drafted by Senator John Sherman of Ohio, which declared unlawful all arrangements between persons or corporations that tended to restrict competition or increase prices, was extensively debated, but did not come to a vote.

Over the next two years both houses struggled with a large number

[77] H. R. Seager and C. A. Gulick, Jr., *Trust and Corporation Problems* (New York, 1929), pp. 341–366; Thorelli, *Antitrust Policy*, pp. 155–156; R. C. Cotner, *James Stephen Hogg: A Biography* (Austin, 1959), pp. 164–165; Hurst, *Law and Economic Growth*, p. 475.

[78] Thorelli, *Antitrust Policy*, pp. 149–151, 157–159.

of proposals and counterproposals dealing with the trust problem. No significant party division emerged during these debates. Some congressmen raised serious constitutional objections. The issue became entangled with the tariff question and the determination of federal monetary policy. A number of legislators expressed genuine concern lest, as Senator George F. Hoar of Massachusetts put it, "some crude, hasty legislation which does not cure the evil" be adopted. But finally, in June, 1890, a bill known as the Sherman Antitrust Act was passed with only one dissenting vote in the entire Congress.

In sweeping terms this law declared illegal "every contract, combination in the form of trust or otherwise, or conspiracy, in restraint of trade or commerce among the several States, or with foreign nations." Persons who made such agreements or who "monopolize or attempt to monopolize" such commerce were subject to fines of up to $1,000 and jail terms of up to one year. Furthermore, any private individual who was "injured in his business or property" by persons or corporations violating the act was authorized to sue for triple damages in the federal circuit courts. Thus the law made combinations in restraint of trade both public and private offenses.[79]

That so broad-gauged a law attacking such powerful interests could pass in a predominantly conservative Congress by such an overwhelming vote seems on the surface difficult to explain. Some historians have concluded that a massive explosion of public wrath compelled Congress to act.[80] Others, focusing on the vagueness of the law and seizing upon such evidence as the well-known remark of Senator Orville H. Platt of Connecticut that his colleagues were only looking for "some bill headed: 'A Bill to Punish Trusts' with which to go to the country" have concluded that Congress was engaging in the most cynical kind of politicking and had no intention of actually inhibiting the combination movement.[81] Still others have suggested that the bill went through easily because the

[79] *Ibid.*, pp. 166 n., 169–210; *U.S. Statutes at Large*, XXVI, 209. Thorelli provides a detailed and sensible analysis of these debates.

[80] See for example, H. U. Faulkner, *Politics, Reform and Expansion* (New York, 1959), p. 101; Thurman Arnold, "The Law to Make Free Enterprise Free," *American Heritage*, XI (October, 1960), 52–54.

[81] Matthew Josephson, *The Politicos* (New York, 1938), pp. 458–460.

lawmakers, not yet greatly concerned about industrial concentration, considered it of minor importance.

Each of these explanations has a superficial plausibility. The trend toward monopoly had been widely denounced by reformers, farm organizations, and other critics. Many members of Congress were unblushing admirers of big business. The measure received much less attention than a number of trivial bills; excited no partisan divisions; was passed after being considerably revised in committee almost without discussion.[82] Actually, these interpretations do not seriously contradict one another. The public was aroused but unclear about what should be done. Congressmen felt compelled to move against the trusts but did not want to *injure* business. Few persons expected the Sherman Act to produce drastic results.

Probably the act won such easy acceptance because it made no fundamental change in business law. Conspiracies in restraint of trade and attempts to create monopolies were already technically illegal. Under English and American common law these practices were considered against public policy and many statutes imposed punishments on those who engaged in them. Although judicial definitions of restraint and monopoly shifted from time to time, by the nineteenth century the idea that competition was desirable, monopoly dangerous, had become, it is fair to say, part of western culture. In America the additional principle that corporations could be controlled by the states which chartered them was also well established. What the Sherman Act did essentially was to empower the *federal* government (which had been concerned neither with interpreting the common law nor with the chartering of corporations) to enforce these same general principles. Senator Hoar explained the matter succinctly during the debates: "We have affirmed the old doctrine of the common law . . . and have clothed the United States courts with authority to enforce that doctrine . . . undertaking to curb by national authority an evil which under all our legislative precedents and policies, has been left to be dealt with either by the ordinary laws of trade or, . . . by the States."

Some Americans feared the new industrial combinations like the

---

[82] J. D. Clark, *The Federal Trust Policy* (Baltimore, 1931), p. 30; Merle Fainsod and Lincoln Gordon, *Government and the American Economy* (New York, 1941), pp. 450–451.

plague; others thought them both inevitable and beneficial. Men disagreed about the character of individual trusts and individual business practices. However, Congress and the country were convinced that monopolies ought not to exist totally unchecked and, as we have seen, most observers still believed that competition provided the simplest and most effective method of balancing contending economic forces. Senator Sherman's first antitrust resolution defined the common objective clearly: "To preserve freedom of trade and production, the natural competition of increasing production, the lowering of prices by such competition." In the course of the debate only one congressman, Senator William Stewart of Nevada, a man of small influence, challenged this purpose; others who objected to the various bills did so on constitutional grounds or because they believed specific remedies unworkable.[83]

The weaknesses of the law, most notably its failure to define such terms as restraint of trade and monopoly precisely and its reliance upon Congress' power to regulate interstate commerce to justify federal action, stemmed from genuine constitutional problems and from the fact that the terms were difficult to define. By leaving the interpretation of the law to the courts, Congress was only following centuries of precedent in this area. In any case, to have spelled out every undesirable business practice would have been impossible, given the complex and dynamic conditions of that day. Disturbed and baffled by the growth of trusts, Congress settled for a restatement of old principles and the mobilization of a new force, the federal judiciary, to defend them, fully conscious that it did not know what the exact result would be. "Mr. Speaker," an Arkansas congressman declared at one point, "I am willing to give my sanction to this bill . . . filled with doubts, yet compelled by a sense of the exigency and the emergency of the occasion to do whatever seems best."[84]

Congress could have attacked the trust problem in other ways— for instance, by changing the patent laws, or by reducing tariffs, or by compelling federal incorporation of large enterprises under strict controls. The method it chose bore little immediate fruit. In the decade of the nineties, the executive branch instituted only a

83 *Congressional Record*, 51 Cong. 1 sess., XXI, Part 4, pp. 3146, 3152; *ibid.*, 50 Cong. 1 sess., XIX, Part 7, p. 6041; Thorelli, *Antitrust Policy*, pp. 190–191.
84 Thorelli, *Antitrust Policy*, p. 205.

handful of antitrust suits and in 1895 the Supreme Court sharply limited the scope of the Sherman Act by deciding, in *U.S.* v. *E. C. Knight Company*,[85] that monopolization of the manufacturing of an article by a single combine did not constitute restraint of interstate commerce *per se*, even if the goods later entered into such commerce. The inadequacy of the Sherman Act, however, resulted only partly from the way it was interpreted and executed. The competitive system it sought to buttress was at once less threatened and less effective than the framers of the law had imagined. After 1890 the trend toward industrial combination continued, but so did industrial competition. Soon a battalion of colossi bestrode the industrial world, but it was not a narrow world that these Caesars could really dominate—the expanding American economy bore the weight of the big trusts handily, if not entirely without strain.

Eventually men learned that competition worked less perfectly than they had believed. Then they found supplementary means of regulating business affairs and enforcing a modicum of economic justice. In the early 1890's, however, both understanding and adjustment, along with much travail, lay still in the future. Nevertheless, by that time the basis of the modern American industrial system had been firmly established. We must now consider some of the by-products of this development.

[85] U.S. *v.* E. C. Knight Co. (156 U.S. 1).

CHAPTER 4

The Workingman

THAT the economic expansion of the post–Civil War era produced substantial material benefits for American labor and especially for industrial workers is no longer subject to doubt. Money wages rose by more than 10 per cent between 1870 and 1890. The cost of living declined. According to the best available estimates, the price index (1860 = 100) fell from 141 in 1870 to 98 in 1890. Thus real wages went up sharply—by between 10 and 20 per cent in the seventies and by at least 25 per cent more in the eighties.[1]

The chief cause of this increase in real wages was technological. New machines made labor more productive. The amount of capital invested in industry expanded far more rapidly than the number of workers, and so did the use of mechanical power. Labor itself was also employed more efficiently as manufacturers gradually learned how to simplify work procedures, accelerate the pace of production, and improve plant design. Furthermore, workers did not generally object to the introduction of machinery, recognizing the relationship between increased output and higher wages. Frederick W. Taylor of the Midvale Steel Company made the best-known contributions to this process of rationalization. As early as 1881, he set a man to work with a stop watch to dissect the "millions of different

[1] C. L. Long, *Wages and Earnings in the United States: 1860–1890* (Princeton, 1960), pp. 37, 42, 60, 68, 113; *Historical Statistics of the United States, Colonial Times to 1957* (Washington, 1960), pp. 410, 506. Between 1860 and 1890, the number of persons engaged in manufacturing increased from 885,000 to 3.2 million.

operations" that workers performed. From this data Taylor determined the "comparatively small number" of simple motions that represented the fastest, and thus the cheapest, way of doing each job. Although these time-motion studies had little impact until the twentieth century, eventually they resulted in the standardization of work procedures and the development of an incentive system of wage payments based on piecework. They caused much resentment among workers, for they made factory tasks almost unbearably monotonous, but they boosted output and made possible higher wages.[2]

Whether or not the workingman received his fair share of the fruits of economic growth is another question. Testifying before the Industrial Commission in 1899, Samuel Gompers of the American Federation of Labor said: "The social conditions of the working people have improved very materially within the past 35 years. . . . The laborers' share of the production of wealth has largely increased per dollar of the worth. It has not, however, increased in the ratio that I think labor is entitled to." Gompers, of course, could scarcely have been expected to express entire satisfaction with labor's lot, but few modern students would disagree with his judgment. Summarizing his analysis of the trend of worker income between 1860 and 1890, economist Clarence D. Long concludes that "the pace of wages and earnings during these three decades of almost unparalleled economic advance must, by present standards, be regarded as moderate, a walk followed by a trot, allegretto rather than allegro!"[3]

Expressed differently, despite the improvement, the average industrial worker could not yet earn enough money to support a family decently. Carroll D. Wright, chief of the Massachusetts Bureau of the Statistics of Labor, put the matter plainly in 1882 after an extensive study of the textile industry. "A family of workers can always live well, but the man with a family of small children to

[2] F. B. Copley, *Frederick W. Taylor: Father of Scientific Management* (2 vols., New York, 1923), I, 223, 227–228; E. C. Kirkland, *Industry Comes of Age: Business, Labor, and Public Policy, 1860–1897* (New York, 1961), pp. 172–173, 350; Industrial Commission on Capital and Labor, *Report* (Washington, 1901), VII, 119–123, XIV, 644–647.

[3] Industrial Commission, *Report*, VII, 615; Long, *Wages*, p. 118.

support, unless his wife works also, has a small chance of living properly."[4]

Besides being far from spectacular, the advance of the standard of living of workingmen was neither uniform nor achieved without corresponding disadvantages. Much depended on whether or not a laborer was fully employed. There are no accurate figures on unemployment for these years. Probably something approaching full employment existed in good times, but economic downturns caused the number of jobless to soar, and sharp fluctuations in industrial activity were common. In 1878, near the end of the "great depression," somewhere between 570,000 and a million persons were out of work in the United States. However, a few years later, during boom times, an informed financial periodical expressed the belief that anyone seeking work could find it. Shortly after that, following another slump, Terence V. Powderly of the Knights of Labor claimed that two million men were jobless. Most guesses made during depressions by labor leaders tended to exaggerate unemployment, but that it became serious at such times is unquestionable.[5]

Skilled workers naturally commanded higher wages than ordinary factory hands—on the average nearly half again as much per hour. White-collar workers, in turn, could command at least twice as much as manual laborers. For the same type of work, however, regional and industrial differentials were very large. Around 1880, wages in the South averaged only about 70 per cent of those in the East and Middle West, while those on the Pacific coast were nearly 40 per cent higher than eastern standards. However, the wages of southern sawmill workers were only 16 per cent lower than those in the North, whereas southern tobacco workers made scarcely half as

---

4 Massachusetts Bureau of the Statistics of Labor (hereafter MBLS), *13th Report* (Boston, 1882), p. 300. A Massachusetts textile worker made the same point before a congressional committee in 1883. "If a man has not got a boy to act as 'back-boy' it is very hard for him to get along." U.S. Senate, *Report on . . . Labor and Capital* (Washington, 1885), III, 451.

5 Rendigs Fels, *American Business Cycles: 1865–1897* (Chapel Hill, 1959), p. 123; MBLS, *10th Report* (Boston, 1879), p. 9; R. V. Bruce, *1877: Year of Violence* (Indianapolis, 1959), p. 19; Samuel Bernstein, "Labor and the Long Depression," *Science and Society*, XX (1956), 81–82; G. E. McNeill (ed.), *The Labor Movement: The Problem of Today* (Boston, 1887), p. 575; Samuel Rezneck, "Patterns of Thought and Action in an American Industrial Depression," *American Historical Review*, LXI (1956), 286–287.

much as Northerners. West Coast clothing manufacturers paid more than twice as much for labor as their eastern competitors, but western paper manufacturers paid about 25 per cent less for labor than Easterners did. According to one witness, the wages of printers in Massachusetts in 1883 ranged all the way from $8 to $25 a week. In 1890, and speaking now of national averages, brewery workers made about $700 a year, steelworkers about $450, textile workers less than $350.[6]

Sex and age differentials exaggerated these variations; adult males received about 75 per cent more for similar work than women, two and a half or three times as much as children, even for piecework. Race and nationality also affected worker income: generally European immigrants, Negroes, and Chinese were relegated to low-paying jobs, and even when they performed similar tasks they earned less money than native-born white workers. In 1890, fewer than one-third as many Negroes in proportion to their numbers had industrial jobs as white Americans.[7]

It is also difficult to generalize about the length of the working day. To say that in 1890 the typical hand worked ten hours a day, six days a week, obscures the fact that bakers averaged over 65 hours a week, steelworkers over 66, canners nearly 77. In the construction industry, on the other hand, the work week averaged only a little more than fifty-five hours; in 1886 over 17,000 Illinois workers, most of them in the building trades, had achieved the eight-hour day. Conditions also differed within industries. In steelmaking, where certain operations had to be conducted round the clock, the twelve-hour day and the seven-day week were standard for blast-furnace workers, but the men who handled the Bessemer converters worked only sixty-three hours a week and those employed in rolling steel

[6] R. A. Easterlin, "Interregional Differences in Per Capita Income, Population, and Total Income, 1840–1950," National Bureau of Economic Research, *Trends in the American Economy in the Nineteenth Century* (Princeton, 1960), pp. 73–140, esp. p. 96; Long, *Wages*, pp. 79, 80, 100, 155; R. K. Burn, "The Comparative Economic Position of Manufacturing and White Collar Employees," *Journal of Business*, XXVII (1954), 257–267; U.S. Senate, *Report . . . on Labor and Capital*, I, 41. The wages of 1,734 Western Union telegraphers varied from $30 to $150 a month in 1883, the average being $70. *Ibid.*, I, 963. Similar variations characterized the wage scales of the Standard Oil Company. R. W. and M. E. Hidy, *Pioneering in Big Business: 1882–1911* (New York, 1955), pp. 591–592.

[7] Long, *Wages*, pp. 109–110; R. W. Logan, *The Negro in American Life and Thought: The Nadir, 1877–1901* (New York, 1954), p. 154.

rails only fifty-nine hours. Seasonal and cyclical variations in the hours of labor were also very large.[8]

The problem of generalizing about the economic state of workers can be further elucidated by comparing the circumstances of some of the 2,129 families which were studied by agents of the Illinois Bureau of Labor Statistics in 1883. First, consider two coal miners. Both were men of steady habits with large families; union men, they earned wages of $1.50 per day. Their standards of living, however, differed greatly. One, who lived in Belleville, Illinois, worked only thirty weeks in 1883; his total income was $250. He paid $6 a month for a two-room tenement which he shared with his wife and five children, aged three to nineteen. The family food bill for the entire year came to only $80, spent mainly on bread, salt meat, and coffee. By dint of shrewdness and the most careful economy, this man maintained a decent home. Three of his children attended the public school, and the investigator reported the family's crowded flat to be neat and clean, if very scantily furnished. "The figures for cost of living are actual," he wrote, "and there is no doubt the family lived on the amount specified."

The other miner was a resident of Streator, Illinois; his family consisted of himself, his wife, and their four children. He worked full time in 1883, earning $420. In addition, his three sons, also miners, brought in nearly $1,000 more. He owned a well-furnished six-room house and an acre of land, on which the family raised vegetables for home consumption. Their food bill came to $900 a year (a typical breakfast was made up of steak, butter, potatoes, bacon, and coffee), and they spent well over $100 on books, insurance, and "sundries." Statistically these two miners fall into the same class as workers, and both apparently lived rewarding lives, yet their manner of existence was very different.[9]

Another type of variation obscured by the statistics is illustrated

8 Illinois Bureau of Labor Statistics (hereafter IBLS), *4th Report* (Springfield, 1886), p. 170; Leo Wolman, "Hours of Work in American Industry," National Bureau of Economic Research, *Bulletin No. 71* (New York, 1938), pp. 2, 8–9. The steel industry also defied the trend toward shorter hours. The introduction of improved machinery, by lessening the physical burdens of steelmaking, enabled the manufacturers to lengthen the work day. David Brody, *Steelworkers in America: The Nonunion Era* (Cambridge, Mass., 1960), pp. 36–37.

9 IBLS, *3rd Report* (Springfield, 1884), pp. 187, 191, 395, 401. Close-knit family groups often achieved very substantial incomes without any single member rising out of the working class. In 1888, for example, the Wisconsin Bureau of Labor

by the case of two railroad brakemen. One, who lived in Joliet, Illinois, was barely existing. To support his wife and their eight children, he earned in 1883 only $360. These ten people were jammed into a three-room house renting for $5 per month; they ate chiefly bread, "syrup," and potatoes. "Clothes ragged, children half-dressed and dirty," the state investigator reported. "They all sleep in one room regardless of sex. The house is devoid of furniture, and the entire concern is as wretched as could be imagined. Father is shiftless and does not keep any one place for any length of time. Wife is without ambition or industry."

The second brakeman, a resident of Aurora, had only a wife and two children to support and earned more money in 1883, $484, yet even considering these facts his standard of living was infinitely more comfortable. He owned a well-furnished five-room house in a pleasant neighborhood. The family kept a cow and tended a vegetable garden in the summer. Their fare was simple but well-balanced and they were able to invest nearly $50 a year in insurance, reading matter, and small luxuries. Endless similar examples could be cited from this Illinois study alone. The relative prosperity of individual familes depended upon many conditions that had little to do with pay rates.

To generalize about the feelings of workingmen in this period calls for deduction, projection—some would simply say guesswork. Relatively few ordinary workers recorded their opinions, and those who did were not of one mind. In 1878 the Massachusetts Bureau of the Statistics of Labor distributed a questionnaire aimed at discovering the views of workers. Although the bureau mailed notices of the project to 5,000 persons and published announcements in the press, only 638 workers asked for the questionnaire and of these only 230 submitted usable replies.[10] Both the uniqueness and the inadequacy of this investigation make it hard to evaluate: it was

---

Statistics reported an iron molder, earning about $925 a year, whose family's income exceeded $2,475. Wisconsin Bureau of Labor Statistics (hereafter WBLS), *3rd Report* (Madison, 1888), p. xiv.

[10] IBLS, *3rd Report*, pp. 171, 393; MBLS, *10th Report*, pp. 100–103. On the difficulty of discovering the views of workers, see Carroll D. Wright's testimony, U.S. Senate, *Report . . . on Labor and Capital*, III, 279; James Leiby, *Carroll Wright and Labor Reform* (Cambridge, Mass., 1960), pp. 47, 56; and Ohio Bureau of Labor Statistics (hereafter OBLS), *9th Report* (Columbus, 1886), p. 6.

conducted at the tail end of a depression; the sample consisted chiefly of skilled workers; it drew entirely upon literate respondents at a time when, for example, about 10 per cent of the textile workers in the state could not read or write. Furthermore, both the workers' answers to particular questions and their general attitudes were far from uniform. About half the men thought they were overworked, but only a slightly larger percentage responded affirmatively to such slanted questions as "Do you consider yourself underpaid?" and "Do you consider your employer unfairly profits from your labor?" Ninety per cent thought their children were receiving an adequate education, but only a quarter expected to be able to lay aside enough money to care for themselves in old age. A Wisconsin investigation in 1887–88 also suggests that there was no unanimity among workingmen about the value of unions, the need for labor legislation, the proper length of the working day, and the importance of competition. For example, in answer to the question: "What new laws, in your opinion, ought to be enacted?" one carpenter replied: "Keep down strikes and rioters. Let every man attend to his own business," while another wrote: "Complete nationalization of land and all ways of transportation. Burn all government bonds. A graduated income tax. Tax bonds and mortgages. . . . Abolish child labor and [pass] any other act that capitalists say is wrong."[11]

In 1881 the Massachusetts bureau conducted a detailed investigation of the textile industry in Fall River, Lowell, and Lawrence, questioning about 700 persons—workers, manufacturers, and "leading citizens." This study revealed a wide difference between the attitudes of operatives in Fall River and the other two towns. In Fall River nearly all the hands complained of overwork, poor housing, harsh employers, and a dozen other grievances. "I get so exhausted that I can scarcely drag myself home when night comes," a typical worker declared. While some Lowell and Lawrence operatives complained of specific aspects of their work, the general view, according to the investigators, was that expressed by a Lawrence worker: "There is no reason for discontent. . . . I get a good pay, and so does my wife, at present; my pay supplies us with all we

11 MBLS, *10th Report*, pp. 104–116; MBLS, *13th Report*, pp. 205–208; WBLS, *3rd Report*, pp. 64–79, esp. p. 66.

want . . . [and] her wages have gone in the bank." One female operative in Lawrence even said: "If you will stand by the mill, and see the people come out, you will be surprised to see the happy, contented look they all have . . . as cheerful and as happy as though coming out of church."

The investigators probably exaggerated the differences, which they attributed to the newness of the industry in Fall River and its concentration on mass-produced, cheap-quality cloth, the presence of querulous foreign labor agitators in that town, and the Lowell and Lawrence manufacturers' tradition of enlightened paternalism. The study demonstrated clearly, however, that differences did exist.[12] It is perhaps belaboring the obvious to note that since the growing millions of industrial workers varied widely in origin, experience, and fortune and were largely unorganized, they differed also in their opinions and attitudes.

Nevertheless, the weight of evidence suggests a strong and growing dissatisfaction. Dramatic instances of industrial violence punctuated the period: from the great railroad strike of 1877, marked by arson, rioting, murder, which paralyzed almost two-thirds of the railroad mileage of the nation; to the Homestead strike of 1892 in the steel industry, with its pitched battle between workers and Pinkerton dectectives; and the Pullman strike of 1894, which again tied up most of the railroads of the country. The significance of such disturbances can be overstated, but the disturbances cannot be ignored. In 1881, a year of general prosperity, there were 477 work stoppages in the United States involving 130,000 workers. In 1886 there were 1,572 involving 610,000 men, and thereafter the number of strikes fell below a thousand a year only once in the remainder of the century. In the state of Massachusetts, 159 strikes were recorded between 1830 and 1879. Between 1881 and 1886, an estimated 175 took place in Massachusetts and at least that many in Illinois. During 1886 alone, some 500 business establishments in the city of Boston were shut down by labor troubles.[13]

---

[12] MBLS, *13th Report*, pp. 202, 216–217, 272–275, 301, 338–339, 343, 345, 409–415. See also U.S. Senate, *Report . . . on Labor and Capital*, III, 407–415, in which many witnesses commented on the differences between Fall River and other textile towns in Massachusetts and New Hampshire.

[13] Bruce, *Year of Violence, passim*; Leon Wolff, *Lockout, the Story of the Homestead Strike of 1892* (New York, 1965), pp. 100–116, *passim;* Almont

Contemporary observers commented frequently on the disgruntled attitudes of workingmen. "That a deep-rooted feeling of discontent pervades the masses, none can deny," labor leader Terence V. Powderly wrote in 1885; "that there is just cause for it, must be admitted." In June, 1887, Samuel M. Hotchkiss, newly appointed commissioner of the Connecticut Bureau of Labor Statistics, made an informal study of working-class opinion in his state. "I mingled freely with the people of the State, became acquainted with their affairs, especially the relations existing between employers and employed, and endeavored to learn as far as possible what all classes desired of the Bureau," he reported. His conversations with workingmen were both eye-opening and unnerving. He commented on "the feeling of bitterness which so frequently manifests itself in their utterances," their "distrust of employers," and their general "discontent and unrest." To test the soundness of his conclusions, he asked a prominent businessman, a labor leader, a lawyer, a socialist, and a land reformer to prepare papers on the subject of labor discontent. Of course the views of these five individuals differed widely, but all agreed that the discontent was both deep and pervasive.[14]

Many elements contributed to the militancy and dissatisfaction of industrial workers. In the first place, large numbers remained desperately poor; the slow advance in the standard of living did not affect everyone. In 1877, coal miners in eastern Pennsylvania were trying to support families on earnings of $200 a year or less. They lived in rickety unpainted shacks and subsisted on mush and potatoes. In 1889 a Wisconsin factory inspector reported twenty-

Lindsey, *The Pullman Strike* (Chicago, 1942), *passim; Hist. Stat.*, p. 99; MBLS, *11th Report* (Boston, 1880), p. 63; MBLS, *19th Report* (Boston, 1888), pp. 66, 73; IBLS, *4th Report*, p. 403.

14 T. V. Powderly, "The Army of the Discontented," *North American Review,* CXL (1885), 371; Connecticut Bureau of Labor Statistics (hereafter CBLS), *3rd Report* (Hartford, 1887), pp. 9–17, 281–350. Dozens of labor leaders (informed if not disinterested observers) expressed similar views during the 1883 Senate investigation of the relations of labor and capital. E.g., Senator James Z. George: "Do you think the general sentiment among wage receivers . . . is that of unrest and discontent?" P. J. McGuire, secretary of the Brotherhood of Carpenters and Joiners: "Yes sir; and it is rapidly growing." The reformer Henry George told the committee: "There exists among the laboring classes of the United States a great and growing feeling of dissatisfaction and discontent." *Report . . . on Labor and Capital,* I, 358, 467.

four Italian miners living in *one-half* of a fourteen-by-twenty-four-foot shanty. In 1892, after a decade and a half of remarkable economic growth and at the peak of a business cycle, investigators in Chicago found nearly 11,000 persons laboring in 666 sweatshops under the most wretched conditions imaginable. They described case after case of men, women, and children working in dark, crowded, ill-ventilated hovels, surrounded by filth and laboring endlessly for a pittance. In a typical instance a family of eight lived and worked in a three-room rear tenement. "The father, mother, two daughters and a cousin work together making trousers at 65 cents a dozen pairs. . . . They work 7 days a week. . . . Their destitution is very great."[15] Only the poorest suffered this badly, but the general picture was dark enough. After completing his 1878 investigation of unemployment in Massachusetts, which some observers attacked as tending to minimize the harshness of conditions, Carroll D. Wright wrote: "We do not wish it to be understood for a moment that we do not think the people are poor: they are poor indeed." The 1883 Illinois study of working conditions turned up dozens of examples of destitution, both among unskilled laborers in small towns and among craftsmen in Chicago. A score of witnesses testified to the poverty of many classes of workers during the Senate investigation of that year.[16]

Despite the fact that all the systematic contemporary studies of working conditions depended heavily upon the experiences and state of skilled workers, the findings were depressing. The Illinois investigators, for example, estimated that a quarter of the state's workingmen "fail to make a living." Reporters, reformers, and others, who wrote more impressionistically about unskilled laborers, reached similar conclusions.[17]

Even for those wage earners who were able to maintain a decent

[15] Bruce, *Year of Violence*, pp. 294–295; WBLS, *4th Report* (Madison, 1890), p. 21a; IBLS, *7th Report*, pp. 369, 364–366, 405, *passim*.

[16] MBLS, *10th Report*, p. 8; IBLS, *3rd Report* (Springfield, 1884), pp. 338–339, 405–406; R. H. Bremner, *From the Depths: The Discovery of Poverty in the United States* (New York, 1956), p. 73.

[17] IBLS, *3rd Report*, p. 267. In 1882 Theodore Roosevelt, then a youthful New York assemblyman, served on a committee studying the condition of New York City cigar makers. He was appalled by what he saw: five adults and several children living and working in a single room, surrounded by garbage, tobacco scraps, and foul bedding. Theodore Roosevelt, *Autobiography* (New York, 1913), p. 89; H. A. Hurwitz, *Theodore Roosevelt and Labor in New York State: 1880–*

standard of living and whose lot was actually improving, progress often served only to whet appetites without bringing real satisfaction. The well-publicized industrial wonders of the age promised more than they were in fact delivering for the mass of workers, while for a relative handful of owners and managers the new order yielded riches unimaginable a few decades earlier. Much of the bitterness of laboring men is best explained by the growing gap between their ambitions and their expectations. We know little about the social and economic mobility of nineteenth-century Americans. According to the folklore of the times, opportunities for advancement knew no limit. John W. Britton, a New York manufacturer and banker, voiced this popular belief in typical fashion in 1883. "A man here may be a common day laborer," he said, "but if he has the right material in him there is no reason why he should not occupy the best place in the nation."[18] Yet Britton's personal experience did not justify this optimism—his father had been a skilled craftsman; he himself began as a carriage maker. The evidence indicates that only an unmeasurable minority of unskilled laborers achieved the kind of rags-to-riches rise that Britton and many other Americans assumed to be so common. Stephan Thernstrom's pioneering study of workingmen in Newburyport, Massachusetts, based on manuscript census records, shows that over the period from 1850 to 1880, few unskilled workers rose beyond the ranks of the semiskilled and almost none achieved middle-class status. The sons of manual laborers tended to become semiskilled workers, "but the barriers against moving more than one notch upward were fairly high." Poor men in Newburyport did improve their condition over time; by putting their wives and children to work and by rigorous economizing—Thernstrom calls it "ruthless underconsumption"— many accumulated enough money to buy their own homes and provide for their old age. However, nearly all remained in the ranks of the laboring class.[19]

Historians who have examined the subject of mobility from the

---

1900 (New York, 1943), pp. 79–80. The most famous and influential of the impressionistic accounts was Jacob Riis's *How the Other Half Lives* (New York, 1890).

[18] U.S. Senate, *Report on . . . Labor and Capital*, II, 1127.

[19] Stephan Thernstrom, *Poverty and Progress: Social Mobility in a Nineteenth Century City* (Cambridge, Mass., 1964), pp. 114, 136, 160.

other end of the scale have arrived at related conclusions. Andrew Carnegie began as a bobbin boy earning $1.20 a week in a Pennsylvania textile mill, Jay Gould as a clerk in a country store, but even their most sanguine contemporaries admitted that such success was rare. Less dramatic, but still exceptional, was advancement of the kind made by the piano maker Henry Steinway (Steinweg) and his sons, who migrated to the United States from Germany in the early fifties. After working for others for a few years, they established their own shop and soon won both fame and fortune. Thirty years after founding their business, the Steinways were turning out 3,000 pianos a year and employing about a thousand workers. This example can be duplicated dozens of times. But when the historian William Miller studied the origins of 200 late-nineteenth-century business leaders, he found that a large majority came from well-to-do or middle-class families of old American stock. "Poor immigrant boys and poor farm boys together actually make up no more than 3 per cent of the business leaders," he reported. Most successful executives had "social characteristics that distinguished them sharply from the common run." While further research may modify the conclusion, it seems fairly clear that the most downtrodden seldom improved themselves substantially and that only a handful truly rose from rags to riches.[20]

For evidence of the economic mobility of the vast majority of the people, one must depend upon contemporary impressionistic estimates. These are profuse but inconclusive, for when knowledgeable persons generalized, they were usually trying to prove a point. In 1883, for example, a Pittsburgh labor leader told a Senate committee that he could name only two men in the area who had risen from the wage-earning class to important business positions, but the manager of a Pittsburgh factory testified: "I find, at least in our city, that nearly all the men who are now capitalists have been workingmen," and Jay Gould claimed that "nearly every one that occupies a prominent position has come up from the ranks, worked his own way along up." The majority of those who commented

20 "Henry Steinway" and "William Steinway," *Dictionary of American Biography*, XVII, 567–569; U.S. Senate, *Report on . . . Labor and Capital*, II, 1085, 1089; William Miller, "American Historians and the Business Elite," *Journal of Economic History*, IX (1949), 184–208, and "The Recruitment of the American Business Elite," *Quarterly Journal of Economics*, LXIV (1950), 242–253.

stressed the opportunities for advancement that America provided. They were probably justified in doing so, but we must remember that those who rose tended to generalize from their own experiences, and that most of the unsuccessful have left no record of their failure.[21]

Apparently, the growth of big corporations did not lessen mobility, yet by seeming to widen the gap between rich and poor it encouraged the poor to think that it did. Great mechanized corporations and their multimillionaire masters might in fact be benefiting workingmen by increasing the productivity of labor and creating new job opportunities, but they simultaneously undermined their confidence in their ability to rise and bred envy and resentment. In the late seventies a carpenter wrote: "We are fast drifting to that condition of society which has preceded the downfall of Sparta, Macedonia, Athens, and Rome, where a few were very rich, and the many very poor," and a steam fitter predicted: "In fifteen years this country will be worse off than the old countries of Europe and Asia. The rich will be very rich, the poor very poor, and the government will be controlled by the moneyed class." Similar denunciations were made repeatedly over the next two decades; in 1900, for example, a union official, testifying before the Industrial Commission, drew a vivid comparison between the steel magnate Andrew Carnegie and big concerns like Standard Oil, with their individual and corporate profits running annually into the tens of millions, and the ordinary worker earning (he said) a dollar a day. When, "seeing . . . these enormous profits that are made possible through his skill and industry," the worker asks for a modest raise, his reward is "the ball and chain," this spokesman for labor declared.[22]

How many Americans took such statements seriously is hard to determine; probably far fewer than the number who accepted the myth, popularized by Horatio Alger and others, that anyone who would work hard, practice thrift, and live virtuously could—with a little luck—become a millionaire. That the majority of workers accepted these middle-class, capitalistic values is demonstrated by the thousands who scrimped and saved to start small shops and buy

[21] U.S. Senate, *Report on . . . Labor and Capital,* I, 28, 1089; II, 25, 1126–1129.
[22] MBLS, *10th Report,* pp. 112, 131; Industrial Commission, *Report,* VII, 716.

their own homes, and by the popularity of literature glorifying the methods and objectives of American capitalism. Uncounted multitudes who did not have middle-class incomes were nonetheless middle class in their habits and attitudes.

Yet if the new, highly mechanized industries were not converting the workingman into a wage slave, they did confront him with new problems, material and psychological. Some contemporaries feared that mechanization would lead to permanent mass unemployment and destroy the need for skilled labor. This fear was illusory. The labor market expanded steadily and technology actually increased the importance of human skills, although in the short run it might appear to displace individual skilled workers. Mechanization did, however, make factory labor more routine, less interesting, and sometimes more dangerous and nerve-racking. More important, in combination with the growth of large corporations it undermined the skilled worker's self-confidence by making him more dependent upon others—the capitalists who supplied the machines and, because mechanization led to the subdivision of production into many separate elements, upon other workers, too. Skill continued to command a premium, but the machine ended the day of the independent artisan who made an entire product from start to finish by himself. Terence V. Powderly caught the implications of this loss of independence in his *Thirty Years of Labor*. After describing how specialization and mechanization were affecting workingmen, he wrote: "They no longer carried the keys of the workshop, for workshop, tools and keys belonged not to them, but to their master. . . . They saw that they no longer were engaged in that competition which is 'the life of trade,' they realized that it was a competition which ultimately meant death to manhood and independence, unless through some means it became directed into a different channel."[23]

Immigration seemed a further threat. In 1870 about one-third of all workers in manufacturing industries were foreign-born. This percentage did not increase thereafter, but the heavy influx of foreigners alarmed many workingmen. From a low point of about

[23] S. B. Warner, Jr., *Streetcar Suburbs* (Cambridge, Mass., 1962), pp. 7–83; T. V. Powderly, *Thirty Years of Labor: 1859 to 1889* (Columbus, 1889), pp. 26–27. For an excellent contemporary analysis of this subject, see D. A. Wells, *Recent Economic Changes* (New York, 1889), pp. 364–400.

138,000 in 1878, immigration soared to a peak of almost 789,000 in 1882. All in all, more than 6.3 million foreigners entered the United States between 1877 and 1890. Most of these newcomers were job-seekers: well over 60 per cent were males, and roughly three of every five were between the ages of fifteen and forty. Most were also poor and unskilled; in 1882, for instance, 612,000 of the 789,000 new arrivals were manual laborers or persons without any occupation.[24]

That established wage earners should fear and resent these newcomers was understandable enough. Their poverty and lack of experience often led them to work for wages that Americans considered substandard. When the Wisconsin Bureau of Labor and Industrial Statistics asked men in dozens of crafts if immigration was injuring them, "the verdict [was] practically unanimous." An iron worker said: "Immigrants work for almost nothing and seem to be able to live on wind—something which I can not do." Another worker objected on the ground that immigration "brings wages down below the breadline."

Union men particularly objected to unlimited immigration. The view of John Jarrett, president of the Amalgamated Association of Iron and Steel Workers, was typical of many. He claimed that the Hungarians, Poles, Italians, and other immigrant workers who were beginning to enter the iron and steel industry in the eighties did not "know the difference" between good wages and bad, light work and heavy. "I have been disgusted to find," Jarrett said, "that those people can live where I think a decent man would die; they can live on . . . food that other men would not touch." Through an interpreter, he once tried to interest a Hungarian laborer in organizing his fellows. The man became confused and frightened, and Jarrett gave up the effort. "All I know about these men," he reported, "is that I have been astonished and astounded at the little they do know, and when you go to talk with them they are fairly afraid to speak with you."[25]

Immigrant workers, especially those without industrial experience, were sometimes difficult to organize, but the charge that they

---

[24] John Higham, *Strangers in the Land: Patterns of American Nativism, 1860–1925* (New Brunswick, 1955), p. 16; *Hist. Stat.*, 56–57, 61–62. Of course, immigration authorities classified the children and many of the women as having no occupation.

[25] WBLS, *3rd Report*, pp. xxvi, 1, 10; U.S. Senate, *Report on . . . Labor and Capital*, I, 1139–1140.

1. Holt Combine, powered by five men and thirty-three mules

(Caterpillar Tractor Company)

2.   The factory—romance: Homestead Mill near Pittsburgh by William C. Wall

(Courtesy, Mr. and Mrs. Charles J. Rosenbloom)

3.   The factory—reality: Illinois Steel Works, South Chicago

(Library of Congress)

4. Advertisement of Illinois Central Railroad (1882)

(Library of Congress)

5. Randolph Street Railroad Station, Chicago

(Chicago Historical Society)

6. Acme Refinery, Titusville, Pennsylvania, an affiliate of Standard Oil

(Drake Well Museum)

7. Edison's Pearl Street Power Station, New York City

(Edison National Historic Site)

8. Thomas A. Edison in his laboratory, West Orange, New Jersey
(Library of Congress)

9. Brooklyn Bridge (1889)

(J. Clarence Davies Collection, Museum of the City of New York)

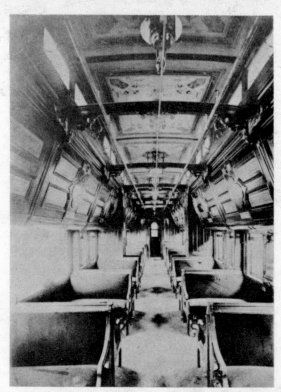

10. George Pullman's first sleeping car, the "Pioneer"

(Pullman Company)

11. "New York a Few Years from Now" (1881)

(Harper's Weekly, August 27, 1881)

12. Electric streetcar, Holbrook, Massachusetts (1892)

(Library of Congress)

13. Mulberry Bend, New York's Lower East Side, in the late 1880's
(Photo by Jacob A. Riis, Museum of the City of New York)

14. Immigrants arriving in steerage on S.S. *Pennland* (1893) (Byron Collection, Museum of the City of New York)

15. A slum boarding house, New York, c. 1889

(Photo by Jacob A. Riis, Museum of the City of New York)

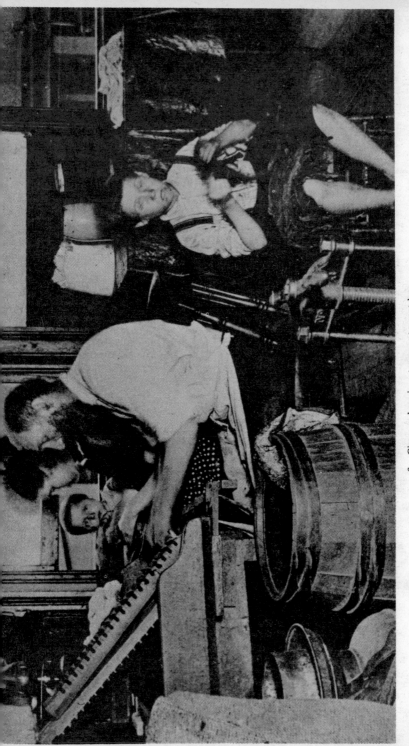

16. Cigarworkers in a tenement-sweatshop
(Photo by Jacob A. Riis, Museum of the City of New York)

17. Railroad riots in Baltimore, 1877

(New York Public Library)

Attention Workingmen!

═══════ GREAT ═══════

MASS-MEETING

TO-NIGHT, at 7.30 o'clock,

═══ AT THE ═══

HAYMARKET, Randolph St, Bet. Desplaines and Halsted.

Good Speakers will be present to denounce the latest
atrocious act of the police, the shooting of our
fellow-workmen yesterday afternoon.

Workingmen Arm Yourselves and Appear in Full Force!

THE EXECUTIVE COMMITTEE

Achtung, Arbeiter!

Große

Massen-Versammlung

Heute Abend, ½8 Uhr, auf dem

Heumarkt, Randolph-Straße, zwischen

Desplaines- u. Halsted-Str.

☞ Gute Redner werden den neuesten Schurkenstreich der Polizei,
indem sie gestern Nachmittag unsere Brüder erschoß, geißeln.

☛ Arbeiter, bewaffnet Euch und erscheint massenhaft!

Das Executiv-Comite.

18. Anarchist handbill summoning
the meeting which led to the Haymarket bombing

(New York Public Library)

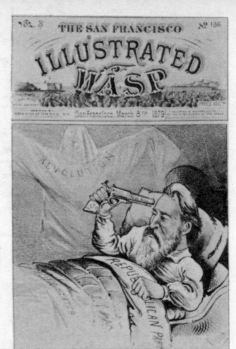

19. California comment on Hayes's veto of the Chinese Exclusion Bill (1879)

(Bancroft Library, University of California)

20. Currier and Ives print in praise of James A. Garfield

(Library of Congress)

21. *Puck's* view of Arthur's campaign for renomination (1884)

(Chicago Historical Society)

22. *Judge* comments on Cleveland (1884)

(New York State Historical Association)

23. Benjamin Harrison

(William Henry Smith Memorial Library, Indiana Historical Society)

objected to unions was in the main untrue. Indeed, a large if not exactly determinable fraction of union members was of foreign birth, and most of the tactics employed by labor leaders were derived from the experience of European, especially British, unionists. Immigrants dominated the coal-mining unions, those in textiles, and many others. One cause of the militancy of Fall River textile hands in the seventies and eighties, for example, was the fact that British and Irish workers in Fall River outnumbered the native-born by better than two to one, whereas in Lowell and Lawrence the two groups were of equal size. "The one great trouble with Fall River," a worker explained in describing the city's labor conflicts, "is the existence of so much English help."

It is true that immigrants were occasionally used as scabs. Employers in the Pennsylvania coal fields often broke strikes by importing carloads of them, recruited by the agents of "labor exchanges" in the eastern seaports. So, from time to time, did steel companies, railroads, and textile manufacturers. However, by no means all the strikebreakers were immigrants, and many immigrants who were imported for that purpose promptly quit once they discovered what was going on. The trade unions were also partly responsible, for they played into the employers' hands by refusing to enroll unskilled men in their ranks. A recent student, Charlotte Erickson, has concluded that the labor movement was guilty of "confused and unrealistic thinking about immigration" in these years.[26]

The attitudes and actions of employers aggravated the fears and discontents of industrial workers in other ways. To the modern

[26] Higham, *Strangers in the Land*, pp. 48–50; MBLS, *13th Report*, pp. 204–206; R. T. Berthoff, *British Immigrants in Industrial America: 1790–1950* (Cambridge, Mass., 1953), pp. 88–96; C. K. Yearley, Jr., *Britons in American Labor: A History of the Influence of the United Kingdom Immigrants on American Labor, 1820–1914* (Baltimore, 1957), pp. 311–317, *passim;* Charlotte Erickson, *American Industry and European Immigration: 1860–1885* (Cambridge, Mass., 1957), pp. 106–136, 186. American labor unions were not at this time officially opposed to free immigration; their prejudice was against unskilled labor, not against foreigners as such, and against contract labor, that is, the recruiting and transportation of European workers by American firms. Yet, as Erickson has shown, few unskilled workers were brought in under contract. When contract labor was outlawed by the Foran Act in 1885, it was chiefly at the instigation of the highly skilled Window Glass Workers of America, who were concerned about the importation of Belgian and English glassworkers. *Ibid.*, pp. 139–165.

mind, the labor policy of post-Civil War manufacturers seems both callous and stupid. The subject presents a special challenge. Unless one succumbs to the temptation of arguing that businessmen were a special breed of fool or monster, one must attempt to explain their policies, and this is difficult to do without descending to apologetics. The record is clear. Consider the following statements, each typical of dozens to be found in contemporary documents:

John I. Blair, railroad president: I was informed your main boss carpenter said he had not reduced wages. . . . You have got to do it. . . . Now is the time to reduce labour while so many manufactures are suspending.[27]

Henry V. Rothschild, clothing manufacturer: I say the legislature has no right to encroach upon me as to whether I shall employ men eight hours, or ten, or fifteen.[28]

A Massachusetts textile manufacturer: As far as arbitration [collective bargaining] is concerned, we will not agree to that. Our money built these mills, and we propose to secure whatever benefits may be derived from the business.[29]

A Massachusetts shoe manufacturer: Experience with laboring men for twenty-one years and more has convinced me that nothing saves men from debauchery and crime so much as labor—and that, till one is tired and ready to return to the domestic joys and duties of home. The dram-shop and the saloon are all favorable to a reduction of the hours of labor.[30]

John H. Devereux, railroad general manager: I would proceed to discharge every man on the Buffalo Division who continued to foment, and cause a disturbance. . . . It would be a sad thing for some of the old white-haired Engineers . . . to be thrown out of work, but I told the Committee I should strike with an unsparing hand.[31]

Joseph Medill, newspaper publisher: The chief cause of the impecunious condition of millions of the wage classes of this country is due to their own improvidence and misdirected efforts. . . . The wage classes cannot support in idleness a quarter of a million saloon-keepers . . . and at the same time hope to prosper themselves.[32]

Thomas L. Livermore, textile company manager: There is such a thing

[27] T. C. Cochran, *Railroad Leaders: 1845–1890* (Cambridge, Mass., 1953), p. 263.

[28] Sidney Fine, *Laissez Faire and the General-Welfare State* (Ann Arbor, 1956), p. 106.

[29] MBLS, *13th Report*, p. 366.

[30] MBLS, *10th Report*, p. 149.

[31] Cochran, *Railroad Leaders*, p. 314.

[32] U.S. Senate, *Report on . . . Labor and Capital*, II, 959–961.

as too much education for working people sometimes. . . . I have seen cases where young people were spoiled for labor by being educated to a little too much refinement.[33]

N. F. Thompson, secretary, Southern Industrial Convention: Labor organizations are to-day the greatest menace to this Government that exists. . . . Their influence for disruption . . . is far more dangerous to the perpetuation of our Government in its purity and power than would be the hostile array on our borders of the army of the entire world combined. . . . [A] law should be enacted that would make it justifiable homicide for any killing that occurred in defense of any lawful occupation.[34]

Few industrialists formulated their views on labor relations in any organized way. Nearly all adopted a pragmatic approach when dealing with employees. When labor was plentiful they justified holding down wages by referring to the law of supply and demand, but when it was scarce they opposed increases by arguing that wage rates were directly related to productivity.[35] They insisted that capital and labor had mutual interests, yet refused labor a share in the decision-making that determined their common fate. They professed to believe in democracy, but assumed that they knew what was best for "the men." Few objected in principle to labor unions so long as they functioned only as fraternal organizations or mutual-benefit societies, but most refused to engage in collective bargaining. They equated labor organizers with labor agitators, and thought that unions made workingmen inefficient, discontented, and unenterprising. They appreciated the advantages of combination and centralization for management, but would not concede that labor might also find combination attractive, and for essentially the same reasons.[36]

No single cause or influence explains their confusion. Undoubtedly smugness and selfishness played a part. Some who pos-

[33] *Ibid.,* III, 15.

[34] Industrial Commission, *Report,* VII, 756–757.

[35] When asked by a senator why the wages of female telegraphers were lower than those of male operators, Norvin Green, president of Western Union, replied: "They are as well paid for the work they do as the men are. . . . I doubt whether they do as much work as the men." But when asked whether the company had "substantially the power to dictate . . . wages," Green answered: "All employment, all forms of labor, are governed by the laws of supply and demand." U.S. Senate, *Report on . . . Labor and Capital,* I, 895, 907.

[36] *Ibid.,* I, 892, 911, 1084, 1088; II, 361, 1122–1124.

sessed immense wealth and power came to think themselves better than their fellows and to attribute to the system as it existed a degree of perfection it did not deserve. Many statements of the age reek with hypocrisy and rationalization, as when William H. Vanderbilt said in 1877: "Our men feel that, although I . . . may have my millions and they the rewards of their daily toil, still we are about equal in the end. If they suffer I suffer, and if I suffer they cannot escape." It is also true, however, that the uncertainties and fears which plagued businessmen in a period of fierce competition, rapid technological innovation, and sharp changes in the level of economic activity made calm, rational analysis difficult. Steelmaking, according to one close observer, was "a merciless game"; demand fluctuated so chaotically that the manufacturers were either "panic-stricken" or "strained to utmost capacity." When industrialists insisted that men could not change the "natural laws" that governed the market place, they were reassuring themselves in the face of the monumental uncertainties of the time: the risks connected with every investment, the sudden panics and depressions, the lumbering but apparently inexorable downward trend of prices, the inability of either economists or practical men of affairs to explain, let alone control, the course of economic events.[37]

The inertia of tradition in conflict with changing economic realities also confused industrialists. Americans were conditioned to think of themselves as individualists, their society as egalitarian, opportunity as omnipresent, progress as inevitable. They found no difficulty in revering both entrenched wealth and social equality. Large numbers of men in every walk of life argued that property was sacrosanct, and that workers who banded together to extract a larger share of the fruits of industry from its owners were immoral. Yet William Vanderbilt's smooth assertion that rich and poor were "about equal in the end" aroused few rebuttals. The majority paid lip service to the idea that there was no permanent working class in the United States, but businessmen, with increasing frequency, referred to the labor force as a special group with its own customs, values, and status in society.

Workingmen themselves hesitated to believe that they repre-

37 Bruce, *Year of Violence*, p. 302; Brody, *Steelworkers*, p. 2; Wells, *Recent Economic Changes*, pp. 12–14; E. C. Kirkland, *Dream and Thought in the Business Community: 1860–1900* (Ithaca, 1956) , pp. 23–26.

sented a special interest; James Bryce noted in the eighties that in America common laborers formed "a less well-marked class" than in any European country. "You cannot appeal from the classes to the masses," he wrote. "What the employer thinks, his workmen think."[38] "Of course," Bryce quickly added, "I do not include questions specially relating to labour, in which there may be a direct conflict of interest." Their lack of class consciousness seldom prevented workers from fighting bitterly with employers over wages and conditions. Nevertheless, many were as conservative as their bosses in their view of labor relations. "The sooner working-people get rid of the idea that somebody or something is going to help them, the better it will be for them," a Massachusetts shoemaker wrote in 1878. "The best way for working people to get help is to help themselves." "Dissolve all unions," a Wisconsin paperhanger suggested in 1887. "I was a journeyman for thirty years; never struck for higher wages; always got the best work by working for the interests of my employers. I do not believe in organizations, because they compel a man to pay more than his business will allow." After its agents had talked to large numbers of textile hands, the Massachusetts Bureau of the Statistics of Labor reported that while most workers believed in unions "in the abstract," many considered the local organizations "simply vehicles for the fomentation of incipient riots and disorderly conduct." If individualism died hard among laboring men, its persistence among employers is not difficult to understand.[39]

However, industrial growth was subjecting the individualistic tradition to heavy strains. Craftsmen in small shops might bargain man to man with their employers on a fairly equal basis, but unskilled laborers in large factories obviously could not. Nor could the masters of great mechanized enterprises keep track of the aptitudes and character of each of their thousands of hired hands. Furthermore, the social and economic gulf that separated big industrialists from their employees increased what one skilled worker called the bosses' "strong disinclination" to deal with labor on an equal basis. "There might be an improvement," a Wisconsin metalworker ar-

---

[38] James Bryce, *The American Commonwealth* (2 vols., New York, 1895), II, 296, 269.

[39] *Ibid.*, II, 269 n.; MBLS, *10th Report*, p. 127; WBLS, *3rd Report*, p. 58; MBLS, *13th Report*, pp. 361–362.

gued, "if employers would be a little more free with their employes; that is, get together and explain matters . . . instead of bull dozing and overawing them as many do." A "new feudalism" was developing, the clergyman R. Heber Newton declared in 1883; "the old common feeling" between boss and worker no longer existed. After sharply criticizing the behavior of striking railroad workers in 1886, the economist F. W. Taussig wrote: "The nature of the service demands that [the men] should be more or less like machines, and little is done to show that they are considered anything more than machines. No attempt is made to bind the rank and file to the roads by ties of sympathy or advantage. Whatever may have been the objects of the leaders . . . the mass of the strikers sympathized with that demand as for a recognition of their manhood."[40]

Yet the same gulf that gave employers a sense of superiority over their men also kept them ignorant of the workers' condition and needs, and therefore incapable of dealing with labor-related industrial problems intelligently. Employers who condemned their men for squandering their wages on drink generally knew little about the grinding toil that drove men to seek relief in alcohol, or the squalid tenement homes and dreary boardinghouses that led them to look for comfort and sociability in saloons. They became furious when workers placed loyalty to a union above loyalty to the company, not understanding why the ordinary hired hand had little reason to identify with a corporate employer. Repeatedly men were fired for trying to organize unions, even for presenting the grievances of their fellows to their bosses. "[If] a man employed on this railroad . . . is appointed on a committee to adjust a grievance," a Texas and Pacific worker told a congressional committee in 1886, "he is liable to be discharged for it."[41] In 1886 the managers of the Chicago, Burlington and Quincy Railroad decided to fire every man who belonged to the Knights of Labor, "inasmuch as the Knights of Labor owe allegiance to somebody else, and not to the railroad." They saw no contradiction between the demand for employee loyalty and their declared policy, enunciated by general

40 U.S. Senate, *Report on . . . Labor and Capital*, I, 219, 290, 578, 681; II, 552; WBLS, *3rd Report*, p. 60; F. W. Taussig, "The South-Western Strike of 1886," *Quarterly Journal of Economics*, I (1886), 221.

41 49 Cong. 2 sess., *House Report No. 4174*, Part II, 358. See also Robert Ozanne, "Union-Management Relations: McCormick Harvesting Machine Company," *Labor History*, IV (1963), 148.

manager Henry B. Stone: "If I wanted boiler iron I would go out on the market and buy it where I could get it cheapest, and if I wanted to employ men I would do the same." In 1883 the Western Union telegraphers struck for a 15 per cent wage increase. They did so, however, only after the company had several times refused even to respond to petitions. The direct cause of the strike, one telegrapher testified, "was the insult offered to our executive committee by the officials of the Western Union Telegraph Company. . . . If our committee had been met in a gentlemanly manner . . . there would probably have been no strike."

Employers were so conditioned to considering labor as a rival contending for the profits of business that, with only a handful of exceptions, they did not see the relationship between shorter hours and efficiency, or between high wages and an increased demand for manufactured goods. They even failed to appreciate the advantages that would accrue to themselves if they could deal with their workingmen as a unit through unions.[42]

The hostility that characterized labor relations resulted chiefly from this lack of understanding. No effective authority, public or private, seriously checked the power of management. While sometimes undisciplined, labor was neither strong nor overly demanding. The average industrialist treated his workers in the same spirit that the mighty Cyclops treated Ulysses and his men, and when the workers objected to being confined and fed upon, he flailed about in his rage like the Cyclops, powerfully but blindly. If workingmen did not always realize that their employers lacked vision, they suffered heavily from their employers' misdirected, yet potent assaults.

What this meant in practical terms was made abundantly clear in 1883 by testimony presented before a special Senate committee charged with looking into the relations of labor and capital and the condition of workingmen. The first witness, Robert D. Layton, an axmaker and union official, summarized the situation in a sentence. "The relation existing between employed and employer," he said, "with a few honorable exceptions is not of that cordial nature that

---

[42] D. L. McMurry, *The Great Burlington Strike of 1888* (Cambridge, Mass., 1956), pp. 16, 21; N. J. Ware, *The Labor Movement in the United States: 1860–1895* (New York, 1929), pp. 128–129; McNeill, *Labor Movement*, pp. 390–392; U.S. Senate, *Report on . . . Capital and Labor*, I, 110, 122, 129.

it should be." Layton went on to describe the objectionable tactics of employers in some detail: The discharging and blacklisting of workers merely for joining unions. The employment of scabs (also known as "scads," "blacklegs," and "rats") to break strikes. The closing of plants (the lockout) until workers promised never to join a union. The imposition of arbitrary and degrading work rules, ranging from the niggardly dispensing of drinking water to the assessment of fines for tardiness and breakage. The cheating of pieceworkers and miners by false weighing and the downgrading of output. The refusal of employers to allow workers access to their books to verify statements about the profitability of their businesses during disputes over wages. The gouging of employees who lived in company-owned housing and shopped at company ("pluck-me") stores.[43]

A parade of later witnesses elaborated upon Layton's charges. They described "minute thieves" who shaved time off lunch periods and kept their plants running after the official closing hour to exact extra work from their hands, and other employers who paid their men in scrip convertible into groceries at inflated prices at company-controlled stores.[44] They explained subtle pressures applied to make employees vote as their bosses desired,[45] and denounced the employment of convicts to drive wage rates down.[46] They presented copies of contracts which compelled workers to swear that they would not join a union,[47] gave examples of men who had been blacklisted,[48] and painted bleak pictures of conditions in company-owned towns, in sweatshops, and on cargo vessels.[49] A union organizer described a study of over 500 New York bakers, which revealed that their average workday was more than sixteen hours long. A carpenter summed up the prevailing sentiment of most of the laborers who testified when he said of his fellows: "They hate the bosses, and the foremen more than the bosses, and that feeling is deep."[50]

43 U.S. Senate, *Report on . . . Labor and Capital*, I, 1–41, esp. pp. 8–9, 11, 18, 32–34, 40.

44 *Ibid.*, I, 44, 271, 455, 1154.

45 *Ibid.*, I, 342, 444.

46 *Ibid.*, I, 452–453, 581.

47 *Ibid.*, I, 198, 200.

48 *Ibid.*, I, 113, 181, 651–652; III, 529–536.

49 *Ibid.*, I, 276, 426; II, 291.

50 *Ibid.*, I, 438, 416.

The employers who testified during this investigation did not really present a different picture, although they interpreted the facts differently. Many expressed concern for the welfare of their employees; most supported labor's right to organize into unions; a number spoke proudly of their humane treatment of their men. But none was ready to deal with labor as an organized force or to concede that he had any moral or social obligation to allow labor a role in determining how the profits of production should be shared. Norvin Green, president of Western Union, said: "My sympathies are with the laboring people. I would like to see them prosper. . . . There is no question at all of the right of laborers to organize. . . . [But unions] must necessarily do more harm than good. . . . Whenever they assume to dictate the terms of their employment, just to the extent that they do that they react upon their members, and do them harm, as a general thing, instead of good." Green made much of Western Union's benevolence as an employer, describing, for example, the case of an incurably ill telegrapher whose salary was paid for nearly a year while he was out sick, and for several months after his death. "We knew he would never come back," Green said, "but he had been in our employ a number of years, twelve or fifteen, and had been a very faithful man, and so we thought it right to treat him generously." Yet when asked why the company had no insurance plan, he replied: "It is not in accordance with the genius of our Government or our country to pay pensions." Other examples of employer benevolence seem equally inadequate by modern standards. A cotton manufacturer described a company library of 6,000 volumes that was "practically" free to his workers. The manufacturer and publicist Edward Atkinson urged the committee to make a special trip to Philadelphia to inspect a hat factory where the employer gave "every man, woman, and child" a daily pint of free milk "to keep up the steam" in their "continuous and exhausting work." This, Atkinson said, was "the best kind of philanthropy that I know of—it does good both to him who gives and him who receives."[51]

[51] *Ibid.*, I, 954–957, 940; III, 204, 419–420. A study of the welfare practices of Milwaukee business concerns reveals that before 1900 such practices as the providing of accident benefits "on an individual basis" and the subsidization of voluntary benefit societies organized by employees were fairly common. Other types of welfare included contributing money and land to workers' religious organizations, selling home sites to workers at low prices, and an assortment of picnics and outings. Gerd Korman, *Industrialization, Immigrants and Ameri-*

George Storm, a New York cigar manufacturer, professed, like Norvin Green, to be prounion. "It is a great species of tyranny when a corporation . . . will demand of working people, as a condition of employment, that they shall pledge themselves not to belong to any association." But he also said: "I draw a line between the people who belong to those organizations and those who pretend to speak for them. So far as we are concerned, it matters little to me if a man belongs to ten organizations; but those organizations, whatever they may be, can exercise no influence directly in the adjustment of anything that may occur between ourselves and our men."[52]

"Labor questions," another manufacturer testified, "have not given us a great deal of trouble in connection with our works. While we employ a very large number of people, yet peace and quietness exists with us from one end of the year to the other, usually. . . . We endeavor, in all our intercourse with our workpeople, to treat them as human beings." He was always ready to "reason" with dissatisfied workers, even to meet with elected committees when trouble occurred. Yet the illustrations he used to explain his policy make it clear that he considered employees who were not persuaded by his explanations "obstinate and obdurate," or "fractious and unruly." Such persons were told "that they had to submit to our orders, otherwise their places would be vacant."[53]

Evidence drawn from other sources confirms the impression created by this Senate committee testimony. Among the most liberal of employers was the Standard Oil Company. It paid good wages and treated its employees decently, providing reading rooms and recreational facilities, and adopting a remarkably enlightened industrial-accident policy. But when strikes occurred, the company responded ruthlessly. During a walkout of barrelmakers in 1877, Standard hired over 300 special policemen and turned them loose on a crowd of strikers who were trying to prevent scabs from entering the Cleveland plant. The trouble had been precipitated by a wage cut, which Standard justified on the ground that its business was in poor

---

canizers: *The View from Milwaukee, 1866–1921* (Madison, Wis., 1967), pp. 69–72. The *5th Annual Report* of the U.S. Commissioner of Labor (Washington, 1890), pp. 21–37, summarizes the welfare programs of the railroads in 1890.
[52] U.S. Senate, *Report on . . . Labor and Capital*, II, 827, 816.
[53] *Ibid.*, II, 1152–1153.

shape. Nevertheless, during the first six months of 1877, it paid out $80 in dividends on each $100 share of its stock. The historian Herbert G. Gutman estimates that John D. Rockefeller was collecting dividends in 1877 at a rate of at least $720 an hour, more than most of his workers earned in an entire year. Even the friendly historians of Standard Oil, Ralph W. and Muriel E. Hidy, have described its labor policy as "opportunistic and patriarchal," combining "sympathetic interest in the welfare of workers and resolute determination not to bargain with unions."

Another company that paid relatively high wages was the McCormick Harvesting Machine Company, but it too resisted unionization with all its forces. When a strike occurred at its Chicago plant after wages had been reduced sharply in the face of record-breaking profits, it employed strikebreakers and built emergency barracks within the plant so that they would not have to face angry pickets. After being forced to give in to the workers' demands, it promptly introduced new machinery to do away with the jobs of the skilled workers who had led the walkout.

Of course conditions varied from industry to industry and from one company to another within industries. The difference between working conditions in the Fall River textile mills and those in other Massachusetts towns has already been mentioned. Similar differences existed in the textile mills of Maine. Among carpet manufacturers, the Lowell Manufacturing Company had excellent labor relations in the eighties, whereas Philadelphia and New York carpetmakers experienced repeated difficulties with their men. The old, paternalistic boardinghouse system at Lowell was abandoned, hours were reduced, weekly paydays substituted for the monthly system. According to a labor leader, working conditions were the best in the industry. Only one serious strike occurred in the decade, in protest against a wage cut. During the walkout the management treated the strikers courteously and made no effort to bring in scabs. The strike failed, but when the men returned to work, no reprisals were taken against their leaders. As soon as business improved, the cuts were restored.

But at the Hartford Carpet Company, by no means the least enlightened of the carpet manufacturers, the Irish and French Canadian work force was subjected to repeated indignities by callous overseers. When the workers requested the firing of a particularly brutal boss—"where Bill Martin is," the saying went, "there is neither God nor good"—their petition was ignored. The company dominated the town of Thompsonville, owning the workers' homes and supplying most community facilities. On election day the plant superintendent "took his stand at the ballot box to watch the pink and white slips go in."[54] Elsewhere carpet makers were even more antilabor. When a strike of dye workers at the Bigelow Carpet Company failed in 1886, the management rehired less than a third of those who had walked out, even after the men had voted to dissolve their union.[55]

The attitude of Illinois coal companies toward their labor displayed similar contrasts. When 200 Macoupin County miners struck in 1885, the controversy, according to the local union, was "settled by a conference through committee" in a single day. "[We] favor the settlement of all disputes by arbitration," the union reported. But more typically, when a strike occurred in a Vermilion County mine the next year, "the company sent an agent to Kentucky, and engaged negroes to work the mines." As a union spokesman explained: "The old miners have been forcibly ejected from their homes, and live in the woods."

In the eastern and central Ohio coal fields, miners were paid in cash; but in the Hocking Valley, employers systematically gouged them by paying them in scrip redeemable at company-owned stores. Prices at these stores averaged 15 or 25 per cent higher than at other stores, and while independent storekeepers accepted the scrip, they discounted it proportionately. Even when a miner was paid in cash, he was expected to trade at the company store. What happened

54 H. G. Gutman, "The Labor Policies of the Large Corporation in the Gilded Age: The Case of the Standard Oil Company," unpublished MS., cited with the kind permission of the author; Hidy and Hidy, *Pioneering in Big Business*, pp. 587–599; Ozanne, "Union-Management Relations," pp. 140–149; J. S. Ewing and N. P. Norton, *Broadlooms and Businessmen* (Cambridge, Mass., 1955), pp. 89–91, 115–117. One of the most common difficulties involved in labor management in these years resulted from the great degree of independence afforded to individual foremen, who usually controlled hiring and firing and whose personal dealings with each worker were subject to few checks from above. See Hidy and Hidy, *Pioneering in Big Business*, p. 587; Korman, *Industrialization, Immigrants, and Americanizers*, pp. 62–63; Kirkland, *Industry Comes of Age*, pp. 337–338. On the use of political pressure in the textile towns, see G. S. Gibb, *The Saco-Lowell Shops* (Cambridge, Mass., 1950), p. 396.

55 Ewing and Norton, *Broadlooms*, pp. 151–152.

when he did not was described by one worker as follows: "No direct compulsion is used. . . . A hint is conveyed to him in a round-about way, that his prospects at the mine would be improved by trading at the store of his employer. If this has not the desired effect, he is laid off for a few days. . . . This failing, the next move is to make the miner's situation so unpleasant by a system of persecution that life becomes a burden."[56] Miners were also expected to supply their own blasting powder and to buy it from their employers at inflated prices. One company cleared a thousand dollars a month by selling powder to its men at $3.25 a keg when the going rate was $1.90. "If the miner dared . . . to buy his powder where he could obtain it on more reasonable terms, the threat of discharge soon brought him back to the company's powder-house."

The Ohio legislature outlawed scrip and forbade employers to compel their men to buy at any particular store, but, according to one local lawyer, this law "was not worth the paper upon which it was written." The Ohio Bureau of Labor Statistics repeatedly printed facsimiles of company scrip dated long after the law was passed. Its 1878 *Report* pointed out that antiscrip laws were being "daily and hourly violated"; the miners were "virtually the slaves" of the scrip system and "dare not attempt to enforce the provisions of the laws." Years later the situation remained unchanged. "We visited Shawnee, Perry County," state investigators reported in 1885, "and found the place flooded with 'scrip' in denominations from one (1) cent to five (5) dollars." As a result of the attitude of the mine operators, labor relations in the area were bitter and turbulent. Conservatives claimed that miners were "in their normal element only when on a strike," the Commissioner of Labor Statistics wrote, "but where villanies . . . are practiced upon a class of men, the wonder is that they have contented themselves with strikes as remedies for their grievances. In many other communities under similar circumstances furnishing subjects for first class funerals would have been resorted to."[57]

Although the responses of American workingmen to the assump-

---

[56] IBLS, *4th Report*, pp. 397, 401; OBLS, *7th Report* (Columbus, 1884), p. 187; OBLS, *9th Report*, p. 214.

[57] OBLS, *7th Report*, p. 185; *2nd Report* (Columbus, 1879), p. 116; *9th Report*, pp. 215–224, 226.

tions, attitudes, and actions of their employers varied, most accepted existing conditions as inevitable and made the best of them; discontent did not necessarily lead to protest. The United States was a predominantly agricultural nation in the process of rapid industrialization. Industrial workers were a minority group much influenced by American rural values, either because they had grown up on farms or, if they were recent immigrants, because they were impressed (perhaps overwhelmed) by the new culture in which they were immersed. At the same time, the immense achievements of the new industry acted to mute criticism; discontented farmers might mutter about a lost golden age (although they, too, found the new order impressive), but workingmen, observing what the new machines were accomplishing close up, were often awed and sometimes made proud in spite of themselves by the experience.

American workingmen were also, as a class, remarkably silent. A large if not exactly determinable percentage of the labor force was unskilled, poorly educated, and socially underprivileged. Negroes and immigrants particularly had little influence, and lacked the self-confidence necessary to seek influence aggressively. At the other extreme, upwardly mobile types tended to identify with their employers and adopt the values of American capitalism enthusiastically. Studying their situation, a modern economist or sociologist might rank such men as members of the working class, but psychologically their point of view was middle class. Whatever the facts of their existence, they did not consider themselves as exploited or underprivileged; or if they did, they assumed that their condition was temporary. For these reasons the discontent of workingmen was largely stifled. If the idea of protesting their fate was not actually unthinkable, to protest seemed either hopeless, shortsighted, or impolitic. This helps to explain why expressions of discontent, when they did occur, took the form of violent explosions, which subsided as quickly as they burst forth and which produced little or no apparent change.

The social climate of the times was unfavorable to the growth of a strong labor movement, as was the historic division of the movement into a practical-minded wing concerned only with wages and working conditions and a reformist element seeking basic social and economic changes to be achieved through political action or revolution. The same pressures that were causing manufacturers to mechanize, consolidate, and develop complex organizations were also affecting labor, but workers adjusted to these pressures very slowly. The growth of unions was hesitant, sporadic, and marked by internal conflict. In the Pennsylvania coal fields, for example, only a few local unions existed in the 1860's. By 1873, however, John Siney's Workingmen's Benevolent Association had enlisted 50,000–60,000 miners and wrested important concessions from the operators. In 1875 the Association waged a six-month strike in protest against a wage cut, only to meet with complete defeat. By 1876, union membership in the Pennsylvania fields was down to almost nothing. The Knights of St. Crispin, a shoemakers' union, claimed 50,000 members in 1870; in 1878 it no longer existed. The Typographical Union had 9,800 members in 1874, less than half that many four years later. For reasons that are far from clear, such sudden shifts in union activity occurred repeatedly. Viewing the period as a whole, the union movement made very little progress. Trade unions had about 300,000 members in 1870, only 370,000 in 1890, although the labor force more than doubled in these decades.[58]

The deflationary trend of the post–Civil War years hurt the labor movement in two ways. Reform-oriented unionists diverted much of their energy into the greenback movement and other attempts to inflate the currency, while practical men found the going extremely difficult when they tried to win wage increases and other concessions from hard-pressed employers. During the bad times of the seventies, unions in nearly every trade lost members and became, if not less militant, far more cautious about their use of the strike device. By the late seventies a few trade union leaders were arguing that the strike was anachronistic as a method of improving the lot of labor. Some conservative unions, most notably the Brotherhood of Locomotive Engineers, adopted a policy of avoiding walkouts and winning concessions from employers by "cooperation" (demonstrating the good character and reliability of members) and by "arbitration" (peaceful collective bargaining).[59]

Yet the bad times angered and frustrated wage earners. Railroad

[58] Long, *Wages*, p. 42; Lloyd Ulman, *The Rise of the National Trade Union* (Cambridge, Mass., 1955), p. 19; Philip Taft, *Organized Labor in American History* (New York, 1964), pp. 70–73; McNeill, *Labor Movement*, pp. 249–251; Ware, *Labor Movement*, pp. 18–19, 51, 117.

[59] McMurry, *Burlington Strike*, pp. 29–31; J. R. Commons *et al.*, *History of Labour in the United States* (New York, 1918), II, 176–177.

workers were especially hard hit, for the competitive rate-cutting of the depression years led employers to try to recoup by reducing labor costs. An explosive mood developed. Symptomatic was the changing attitude of the Brotherhood of Locomotive Engineers. These skilled, conservative, and relatively well-paid men elected a new president, Peter M. Arthur, and in 1876 successfully struck the Central of New Jersey and the Grand Trunk system.[60] However, when the engineers struck the Boston and Maine in February, 1877, that company rushed in strikebreakers and starved the union into submission. The discontent of railroad workers was compounded by the attitude of public-spirited conservatives like Charles Francis Adams, Jr., of the Massachusetts Railroad Commission. Employers should treat their men fairly, paying decent wages and providing insurance benefits, Adams insisted; but since railroads were public utilities, strikes should be outlawed. Workers who abandoned trains, refused to handle the cars of struck lines, or tried to dissuade other men from doing so should be fined and imprisoned. "The Brotherhood of Locomotive Engineers has got to be broken up," he wrote. "It has become . . . a standing public menace."[61]

When, during the summer of 1877, the major lines again slashed wages, a true mass uprising followed. The engineers, chastened by the failure of the Boston and Maine and other strikes, took a back seat in these disturbances; a new group, the Trainmen's Union, organized to include low-paid brakemen, conductors, and switchmen as well as engineers and firemen, initiated the trouble by striking against the Baltimore and Ohio on July 16. Baltimore police promptly dispersed the pickets, but the next day Baltimore and Ohio workers seized a vital junction at Martinsburg, West Virginia. Local police tried to drive them off. A mob formed. State militiamen were called in, then federal troops, and order was restored.

This, however, was only the beginning; the strike, erupting in a dozen rail centers, spread quickly. Wherever police and soldiers tried to disperse the strikers, the men, defending what they con-

---

[60] Bruce, *Year of Violence*, pp. 29, 33–36. Bruce provides an interesting but rather highly colored account of the discontent of railroad workers and of economic conditions generally in the late seventies.

[61] *Ibid.*, p. 36; E. C. Kirkland, *Charles Francis Adams, Jr.; The Patrician at Bay* (Cambridge, Mass., 1965), pp. 54–55.

sidered their rights, resisted. Fighting broke out at widely scattered points; for a week the nation seemed on the verge of a revolution. In Baltimore, when a mob tried to prevent a militia regiment from leaving its armory, the soldiers opened fire, killing ten persons. At Pittsburgh, rioters burned 2,000 freight cars and much other railroad property, looted stores, exchanged heavy fire with troops. By July 25, all the lines outside of New England and the South had been affected. Strikers in Indianapolis seized the Union Depot, disconnecting cars and halting all but mail trains. When the governor and local officials hesitated to use force, local citizens, led by Benjamin Harrison, recently defeated Republican candidate for governor, organized a Committee of Public Safety and recruited two hundred men to preserve order. In Chicago, armed businessmen patrolled residential areas. In Buffalo, crowds surged through the New York Central yards, occupied the facilities of the Lake Shore and Erie railroads, attacked militia units. Everywhere that violence occurred, toughs and teen-age hoodlums swelled the ranks of the strikers.[62]

Yet the uprising collapsed as swiftly as it had started. Lacking central leadership, strikers lost heart when isolated groups gave up the fight in the face of overwhelming state and federal force. Moderates among the strikers became alarmed at the destruction of life and property. Unemployed men succumbed to the calls of the lines for strikebreakers. Although frightened reactionaries called for ruthless suppression of the rioters, sensible conservatives, realizing that the strikers had legitimate grievances, urged compromise. Benjamin Harrison combined his vigorous efforts to maintain law and order in Indianapolis with a call for a citizens' mediation committee to consider the complaints of the strikers. Railroad wage rates, Harrison said, were "too low"; he promised to "use his influence with those in authority" to see that they were raised once the men had gone back to their jobs. Many railroad executives, concerned about the losses they were suffering, promised to discuss the strikers' complaints if they would return to work. By August 3 the last holdouts had given up the struggle.[63]

These 1877 disturbances produced mixed results. Superficially

[62] Bruce, *Year of Violence*, pp. 198–201; H. J. Sievers, *Benjamin Harrison: Hoosier Statesman* (New York, 1959), pp. 135–137; Ray Ginger, *Altgeld's America* (New York, 1958), p. 37.

[63] Bruce, *Year of Violence*, pp. 103–114, 282–291; Sievers, *Harrison*, pp. 137–138.

labor was thoroughly defeated; the men straggled back to work without achieving their demands and many were thrown in jail for their riotous behavior. The press resounded with demands that unions be restricted or even made illegal. The strike was called "un-American," an "insanity of passion," the work of communist agitators. It led to the strengthening of state militia units and the construction of many ugly armories, monuments to middle-class fears of social revolution. Yet it focused national attention on the legitimate complaints of workingmen: level-headed observers realized that this outburst of mass resentment could not be explained away as the work of a handful of agitators or malcontents. For example, while most clergymen denounced the strikers—the Reverend Lyman Atwater blamed the troubles on "a junto of men, who stand ready to strike in the dark, from their secret conclave, at everything we hold dear"—a few liberal ministers were roused to take a greater interest in the problems of labor, an interest that soon grew into the Social Gospel movement. The economic disruption resulting from the tie-up also stimulated the movement for federal regulation of the railroads.[64]

To labor and to employers the strike offered clear but not easily assimilated lessons. It showed workers the advantages of organizing on an industry-wide basis rather than by specific crafts, and of striking whole industries rather than individual companies. When enough men walked out, they were fairly safe against reprisals even if they lost the strike; wages and working conditions actually improved after the collapse of the uprising, and only in part because the railroad business became more prosperous. After 1877, railroad executives began to pay more attention to labor relations and to develop benefit and insurance plans to mollify their employees. On the other hand, the affair showed how difficult it was to control a nationwide strike and how antithetical to labor's interest was violence, which frightened and infuriated the middle-class majority. The labor movement had not yet developed either the administrative skills or the unity of purpose to operate effectively on a national basis.[65]

[64] Bruce, *Year of Violence*, p. 311; T. A. Scott, "The Recent Strikes," *North American Review*, CXXV (1877), 352; Fine, *Laissez Faire*, pp. 120–123, 169 n.; Allan Nevins, *The Emergence of Modern America* (New York, 1927), p. 392; H. F. May, *Protestant Churches and Industrial America* (New York, 1949), p. 91.
[65] Bruce, *Year of Violence*, pp. 301–302; Cochran, *Railroad Leaders*, pp. 175–

The return of boom times around 1879 provided a more favorable climate for unionization, and the next few years proved crucial in the history of organized labor. Nearly all union leaders sensed the need for combining their interests, but they could not agree on how to do so or for what purpose. The old-fashioned trade unions experienced a modest revival. Dozens of new "international" craft unions sprang up, and the leaders of these organizations made a few fumbling efforts to create a national federation. At a meeting in Pittsburgh in 1881, over 100 delegates established a Federation of Trades and Labor Unions of the United States and Canada, but to carry on what they called the "struggle between capital and labor, which must grow in intensity from year to year and work disastrous results to the toiling millions of all nations if not combined for mutual protection and benefit," the founders of this imposing-sounding institution could collect among themselves only $56. Most trade-union men were too narrowly local in their interests and too poor to form a strong centralized organization.[66]

One group, however, was trying to transcend the limitations imposed by organization according to separate crafts. The Noble Order of the Knights of Labor originated as an ordinary trade union of Philadelphia garment cutters. A secret order with an elaborate ritual—its leader, Uriah S. Stephens, belonged to the Masons, the Odd Fellows, and the Knights of Pythias—it remained insignificant from its foundation in the sixties until the late seventies. But the great strike of 1877 changed its character. Stephens, a broad-gauged labor reformer in the tradition of the Jacksonian era, had always advocated the "amalgamation and affiliation" of all workers into one "great brotherhood." Trade unions, he said, were "too narrow in their ideas and too circumscribed in their field of operations." In practice Stephens' rhetoric had produced relatively few results; local assemblies of the Knights had admitted "sojourners"—non-dues-paying members of other trades who were supposed to proselytize among their fellows—but as late as 1876 the three-dozen-odd locals were primarily organized along trade lines. After 1877, however, many workers found the idea of a brotherhood of labor appealing. Men flocked to the Knights spontaneously. By

178; Stanley Buder, *Pullman: An Experiment in Industrial Order and Community Planning, 1880–1930* (New York, 1967), p. 39.

[66] Ulman, *National Trade Union*, p. 4; Taft, *Organized Labor*, pp. 95–96.

1879 it had over 9,000 members, by 1882 over 42,000, by 1885 over 110,000.[67]

The leaders of the Knights proved incapable of welding these eager converts into an effective organization. Stephens' labor philosophy was largely religious in inspiration; he had no very deep insight into contemporary labor problems. He squabbled with other leaders over petty details of the ritual and left the order. His successor, Terence V. Powderly, was a controversial character, part idealist, part politician, part mountebank. In some respects he was very forward-looking. Under him the Knights cast off secrecy and mumbo jumbo. They came out for the eight-hour day, employing the argument, developed by union leaders in the sixties, that more leisure would give workers time to improve themselves and thus elevate both their productivity and their aspirations. They opened their ranks to unskilled workers, to Negroes and immigrants, to women. They believed, as one contemporary historian put it, that "the general introduction of machinery has so revolutionized the methods of industry that there are practically very few trades remaining." However, Powderly had no more profound a grasp of current social and economic problems than Stephens, and no understanding at all of how to improve the economic situation of workingmen. Collective bargaining and striking did not interest him. Although he believed in organizing Negroes, he preferred that they set up segregated locals, and he insisted repeatedly that he was opposed to social equality for the races. Without being a rigorous socialist, he deplored the wage system, a means, he said, whereby "the Shylock of labor . . . could strike the toiler to the dust." Apparently not realizing that success in industry was becoming steadily more dependent upon the amassing of large amounts of capital, he claimed that "there is no good reason why labor cannot, through co-operation, own and operate mines, factories, and railroads."

The statements of Powderly and other prominent Knights were full of radical bombast. "There is no mutuality of interests . . . [between] capital and labor," declared George E. McNeill, chief organizer of the Knights in Massachusetts. "It is the iron heel of a soulless monopoly, crushing the manhood out of sovereign citizens."

---

[67] Ware, *Labor Movement,* pp. 37–39, 66, 155–156; G. N. Grob, *Workers and Utopia* (Evanston, 1961) , pp. 34–36.

But they believed the millennium could be achieved through "co-operation." In his muddleheadedness Powderly saw no contradiction between this kind of rhetoric and his argument that all men were brothers. The talk of most leading Knights closely resembled that of the Grangers and Populists: it contained the same curious mixture of fanaticism, utopianism, and hard common sense. "I can see ahead of me," Stephens once said, "an organization that will cover the globe. It will include men and women of every craft, creed and color; it will cover every race *worth saving*." "No drones," Powderly insisted. "No lawyers, no bankers, no doctors, no professional politicians." Yet in the next breath he could speak of "combining all branches of trade in one common brotherhood."[68]

As with the trade-union federation, the hierarchy of the Knights had little control over local groups. Although many semiskilled factory workers joined, so did thousands of craftsmen, often transferring en masse from the trade unions. "Two card" men became common—Samuel Gompers of the Cigarmakers' International Union, a founder of the trade-union federation, was also a member of the Knights. By 1882, 318 of the organization's 484 assemblies were actually trade unions. However, thousands of unskilled southern cotton and sugar hands were beginning to enroll as well. As early as 1878, the Knights had fifteen organizers in the South, and their appeal for "solidarity" won many converts among supposedly unorganizable Negro farm laborers and also among white railroad workers and miners. These men were not oriented toward trade unions. Militantly in favor of striking to achieve their own objectives, they opposed the antistrike policy of men like Powderly, but they resented any suggestion that the Knights assess the membership to provide strike benefits for skilled tradesmen who were far better off than themselves. Powderly and other leaders of the Knights did not give much direction to the diverse elements that were flocking into the order. Official policy fluctuated from year to year and the separate assemblies paid very little attention to official policy in any case.

[68] IBLS, *4th Report*, p. 162; G. N. Grob, "Organized Labor and the Negro Worker: 1865–1900," *Labor History*, I (1960), 167–168; McNeill, *Labor Movement*, pp. 411–412, 460; Ware, *Labor Movement*, p. 156; Taft, *Organized Labor*, p. 91; Grob, *Workers and Utopia*, pp. 36–47, 135–136; Arthur Mann, *Yankee Reformers in the Urban Age* (Cambridge, Mass., 1954), pp. 178–182.

Nevertheless, trade-oriented assemblies always had to struggle against a hierarchy that was philosophically opposed to concentrating on short-term practical objectives, such as higher wages and shorter hours, and that sought systematically to dilute the strength of craft groups by submerging them in mixed assemblies.[69]

The national assembly of the Knights of Labor had little to do with the wave of strikes which contributed so largely to the growth of the organization in the early eighties. The first of these strikes was the Western Union walkout in the summer of 1883. Powderly gave the telegraphers practically no help, and their organization suffered a shattering defeat. Responding to resulting criticism, the national assembly of the Knights then reversed itself and voted to create an Assistance Fund to support strikes; but when the glass-workers, a powerful local organized on industrial lines, struck in protest against a wage cut in the fall of 1883, an attempt to levy a five-cent assessment on all Knights produced very disappointing results.[70]

Then, in 1884, began what labor historians have called "the great upheaval." In May unorganized shopmen struck the Union Pacific Railroad in protest against a wage cut; in two days the Union Pacific management capitulated. The men promptly joined the Knights of Labor. The next month almost 4,000 miners in the Hocking Valley of Ohio walked out in protest against a similar reduction. The mine owners refused to make any concessions and eventually broke the strike, but the men had managed to hold out for six months and to raise over $100,000 in strike benefits. In March, 1885, workers of the Missouri Pacific Railroad struck against a pay cut. The walkout spread to the entire Southwestern system, dominated by Jay Gould. After the governors of Missouri and Kansas had intervened in the men's behalf, Gould surrendered. That summer, the Gould system was struck again; this time a rather

[69] Ware, *Labor Movement*, pp. 137–138, 158; U.S. Senate, *Report on . . . Labor and Capital*, I, 270; C. V. Woodward, *Origins of the New South* (Baton Rouge, 1951) , pp. 229–230; Grob, *Workers and Utopia*, pp. 48–52, and Grob, "The Knights of Labor and the Trade Unions," *Journal of Economic History*, XVIII (1958) , 176–192.

[70] Ware, *Labor Movement*, pp. 133–134; Pearce Davis, *The Development of the American Glass Industry* (Cambridge, Mass., 1949) , pp. 127–132.

inconclusive settlement was reached, but Gould agreed to recognize the union and promised not to retaliate against the strikers.[71]

Although Powderly and his associates had had almost nothing to do with the "upheaval," the defeat of the mighty Jay Gould attracted recruits to the Knights by the thousands and infused the whole labor movement with a new militancy. The Brotherhood of Locomotive Firemen, for example, a conservative benevolent association committed to co-operation, voted in 1885 to become a full-fledged labor union and to strike when necessary to achieve its ends. Between mid-1885 and mid-1886, the membership of the Knights of Labor soared from about 100,000 to over 700,000.[72]

However, this sudden growth of aggressive unionism was built on quicksand. Public opinion appears to have been fairly sympathetic to the unions at this time, partly because wage reductions and rising unemployment were causing much distress and partly because of the Knights' successful defiance of the notorious robber baron, Jay Gould. But the national leaders of the Knights, confused about their objectives, were ill-prepared, as a trade-union newspaper put it, for "the management of strikes or aught else pertaining to wages and terms of labor." Moreover, in many local organizations, hotheads among the rank and file forced strikes in hopeless situations and engaged in acts of violence and intimidation that caused employers to dig in their heels and alienated not only the general public but also many workingmen. During the Knights' strikes against the Gould lines, nonstriking workers received bloodthirsty threats, signed "Knights of Labor Cow Boys, Mob No. 1," and some were badly beaten when they insisted on working.[73] Men like Powderly deplored such violence, but were powerless to check it. Of course, lawless behavior by strikers led, as the prounion Ohio Commissioner of Labor Statistics put it, "only to disaster and defeat."[74]

---

[71] Commons, *History of Labour*, II, 363–364, 367–371; Taft, *Organized Labor*, pp. 98–100; Ware, *Labor Movement*, pp. 134–136, 140–144.

[72] McMurry, *Burlington Strike*, p. 34; Ware, *Labor Movement*, p. 66.

[73] Commons, *History of Labour*, II, 353. "We have selected a man out of our gang for the purpose of lynching you all, and he will get you sooner or later, if you don't leave," one threat ran. A roundhouse worker testified stoically: "They put a couple of black eyes on me and put a few lumps on the top of my head." *House Report No. 4174*, Part II, 150, 152.

[74] OBLS, *9th Report*, p. 26.

Industrialists were becoming thoroughly alarmed both by the success of the unions and by the belligerency of labor generally. The radical-sounding talk of many labor leaders and their overly ambitious plans (as early as 1884 the feeble trade union federation called for a general strike in 1886 for the eight-hour day) strengthened the determination of employers to fight back, and alarmed the middle-class majority of the country.

Although the union movement was expanding fast, growth was spotty and still relatively insignificant. Organizers were particularly successful in Illinois, but by mid-1886 only about 100,000 Illinois wage earners carried union cards, barely more than half the total employed in manufacturing, transportation, and mining alone. These union men were heavily concentrated in Chicago—a study made by the Illinois Bureau of Labor Statistics revealed that 60,000 of the 89,000 union members investigated worked in Cook County, although only 55 per cent of all Illinois workers resided there.[75] In the nation as a whole, no more than one wage earner in four belonged to a union in 1886 and a large percentage of those who did were very recent converts, not really indoctrinated with the union point of view.

The "great upheaval" reached a climax in the spring of 1886. In March the Knights again struck what they called "the contemptible and blood-sucking corporations" of Gould's Southwestern system. This time the little tycoon was ready for a showdown. Although the workers seized control of yards and dismantled locomotives, stripping "the roads . . . in an instant of men indispensable for the movement of trains," he would not yield, and by early May the strike had been crushed.[76] Meanwhile a number of trade unions had gone ahead with the planned general strike for the eight-hour day. Powderly had tried to keep the Knights from participating, arguing that the time was not ripe, but many local assemblies ignored him. The strike began on May 1. Although about 190,000 men laid down their tools, the walkout was anything but a national movement. Nearly 80 per cent of the strikers came from three cities—Chicago, New York, and Cincinnati, and, except for 35,000

75 IBLS, *4th Report*, pp. 192–193, 218, 221. Excluding coal miners, 88 per cent of all Illinois trade-union members were Chicagoans.

76 Taussig, "South-Western Strike," pp. 184–222; Ware, *Labor Movement*, pp. 145–158.

Chicago meat packers, almost all were craftsmen rather than industrial workers—cigarmakers, carpenters, bricklayers, and the like. Miners, railroad workers, and factory hands were not involved.[77]

In Chicago, center of the movement, social tensions were heightened by a totally unrelated strike at the McCormick Harvester plant. This strike had been going on since February, and it had been marked by a number of violent disturbances. On May 3 a clash between strikers, scabs, and police caused one death and a number of injuries. Next day a circular appeared on the streets:

REVENGE! WORKINGMEN! TO ARMS!

Your masters sent out their bloodhounds—the police—they killed six of your brothers at McCormick's this afternoon. . . . If you are men . . . then you will rise in your might Hercules, and destroy the hideous monster that seeks to destroy you.

This circular, printed in German and English, was the work of August Spies, one of a small group of anarchist revolutionaries, mostly of German birth, advocates of the "propaganda of the deed," who were trying to take advantage of the local unrest. Next evening, Spies and some of his associates addressed a public gathering in Haymarket Square called "to denounce the latest atrocious act of the police, the shooting of our fellow-workmen yesterday afternoon."

The meeting was a disaster from every viewpoint. The turnout in cavernous Haymarket Square was disappointingly small—perhaps 1,200—and it dwindled rapidly after rain began to fall. The meeting was about to break up a little after ten o'clock when a column of 180 policemen suddenly appeared and ordered the crowd to disperse. Then someone threw a bomb. One policeman was killed, 70 injured. The angry policemen reformed their ranks and charged the crowd, guns blazing, clubs swinging. In a few moments it was all over, the rain-soaked square silent except for the moans of the wounded.[78]

Although the nation's newspapers, thundering against this outrage, tended to connect it with the industrial unrest of the period, its impact on the labor movement was chiefly indirect. Union

---

[77] Henry David, *The History of the Haymarket Affair* (New York, 1936), pp. 157–167, 176–177; Commons, *History of Labour*, II, 385.

[78] David, *Haymarket Affair*, pp. 191–206.

leaders denounced the bombing as vigorously as anyone, and the reaction of the business community was remarkably mild. A Chicago newspaper quoted Powderly as saying: "There is not a Trade-Union in America that will uphold those men in Chicago. . . . The anarchist idea is unAmerican." The *Commercial and Financial Chronicle* editorialized: "There is no evidence to show and much to disprove that such methods have to any considerable extent the sympathy of the striking employees." Writing in the *Forum*, Andrew Carnegie held that labor was "not justly chargeable" with the actions of radical agitators, and praised the "promptitude" with which labor leaders had denounced the affair and the "solid basis of virtue in the wage-receiving class." Aside from the eight anarchists who were convicted of complicity in the crime after a grossly unfair trail, the main sufferers were immigrants, for the incident produced the worst outburst of nativist sentiment of the entire post-Civil War period.[79]

Nevertheless, after the explosion every instance of labor violence gave a measure of plausibility to the attacks of reactionaries on unions and strikes. The eight-hour movement could not have succeeded totally in any case at this time, but the incident certainly took much of the steam out of the drive for shorter hours and operated to make labor less aggressive in the pursuit of all its goals. "The explosion of the bomb on the Haymarket square abruptly ended [the movement]," a report of the Illinois Bureau of Labor Statistics concluded. "Men who would have ventured far in behalf of the principle underlying the demonstration shrank from any assertion of that principle under conditions which could hardly fail to involve misinterpretation." Two years later the Wisconsin Bureau of Labor Statistics observed that "everywhere the life and spirit of 1886 have departed."[80]

Other reactions were generally in line with these conclusions. "We arbitrated with employers as to a scale of wages and hours of labor last May," a Chicago bakers' union reported late in 1886,

[79] *Ibid.*, pp. 211, 214, 221-525; Andrew Carnegie, "Results of the Labor Struggle," *Forum*, I (1886), 538-551; Higham, *Strangers in the Land*, pp. 54-56. Four of the anarchists were executed; another committed suicide. The other three received long prison terms, but were pardoned in 1893 by Governor John Peter Altgeld of Illinois. For a sampling of antilabor comment after the bombing, see Reznenck, "American Depression," p. 305.

[80] IBLS, *4th Report*, p. 498; WBLS, *3rd Report*, p. xxvii.

"but after the general trouble, existing at that time, the employers broke the contract. Some of our men now work 16 hours as a day's labor." The records of the Illinois Bureau of Labor Statistics suggest that employer resistance to the comparatively few strikes that occurred in that state in the latter half of 1886 was much stiffer than it had been before the bomb burst.[81] "Our observation as to the [eight-hour] strike," a lumber company official stated, "was that it was decidedly disastrous both to employers and workmen. . . . The shorter day may obtain sometime in the future, but the strike of last May delayed that date a long time." To which a building contractor added smugly: "I anticipate no more attempts to prevent me from employing carpenters for ten hours for some time." Yet labor made substantial gains in 1886, and did not lose all of them in the reaction following the Haymarket bombing. Nationally, the average workday in thirteen important industries fell from 10.2 to 10 hours, the sharpest single decline of the period 1860–90.[82]

Whether the events of 1886 explain the decline of the Knights of Labor is a different question. The failure of the strike against the Gould railroads more than the Haymarket catastrophe marked the turning point in the Knights' history, but the inability of the officers of the organization to control rank-and-file members and (more significantly) give them intelligent direction probably ensured that it would soon have begun to crumble in any case. Conflicts between the Powderly faction and trade-union leaders within and without the order had been increasing steadily, the trade-union men feeling that the Knights, besides competing with them for members, were injuring the whole labor movement by admitting insufficiently trained craftsmen to their ranks and neglecting bread-and-butter issues in favor of general social reform. A bitter dispute within the Cigarmakers' International Union, which resulted in one group joining the Knights and attaching a "white label" to its cigars in competition with the blue union label of the International, was the most notable of many clashes.[83]

Although the trade unions seemed minuscule in 1886 compared

81 IBLS, *4th Report,* pp. 367–402; see esp. pp. 367, 392, 393, 401.

82 *Ibid.,* pp. 495, 496; Long, *Wages,* p. 37; David, *Haymarket Affair,* pp. 538–540.

83 Ware, *Labor Movement,* pp. 63, 258–279; Taft, *Organized Labor,* pp. 108–109.

to the Knights, their leaders were more professional and level headed—focusing on more limited immediate objectives, they pursued them more patiently and consistently. The testimony of prominent trade unionists before the Senate committee on the relations of labor and capital in 1883 reveals their thinking clearly. When Senator Henry W. Blair of New Hampshire asked President Adolph Strasser of the Cigarmakers: "Do you not contemplate, in the end, the participation of all labor and of all men in the benefits of trades unions?" Strasser answered: "Our organization does not consist of idealists. . . . We do not control the production of the world. That is controlled by the employers. . . . I look first to cigars."

"I was only asking you in regard to your ultimate ends," Blair explained. To which Strasser replied: "We have no ultimate ends. We are going on from day to day. We are fighting only for immediate objects—objects that can be realized in a few years." Samuel Gompers of the same union put it this way: "Whatever ideas we may have as to the future state of society . . . they must remain in the background, and we must subordinate our convictions . . . to the general good that the trades-union movement brings to the laborer."[84]

These statements contain the germ of the "pure and simple unionism" that was characteristic of the early twentieth-century labor movement. Men like Strasser and Gompers, however, had not yet actually repudiated the ambitious social objectives of the Knights. They considered themselves socialists, although, despite Gompers' contrary statement in his autobiography, they were probably not Marxians. They did not even in this period abjure the old idea of a workingmen's political party. But they were rapidly learning to separate their philosophical beliefs from their professional labor-union activities. They objected to the Knights' talk about brotherhood and co-operation as *substitutes* for economic pressure. Theirs was a "hard, cold cruel school" (as Gompers put it) with no place for "mere word mongers." They opposed organizing *everyone,* but advocated toughness in dealing with employers. "No strike is a loss or failure to the workers, even if the point sought is not gained for the time being," Peter J. McGuire of the Brotherhood of Carpenters and Joiners insisted. "If naught else,

84 U.S. Senate, *Report on . . . Labor and Capital,* I, 374, 460.

they at least teach the capitalists that they are expensive luxuries to be indulged in." To which Gompers added, boasting of the Cigar-makers' $150,000 strike fund: "When the employers know that the workingmen are organized and have got a good treasury strikes are very frequently avoided."[85]

During the hectic last months of the "great upheaval," a small group of trade unionists, including Strasser and McGuire, drafted a "treaty" for the consideration of the Knights that was really a declaration of war. It demanded that the Knights cease accepting members of all crafts where trade unions already existed, and that the trade assemblies in the Knights be disbanded. Naturally enough, the Knights refused to ratify this "treaty," whereupon representatives of the trade unions, gathered in Columbus, Ohio, in December, 1886, organized the American Federation of Labor. Samuel Gompers was chosen president. The new organization levied an assessment of one-half cent a month on all members and "condemned" the policies of the Knights of Labor. Gompers considered the Knights as much an enemy of the A. F. of L. as any employer. "They will give us no quarter and I would give them their own medicine in return. It is no use trying to placate them or even to be friendly."[86]

Although both the new Federation and the Knights squandered much of their resources over the next few years in fighting with each other, the fact that the Federation survived while the Knights collapsed was not a result of their conflict. The A. F. of L. remained for years a feeble institution. Membership in its loosely affiliated unions—about 138,000 workers in 1886—increased very slowly; in 1887 the monthly assessment was reduced to one-quarter of a cent per member and the total collected came only to $2,100.34. In that year the Knights took in $267,000. Nevertheless, the Knights disintegrated rapidly. Membership declined to about 250,000 in 1888. By 1890 it had fallen to approximately 100,000, and Powderly was writing: "Something must be done or we must let the sheriff run the

85 *Ibid.*, I, 322, 373; Grob, *Workers and Utopia*, p. 147; R. A. Christie, *Empire in Wood: A History of the Carpenters' Union* (Ithaca, 1956) , pp. 33–37.

86 Ware, *Labor Movement*, pp. 280–284, 294–296; Taft, *Organized Labor*, pp. 113–115; Grob, *Workers and Utopia*, p. 119. Grob argues that the treaty was an attempt to persuade the Knights to concentrate on long-range goals and leave bread-and-butter issues to the trade unions. *Ibid.*, pp. 112–113.

concern." But when Powderly attempted to explain the causes of the decline of the order a few years later, he did not place any of the blame on the A. F. of L.[87] The Knights of Labor broke up partly because its leaders were disorganized and uninspired; but the fact that the trade unions, which were led by shrewd and dedicated men, could not profit much from its collapse suggests that American workingmen were still too diffuse in background and training and too confused by the onrushing changes that industrialization was producing to co-operate with one another without regard for particular industries or crafts. There were many strikes, but, except when railroad workers were involved, they took the form of local battles with individual firms. Talk of general strikes subsided along with serious efforts to organize unskilled laborers and semiskilled factory hands. As the eighties gave way to the nineties, the vast majority of American wage earners remained outside the union movement.

However, workingmen were not left entirely to their own devices in their struggle to increase their share of the profits of manufacturing. To a steadily increasing extent, government interjected itself into this struggle, sometimes on one side, sometimes on the other. By the late eighties a sizable body of labor legislation had been enacted by state governments. Massachusetts had the most extensive system; its laws provided machinery for arbitrating labor disputes, restricted the hours of work of women and children, made employers liable for certain industrial accidents, enforced safety standards in factories, and protected the wages of workers in various ways. New York also had a fairly comprehensive body of labor law, including an especially well-designed child-labor act, and all the other industrialized states had passed at least some legislation in this broad field.[88] Most states with important mineral deposits had, by the eighties, enacted mine-safety laws and appointed inspectors to enforce the regulations.[89]

[87] Ware, *Labor Movement,* pp. 66, 294 n., 298, 373–376; Taft, *Organized Labor,* pp. 117–119.

[88] MBLS, *21st Report* (Boston, 1890), pp. 3–106; New York Bureau of Labor Statistics (hereafter NYBLS), *10th Report* (Albany, 1893), Part I, 11–38. For a summary of state labor legislation in 1886, see U.S. Commissioner of Labor, *1st Report* (Washington, 1886), pp. 457–485.

[89] IBLS, *2nd Report* (Springfield, 1882), pp. 389–397.

However, few southern and western states enacted labor legislation during this period, and when they did their laws were usually either antilabor, like the Oregon and Texas measures limiting the activities of union organizers and pickets, or, like the Georgia law restricting the working day in manufacturing establishments to the time from sunrise to sunset, so broad as to offer workers no protection at all.[90] Of course, the absence of strong laws in some states enabled reactionaries in other states to argue that by increasing labor costs reform would subject local manufacturers to ruinous competition. Furthermore, even in states with considerable labor legislation, enforcement was often spotty. Many employers (and sometimes their workers as well) objected to the regulations, and the states frequently failed to make them comply. In 1881, New York required factory owners to supply seats for female workers. A decade later the state factory inspector reported: "The seats may be and as a rule are provided; but the well-known penalty for occupying them is instant discharge. The trouble about the law, which is a very good and humane one, is that there is no one to enforce it."

Poverty compelled many parents to put children to work in violation of child-labor laws. When, for example, a Wisconsin factory inspector found several boys who seemed younger than the twelve-year limit working in a textile mill, the superintendent told him "he did not want to hire children under the lawful age, and if he did he was not to blame, as the statements of the boys as to their age was verified by their parents." The Chicago social worker Jane Addams complained bitterly about parents who "hold their children in a stern bondage which requires a surrender of all their wages and concedes no time or money for pleasures," but many poor families had little choice. "Why, there's lots of talk about free education and the advantages to the working man of our public school system," a Cleveland barrelmaker told a reporter in 1877. "Do you suppose, sir, at the wages we have to work for now-a-days, we can afford to send our children to school? No, sir!" The detailed reports of the Wisconsin factory inspectors in the late eighties throw much light on the difficulty of making labor legislation effective. In some cases, employers even refused entry to inspectors. "I have no use for idlers prowling around," the owner of a lumber mill stated.

90 Commissioner of Labor, *1st Report*, pp. 461, 478, 483.

"I am able to conduct my own affairs without the aid of any kind of officer."[91]

Beginning with Massachusetts in 1869, a number of states created bureaus of labor statistics. The pioneering Massachusetts bureau was authorized to "collect, assort, systematize, and present . . . statistical details relating to all departments of labor." After Carroll D. Wright, a patent lawyer and state senator, became its chief in 1873, it began to turn out masses of statistical data on wages, hours, and working conditions in the state, to conduct useful surveys of opinion, and to make special studies of matters ranging from labor disputes, immigration, and unemployment to the liquor problem, the abandonment of agricultural areas, and prison labor. Businessmen often resented Wright's "prying," and many workingmen claimed that he was too eager to smooth away conflicts and point out the wastefulness of strikes, but his tact, his obvious effort to be objective, and his repeated insistence that labor bureaus should be nonpartisan and should avoid suggesting specific reforms soon won him and the bureau widespread support. By 1879 six other states had labor bureaus, and by 1890 the number had grown to 25.[92]

Most of these bureaus had no powers beyond the right to collect and publish data, the theory being that when the facts were known, the public would insist that evils be corrected, inequities adjusted. "Public sentiment is nearly all the power that is necessary in reforming industrial evils," Wright insisted.[93] Obtaining data was far from easy: many manufacturers left requests for information unanswered or submitted hastily prepared, inaccurate reports, while efforts to gather facts and opinions from workingmen by mail led only to repeated frustration. Since workers were also reluctant to testify at public hearings, Wright and other pioneers soon began

91 NYBLS, *10th Report,* Part I, 26; WBLS, *4th Report,* p. 8a; WBLS, *3rd Report,* p. 277; Jane Addams, *Twenty Years at Hull-House* (New York, 1910), p. 248; Gutman, "Labor Policies of the Large Corporation," p. 26. By the late eighties the courts were also making the enforcement of labor legislation difficult by interpreting the police powers of the states very narrowly. See A. M. Paul, *Conservative Crisis and the Rule of Law: Attitudes of Bar and Bench, 1887–1895* (Ithaca, 1960), pp. 61–81, 104–130.

92 Leiby, *Wright,* pp. 54–80; "Carroll D. Wright," *Dictionary of American Biography,* XX, pp. 544–545; MBLS, *40th Report* (Boston, 1911), pp. 359–400; OBLS, *2nd Report* (Columbus, 1879), pp. 34–35; U.S. Senate, *Report on . . . Labor and Capital,* III, 277–283; NYBLS, *10th Report,* Part I, 344–345.

93 U.S. Senate, *Report on . . . Labor and Capital,* III, 282–283; Leiby, *Wright,* pp. 5, 79, 140; MBLS, *40th Report,* pp. 388–389.

sending agents to interview workers on the job and in their homes. Although fragmentary and, even according to the standards of the day, methodologically unsophisticated, the statistical data collected provided valuable material for the study of working conditions, and some of the special reports of the bureaus had considerable influence on public opinion, and thus on legislation. The bureaus all operated on a shoestring; in 1885, the Ohio commissioner, who had only $1,500 a year to carry on his work, pointed jealously to the affluence of the bureaus of New York and Massachusetts, each of which luxuriated in annual appropriations of over $6,000. But when intelligently directed, as was particularly the case in these years in Massachusetts and Illinois, remarkable results were achieved with these tiny sums.[94]

Little that the federal government did during these years related directly and specifically to the workingman. Politicians and manufacturers insisted that the protective tariff was a prop necessary to keep American wages from descending to European levels, and, in general, labor accepted their reasoning. Most wage earners also favored the restriction of immigration, but the Chinese Exclusion Act of 1882 and the Foran Act of 1885 outlawing contract labor were the only curbs applied during this era. As early as 1868 Congress had enacted an eight-hour law for federal workers, but it was emasculated by the Supreme Court in 1876. Labor leaders repeatedly demanded that it be strengthened and enforced, some even asking that the patent laws be changed to require all manufacturers operating under patents to adopt the eight-hour day, but nearly everyone conceded that federal regulation of the hours of labor, except for those of its own employees, was unconstitutional. Congress stiffened the eight-hour law somewhat in 1888, but only after further amendment in the early nineties did it become reasonably effective.[95]

Union leaders also sought a law authorizing the federal incorpo-

[94] OBLS, *9th Report*, p. 5; Leiby, *Wright*, pp. 84–85. Wright conducted his normal operations with the help of a single clerk. He focused his investigations on particular problems for relatively brief periods, hiring as many as fifteen or twenty agents on a temporary basis. "This is the only method we can adopt to secure the greatest results from the small amount of money at our disposal," he explained. U.S. Senate, *Report on . . . Labor and Capital*, III, 279.

[95] *Ibid.*, I, 461; Taft, *Organized Labor*, pp. 123–124; M. A. Kelly, "Early Federal Regulations of Hours of Labor in the United States," *Industrial and Labor Relations Review*, III (1950), 367–374.

ration of unions, not primarily as a guarantee of labor's right to organize, but to afford legal protections related to their holding and use of property denied them under common law. Senator Blair of New Hampshire introduced such a measure in the early eighties, but no action was taken, again in part because of the constitutional scruples of many congressmen.[96] Labor pressure for a federal bureau of labor statistics did, however, produce results. Peter J. McGuire of the carpenters' union presented the case for a federal bureau forcefully in 1883, stressing the "vast amount of material connected with this labor queston that is scattered through the different Departments that requires systematizing," and the need to "summarize" the work of the state bureaus. The next year Congress created a bureau of labor to "collect information upon the subject of labor, its relation to capital, the hours of labor, and the earnings of laboring men and women, and the means of promoting their material, social, intellectual, and moral prosperity." The first commissioner of labor, Carroll D. Wright, interpreted his assignment chiefly in statistical terms, but his prestige and his competence as a compiler of information made the bureau a popular success from the start. In 1888 Congress converted the bureau into a department, although Commissioner Wright was not made a member of the cabinet.[97]

Although he insisted that he intended to avoid "theoretical discussion," Wright seldom hesitated to arrive at generalizations and make recommendations. For example, in his first report, which dealt with the causes and cures of industrial depressions, he suggested substituting planning and combination for "the ill-advised eagerness of men to push their work individually." The general fear of organized activities was "the chief bugbear" of the times, he said. "If . . . the organization of employers on the one hand and the organization of workmen on the other could be secured, depressions would have but little effect, either in severity or in duration." Other early studies undertaken by the bureau included an investigation of the effect of prison labor on wages, a massive 1,100-page

96 U.S. Senate, *Report on . . . Labor and Capital*, I, 378–381, 461–462.

97 *Ibid.*, I, 327–328; Commissioner of Labor, *1st Report*, p. 7. President Arthur first nominated the trade-union leader John Jarrett, but reneged when he discovered that Jarrett had supported his successful rival, James G. Blaine, for the 1884 Republican presidential nomination. Leiby, *Wright*, pp. 70–72.

analysis of recent strikes, and a study of labor conditions in the railroad industry. In his first report, Wright complained tactfully of "the apprehension of manufacturers that the information required would do them some harm," but after his investigation of the touchy railroad-labor question, he was able to acknowledge the "courtesy and generosity of the managers of railroads," many of whom even sent their payroll records to Washington to assist in the work.[98]

This change of attitude, which others engaged in obtaining information from businessmen for public purposes also noted,[99] was further evidence that men were abandoning laissez faire in practice, however vociferously they still adhered to it in theory. Reacting to the strike against the Gould railroads in 1886, President Grover Cleveland, temperamentally a rugged individualist, paid lip service to the principle that "the Federal Government must be greatly limited by constitutional restrictions," but he immediately added that "something may be done under Federal authority to prevent the disturbances which so often arise from disputes between employers and the employed."[100] Of course, the awareness that labor problems affected the national interest did not always result in actions beneficial to workers. President Hayes's use of federal troops in the great railroad strike of 1877 was an early illustration of this fact, Cleveland's in the Pullman strike of 1894 a later one. State intervention in strikes, far more common, nearly always had the effect of speeding the defeat of the strikers. On the other hand, state labor legislation frequently was invalidated by judges whose belief in laissez faire had not succumbed to the changing needs of an industrial society. The rejection of a New York law prohibiting the manufacture of cigars in tenement houses in 1885 was one of the first (and also the most notorious) of such decisions. In 1886 a Pennsylvania court even threw out a law prohibiting the payment of wages in goods, which it described as "an insulting attempt to put the laborer under a legislative tutelage . . . degrading to his

---

[98] Commissioner of Labor, *1st Report*, pp. 6, 287, 293; *5th Report* (Washington, 1890) , p. 8.

[99] See for example, WBLS, *4th Report*, p. vi.

[100] J. D. Richardson (ed.) , *Messages and Papers of the Presidents* (10 vols., Washington, 1898) , VIII, 395; Allan Nevins, *Grover Cleveland: A Study in Courage* (New York, 1932) , p. 349.

manhood [and] subversive to his rights."[101] The full impact of these judicial assaults on labor legislation, however, was not felt until the 1890's, and then, of course, it was only temporary. The struggle of the American workingman to improve his lot was to be long and complicated, but by 1890 the underlying social and economic developments that made substantial improvement possible were well under way.

[101] Fine, *Laissez Faire*, pp. 159–161.

CHAPTER 5

Urbanization

W E live in the age of great cities," the Reverend Samuel Lane Loomis told the students of Andover Theological Seminary in 1886. "Each successive year finds a stronger and more irresistible current sweeping in toward the centres of life."[1] This was indeed the case. As the population of the United States expanded during the 1870's and 1880's, the nation became steadily more urbanized. In 1870, about one-fifth of the people lived in towns and cities ranging in size from 8,000 to nearly a million people. Twenty years later, about one-third of a much larger population lived in communities of more than 8,000 persons, and three cities—New York, Chicago, and Philadelphia—had soared beyond the million mark.

Urbanization was not a new trend in the United States, but during these decades its speeding pace altered the character of American life substantially. The rural sections of the country continued to grow, but they yielded human surpluses which poured into the cities along with the grain and livestock and other products of the soil. This flow met and mingled with the rising stream of foreign immigrants, many of whom also collected in urban areas. The interaction of these newcomers with the established urban population created the same kind of swirling confusion that occurs in the mouth of a harbor when a river discharges its waters against the force of a rising ocean tide.

Whereas in earlier times large American cities had been chiefly

[1] S. L. Loomis, *Modern Cities and Their Religious Problems* (New York, 1887), pp. 18–19.

centers of commerce, post-Civil War urban growth was related primarily to industrialization. This explains why most of the great cities were located in the northeastern part of the country. In 1870 the only communities outside this area with more than 100,000 inhabitants were New Orleans and San Francisco, both mainly trading centers, and even in 1890 over 80 per cent of all city dwellers lived in the North Atlantic and North Central states. At the latter date the ten largest cities were New York with nearly 1.5 million; Chicago and Philadelphia, each with slightly more than a million; Brooklyn with over 800,000; St. Louis, Boston, and Baltimore with almost 450,000 each; and Pittsburgh, San Francisco, and Cincinnati with populations in the neighborhood of 300,000.[2]

However, the phenomenon of urbanization was nationwide: many smaller, newer cities on the fringes of this area and in other sections of the country were actually growing faster than these giants. Denver, a town of 4,700 in 1870, had over 107,000 in 1890. Minneapolis had 13,000 in 1870, 165,000 twenty years later, while Omaha, St. Paul, and Kansas City, Missouri, grew at about the same pace. The new steel town of Birmingham, nonexistent in 1870 and with only 3,000 inhabitants in 1880, had 26,000 in 1890. Duluth jumped from 3,400 to 33,000 in the eighties, Kansas City, Kansas, from 3,200 to 38,000, Wichita from 4,900 to 24,000, Los Angeles from 11,000 to 50,000. In the Far West a larger *percentage* of the population lived in cities in 1890 than in the "urbanized" Northeast. Although later developments would cause the growth curves of some of these communities to flatten out, others to accelerate still faster, all seemed at this time merely at earlier stages of the same march toward giantism that was affecting the great metropolises. The growth of Omaha, for example, roughly paralleled that of Chicago in 1840–60, while Los Angeles was expanding at about the same pace that Buffalo had in 1830–50.[3]

Attempts to explain this rapid urban expansion are complicated

[2] A. F. Weber, *The Growth of Cities in the Nineteenth Century: A Study in Statistics* (New York, 1899), pp. 22, 28; U.S. Bureau of the Census, 15th Census, *Population* (Washington, 1931), I, p. 18. Brooklyn was a separate city until 1898, and while its economy was closely connected with New York's, it was no mere suburb, having a thriving, independent existence of its own. H. C. Syrett, *The City of Brooklyn: 1865–1898* (New York, 1944), pp. 20, 242–243.

[3] 1930 Census, *Population*, pp. 18–20; W. Z. Hirsch (ed.), *Urban Life and Form* (New York, 1963), p. 62.

by the fact that conditions differed greatly from place to place. Furthermore, changes occurred so swiftly that cause and effect are often impossible to untangle. Economic specialization and integration were certainly essential. Conditions that fostered the growth of large manufacturing units inevitably led laborers to concentrate around the factories, and further growth followed as merchants, storekeepers, and artisans flocked to supply the needs of the new workers. Yet these trends also stimulated the rural economy by creating new demands for farm products, and agricultural expansion triggered further urbanization, for it caused the rise of large food storage and processing centers, and stimulated the manufacture of farm machinery and the consumer goods that farmers desired.

The growth of cities also depended upon technological advances of many kinds. Without the railroad network the concentration of population in great metropolitan centers would have occurred more slowly, chiefly because an efficient transportation system was basic to the appearance of big industries and of national markets. Countless other technical and scientific discoveries contributed to the development of cities: the invention of the electric light and of electric street railways, improvements in the design of water and sewage systems, the skyscraper, the elevator, new medical knowledge leading to the control of contagious diseases, and many, many others. Yet technology was itself largely a product of the city, both in its relation to the factory and in its dependence upon an intellectual creativity that found its most congenial environment there.[4]

Similarly, while the opportunities that cities offered in the way of cultural and social stimulation were obviously created by urban growth (men did not found cities in order to establish universities and museums and theaters or to increase and vary the circle of their acquaintances), these advantages surely attracted outsiders once they had come into being. On the other hand, city life produced in many residents a desperate urge to escape to the fresh air and serenity of the countryside. Throughout the period every major city experienced a continual movement of people in and out—young men from the farms and European immigrants entering, middle-class residents leaving for the suburbs, and foreign-born persons

4 F. J. Kingsbury, "The Tendency of Men to Live in Cities," *Journal of Social Sciences*, XXXIII (1895), 5–18.

returning home either disillusioned by their American adventure or laden with money earned in the land of opportunity. Unknown numbers of floaters drifted in and out of the cities on the alternating tides of prosperity and depression.[5]

Another way of trying to understand the growth of cities in this era is to examine the motives of the millions of persons who crowded into them. The foreign immigrants who entered the country in such numbers had often little choice but to become city dwellers. Most arrived in America with almost no money; for such persons, acquiring a farm was out of the question. An English settler in Minnesota in the seventies, for example, advised his compatriots that they would need about £500 to get established. While many immigrants, especially those from Scandinavia and Germany, were able to obtain land, most became wage workers, the great majority perforce in urban communities. Most were unskilled, and the cities offered the best opportunity for persons without special training to find employment. By 1890 the immigrant population of fast-growing cities like Chicago and Brooklyn was almost as large as their total population a decade earlier. New York, the chief port of entry for immigrants, had a foreign-born population of nearly 40 per cent by 1890, while about a third of all Bostonians and a quarter of all Philadelphians were of foreign birth in that year. The presence of established communities of their fellow countrymen in the cities acted as a further, noneconomic attraction to later arrivals. Lonely, confused, poor, often with little or no command of English, new immigrants were looking for understanding and for something familiar, as well as for jobs. Every major city had many districts, usually the poorest and dingiest, to which Poles, Italians, Germans, Irish, and other ethnic groups gravitated, each crowding together as though for mutual protection and support in an alien world.[6]

[5] On the difficulty of determining exactly the movement of population within the United States, see E. S. and A. S. Lee, "Internal Migration Statistics for the United States," *Journal of the American Statistical Association*, LV (1960), 664–697.

[6] M. A. Jones, *American Immigration* (Chicago, 1960), pp. 214, 223–225; R. T. Berthoff, *British Immigrants in Industrial America: 1790–1950* (Cambridge, Mass., 1953), p. 110; A. M. Schlesinger, *The Rise of the City* (New York, 1933), pp. 65, 72–73; Syrett, *Brooklyn*, p. 235; Oscar Handlin, *The Uprooted* (Boston, 1951), *passim;* B. L. Pierce, *A History of Chicago* (3 vols., New York, 1957), III, 20–47; Moses Rischin, *The Promised City: New York's Jews, 1870–1914* (Cambridge, Mass., 1962), pp. 76–81.

Rural Americans migrated to the cities for a host of reasons. In the older sections, where farms were small and all the arable land already occupied, a steady stream of young men and women left the countryside in search of work. After about 1890, when agriculture actually began to decline in New England, many rural people abandoned their farms altogether, joining the migration to urban centers. Even in the West, ambitious young people, impressed by the success of industrial tycoons and merchant princes, often decided to play for higher stakes, giving up the relatively secure but modest rewards of tilling the soil in hope of becoming millionaires in the cities.[7]

Equally compelling were the harshness and intellectual sterility of rural life and the corresponding attractiveness of the social and cultural opportunities available in the cities. Many migrated because of the superior educational facilities of urban communities, and because of their theaters, music, and art (without regard for quality, since tastes differed enormously). More generally, the excitement and stimulation of city life along with its fleshpots and titillating vices attracted thousands. Observers noted the "energy and enterprise" and the "roar and bustle and energy" of cities like Chicago, and the tendency of "the most important and successful men in all branches of activity" to gravitate to such places as Washington and New York. This aspect of the magnetic pull of urban life on rural Americans is well revealed in William Allen White's *Autobiography*. Arriving in the "gilded metropolis" of Kansas City in 1891, young White was overwhelmed and amazed by its "marvels." He quickly fulfilled a lifelong ambition by purchasing a secondhand dress suit. He thrilled to the music of a sixty-piece orchestra. ("The clarion notes entwined in the harmonics from the various instruments kept calling in my heart—for the first time—tunes that I could not whistle.") He attended concerts and plays, heard James Whitcomb Riley recite poetry. ("It got me. I went raving mad. I kept saying over and over and with variations, the whole long way home: 'I can do that!' ") "Life was certainly

[7] F. A. Shannon, *The Farmer's Last Frontier: Agriculture, 1860–1897* (New York, 1945), pp. 248–249; W. M. Springer, "City Growth and Party Politics," *Forum*, X (1890), 474. The relative unprofitability of farming has already been discussed in Chapter 2. This was certainly a factor that caused many rural citizens who had no illusions about their chances of actually growing rich to migrate.

one round of joy in Kansas City," White recalled half a century later.[8]

Concerned by the trend of population toward the cities, Massachusetts Commissioner of Labor Statistics Carroll D. Wright prepared in 1879 a kind of inventory designed to discover what social and cultural opportunities were available in the state, which he sent to the heads of all the school boards. He asked them to describe and enumerate the clubs, churches, amusements, organized community activities, even the number of pianos "in use" in their communities. The replies to this questionnaire revealed sharp differences in the social life of rural and urban districts even in densely populated Massachusetts. Surveying them, Wright rated the communities on a scale ranging from excellent to poor. Of the rural townships, only 41 of 234 possessed facilities that seemed to him excellent or very good; he rated 66 either fair or poor. Of the nineteen cities of Massachusetts, twelve fell into his two top categories; none was rated poor. He placed only one city even as low as fair on his admittedly subjective but apparently sensible scale.

The study, Wright decided, proved "the superior social life of the cities" conclusively, and suggested that the "defective social element of our country life" was contributing significantly to the drift of population to the cities.[9] Many of Wright's respondents added comments to his questionnaire that reinforce his statistical conclusions. "Hard work and no holidays," one man wrote in accounting for the migration. "No books, no papers, no games, no young company; 'go to bed John, hard day's work tomorrow.' 'Get up, John, it is most five; how lazy you are getting.'" Another wrote: "The lack of pleasant, public entertainments in this town has much to do with our young people feeling discontented with country life." Still another said: "I was born and bred in Boston, and have been educated and settled in country towns, and feel a little competent to compare the two modes of life. . . . People will not live on the farm as they seemed willing to do a hundred years ago."[10]

[8] James Bryce, *The American Commonwealth* (2 vols., New York, 1895), II, 863–864; B. L. Pierce (ed.), *As Others See Chicago* (Chicago, 1933), pp. 229, 289; Frances Carpenter (ed.), *Carp's Washington* (New York, 1960), p. 93; W. A. White, *Autobiography* (New York, 1946), pp. 205–212.

[9] MBLS, *11th Report* (Boston, 1880), pp. 239–276.

[10] *Ibid.*, pp. 273–274.

Thus people flocked to American cities for many reasons and from widely scattered parts of the world. Urbanization was part of an enormous interaction for which no simplistic explanation is satisfactory. It was part of a process, not its product.[11] Contemporaries were of course aware that urbanization was taking place in the United States at a very rapid rate, but because the process was so complex and dynamic they failed to understand it, or rather tended to focus on those aspects that struck them most directly at any particular time. The ambivalence of rural Americans toward the city has already been mentioned. City dwellers themselves were scarcely less confused in their thinking. A well-to-do merchant studying his balance sheet, dining in a good restaurant, or returning to his comfortable town house after an evening at the theater might contemplate his condition with satisfaction; the same man set upon in the streets by a gang of toughs or caught in a tangle of traffic on his way to business might generalize about urban life in far different terms. The former farm boy or immigrant who found a good job and made friends would have one opinion of the city, another who experienced only grinding toil, slum housing, and loneliness, quite another.

Social commentators and other experts proved little better at reaching valid generalizations—the cities were too large and were changing too fast for any mind to grasp them in their entirety. James Bryce, observing American cities as a political scientist and man of the world, was shocked by their political corruption and repelled by their almost total lack of individuality. "Their monotony haunts one like a nightmare," he wrote. The Reverend Josiah Strong saw only the immorality of the cities and the declining influence of true (by which he meant Protestant) religious values. "The dangerous elements of our civilization are each multiplied and all concentrated in the city," he wrote. Yet Julian Ralph, a widely traveled American journalist, was most impressed by the pride and energy of city dwellers, and their booster spirit, which he called their "supervoluminous civicism." Another professional travel writer even claimed that the choking smoke of Pittsburgh helped prevent "lung and cutaneous diseases," and was "the sure death of malaria and its attendant fevers." The sociologist F. J. Kingsbury, impressed by the inevitability of urban expansion,

11 Hope Tisdale, "The Process of Urbanization," *Social Forces,* XX (1942), 311–316.

emphasized the social efficiency of cities and the mental stimulation they afforded inhabitants. "Everything that is best in life can be better had in the city," he insisted.[12]

If one shifts from trying to find the ultimate significance of late-nineteenth-century urbanization to merely describing it, the task becomes more manageable, although far from simple. Since the founding of Jamestown and Plymouth, Americans had been involved in tasks of construction and development: in supplying themselves with food, clothing, and shelter, in organizing patterns of economic production and distribution, in establishing social and political institutions suitable to their environment. In the burgeoning cities of the post-Civil War era, these basic functions continued to be performed, but the imperatives of urban life required that they be carried out in new ways.

A city would not be a city if it did not have a relatively dense population, but in the seventies and eighties people crowded together in the great American cities on a scale never before experienced in the United States and seldom anywhere in the world. The cities grew physically larger, yet people jammed into them faster than they could expand, faster than houses could be constructed, lots subdivided, roads laid out. Since men had to live near their work, the lack of efficient urban transportation exascerbated the problem. A psychological element was also involved: much of the satisfaction of being a city dweller came from a sense of existing in the midst of an exciting, vital mass of humanity. Congestion was one of the most obvious characteristics of urban life, one that soon began to feed upon itself; for as cities became more thickly settled, movement within them became more difficult and therefore slower. Thus workingmen had to move closer to their places of employment, which meant that still more people had to crowd into smaller areas.

High population densities caused a sharp rise in the price of urban real estate. The contemporary press was full of stories of owners of modest properties who suddenly found themselves rich. A Washington boardinghouse keeper was offered $64,000 in the late

---

12 Bryce, *American Commonwealth*, I, 622, 637; II, 818–819; Josiah Strong, *Our Country* (New York, 1885), p. 177; Pierce, *As Others See Chicago*, p. 288; C. N. Glaab (ed.), *The American City: A Documentary History* (Homewood, Ill., 1963), pp. 237, 367.

1880's for a building purchased twenty years earlier for $4,000. Land in one residential section of Chicago jumped from $160 a front foot to $800 in a decade. A city block in Denver worth $6,500 in 1874 went for $205,000 in 1888. Lots in New York City that sold for as little as $80 in the early forties were worth $8,000 in the early eighties, while between 1880 and 1883 the average price of a fifty-foot lot in Birmingham rose from $260 to $756.80.[13]

Such examples could be multiplied endlessly. Paradoxically, the poorest people were forced to live in areas where real estate was expensive because of their need to be near the crowded business and industrial sections where they worked. In 1880 the Tenth Ward of New York's Lower East Side, an area of forty-five city blocks, contained over 47,000 persons. By 1890 more than 57,000 people lived there, giving the ward a population density of 334,080 per square mile, amost ten times the city's average.[14]

The necessity of housing large numbers of low-income people in areas where land was expensive produced the slum tenement. By 1890 the technology existed for relieving the pressure by building upward. The iron-skeleton skyscraper, developed during the eighties in Chicago, and the elevator had led to the construction of ten- and fifteen-story commercial buildings, and soon the word "skyline" came into the language.[15] But this solution seemed too expensive for ordinary mass housing. Instead, more and more families were squeezed into existing structures. Flats and apartment houses in working-class districts were subdivided and partitioned, and then whole familes were crowded into single rooms. Ramshackle structures rose in back yards without direct access to the street. Owners of private homes succumbed to the temptation of converting their properties into rooming houses. When new housing was constructed, high land costs and greed for profit encouraged builders to utilize every possible square foot of ground and to pack as many separate units as they could under each roof.

13 Carpenter, *Carp's Washington*, p. 306; Pierce, *Chicago*, III, 60; J. A. Garraty, *Right-Hand Man: The Life of George W. Perkins* (New York, 1960), p. 19; U.S. Senate, *Report on . . . Labor and Capital* (Washington, 1885), I, 823; IV, 350.

14 S. B. Warner, Jr., *Streetcar Suburbs: The Process of Growth in Boston, 1870–1900* (Cambridge, Mass., 1962), p. 56; Rischin, *Promised City*, p. 77; Jacob Riis, *How the Other Half Lives* (New York, 1957), pp. 228–229.

15 O. W. Larkin, *Art and Life in America* (New York, 1949), pp. 288–290; John Burchard and Albert Bush-Brown, *The Architecture of America: A Social and Cultural History* (Boston, 1961), pp. 152–154, 243–244.

As the cities became more crowded, efforts were made to improve housing conditions. In New York, for example, some tenements dating from the 1860's had as many as twelve families living on each floor; more than half the rooms in these buildings had no windows. As late as 1879 the average New York tenement, constructed on a lot twenty-five feet wide and one hundred feet deep, had windows only at the narrow ends. The interior rooms lacked outside ventilation, and many of these buildings had no toilets. A tenement-house law of 1879 limited the ground space which could be covered by new buildings, and provided for minimal plumbing facilities and more adequate ventilation. These requirements were satisfied by the "dumbbell" tenement, a five- or six-story building with four apartments to a floor, characterized by narrow indentations along the flanks to allow for windows in every room.[16] Yet even these "improved" dwellings were woefully inadequate, especially as they began to age and as population pressures led to multiple-family occupancy of apartments. As a federal investigator reported in 1895, the air shafts formed by the indented flanks of adjoining dumbbells furnished "imperfect light and ventilation" at best, and with the passage of time "refuse matter or filth of one kind or another [was] very apt to accumulate at the bottom, giving rise to noxious odors."[17]

A few socially minded wealthy men and women, inspired by the efforts of British and other European philanthropists, put up model tenements to prove that decent housing for workingmen could be a money-making proposition. The first of these was Alfred T. White, whose Home Building development in Brooklyn was completed in 1877. By 1890 White had constructed three such projects in Brooklyn, containing over 500 units and housing more than 2,000 persons,

[16] Riis, How the Other Half Lives, pp. 5–10; Rischin, Promised City, p. 82; U.S. Commissioner of Labor, Eighth Special Report (Washington, 1895), p. 128, plans 5, 6, 9; Gordon Atkins, Health, Housing, and Poverty in New York City: 1865–1898 (New York, 1947), pp. 111–118. The original dumbbell design, the work of James E. Ware, was one of about 200 plans submitted in a prize competition sponsored by a trade journal, the Plumber and Sanitary Engineer. Roy Lubove, The Progressives and the Slums (Pittsburgh, 1962), pp. 29–31.

[17] Commissioner of Labor, 8th Special Report, p. 129. When a U.S. senator asked the secretary of the New York City Board of Health if the law allowing builders to cover 78 per cent of a lot was not literally stultifying, the secretary replied: "It is regarded as reasonable in this city, where the land is so valuable." U.S. Senate, Report on . . . Labor and Capital, II, 653.

and at least six other projects were operating in the New York and Boston areas. Typically, model tenements were built around courtyards, thus providing playground space, and they usually offered other communal facilities, such as reading rooms and baths. These buildings were safe, clean, and possessed of decent plumbing, but they lacked central heat. However, the rents, while modest considering the facilities offered, placed these dwellings beyond the reach of the poor. An analysis of White's Riverside project, made in the early 1890's, revealed that only a small percentage of the tenants were unskilled laborers and that nearly all were either native Americans or representatives of the "older," better-established immigrant groups from northern Europe. The sponsors of model tenements, while genuinely desirous of improving working-class districts, were convinced that this could only be done if investors could count on making a profit—all these projects aimed at clearing about 5 percent yearly, and most succeeded. Even so, they found few imitators and had no appreciable effect on the urban housing problem.[18]

Many American manufacturers constructed homes for their workers. This practice dated back to the 1830's, when the Lowell Associates erected boarding houses for their female operatives at the new town of Lowell, in Massachusetts. In later years, whenever mills were built at undeveloped sites or when mining companies began to exploit new mineral regions, the owners usually had to create entire "company towns." Although the housing in these communities was more often than not jerry-built and totally lacking in architectural distinction, and although the employer-landlords often subjected residents to a variety of petty tyrannies, the histories of most of these developments throw little light on the problems of late-nineteenth-century urbanization. They seldom achieved very great size and·were unrelated to the growth of great metropolitan centers.[19]

[18] Commissioner of Labor, *8th Special Report*, pp. 169–214, especially p. 182. This report contains descriptions, including architect's drawings, of all the model housing developments existing in 1890. See also "Alfred Treadway White," *Dictionary of American Biography*, XX, pp. 86–87; A. T. White, *Better Homes for Working People* (New York, 1885); Lubove, *Progressives and the Slums*, pp. 34–39; R. T. Paine, Jr., "Homes for the People," American Social Science Association, *Journal*, XV (1882), 104–120.

[19] J. W. Reps, *The Making of Urban America* (Princeton, 1965), p. 421. After visiting the town of Cohoes, New York, a satrapy of the Harmony Mills, in 1882,

The most notable exception was the town of Pullman, Illinois, a suburb of Chicago created in the early 1880's by George Pullman, the inventor of the sleeping car. This community of over 8,000 was carefully planned by an architect, Solon Beman, and a landscape designer, Nathan Barrett; the houses were well built and surrounded by greenery. The Pullman Company also provided a church, a fourteen-room schoolhouse, a library, and a park, with tennis courts, a baseball field, and other recreational facilities. Monthly rents averaged $3.30 per room, slightly higher than equivalent space in Chicago, but all observers agreed that the quality of the housing and the surroundings fully justified the difference. In 1884, the heads of ten state bureaus of labor statistics visited the town. The reaction of these firmly prolabor investigators was ecstatic: "One of the most attractive experiments of the age. . . . The women were in love with the place. . . . Beauty, order, and cleanliness prevail. . . . We found the *morale* of the place even better than we expected."[20] But with a few exceptions, such as the Diamond Match Company development at Barberton, Ohio, and the Apollo Iron and Steel Company's town near Pittsburgh, designed by the landscape architect Frederick Law Olmsted, other manufacturers did not follow George Pullman's example.[21]

The great mass of urban workers lived in privately owned tenement houses operated strictly for profit. These buildings were almost always very crowded. In 1883 a Senate committee visited a number of New York tenements. Here is its report on one of the better ones, located on the Upper East Side:

Samuel Gompers claimed that when the river was low the company shut off the water supply of company-owned houses in order to be able to preserve the water power needed to run the plant. U.S. Senate, *Report on . . . Labor and Capital,* I, 277.

[20] Stanley Buder, *Pullman: An Experiment in Industrial Order and Community Planning, 1880–1930* (New York, 1967), pp. 41–59, 62–69, 92–104; Reps, *Making of Urban America,* pp. 421–422; IBLS, *3rd Report* (Springfield, 1884), pp. 638–654. For other contemporary accounts, see Pierce, *As Others See Chicago,* pp. 245–249, 266–273. The unanimity of the praise was marred by an article by the economist Richard T. Ely, who spent his honeymoon in Pullman in 1884. Ely, alarmed by the undemocratic character of the community, wrote that "the idea of Pullman is un-American." B. G. Rader, *The Academic Mind and Reform: The Influence of Richard T. Ely in American Life* (Lexington, 1966), pp. 54–56. It was of course ironic that, a decade later, labor trouble in Pullman was to trigger one of the most serious strikes in American history and give the founder of the town the reputation of being a tyrannical exploiter of labor.

[21] Reps, *Making of Urban America,* p. 424.

Each set of apartments was four rooms deep, and on each floor there were two sets, with a hall separating them. In one set of these apartments which the committee inspected . . . the front room was used as a parlor, the rear room as a kitchen and dining-room, and those intervening as bed-rooms. The "parlor" was about 16 x 12. . . . A conversation took place between the chairman and the wife of the tenant, in part as follows: Q. How many children have you?—A. We have had seven. We lost the first; the others are alive. . . . Q. You manage to live and be tolerably happy in this world, though?—A. Yes sir; we are quite happy.

An *average* New York tenement was described as follows in the late 1870's by an investigator of the New York Charities Aid Association:

This building is six stories high. Its middle rooms throughout receive almost no daylight. In one room servant girls out of employment find board at 10 cents per night. On the fourth floor in a rear room lives a widow, who takes five boarders. On the sixth floor lives a laborer; has wife and four children. . . . In this house live 90 persons; of these 17 are men, 36 women, and 37 children.

The same observer recorded this impression of a *bad* tenement:

A structure of the poorest class. A basement room was unfurnished except with a stove, a keg of stale beer, and boxes used for seats. Around the former were huddled four men and three women, four others being in the room. . . . The proprietor of this room (which is 14½ by 10 feet in extent) takes from eight to twelve lodgers at night. . . . Another room, the darkest in the house, is occupied by two Italian men and three women. In only four rooms was there anything like a family organization. . . . In this house are 14 rooms, occupied by 72 persons.[22]

The historical record is full of similar accounts of crowding in other industrial cities:

Fall River, Massachusetts: One operative, a spinner, used strong language when speaking of the mill tenements. He had a kitchen, two bedrooms, and a wash-room; and he spoke bitterly of the fact that such close quarters had a demoralizing effect upon the young of his family, it being necessary for himself and wife, owing to the smallness of their sleeping-rooms, to dress in the kitchen before their children, one boy sleeping in the kitchen, while the two younger children . . . slept in the smaller bedroom.[23]

22 U.S. Senate, *Report on . . . Labor and Capital,* I, 97–98; II, 1047–1048.
23 MBLS, *13th Report* (Boston, 1882) , pp. 273–274.

Lowell, Massachusetts: "Little Canada" . . . is a settlement of French Canadians. . . . In the census of 1880 it was found that in the 36 tenements [of one building] there were 396 persons. . . . The general appearance of "Little Canada" was very demoralizing, the people being crowded into the smallest possible space.[24]

Albany, New York: I asked her how much of a family she had, and she said seven children; she says "we do not want a large house"; she said they had three rooms in Albany; I asked her how they got along with three rooms, and she said, "after the day's work is done in the kitchen, we let down two or three beds in the kitchen, and sleep in it."[25]

Cincinnati, Ohio: Cincinnati contains 5,616 tenement houses, having an aggregate of 54,065 rooms. . . . These rooms shelter 24,983 families, numbering 105,488 souls. . . . High houses, narrow streets, damp and shady courts and alleys, over-crowded rooms, can hardly be regarded as conducive to good health.[26]

Urban crowding gave rise to serious public-health problems. In city after city, the needs of rapidly expanding populations made existing facilities for the disposal of sewage and garbage obsolete. Dozens of commentators complained that American cities, and many of their residents, literally stank. The evidence ranges from H. L. Mencken's hyperbolic 1940 account of Baltimore in the 1880's, which, he said, smelled "like a billion polecats," to the statement of Dr. Charles V. Chapin, the nation's leading late-nineteenth-century authority on public health, that the most annoying nuisance connected with urbanization was the prevalence of the privy, "a single one of [which] may render life in a whole neighborhood almost unendurable in the summer." The inadequacy of the sewage system of Rochester "became painfully evident even in choice residential sections." The mayor of Cleveland, in 1881, called the Cuyahoga River "an open sewer through the center of the city." The New York City Board of Health reported at about the same date that "foul-smelling privies" were one of the chief "sources of discomfort and disease" in the metropolis; and when the New York Association for Improving the Condition of the Poor published a notice asking tenants to report housing violations, it was deluged with hundreds of complaints about inadequate sewage facilities. "The stench is something terrible," one sufferer wrote.

24 *Ibid.,* pp. 282–284.
25 NYBLS, *2nd Report* (Albany, 1885) , p. 62.
26 OBLS, *3rd Report* (Columbus, 1880) , p. 236.

"The stink is enough to knock you down," another reported. According to the Chicago *Times,* a "solid stink" permeated that city. "No other word expresses it so well as stink," the paper added. "A stench means something finite. Stink reaches the infinite and becomes sublime in the magnitude of odiousness." In 1892 one neighborhood of Chicago covering a third of a square mile contained only three bathtubs.[27]

Descriptions of alleys filled with garbage and rubble, of streets choked with refuse, are equally easy to collect, yet to focus entirely upon the inadequacies of urban sanitation would be to ignore both the difficulties imposed by urban growth and the progress that was made in overcoming these difficulties. Cities needed enormous amounts of pure water and complicated sewage systems to carry this water to a safe place after it was used, and to drain off rainfall quickly. They also required adequate systems to collect and dispose of garbage and trash, and other sanitary improvements. These facilities were expensive; Boston, for example, devoted about 30 per cent of its budget to sanitary projects throughout the last third of the century. The cost aside, it was next to impossible to plan the necessary work and find the labor to carry it out fast enough to keep pace with population growth. In 1888 a committee of the American Economic Association estimated that about half the municipal water systems then operating in the United States had been constructed since 1880.[28] It was also hard to concentrate civic energies for such purposes in an age when technology was in such a state of flux that authorities disagreed about how best to deal with sanitation problems, and when developments were coming so rapidly that new systems often became obsolete before they were completed.

The progress made in the area of water supply and sanitation was therefore somewhat spotty. Brooklyn had an excellent water supply

27 Alistair Cooke (ed.), *The Vintage Mencken* (New York, 1956), p. 16; C. V. Chapin, *Municipal Sanitation in the United States* (Providence, 1901), p. 172; Blake McKelvey, *Rochester: The Flower City, 1855–1890* (Cambridge, Mass., 1949), p. 263; W. G. Rose, *Cleveland: The Making of a City* (Cleveland, 1950), p. 447; U.S. Senate, *Report on . . . Labor and Capital,* II, 1043–1044; Pierce, *Chicago,* III, 311; Jane Addams, *Twenty Years at Hull-House* (New York, 1910), p. 313. See also Gerd Korman, *Industrialization, Immigrants, and Americanization: The View from Milwaukee, 1866–1921* (Madison, 1967), p. 113.

28 Warner, *Streetcar Suburbs,* p. 30; H. C. Adams, "The Relation of Modern Municipalities to *Quasi*-Public Works," American Economic Association *Publications,* II (1888), 520.

system, but Philadelphia's was so poor that a group of leading citizens characterized their water in 1883 as "not only distasteful and unwholesome for drinking, but offensive for bathing purposes." The increasing demands of its rising population so severely taxed New York's excellent pre–Civil War water system that by 1883 low water pressure in many neighborhoods forced families in the upper stories of buildings to carry their supplies in pails from the lower floors. "In some parts of the city at certain times of the day, you will only be able to turn the water on in the basement," the secretary of the Board of Health admitted. Yet by the early nineties expansion of the New York reservoir system had again given the city a plentiful supply of pure water, although its waste-disposal system still left much to be desired. Fewer than one Washington house in three was connected to a sewer in the early eighties, and progress over the next decade was painfully slow. In Rochester, however, where only an antiquated system for draining off rainwater existed in 1875, the city, after much debate, employed an engineer to design a comprehensive sewer network and by the early nineties had a first-rate system.[29]

No city had more monumental sanitation problems than Chicago. In the early seventies it undertook to keep its sewage out of Lake Michigan by diverting the flow of the Chicago River into the Illinois River and thus into the Mississippi. But besides befouling the water supply of Joliet and other towns, this method worked poorly. In wet seasons, rising waters backed up in the Chicago, discharging tons of waste into the lake. The city's water had to be dosed with chemicals until it tasted like creosote. Over the years Chicago built six pumping stations that drew water from far out in the lake, and it deepened and extended the canals that reversed the flow of the Chicago River. The garbage collection system of Chicago, even in the nineties, was totally inadequate. Residents dumped their trash and discarded food in huge wooden boxes on the streets, where it often lay putrefying for days on end before being hauled away. The filth and smell of the city led the social worker Jane Addams to investigate. Aided by a small committee,

[29] Bryce, *American Commonwealth*, I, 635; U.S. Senate, *Report on . . . Labor and Capital*, II, 658; Atkins, *Health, Housing, and Poverty*, pp. 167–168, 198–199, 241; Schlesinger, *Rise of the City*, p. 104; C. M. Green, *Washington: Capital City, 1879–1950* (Princeton, 1963), p. 45; McKelvey, *Rochester*, p. 263.

she noted and reported over a thousand illegal sanitary hazards in a two-month period. When nothing was done by corrupt officials, she persuaded the mayor to make her a garbage inspector in her neighborhood and managed to improve the service substantially. Her most notable achievement was the discovery, in one street, of a forgotten layer of pavement buried under eighteen inches of accumulated debris. It was not until 1900 that Chicago could be said to have solved its water and sewer problems.[30]

The same difficulties that vexed urban water and sewage systems affected the laying out and surfacing of streets, the provision of light and power, the creation of parks and playgrounds, and the development of local transport. The construction and maintenance of streets, for example, was complicated by the rapid settlement of outlying districts, the ever-heavier pounding taken by those in crowded downtown sections, the installation of public utilities, and the introduction of new types of paving, chiefly cobblestones and brick, but also asphalt, which was far smoother and easier to repair. In most cities, new streets were laid out far more swiftly than they could be properly surfaced. Between 1870 and 1890, Cleveland almost tripled in population. It began this period with less than twenty miles of paved streets, and added, on the average, only two miles a year over the next two decades. Thus, in 1889, most of the city's 440 miles of street were mere sand and gravel. Chicago proved almost equally laggard; in 1890 nearly three-quarters of its 2,048 miles of street were unsurfaced, and most of the rest were paved with unsatisfactory wooden blocks. At least in part, such conditions resulted from the necessity of each community to choose among competing demands for civic funds and energies. Washington had, for the era, remarkably clean and well-paved streets, but inadequate sewage-disposal facilities; Chicago put more effort into the latter, far more pressing problem. Only the smaller, less rapidly growing cities—New Haven was a good example—could simultaneously spend money on paving streets and building a good network of sewers.[31]

30 Pierce, *Chicago*, III, pp. 309–313; Addams, *Hull-House*, pp. 281–287.
31 Rose, *Cleveland*, pp. 361, 371, 495, 500; Schlesinger, *Rise of the City*, p. 89; H. U. Faulkner, *Politics, Reform, and Expansion* (New York, 1959), p. 38; N. P. Lewis, "Modern City Roadways," *Popular Science Monthly*, LVI (1900), 524–539; Green, *Washington*, pp. 47–49; R. G. Osterweis, *Three Centuries of New Haven* (New Haven, 1953), pp. 331, 334–335. New Haven grew from 50,000 to 81,000

Pressure for urban investment in public utilities also mounted steadily. Here new technology stimulated immensely the demands caused by mere growth. The late seventies saw the first use of the telephone, of arc lamps for street lighting, of "water" gas (a compound of hydrogen and oil formed by blowing steam over incandescent coal) for home illumination and cooking. The next decade saw the rapid development of Edison's electric light. The voracious appetite of cities for all these conveniences may be seen in the experience of Chicago. The city got its first telephone in 1877. By 1881, over 3,400 were in use; by 1893, over 10,300. Its first arc lights began to sputter in 1878; the first incandescent electric light bulb was switched on in 1880. By 1884, eleven electric companies were doing an annual business totaling over $1 million and thereafter output soared, multiplying ten times between 1888 and 1893. Between 1887 and 1890, the capital invested in Chicago gas companies increased from about $25.5 million to $40.9 million.[32]

Central among the requirements of urban development was the improvement of local transportation to relieve congestion. Although city street paving tended to lag, bridge building made great strides, beginning with the opening of the Eads Bridge across the Mississippi at St. Louis in 1874. John Roebling's magnificent Brooklyn Bridge over the East River, completed in 1883, appeared to contemporaries to symbolize the new age of the city, and later generations have judged it one of the major monuments of that or any age. The importance of such conveniences in stimulating both urban and suburban growth scarcely requires demonstration. In its first year, over 11 million persons crossed the Brooklyn Bridge, and by 1887 the volume of traffic had tripled.[33]

---

between 1870 and 1890. Rochester, a more rapidly growing city of medium size (62,000 to 134,000), found itself in a position similar to Chicago's. By 1890 it had good sewers, but only one-quarter of its streets were paved. McKelvey, *Rochester*, p. 261.

[32] Schlesinger, *Rise of the City*, pp. 93–102; E. C. Kirkland, *Industry Comes of Age: Business, Labor, and Public Policy, 1860–1897* (New York, 1961), pp. 243–244; "Charles F. Brush," *Dictionary of American Biography*, XXI, 129–130; Matthew Josephson, *Edison: A Biography* (New York, 1959), p. 358; Pierce, *Chicago*, III, 221–229.

[33] "James Buchanan Eads," *Dictionary of American Biography*, V, 587–589; Syrett, *Brooklyn*, pp. 148–153; Alan Trachtenberg, *Brooklyn Bridge: Fact and Symbol* (New York, 1965), pp. 7–9, 67–68, 93–127; D. A. Wells, *Recent Economic Changes* (New York, 1889), pp. 385–386.

Not much could be done to speed up the flow of goods that poured in and out of the great cities by rail and water in ever-increasing volume. The linking of railroad terminals helped considerably by eliminating transfers, and large manufacturers usually received and shipped out their materials at sidings on railroad spurs built directly into their plants. But local deliveries of food, manufactured goods, fuel, and other supplies were still made by horse and wagon, usually through narrow, ill-paved streets and in competition with heavy pedestrian traffic.

However, a better way of moving people about the cities was developed: the streetcar. Consider Boston. In the early seventies, the area of Boston was limited by the distance men could conveniently walk to work; this "walking city" extended about two and a half miles from the center of town. Well-to-do individuals resided farther out and commuted to their businesses by steam railroads, but the trains were relatively expensive and offered only limited service; most ordinary workingmen lived within the city limits.[34] Between 1873 and 1887, however, streetcars pulled by horses extended a flexible network another mile and a half beyond the walking city. Then the faster electric streetcars quickly pushed their tracks about two miles farther into the countryside. Each extension of the city's perimeter increased its size enormously: multiplying the city's radius two and a half times expanded its area over 600 per cent.[35]

The shift of population outward into the suburbs was characteristic of every important American city in these years, and nearly always resulted from the construction of streetcar lines. Even more important, however, was the effect of these street railways on movement within the cities themselves. By 1890 Brooklyn had 164 miles of track and peaceful rural sections like New Utrecht, Flatbush, and Bay Ridge were rapidly being integrated into the urban way of life. In the outlying sections of Boston the population increased far more rapidly than in the center of the city.

As early as 1882, the nation's 400-odd streetcar companies were

[34] Warner, *Streetcar Suburbs*, pp. 17, 22. As early as 1870 New York had built an elevated steam railway. In the next decade Brooklyn constructed an "L." Chicago did so, too, beginning in 1892. But this noisy and dirty mode of transportation depressed property values and was too expensive for small cities. Allan Nevins, *The Emergence of Modern America* (New York, 1927), p. 82; Schlesinger, *Rise of the City*, p. 91; Syrett, *Brooklyn*, pp. 144–145.

[35] Warner, *Streetcar Suburbs*, pp. 22, 23, 63.

operating about 18,000 cars over some 3,000 miles of track and carrying 1.2 billion passengers a year. These figures rose spectacularly after Frank J. Sprague set up the first practical electric trolley line in Richmond, Virginia, in 1888. In 1890 there were 5,661 miles of horsecar lines in the United States, and 5,783 of electric, the latter alone transporting over 2 billion passengers annually.[36]

Sam B. Warner's investigation of the relation between Boston's growth and the spread of its streetcar network suggests many interesting generalizations about late-nineteenth-century urbanization. Before the coming of the streetcar, peripheral towns were not true suburbs; although many residents commuted to the metropolis, these communities still had self-contained economies of their own. These broke down fast once the horsecar and the trolley bound the suburbs to central sections. Streetcars, with their frequent stops, made for continuous development, whereas towns that relied upon railroads clustered around the more widely spaced stations. Suburbs separated people by income but not by ethnic origin; they provided a ladder for upwardly mobile individuals, who tended to move farther and farther from the center of town, leaving the older suburbs for lower-middle-class families.[37]

The construction of suburbs required an enormous effort: huge investments by private builders and developers, and also public expenditures for schools, utilities, and other community services. In most metropolitan areas, it seems to have been public policy to encourage suburban growth as a means of dealing with congestion and the slum problem, but probably also because of the prevailing American idealization of rural life. In his *Modern Cities* (1887), Samuel Lane Loomis wrote of "sprightly little villages springing up . . . each in the center of its patch of green," from which happy commuters streamed each morning toward the city. The Boston minister Edward Everett Hale praised the "villages where workingmen can live with their families in homes of their own, where the

36 *Ibid.*, p. 180; Syrett, *Brooklyn*, pp. 233, 241; Federal Electric Railways Commission, *Proceedings* (Washington, 1919), III, 2164-2165, 2221-2222. Sprague, who had previously experimented with electric traction on a "private track" of the New York City elevated railway, installed the Richmond line for "a lot of New York politicians" who had obtained a franchise. He and his backers lost about $100,000 on the venture, but they started a revolution. See Sprague's testimony, *ibid.*, I, 751-752, and also that of William J. Clark, I, 135-137.

37 Warner, *Streetcar Suburbs*, pp. 19, 43, 56, 66, 75-79.

children can have the advantages of country life." Willard Glazier, a travel writer, described the suburbs of Cincinnati as a "paradise of grass, gardens, lawns, and tree-shaded roads."[38]

Other contemporaries confused the same values when they complained of the absence of greenery in the cities. Boosters referred to Cleveland as "the Forest City" and to New Haven as "the City of Elms," but in fact most urban centers were almost as barren of vegetation as the Sahara. "If there is any grass on the south side of Pittsburgh," one witness told Senate investigators in 1883, "it is in a little box sitting on a window sill," and another, Samuel Gompers, describing New York City tenement life, said: "The only 'grass' that I could see was the green paint on the walls." An Englishwoman visiting Chicago was struck by "the dearth of trees" and the absence of "pleasant green shade." Actually, as at least Edward Everett Hale, a lifelong resident of the Roxbury section of Boston, should have known, except in the more distant districts inhabited by the wealthy, suburbs quickly lost their rural character. Built largely without plan, most were dominated by rank upon rank of "three-deckers" and small frame houses, laid out in the traditional urban grid, on narrow lots.[39]

Civic leaders tried to compensate for the lack of rural atmosphere by creating parks, but the high cost of land forced them to lay out most of their parks on the outskirts of the cities, far from the crowded slums that needed them most. Central Park, Frederick Law Olmsted's masterpiece of landscape design, was on the fringes of New York even when it was completed after twenty years' labor in 1876. Prospect Park in Brooklyn, Fairmont Park in Philadelphia, the South Park system of Chicago, and most other parks of any size dating from the seventies and eighties were similarly situated.[40] Yet the streetcar helped to ease this problem too, providing cheap and rapid service to outlying parks and amusement areas, as well as to

38 *Ibid.*, pp. 5, 32–33, 156–157; Loomis, *Modern Cities*, p. 64; E. E. Hale, "The Congestion of Cities," *Forum*, IV (1888), 532; Willard Glazier, *Peculiarities of American Cities* (Philadelphia, 1883), p. 128.

39 U.S. Senate, *Report on . . . Labor and Capital*, I, 31, 272; Pierce, *As Others See Chicago*, p. 228; Warner, *Streetcar Suburbs*, p. 158.

40 Buchard and Bush-Brown, *Architecture in America*, pp. 161–162; Syrett, *Brooklyn*, p. 141; Pierce, *Chicago*, III, 317. Of course, later growth left many of these large parks admirably situated, but, for the working people of that era, enjoying city parks meant traveling considerable distances.

the open country. Park building expanded rapidly; between 1888 and 1898, park acreage in the nation's twenty-five largest cities more than doubled.[41]

Considering the speed of urbanization in the post–Civil War decades, the failings of cities seem less important than their achievements. The squalor of the slums and the unimaginative dinginess of the suburbs should be balanced against the fact that merely raising enough roofs to shelter so many millions was a gigantic task. The installation of electric utilities proceeded at such a pace that when aesthetically minded community officials tried to bury the forest of wires that threatened to block off the sky, they discovered, as Mayor Seth Low of Brooklyn wrote in 1888, that "the multiplication of the wires is so constant and at so rapid a rate that as fast as some are placed beneath the surface, those which have been strung up while this process has been going on seem as numerous as before the underground movement began."[42] Even the corruption so commonly associated with the granting of municipal gas, electric, and streetcar franchises has to be viewed in the context of the voracious appetite of city residents for these utilities.

Moreover, any social system that crowds very large numbers of persons engaged in hundreds of independent activities into a small space is sure to create a great deal of social friction. This is the price that city dwellers always pay for the benefits that come from the massing of many talents. The men and women of this generation paid a particularly high price partly because their institutions, evolved in a simpler, rural environment, encouraged individualism and led them to value especially some aspects of life that had to be sacrificed in an urban situation. The times also conspired to subject American urban society, like that of the great cities of Europe, to an

41 MBLS, 11th Report, pp. 263–265; Warner, Streetcar Suburbs, p. 60; C. M. Robinson, The Improvement of Towns and Cities (New York, 1901), pp. 154–155; A. W. Crawford, "The Development of Park Systems in American Cities," American Academy of Political and Social Science, Annals, XXV (1905), 218–234.

42 Bryce, American Commonwealth, I, 665. An English visitor to New York in the late seventies commented on the "perfect maze of telephone and telegraph wires crossing and recrossing each other. . . . The sky, indeed, is blackened with them, and it is as if you were looking through the meshes of a net." W. G. Marshall, Through America, quoted in Bayard Still (ed.), Mirror for Gotham: New York as Seen by Contemporaries from Dutch Days to the Present (New York, 1956), p. 231.

additional strain. Besides adjusting to the world of the city, Americans had to absorb immigrants in unprecedented numbers, many of them unprepared by previous experience either for the old American way or for the new.

The juxtaposition of urbanization and immigration led many observers to conclude that the difficulties associated with the former phenomenon were caused by the latter. It was a long-standing habit of Americans to blame recent immigrants for every failing their civilization exhibited, and to characterize each wave of newcomers in unflattering terms. As early as the seventeenth century the welcome afforded new arrivals by established citizens was often touched with misgivings. Over the years these misgivings persisted, rising out of ignorance and suspicion of the languages, customs, and religions of the aliens, and also, more rationally, out of their poverty, which often made them seem, at least temporarily, a threat to the well-being of older inhabitants. Periodically, in bad times, anti-immigrant feeling mounted, and when these outbursts coincided with some danger to the national interest, real or presumed, they took on ultranationalistic overtones, producing such ugly incidents as the Alien and Sedition Acts of 1798 and the Know-Nothing movement of the 1850's.

For a decade after the Civil War, boom conditions attracted an average of 300,000 to 400,000 immigrants a year to the United States. The economic stagnation of the seventies reduced the flow, but the return of prosperity brought a still greater influx, well over 2.5 million in 1881–84. Actually, the foreign-born percentage of the population did not change significantly; all through the second half of the nineteenth century, about one person in seven in the country was foreign-born. However, the tendency of immigrants to settle in the cities and thus to be caught up in the dynamics of urbanization made them, by the mid-eighties, more noticeable. At the same time the sources of immigration were beginning to change. As late as 1880, the British Isles, Germany, and Scandinavia supplied nearly three-fourths of all immigrants; by 1890, their proportion was down to about 60 per cent. Concurrently, southern and eastern Europeans were becoming more important in the immigration statistics. In the seventies, about 45,000 Italians came to America, in the eighties nearly 270,000. Before 1872, Polish immigration had never approached 1,000 a year; in the eighties it averaged over 4,000, then rose to 11,000 in 1890 and 40,000 in 1892. Beginning in 1881, legal discriminations and violent persecution in Russia led masses of Russian Jews—over 200,000 in the next dozen years—to seek refuge in America.[43]

Not many people grasped the significance of this "new" immigration, which was still in its early stages in the eighties. Every immigrant must make painful adjustments: learning to bear the absence of relatives, friends, and familiar sights; mastering a new tongue and new customs; finding a place to live, a job; re-establishing the thousand ties that bind a man to his community. But these newcomers, wrenched from almost medievally primitive surroundings, often illiterate, and desperately poor, were especially unready for life in industrialized cities.[44] Their poverty, isolation, and rootlessness inspired the contempt of many Americans and gravely undermined their own self-confidence, further inhibiting their ability to adjust to their new surroundings. Jane Addams, a woman of great idealism and sensibility who saw the process from Hull House on Chicago's Halstead Street, wrote of "the pathetic stupidity of agricultural people crowded into city tenements."[45]

Had immigrants been able to stand aside even briefly to decide where to settle and to ready themselves for some particular line of work, they would have fared better and probably been more cordially received. Such a respite was denied them; they had no resources and were given no choice. The swirling urban crowd engulfed them. Sharpsters and confidence men dogged their first footsteps; cynical employers exploited their necessity. Hundreds were rounded up and marched off to break strikes and undercut established wage rates. (Money itself, to men accustomed to a barter economy, was a bewildering commodity.) Either in igno-

[43] Jones, *American Immigration*, pp. 40, 45; John Higham, *Strangers in the Land: Patterns of American Nativism, 1860–1925* (New Brunswick, 1955), pp. 3–4; *Historical Statistics of the United States, Colonial Times to 1957* (Washington, 1960), pp. 56–57; Rischin, *Promised City*, pp. 24–31, 270.

[44] Except for their ignorance of the English language, the southern and eastern Europeans were probably no more ill-prepared for American conditions than the poor Irish peasants who had flocked to the United States by the hundreds of thousands over the past four decades. But the society itself was more complicated and change was proceeding at a faster pace. T. N. Brown, *Irish-American Nationalism: 1870–1890* (New York, 1966), pp. 18–21.

[45] Higham, *Strangers in the Land*, pp. 64–65; Handlin, *Uprooted, passim*, esp. pp. 73, 79; Addams, *Hull-House*, p. 232.

rance or in panic—like placid stockyard sheep trailing the Judas goat or like herring huddling to escape the savage barracuda—they clotted together, finding a measure of security, but surrendering the best hope of swiftly improving their lot.

Thus distinct ethnic neighborhoods developed in most of the great cities. The southern end of Manhattan Island housed groups from every corner of the globe. Italians dominated the East Side, Irish the West, Jews the "landlocked" center.[46] Everywhere were pockets of Chinese, Poles, Greeks, Bohemians, and a dozen other nationalities. "A map of the city, colored to designate nationalities," Jacob Riis wrote in 1890, "would show more stripes than on the skin of a zebra, and more colors than any rainbow." In Chicago, the Near North Side was German, the Southwest Side Irish, the area along the south branch of the Chicago River Czech, the Northwest Side Polish, while the Jews clustered in a dense section in the heart of the city. In many neighborhoods of any great city of the 1880's, one could wander for blocks without hearing a word of English spoken.[47]

However, immigrants did not concentrate in particular neighborhoods entirely as a matter of choice. They settled in sections that were declining in attractiveness as residential areas either because they were being invaded by commercial enterprises or because shifts in taste or changing economic conditions made them less suitable for single-family and other low-density housing. Thus the newcomer, already in a psychologically and socially unstable state by virtue of the fact that he was a migrant, plunged into local communities that were themselves unstable. Local institutions which had been created to meet the needs of one type of person were often poorly adapted to serve those of quite different types. Schools, for example, quickly became overcrowded as neighborhoods became more densely settled. Teachers accustomed to working with native-born students had suddenly to deal with youngsters from strange cultural backgrounds, many totally ignorant of English. Textbooks

[46] "I have always wondered why so few Jewish boys learned to swim. With the Italians and the Irish holding the river beachheads, the Jews were landlocked." Harry Golden in his introduction to Hutchins Hapgood, *The Spirit of the Ghetto* (New York, 1965), p. viii.

[47] Handlin, *Uprooted*, pp. 64, 66–70; Charlotte Erickson, *American Industry and the European Immigrant* (Cambridge, Mass., 1957), pp. 88–105; Riis, *How the Other Half Lives*, p. 18; Pierce, *Chicago*, III, 22–38.

—entire curricula—failed to meet the practical needs of such students. Educators accepted their responsibility for "Americanizing" the immigrants, but adjusted their methods only slowly.[48] Not until the early years of the twentieth century did schools in immigrant districts begin to put proper stress on elementary instruction in English and on the simple training in hygiene and the household arts that peasant children in an urban environment required.[49]

The immigrant influx also disrupted neighborhood religious patterns. In general, middle-class Protestant populations were replaced by poor Jews and Catholics. The task of erecting churches and maintaining religious social services taxed the resources of these newcomers severely. While they struggled to provide religious facilities for themselves, the established, well-to-do Protestants either moved away or withdrew from participation in community affairs. Dozens of congregations abandoned lower Manhattan in the seventies and eighties. Everywhere, Samuel Lane Loomis claimed in 1886, city churches "stand idle and empty, or serve the purposes of trade, while the population about them grows ever denser." By the eighties a number of Protestant clergymen were, like Loomis, taking a revived interest in urban social problems, but the problems were increasing in number and complexity so rapidly that these earnest souls could not do much about them.[50]

---

[48] Although concerned primarily with the situation a decade or more later, Grace Abbott's *The Immigrant and the Community* (New York, 1917), contains an excellent discussion (pp. 221–246) of the problem of educating immigrant children.

[49] L. A. Cremin, *The Transformation of the School: Progressivism in American Education, 1876–1957* (New York, 1961), pp. 66–73; Handlin, *Uprooted*, pp. 244–248; Addams, *Hull-House*, pp. 253–255; Rischin, *Promised City*, pp. 100–102, 199–200; A. M. Shaw, "The True Character of the New York Public Schools," *World's Work*, VII (1903), 4204–4221. On the other hand, Catholic and Jewish immigrants, fearing that secular public education would undermine the faith of their children, made great sacrifices to maintain their own religious and parochial schools. One sad by-product of successful assimilation was the loss of contact between the immigrants and their children. See, for example, the testimony of the social worker David Blaustein in United States Industrial Commission, *Report*, XIV (Washington, 1901), 115.

[50] For a lucid discussion of the impact of urbanization on religion, see R. D. Cross's introduction to his collection of sources, *The Church and the City: 1865–1910* (Indianapolis, 1967), pp. xi–xlii. See also Loomis, *Modern Cities*, p. 83; A. I. Abell, *The Urban Impact on American Protestantism: 1865–1900* (Cambridge, Mass., 1943), pp. 3–8; H. F. May, *Protestant Churches and Industrial America* (New York, 1949), pp. 112–123. One reason for the growth of the Catholic Church was the fact that it did not have to depend entirely on the resources of local parishioners.

Poverty, bad housing, lack of necessary skills (including the language and knowledge of American ways), their insulation in ethnic enclaves, and the psychic distress resulting from these circumstances acted to slow the adjustment of immigrants to life in the United States and to convince many citizens that they could not be assimilated. Actually, the particular characteristics of the southern and eastern Europeans only exaggerated the difficulties of adjustment. Older immigrant strains had frequently tended to stick together and to preserve their European culture, as witness the clannishness of the Pennsylvania Dutch after generations of life in the United States, the efforts of the Catholic Irish to develop parochial schools, and the reluctance even of many English immigrants to become American citizens and abandon old habits and attitudes. Furthermore, prejudice against immigrants was as likely to develop out of their success in adapting as out of their failure. Boston's old-line families began to change their attitude toward the Irish in the eighties, for example, more because the Irish were taking over control of (and corrupting) local politics than because they were refusing to be "Americanized." The great increase in total immigration in the eighties and the concentration of so many newcomers in the cities, where social adjustment was difficult to begin with, merely focused attention upon the assimilation problem.[51]

Where poverty was most abject, slums most dirty and crowded, where disease and crime rates were rising—there immigrants were most numerous. Reformers who sincerely wished to help the urban poor, and who realized that most were victims rather than creators of their circumstances, nevertheless slipped into the habit of applying derogatory labels to national groups. In his passionate assault on slum conditions, *How the Other Half Lives* (1890), Jacob Riis glibly characterized the Irish as belligerent, the Italians as dirty, the Jews as grossly materialistic. He wrote of "the impulse that makes the Polish Jew coop himself up in his den with the thermometer at stewing heat," of the supposed fact that in the Italian quarter "the women do . . . all the work" while the men lounge "in the open doors of the saloons smoking black clay pipes, talking and gesticulating." As early as 1881, Senator Justin Morrill of Vermont was

51 B. M. Solomon, *Ancestors and Immigrants: A Changing New England Tradition* (Cambridge, Mass., 1956), pp. 43–53; Berthoff, *British Immigrants*, pp. 139, 143.

demanding that Congress keep out the "many vicious and inconvertible elements" among the "multitude of foreign immigrants" pouring into the country, and soon thereafter statisticians began calling attention to the high percentage of foreign-born and second-generation individuals among the nation's growing criminal population. "The great cities, which are our great crime centers, are also the great centers of our foreign population," one such writer pointed out in 1889.[52]

The restiveness of labor further stimulated anti-immigrant feeling. Once again, the conjunction of urbanization and immigration produced the association in men's minds more than actual immigrant behavior; a large proportion of wage workers were foreign-born and city dwellers, that was enough. Although immigrants were usually either conservative or apolitical, the handful of Marxists in America were mostly of foreign birth, and they congregated in the big cities, chiefly New York and Chicago. The Haymarket bombing thus roused a storm of xenophobia. "This horrible tyranny is wholly of foreign origin," a minister pontificated after the tragedy, while newspapers denounced the "scum and offal of Europe." There were perhaps two sides to the immigration question, a report of the Wisconsin Bureau of Labor and Industrial Statistics concluded in 1888, but on one subject there was "no room for debate." "The moguls, and generally the believers in, and followers of, socialism, confiscation, anarchy, disorder, violence and bomb-throwing, are the offspring of foreign countries."[53]

On the other hand, many critics attributed the corruption and inefficiency of city governments to the ignorance and indifference of immigrants. No one put the case more convincingly than James Bryce, his indictment appearing particularly damning because of his generally sympathetic attitude toward American political institutions. Immigrants, Bryce wrote, "follow blindly leaders of their own race, are not moved by discussion, exercise no judgment of their own." They "are not fit for the suffrage," he concluded. "They know nothing of the institutions of the country, of its statesmen, of its political issues."

[52] Riis, *How the Other Half Lives*, pp. 43, 45; W. M. F. Round, "Immigration and Crime," *Forum*, VIII (1889), 428–429.

[53] Higham, *Strangers in the Land*, pp. 138, 55; WBLS, *3rd Report* (Madison, 1888), p. xxvi.

There was more substance to this charge than to most raised against immigrants, for many came to America with no experience in representative government and with an ingrained distrust of all political authority. Language difficulties and the mere problem of survival also militated against the development of political awareness among them. James Russell Lowell, originally a warm supporter of the Irish, was shocked to observe an Irishman, gaping at a statue of George Washington in the Boston Public Garden, ask a companion who it was. Eventually Lowell came to the conclusion that the Irish would never make good citizens.[54]

Cynical politicians undoubtedly took advantage of the apathy and ignorance of immigrants to control elections. In the late eighties, over a third of the states allowed persons not yet naturalized to vote, and in others the fraudulent registration of aliens was common. Bryce personally saw "droves" of recent arrivals recorded on the voting lists in New York, and a carpenter in Janesville, Wisconsin, stated: "I knew men to take 35 of these new comers to the county clerk's office, get out their "papers" at 35 cts. per head, next take them to a saloon, give them a drink, take them to the polls to vote, while the crowd laughed over the matter, and that's the end."[55]

Confusion between cause and effect where urban immigrants were concerned produced much muddled thinking about immigrants among native-born Americans in the eighties, but no clear-cut conclusions emerged. After a detailed analysis of the 1890 census, the economist Francis A. Walker called attention to the shift in the sources of immigration to southern and eastern Europe, to "peoples that have the least possible adaptation to our political institutions and social life." Most contemporaries dismissed this as a passing phenomenon. Although a number of intellectuals were already arguing that "Anglo-Saxons" were a superior breed, only in the next decade did very many of them began to doubt that other, "inferior" races could be assimilated in the famous American melting pot. Even those who criticized immigrant behavior most

[54] Bryce, *American Commonwealth*, II, 367, 99; Handlin, *Uprooted*, pp. 201–209; Rischin, *Promised City*, pp. 221–222; Solomon, *Ancestors and Immigrants*, pp. 53–55.

[55] Bryce, *American Commonwealth*, I, 419 n.; II, 99; WBLS, *3rd Report*, p. 67; A. B. Callow, Jr., *The Tweed Ring* (New York, 1966), pp. 210–211.

sharply in the eighties usually qualified their attacks with such statements as: "No fair-minded man can be insensible of the debt we owe to immigration. . . . The national interest still demands that we shall give welcome to any element that shall increase useful citizenship."[56]

The tradition of America as a haven for all who sought liberty and opportunity remained strong. When the New York *World* organized a campaign in 1886 to raise $100,000 in small contributions for a pedestal for the Statue of Liberty, the symbol of America's hospitality to the world's underprivileged masses, thousands of individuals opened their meager purses and the sum was collected in a few months. Although wealthy manufacturers might blame the foreign-born for every current of radical thought and every sign of social instability, they were unready to deprive themselves of the cheap labor that immigration provided. Restrictionists, in the main, were men of good will, liberal by their own lights, who advocated checking the influx because it seemed the most humane way to deal with urban problems. Aside from the 1882 law suspending Chinese immigration for ten years, which contemporaries viewed as a completely separate question, and the Foran anti-contract-labor law of 1885, the only limitation imposed upon the admission of foreigners before 1917 was a measure barring convicts, lunatics, idiots, and persons likely to become public charges.[57]

And so the cities grew unchecked, hives of productive activity, vital, rich, and dynamic, but also monuments to waste, social disorganization, poverty, and vice. The process of urbanization, like that of industrialization, with which it was so intimately related, reflected the decisions and subsequent actions of millions of individuals. Hundreds of thousands of homes and tenements were built by independent contractors and paid for out of hard-earned private savings.[58] Private businessmen ran the cities' countless shops; pri-

---

[56] F. A. Walker, "Immigration and Degradation," *Forum,* XI (1891), 644; Higham, *Strangers in the Land,* pp. 136–139; Solomon, *Ancestors and Immigrants,* pp. 59–81; Round, "Immigration and Crime," p. 438.

[57] D. C. Seitz, *Joseph Pulitzer: His Life & Letters* (New York, 1924), pp. 156–158; Jones, *Immigration,* pp. 249–251.

[58] In Brooklyn, for example, enough new residences were constructed between 1881 and 1885 to house about 100,000 persons. Syrett, *Brooklyn,* p. 139. In the three districts of Boston studied by Sam B. Warner, Jr. (Roxbury, West Roxbury,

vate real estate interests subdivided fringe areas and laid out streets; private companies operated urban utilities and transportatin facilities. The creativity and labor of all these separate persons worked wonders, but also generated enormous amounts of social friction. This friction never persuaded any substantial proportion of the population to alter its behavior basically. Urbanization did, however, like industrialization, force people to give more thought to collective activity. The corporation and the labor union (both, of course, essentially urban institutions) were by no means the only associations that city dwellers formed in these years. All manner of business organizations—chambers of commerce, local associations of merchants and manufacturers—proliferated. Poverty and its attendant difficulties inspired a large number of philanthropic activities. By 1878, for example, Philadephia had over 800 charitable organizations. Large concentrations of people of comfortable means, as much a product of urban civilization as poverty, enabled such organizations to flourish, but their number and variety led to wasteful duplication and eventually to combination and co-operation. By 1882 there were twenty-two municipal charity organization societies in existence in cities with a total population of six million, and the trend toward rationalizing and co-ordinating charitable work continued through the decade. "Instead of a poor sectarianism of charitable effort, where petty societies work in the dark," the Reverend D. O. Kellogg wrote as early as 1880, "there should be a community of philanthropists in which the experience of one enriches them all."[59]

The strong religious overtones of urban charitable organizations

and Dorchester), 9,000 individual property owners put up 22,500 houses in the last thirty years of the century. Nearly all were "either men building houses for their own occupancy or small investors who built a house nearby their own residence in order to profit from the rents of one to three tenants." Although what Warner calls "the discipline of history and geography" affected the actions of these builders, "no legislation save the law of nuisance and a few primitive safety codes prevented [them] from doing anything they wanted to with their property." Warner, *Streetcar Suburbs*, p. 37. See also R. M. Fogelson, *The Fragmented Metropolis: Los Angeles, 1850–1930* (Cambridge, Mass., 1967), pp. 39–40.

[59] Schlesinger, *Rise of the City*, p. 350; Roy Lubove, *The Professional Altruist: The Emergence of Social Work as a Career, 1880–1930* (Cambridge, Mass., 1965), p. 2; D. O. Kellogg, "The Principle and Advantage of Association in Charities," American Social Science Association, *Journal*, XII (1880), 88.

tended to moderate as the years passed. Even the Salvation Army, which grew rapidly in the eighties, began late in the decade to supplement its evangelical, revivalistic exhortation of the down-trodden and the depraved with soup kitchens, lodginghouses, and employment bureaus. Gradually a more sociological and professional attitude toward the problems of poverty and the slums emerged, one well suited to the growing stress on organized relief.[60]

The most imaginative and useful of the new organizations were the settlement houses. These centers, modeled after Toynbee Hall in London, brought educated, comfortably-off individuals, mostly idealistic young college girls and recent graduates, to live in slum sections and help local residents to improve themselves and their environment. Each settlement was a combination home, school, and clubhouse. Classes were offered in subjects ranging from elementary English to the study of Shakespeare, from cooking and sewing to stenography and industrial skills. The houses often operated public baths; ran pawnshops, nursery schools, and savings institutions; organized art shows; and provided space for the meetings of labor unions and neighborhood social clubs. Resident workers ranged the district, getting to know the people and their problems, supplying advice, inspiration, and practical aid.

The movement was just beginning in the late eighties; its flowering came in the next decade. Among the first and most influential settlements were Hull House in Chicago (1889), brain child of Jane Addams, and Boston's South End House (1892), directed by Robert A. Woods. Theoretically settlement-house workers were trying to foster democracy and break down barriers between rich and poor. "The dependence of classes on each other is reciprocal," Miss Addams insisted. Immersed in their slum community, Hull House workers had a "genuine preference for residence in an industrial quarter" and were convinced that "the things which make men alike are finer and better than the things that keep them apart." As Woods explained it: "We gradually became acquainted with the people of the neighborhood, and are able to exercise influence on family life, and also on the general social life. . . .

---

60 Schlesinger, *Rise of the City*, p. 336; Lubove, *Professional Altruist*, pp. 10, 18–21.

These settlement houses are intended to be a kind of neutral ground between classes."

Of course, there was a romantic element in the settlement-house workers, capsulized, for example, in Jane Addams' description of a "renowned" college professor "sharing with a group of young men, on the East Side of New York, his ripest conclusions in philosophy" and being "much touched" by their "intelligent interest and absorbed devotion." But they had also a hardheaded, scientific quality; living and working with slum people, they came to understand their needs and their psychology. They developed many valuable programs; brought pressure to bear on municipal agencies for better schools, parks, and community services; collected useful social data. They demonstrated the importance both of firsthand knowledge and of organized effort in dealing with slum conditions and with immigrant populations, and were thus important forerunners of the professional social workers of the twentieth century.[61]

Other urban organizations sprang up during these years which were dedicated to beautifying the cities, improving recreational facilities, and raising the quality and efficiency of government. In hundreds of towns and cities, civic-minded residents founded improvement societies. Although Chicago's Citizens' Association, established in 1874, was one of the earliest, the big cities lagged for a time in organizing such bodies; in 1880, at least twenty-eight Massachusetts towns had societies of this type, but of nineteen Massachusetts cities only Boston had one. As the years passed, however, the improvement society became ubiquitous. "Their number is legion," Charles M. Robinson wrote in *The Improvement of Towns and Cities* (1901). Neighborhood conflicts and the patent advantages of co-operation led both to a national organization of interested city officials, the American Society of Municipal Improvements (1894), and to an association of private groups, the American League for Civic Improvement (1900).[62]

Every large city also had numbers of mixed social and civic

61 Jane Addams, "Hull House, Chicago: An Effort Toward Social Democracy," *Forum*, XIV (1892), 227–229, and *Hull-House*, pp. 89–91, 111–112; U.S. Industrial Commission, *Report*, XIV, 203.

62 Pierce, *Chicago*, III, 321–322; MBLS, *11th Report*, pp. 247, 257; Robinson, *Improvement of Cities*, pp. 255, 262, 273.

organizations established by immigrant groups,[63] along with tax-payers' associations and "good government" clubs. Although the major political parties had powerful machines in nearly every city and generally had matters pretty much to themselves, the number of organizations, some nominally Democratic or Republican, that strove for municipal improvement on nonpartisan lines was large and growing. By 1881, civil-service reformers had set up groups in New York, Brooklyn, Boston, Philadelphia, Cincinnati, Milwaukee, and San Francisco, while citizens in two dozen other cities were in the process of following their lead. A National Civil Service Reform League was founded in that year. Local civic groups designed to reform corrupt city governments were established during the eighties in Philadelphia, Boston, Cincinnati, New Orleans, Albany, and many other cities.[64]

"Private beneficence," Jane Addams concluded after very brief experience at Hull House, "is totally inadequate to deal with the vast numbers of the city's disinherited."[65] In philanthropic work and in many other areas of urban life, the trend toward government intervention and regulation, so noticeable in matters related to the economic changes of these years, was strong. The same principle—that complex interactions made centralized management essential—applied with special force in the cities, where so many people pursued such a great variety of complicated activities.

The question of government intervention in urban affairs was both controversial and fraught with practical difficulties. Since, as we have seen, no mere human could see a city whole, it was in a sense unreasonable to expect anyone to be able to give direction to urban development. Every intelligent contemporary felt the explosive strength that American cities were generating, and sensed that this vitality was a product of the creative energies of millions of separate individuals, each pursuing his own ends. No matter how appalling the waste and human misery that were equally apparent,

[63] City histories contain references to dozens of such organizations founded between 1870 and 1890. See, for example, Pierce, *Chicago*, III, 20–63.

[64] Ari Hoogenboom, *Outlawing the Spoils: A History of the Civil Service Reform Movement, 1865–1883* (Urbana, 1961), pp. 189, 211; F. W. Patton, *The Battle for Municipal Reform: Mobilization and Attack, 1875 to 1900* (Washington, 1940), pp. 29–31.

[65] Addams, *Hull-House*, p. 310.

sober men hesitated to tinker with this awe-inspiring social mechanism. The dynamic state of urban technology caused further misgivings. Should a city spend taxpayers' money to light its streets with gas, or with electricity? Granted that sewage and garbage problems were most pressing, exactly how ought they be tackled? The construction of adequate sewers in Los Angeles was delayed about five years by an argument between those who wished to drain the system into the Pacific and those who claimed that it was technologically and economically feasible to filter the outflow and use the water for irrigation. Implicit in the idea that a local government should assume responsibility for building a garbage-disposal plant was the assumption that experts could agree as to how garbage should be disposed of, yet this was not the case. In 1890, for example, Providence installed a plant for the chemical reduction of the city's garbage. It proved unsatisfactory, and after a few years the city returned to the crude but time-tested practice of allowing farmers to cart the garbage off to feed their swine.[66]

Medical knowledge was also in a state of flux. Public-health officials, battling to control contagious diseases, often disrupted the economic and social life of communities by their overly strict quarantine regulations and fumigation policies. Efforts to do something about high infant-mortality rates in poor districts ran into resistance from Darwinian evolutionists who argued that any attempt to reduce infant mortality might lead to the survival of too many "weaklings" and thus to racial degeneration. On the other hand, bacteriologists were exploding the filth theory of disease by showing that germs were not spontaneously generated, nor did they even thrive, in sewage or dirt. In 1890, after studying the incidence of contagious diseases in Providence tenements, Dr. Charles V. Chapin, city superintendent of health, concluded that there was "no causative relation between unsanitary conditions, as ordinarily understood, and scarlet fever, diphtheria and typhoid fever," and two years later Dr. William H. Welch of Johns Hopkins wrote boldly: "We may drink contaminated water, breathe impure air and live on a polluted soil without getting typhoid . . . or other contagious disease. These influences, . . . do not produce well defined diseases."[67] Medical men paid no serious attention to the survival-of-the-fittest argument and, when confronted by evidence that filth did not cause disease, they either pointed out that dirt and bad drainage ought to be eliminated simply as public nuisances or insisted that the filth theory was "a good thing" even if false.[68] But their tendency to alter their recommendations steadily as medical sophistication increased detracted from the force of their efforts to expand municipal public-health programs.

Beyond all these practical difficulties, honest doubts existed about the morality and justice of municipal regulation of activities that almost no one believed should be regulated on the state and national level. Was it fair to compel citizens with access to private wells to pay for the construction and upkeep of city reservoirs and mains? Should a landlord be deprived of income by making him cut down on the number of rental units in a given building in order to provide tenants with more light and space? Should he be forced to increase his expenses by installing new plumbing and connecting it with municipal sewers? Should owners of private water and utility companies be shorn of the right to invest their capital in such businesses?

No single answer was found for any of these questions during the period. A few extremists even argued that compulsory smallpox vaccination was a violation of the constitutional rights of individuals, but the trend was toward more government-operated facilities and stricter regulations. Providence's Dr. Chapin, a conservative by temperament and upbringing, reflected the predominant view when he wrote in 1889: "When 125,000 people are gathered together on 10 square miles of land they must of necessity give up certain of their liberties. It is the sacrifice they make for the sake of the advantages of city life." An enormous body of law was enacted by state and municipal governments, establishing administrative boards to operate and supervise water, garbage, and sewer systems

---

[67] *Ibid.*, p. 94; F. G. Davenport, "John Henry Rauch and Public Health in Illinois: 1877–1891," *Journal of the Illinois State Historical Society*, L (1957), 282–283, 289; Donald Fleming, *William H. Welch and the Rise of Modern Medicine* (Boston, 1954), pp. 139–140. It was of course true, as demonstrated by Chapin's careful epidemiological research, that when sewage was allowed to contaminate the water supply, the danger that diseases like typhoid would spread was very great. Cassedy, *Chapin*, pp. 53–54.

[68] Fleming, *Welch*, p. 141.

and to regulate other matters connected with public health, and creating elaborate codes dealing with plumbing installations, the abatement of nuisances, the control of disease, the design and safety of multiple dwellings, and other matters.[69]

An increasing number of cities built and operated their own public-utility systems. Although privately operated waterworks did not disappear, the larger cities, beginning with New York and Boston in the 1840's, gradually took over the function of supplying water to their residents. Between 1870 and 1890, the number of publicly owned water systems rose from 116 to 806; then it more than doubled in the next six years. By the end of the century, only nine of the nation's fifty largest cities still had privately owned waterworks. Publicly owned gas and electricity companies were far less numerous. Fewer than a dozen municipal gasworks existed in 1890, Philadelphia's being by far the most important.[70] There were many more publicly owned electric-light companies—about 50 in 1890 and over 350 by 1898—but except for the Chicago and Detroit systems, all were in relatively small communities.[71] Urban transportation remained almost entirely in private hands, and was, in general, very inadequately regulated. Seen in historical perspective, the pattern was one of compromise between private and public development of essential services, and probably this was both inevitable and desirable, given the enormity of the tasks. It was significant, however, that most contemporary students of urban affairs were advocating "municipal socialism," and buttressing their positions with detailed comparative studies of the costs and profits of public and private companies.[72]

The expansion of the functions of municipal government was also handicapped by socioeconomic cleavages which were themselves

[69] Davenport, "Rauch and Public Health," pp. 287–8; Cassedy, *Chapin*, p. 41; Chapin, *Municipal Sanitation*, *passim*.

[70] E. W. Bemis (ed.), *Municipal Monopolies* (New York, 1899), pp. 15–27, 602–607; American Economic Association, *Publications*, II (1888), 523. The other substantial cities with publicly owned gas companies in 1890 were Richmond, Wheeling, and Toledo. Bemis, *Municipal Monopolies*, pp. 607–615.

[71] Bemis, *Municipal Monopolies*, pp. 186–206; Pierce, *Chicago*, III, 331. Chicago established its system in 1887, Detroit in 1895.

[72] M. N. Baker, "Water-Works" in Bemis, *Municipal Monopolies*, pp. 50–52; J. R. Commons, "Municipal Electric Lighting," *ibid.*, pp. 55–180; E. J. James, "The Relation of the Modern Municipality to the Gas Supply," American Economic Association, *Publications*, I (1886), 53–198.

a product of urbanization. As mere creatures of the states, cities were subject to the control of state legislatures, usually rural-dominated. The conflict between city and countryside, part based on genuine economic issues, part on rural prejudices, tended to be resolved in favor of the latter. Within the cities, power struggles between well-to-do and middle-class groups and the poorer elements, largely recently arrived immigrants, also hampered the orderly solution of problems. Economic clashes over such matters as the apportionment of tax burdens were exacerbated by ethnic rivalries and class prejudices. The movement of middle-class citizens to the suburbs deprived the cities of many potential leaders, while those who remained, appalled by the way cynical politicians manipulated the immigrant masses, tended to abjure all participation in local government. When Theodore Roosevelt first interested himself in New York City politics in 1880, his friends told him "that politics were 'low'; that the organizations were not controlled by 'gentlemen' . . . that the men I met would be rough and brutal and unpleasant to deal with." Andrew D. White, former president of Cornell University, characterized municipal officeholders of 1890 as "men who in no other country would think of aspiring to such positions," adding that some "would think themselves lucky in keeping outside the prisons."[73]

The complaints of well-meaning contemporaries are too numerous to be dismissed lightly, but the sordid condition of most local governments resulted to a great extent from a loss of contact between the middle class and the poor that was largely the responsibility of the former group. White, for example, had many intelligent things to say about urban politics. He deplored the extent to which national party alignments influenced the settlement of municipal issues. A city was a corporation; it should be "managed as a piece of property," not as a political unit. He wished to abolish the ward system of neighborhood representation in urban government in order to eliminate petty bickering and logrolling, and to encourage elected officials to take a broad approach to city problems. But his proposals were also designed to weaken the influence of poorer districts. Rule by "a city proletariat mob" must be avoided.

[73] Patton, *Municipal Reform*, pp. 16–17; Herman Hagedorn (ed.), *The Works of Theodore Roosevelt* (20 vols., New York, 1926), XX, 59; A. D. White, "The Government of American Cities," *Forum*, X (1890), 358.

As presently constituted, he insisted, "a crowd of illiterate peasants, freshly raked in from Irish bogs, or Bohemian mines, or Italian robber nests, may exercise virtual control." White's denunciation of American city government as "the worst in Christendom" has to be evaluated in the light of this prejudice.[74] Generalizing about the middle-class urban reformers of a slightly later period, the historian Samuel P. Hays concluded that they "proclaimed an ideology of a popular upheaval against a selfish few [while] they were in practice shaping the structure of municipal government so that political power would no longer be broadly distributed." In a very real sense, the attacks of middle-class city dwellers on the "extravagance, corruption, and mismanagement" (the words are Bryce's) of municipal government were self-serving rationalizations designed to aid them in their struggle for power against the lower-class majority.[75]

From the early seventies, when William Marcy Tweed and his henchmen ruled over the government of New York, to the end of the century and beyond, crooked political machines did dominate most of the large American cities and many of the lesser ones as well. The boss system, according to one student, was merely "experimental" in the immediate post-Civil War years, but by 1890 it had developed into "a fine technique." Cynical politicos stole directly from city treasuries and sold favors to utility companies seeking franchises on a grand scale. They manipulated ignorant immigrant voters and exacted tribute from the panderers of every vice (drunkenness, gambling, gangsterism, prostitution, and so on)

[74] *Ibid.*, pp. 357–372. Neither White's suggestions nor his prejudices were in any sense original. In 1877, a New York commission headed by William M. Evarts called the interjection of national politics into city affairs an "obstacle . . . [which] paralyzes all ordinary efforts for good municipal government" and denounced the control of city affairs by state legislatures. In 1888, Seth Low, former mayor of Brooklyn, wrote: "Charters were framed as though cities were little states. Americans are only now learning, after many years of bitter experience, that they are not so much little states as large corporations." Low and other experts, such as James Bryce, also displayed strong prejudices against immigrants. Bryce, *American Commonwealth*, I, 615, 640–641, 655. The period 1890–1915 saw this line of argument at its peak of influence. W. S. Sayre and N. W. Polsby, "American Political Science and the Study of Urbanization," in P. M. Hauser and L. F. Schnore (eds.) , *The Study of Urbanization* (New York, 1965) , pp. 121–123.

[75] S. P. Hays, "The Politics of Reform in Municipal Government in the Progressive Era," *Pacific Northwest Quarterly*, LV (1964) , 167; R. C. Wade, "The City in History—Some American Perspectives," in Hirsch, *Urban Life and Form*, p. 72; Bryce, *American Commonwealth*, I, 637.

that urban poverty fostered. By their control of hundreds of petty offices, they marshaled armies of voters and then cemented their power by stuffing ballot boxes and falsifying returns.[76]

However, the strength of the bosses was not based entirely upon force and venality; to the slum dweller and especially to the recent immigrant, machine politicians often seemed the only persons in the community who took a positive interest in their plight. The bosses were not dictators. They earned the loyalty of their constituents; they did not simply overawe or intimidate them. They found them jobs as petty city officials and as employees of corporations and small businesses beholden to the machine for favors. They also supplied handouts for the destitute and small gifts for those faced with sudden need. They ran picnics for slum children on hot summer holidays, contributed to dozens of worthy local causes. They mediated between bewildered new immigrants and the harsh impersonalities of the law. Perhaps most important of all, they gave the slum dweller a certain sense of power, the dignity of knowing that he counted, that at least his vote was worth something.

Reformers were appalled to discover that "King" James McManes of Philadelphia controlled the appointments of over 5,600 city employees, but to these employees, along with their families and friends, McManes was a public benefactor—that he accumulated a large personal fortune by shady means alarmed them not at all. When, in the 1890's, Chicago reformers tried to defeat a corrupt alderman in a slum district, they ran into opposition not only from important corporations but also from streetcar conductors, telephone operators, peddlers, and other persons who had obtained jobs, licenses, and a variety of favors from the culprit. These people considered the reformers, not the alderman, a threat to civic stability. Although the recent tendency to romanticize the city boss as a tribune of the common people distorts his motivation, it does more than a little justice to his function.[77]

By the early 1890's, the course of American urban development

---

76 Patton, *Municipal Reform*, pp. 7–13, 18–24.

77 Handlin, *Uprooted*, pp. 212–213; Harold Zink, *City Bosses in the United States: A Study of Twenty Municipal Bosses* (Durham, 1930), pp. 194–201; Addams, *Hull-House*, pp. 315–317; Callow, *Tweed Ring*, pp. 152–160; Brown, *Irish-American Nationalism*, p. 146. For an exceptionally well-balanced contemporary analysis of the role of the boss, see the testimony of Robert A. Woods in U.S. Industrial Commission, *Report*, XIV, 199–200.

for the next half century had been charted. The pace of urban growth did not slacken thereafter, nor did the forces causing that growth change substantially. Cities continued to attract the most talented and wealthy, and also the most underprivileged, to foster both the highest arts and the lowest vices, to be laboratories where new social, economic, and political theories were tested and new tools invented, and where new monuments to man's cultural creativity were produced. Americans continued to grapple with the same urban problems and to profit from the same advantages of city life, and they applied, in many cases more effectively to be sure, and with a good deal less hesitation, techniques of social organization and control that had been suggested and tentatively employed during the so-called Gilded Age.

CHAPTER 6

The Political System

STUDENTS of late-nineteenth-century American political institutions are fortunate in being able to draw upon the observations and insights of four uncommonly knowledgeable contemporary observers: James Bryce, Moisei Ostrogorski, Woodrow Wilson, and Henry Jones Ford. Bryce, a brilliant Scotsman, visited the United States in 1870 and again in 1881 and 1883. He traveled all over the country, talked to hundreds of people, mastered the details of ten state constitutions as well as the federal Constitution, and conducted a voluminous correspondence with intelligent and highly placed American friends. Bryce's *American Commonwealth* (1888) gained immediate recognition as a classic comparable to Alexis de Tocqueville's *Democracy in America*.[1]

Ostrogorski, a Russian trained in law at St. Petersburg and in political science at the *Ecole des Sciences Politiques* in Paris, also visited extensively in the United States in the eighties and nineties, his researches culminating in his book *Democracy and the Organization of Political Parties* (1902). Wilson, a former lawyer turned scholar, was a graduate student at Johns Hopkins in the early eighties. Believing his personal political ambitions to have been hopelessly frustrated, he concentrated his powerful energies on study, producing a remarkable doctoral dissertation, *Congressional Government*, which was published in 1885. Ford was a newspaperman of long experience with the workings of practical politics, having served as an editorial writer for the New York *Sun*, as city

[1] H. A. L. Fisher, *James Bryce* (2 vols., New York, 1927), I, 136–137, 223–239.

editor of the Baltimore *Sun,* and as managing editor of two Pittsburgh papers. His *Rise and Growth of American Politics* (1898) was in some ways the most perceptive of all these remarkable works.[2]

While these writers differed in many of their interpretations, all were critical of current practical politics. "The conditions of public life in this country," wrote Wilson, "are not what they were in the early years of the federal government; they are not what they were even twenty years ago. . . . Since the war . . . we . . . are perplexed at finding ourselves denied a new order of statesmanship to suit the altered conditions of government." Jones complained that "a remarkable nonchalance underlies the sound and fury of partisan politics."[3] "Congress," Ostrogorski concluded, "does not solve the problems, the solution of which is demanded by the life of the nation. . . . The constituted authorities are unequal to their duty; they prove incapable of ensuring the protection of the general interest." And Bryce attacked American political leaders for "clinging too long to outworn issues and . . . neglecting to discover and work out new principles capable of solving the problems which now perplex the country."[4]

These political scientists, and many other close observers of post-Civil War politics, also held a very low opinion of most contemporary statesmen, local, state, and national. An English visitor to a New England women's college provoked only laughter when he asked politely: "I suppose you have a good many young ladies here belonging to the best families, daughters of members of Congress and so forth?" A college professor wrote in 1886: "Not only do men of ability and energy refuse to consider a public position as desirable for themselves, but they regard with supercilious condescension one who is willing to assume public office in a municipality." Bryce concluded that " 'politician' is a term of reproach." He once asked a

[2] "Moisey Yakovelich Ostrogorsky," *Encyclopedia of the Social Sciences,* XI, 503–504; A. S. Link, *Wilson: Road to the White House* (Princeton, 1947), pp. 11–13; "Henry Jones Ford," *Dictionary of American Biography,* VI, 515.

[3] Woodrow Wilson, *Congressional Government* (New York, 1956), pp. 136, 140; H. J. Ford, *The Rise and Growth of American Politics: A Sketch of Constitutional Development* (New York, 1911), p. 304.

[4] S. M. Lipset (ed.), M. Y. Ostrogorski, *Democracy and the Organization of Political Parties* (Garden City, 1964), II, 281, 283; James Bryce, *The American Commonwealth* (2 vols., New York, 1895), II, 28.

casual acquaintance to try to account for a particularly flagrant example of political jobbery. "Why," the man replied, "what can you expect from the politicians?" Ostrogorski observed that "ideas, convictions, character, disqualify a man from public life," and the contemporary literature is full of similar disparaging remarks.[5]

Citizens constantly complained that elected officials refused to stand for principles. "I . . . write this letter," an angry railroad executive told Congressman James A. Garfield in 1875, "simply to express my utter disgust with the character of a Congress, that can flippantly throw aside the proper business of the people to engage in demoralizing [partisan] warfare." In 1882 a young Massachusetts Democrat, William E. Russell, pleaded with his father, a prominent leader of the party, for a program based on "respectable" principles. "I hope whatever resolutions the [state] convention adopts, they will be plain and outspoken; don't let it leave us any longer crying in the wilderness, and wondering why the devil we are Democrats anyway." His plea went unheeded. The next year a trade-union leader complained of the "foolishness that the Republican party, and the Democratic party too, have been indulging in for the past eight years" and demanded that they both "take up some live issue instead of raking over the dead ashes of the past."[6]

Throughout the era, voters gave few solid mandates either to parties or individuals. Between Grant and McKinley, no President won a re-endorsement from the public after his four years in office; none even won a majority of the popular vote. Rutherford B. Hayes owed his election in 1876 to the rankest kind of jobbery; his Democratic opponent, Samuel J. Tilden, actually received 250,000 more popular votes. In 1880, James A. Garfield's margin over the Democrat Winfield Scott Hancock was only 7,368; he got 48.31 per cent of the popular vote to Hancock's 48.23 per cent. Cleveland defeated the Republican James G. Blaine in 1884 by 63,000 votes, his total amounting to less than 49 per cent of all the votes cast. When Benjamin Harrison won over Cleveland four years later, he

5 Bryce, *American Commonwealth*, I, 201 n.; II, 66; H. C. Adams, "Relation of the State to Industrial Action," American Economic Association, *Publications*, I (1887), 536; Ostrogorski, *Democracy and Political Parties*, II, 289.

6 T. C. Cochran, *Railroad Leaders* (Cambridge, Mass., 1953), p. 469; Geoffrey Blodgett, *The Gentle Reformers: Massachusetts Democrats in the Cleveland Era* (Cambridge, Mass., 1966), pp. 13–14; U.S. Senate, *Report on . . . Labor and Capital* (Washington, 1885), I, 614. See also Ford, *American Politics*, p. 308.

received 96,000 *fewer* votes than his opponent, and even in Cleveland's "sweep" of 1892 (he defeated Harrison by 360,000) he failed to obtain a popular majority, for James B. Weaver, the Populist party candidate, attracted over a million supporters.

Party majorities in both houses of Congress were usually paper thin and fluctuated repeatedly. The Democrats won control of the House of Representatives in 1874, lost it in 1880, regained it in 1882, lost it in 1888, won it again in 1890. The Republicans held the Senate throughout the period except for 1879–81, but between 1876 and 1890 they commanded a majority of more than three for only two years. No President during this era had a majority of his own party in both houses of Congress for his full term. The turnover in Congress, particularly in the lower house, was enormous. Wilson pointed out in *Congressional Government* that "a man who has served a dozen terms in Congress is a curiosity," but this statement minimizes the precariousness of the average congressman's tenure. In many Congresses, a majority of the representatives were first-termers. During this period the Ohio delegation in the House consisted of twenty-one members. In the 48th Congress, elected in 1882, only ten of the twenty-one had served in the previous session, and only four of the ten were re-elected in 1884 to the 49th Congress. Only eleven Ohioans in the 49th won seats in the 50th. Thirteen members from Ohio were re-elected to the 51st Congress, but only five of the new delegation survived the overturn of 1890. The situation in many other states was equally unstable.[7]

Tactically, the parties relied heavily upon noise, histrionics, and other primitive techniques for influencing public opinion. Although they distributed campaign documents by the millions of copies in every important election, the spoken word was universally regarded as the most effective weapon in the war to win votes. All the prominent leaders were in great demand, and in close contests popular spellbinders were imported from all over the country in an effort to sway the electorate. Some contributed their services; others collected fees of from $50 to $150 for each speech. In the 1880

[7] *Historical Statistics of the United States: Colonial Times to 1957* (Washington, 1960), pp. 688, 691; Wilson, *Congressional Government*, p. 171; Ford, *American Politics*, p. 241; *Biographical Directory of the American Congress: 1774–1949* (Washington, 1950), pp. 374, 384, 394, 404, 415, 426. "A member of the House can seldom feel safe in the saddle," Bryce noted. *American Commonwealth*, I, 195.

presidential election, the Democratic National Committee paid George W. Julian, a former Republican popular among independent voters, $1,500 plus expenses for his services as a kind of trouble-shooter over a period of two and a half months. Experienced politicians claimed to be able to judge the trend of public opinion by observing the size and enthusiasm of the crowds that orators attracted, and campaign strategists devoted much effort to the planning and management of political rallies, providing bands, special uniforms, badges, torches, and other paraphernalia for parades.

The sums necessary to support these activities, small by modern standards, were obtained by assessing candidates and officeholders and by dunning wealthy party members. Corruption was far from uncommon. Ethical standards were flexible. In the 1880 presidential campaign, for example, Norvil Green of Western Union allowed his cousin William H. English, the Democratic candidate for Vice-President, to send telegrams free, purely because of their relationship.[8]

Apparently few persons were either bored by the meaningless hoopla of the campaigns or repelled by the shady tactics of the campaigners. A substantially larger proportion of the total population voted in every presidential election than at any earlier period, and (still more curious) a larger proportion than voted during the Progressive era, when important issues were clearly at stake. The public seems to have looked upon politics as a kind of national game or spectacle, like baseball, the statesmen being the players, the voters the fans in the bleachers. Political oratory, Bryce remarked, was "not directed towards instruction, but towards stimulation."[9]

Traditionally, this extraordinary political situation has been explained by reference to the newness and complexity of the social and economic problems of the era. "The government was like a ship on a sea dominated by powerful submarine currents," Allan Nevins has written. "The pilots looked to wind, wave, and tide, and made sail by surface indications; and all the while their craft was being hurried on by forces they could neither understand nor calcu-

---

[8] A. V. House, "The Democratic State Central Committee of Indiana in 1880," *Indiana Magazine of History*, LVIII (1962) , 179–210.

[9] Bryce, *American Commonwealth*, II, 287. In every presidential election from 1876 to 1892, between 18 and 19 per cent of the total population voted. Under 15 per cent voted in 1868 and 15.4 per cent in 1912. *Hist. Stat.*, pp. 7, 688.

late."[10] Unable fully to understand the changes taking place, voters and office-seekers concealed their uncertainties and obscure fears by focusing on less challenging questions, by applying stale formulas mindlessly, by repeating past patterns, by concentrating on style rather than performance. Probably, the argument runs, the public's fascination with politics reflected a vague, unconscious awareness that government must eventually provide solutions to the problems of the day. Lacking a clear grasp of how to proceed, men compensated for their ignorance by increasing their commitment to political activity.

The more meaningless the activity, the better, or at least the safer. By the late seventies there was much evidence to suggest that the vaunted American democratic system was collapsing. First the South had refused to abide by majority rule after the election of Lincoln in 1860 and had seceded from the Union. Then, during the Civil War, the civil rights of dissenters had been seriously compromised. Reconstruction had been a conspicuously unsuccessful effort to resolve differences by discussion and compromise; however noble their objectives, northern leaders had imposed their will on the South by military force, had manipulated southern puppet governments, and had tried to remove a President of the United States by impeachment on trumped-up charges. Under the bumbling, complaisant U. S. Grant, the government had sunk into a moral quagmire, becoming more corrupt, probably, than in any period before or since, so despicable that a cabinet officer could say in 1869, when discussing executive-legislative relations: "You can't use tact with a Congressman! A Congressman is a hog! You must take a stick and hit him on the snout!"[11]

Finally, in the presidential election of 1876, the system stumbled to the verge of total collapse. For months after the balloting, politicians schemed, deliberately falsifying returns and seeking to buy the electoral votes of the disputed states, and angry citizens talked of taking up arms to settle the dispute. The resolution of this crisis, in one sense only another sordid transaction, marked a kind of desperate effort to save the federal system by emasculating it. For a long season thereafter, Americans shied away from seeking political solutions for serious problems; having lost confidence in the efficacy

---

[10] Allan Nevins, *Grover Cleveland: A Study in Courage* (New York, 1932), p. 341.

[11] Henry Adams, *The Education of Henry Adams* (Boston, 1918), p. 261.

of democratic government without abandoning their faith in democracy, they preserved, even accentuated, their interest in politics,
but confined their activities in this field to subjects that did not
really matter.

Recent studies of voting behavior suggest a somewhat different
explanation for the character of post-Reconstruction politics. American parties have always been made up of coalitions of groups with
divergent and partially conflicting interests. Since the party in
power, by virtue of its control of the government, has to make
policy decisions, it tends to alienate some of its sympathizers, thus
driving them into the arms of its opponents. On the other hand,
most voters habitually align themselves with a particular party
without much regard for men or measures. They alter their allegiance, once formed, very reluctantly. Sudden shifts in party popularity have occurred only when an especially attractive candidate, in
practice usually a military hero with little or no previous political
experience, has run for President. Long-range changes in party
dominance have taken place when epochal events favoring one
party have influenced masses of new voters (young people and
immigrants) to make their first commitment to that organization.

Neither of these circumstances prevailed during the period 1876–
90. The parties, closely balanced, hesitated to take clear positions
on controversial questions lest by so doing they destroy the precarious balance of power. New voters found no compelling reason
not to identify with the party of their parents or, in the case of
immigrants, with the party that their local compatriots appeared to
prefer. These conditions produced "the most spectacular degree of
equilibrium in American history." Control of Congress and the
White House shifted back and forth, not because of drastic altera-
tions in voter opinion, but because the balance between the parties
was so delicate that minor changes and chance events easily tipped
it one way or the other.[12]

This analysis must remain speculative, but it offers a convincing
explanation of why, when politics seemed so unrelated to the
important problems of the day and when a political career was both

12 Charles Sellers, "The Equilibrium Cycle in Two-Party Politics," *Public
Opinion Quarterly*, XXIX (1965), 16–38. See also D. E. Stokes and G. R. Iverson,
"On the Existence of Forces Restoring Party Competition," *ibid.*, XXVI (1962),
159–171, and P. E. Converse *et al.*, *The American Voter* (New York, 1960).

a precarious and (except at the highest levels) an unprestigious livelihood, elections were fiercely contested and offices eagerly sought, and why public interest in politics remained intense. Great prizes were in easy reach, yet none dared to strike out after them boldly. Corruption was more common than courage, deviousness than candor.

Whatever the explanation of the state of politics, the federal government was to all appearances in a parlous condition. Nowhere was this more obvious than in the executive branch, even in the office of the Presidency itself. The post once held by Washington, Jefferson, Jackson, and Lincoln seemed in the 1870's and 1880's of only minor importance. Ostrogorski commented on "the shrinkage undergone by the presidential office." The President had become, he wrote, simply a party leader, and that chiefly in name. "He was not at liberty to assert his initiative, to give the party a policy, to form comprehensive designs and far-reaching plans." So ineffective were all the inhabitants of the White House in these years that many observers, forgetting how the great Presidents of the past had used their powers, tended to dismiss the office as a mere ceremonial one, if not as a sinecure. Wilson, who wished to see the United States adopt a parliamentary system headed by a prime minister, argued that the President was "part of the official rather than of the political machinery of the government." Since "the business of the President . . . is usually not much above routine," he wrote, the office might "not inconveniently" be made purely administrative, the occupant a sort of tenured civil servant.

Bryce did not fall so completely under the spell of the contemporary situation in his analysis of the Presidency. He recognized that it was a "great office"; that the incumbent's position as representative of the whole nation, as commander in chief of the Army, and as chief administrative officer of the government gave him enormous potential authority. Bryce also understood the positive as well as the negative significance of the veto power. His comments nevertheless reflect the low state of the office. He remarked that a President was "hampered at every turn by the necessity of humouring his party" and was "so much engrossed by the trivial and mechanical parts of his work as to have little leisure for framing large schemes of policy." He even claimed that Presidents had less influence on legislation than the Speaker of the House of Representatives. "The domestic authority of the President is in time of peace small," he wrote, and he devoted a now-famous chapter to the subject: "Why Great Men Are Not Chosen Presidents."[13]

The decline of the Presidency in this period was not significantly related to the quality of the men who held the office. All were vigorous, intelligent, capable, and public-spirited, certainly up to the average of other inhabitants of the White House as individuals, if not in their presidential achievements. Hayes, Garfield, and Harrison had served with real distinction in the Union Army. Hayes had been a successful three-term governor of Ohio; Garfield represented that state continuously in the House of Representatives from 1863 to 1881 and had become a leader among Republican members. Cleveland's integrity and courage were legendary in his own lifetime; his service as mayor of Buffalo and as governor of New York won him the support of reformers and of conservative businessmen alike. Harrison benefited from being the scion of a famous family—his grandfather had been President of the United States, his great-grandfather a signer of the Declaration of Independence—but he was also an excellent lawyer. Even Chester A. Arthur, although known before he became President as an unblushing machine politician, had proved himself an exceptionally fine administrator, both as a Civil War quartermaster general and as head of the huge New York Customs House.[14]

All were also hard-working, honest, patriotic public servants. When Hayes enlisted in the Army in 1861, he wrote in his diary that he would have done so even if he knew he was going to be killed, because the conflict was " a just and necessary war." Garfield possessed a great capacity for work and a highly developed sense of duty. Of his labors as chairman of the House Appropriations Committee, he wrote: "If I find out where every dollar goes, and how it is used, I shall understand the apparatus thoroughly, and know if there are useless or defective parts." A newspaperman of much political experience called Arthur "a man of surpassing sweetness and grace." Cleveland demonstrated repeatedly during his pre-presidential career that he placed adherence to principle above personal advancement, while Harrison's fairness and devotion to

13 Ostrogorski, *Democracy and Political Parties*, p. 279; Wilson, *Congressional Government*, p. 170; Bryce, *American Commonwealth*, I, 45, 54–59, 65, 78–85, 225.

14 For the careers of the Presidents, see the Bibliography, pp. 348–349.

the public interest are well-illustrated by his role in the railroad strike of 1877. "Everybody respects Harrison's ability and integrity," William S. Holman, an Indiana congressman, admitted in an otherwise unfavorable estimate of the man.[15]

How, then, to account for the weakness of the Presidency during the tenure of these men? The argument that the impeachment of Andrew Johnson had shifted the balance of power in the direction of Congress cannot be dismissed, nor can the fact that Johnson's successor, Grant, deferred to Congress on many matters, such as appointments and the framing of legislation, that stronger Presidents had sought to control, or at least influence. The Chief Executives after 1877 were in a position somewhat like that of George III in 1760, when he assumed the throne after his ancestors had allowed the royal prerogative to be chipped away by Parliament for nearly half a century. When Garfield crossed Senator Roscoe Conkling of New York over a political appointment in 1881, Conkling burst in on him unannounced and launched into an hour-long tirade. Garfield was tempted to order him out of his presence, but he did not do so. Conkling was a more than ordinarily arrogant man, Garfield one who, as Hayes put it, "could not face a frowning world," and Garfield did hold his ground and win the fight over the appointment. But that any senator could behave toward any President as Conkling did toward Garfield reflected the relatively low state of presidential prestige at the time.[16]

These Presidents were also hampered by the prevailing belief that they should not meddle in legislative affairs; that they should *execute* the laws, not make them. This was a traditionally Republican philosophy, inherited from the Whigs, who had devised it to cope with what they considered the "executive usurpation" of Andrew Jackson. Even a "strong" Republican President like Lincoln adhered to it where matters unconnected with the national

---

[15] Harry Barnard, *Rutherford B. Hayes and His America* (Indianapolis, 1954), p. 214; L. D. White, *The Republican Era, 1869–1901: A Study in Administrative History* (New York, 1958), pp. 63–64; Henry Watterson, *"Marse Henry": An Autobiography* (2 vols., New York, 1919), II, 103; Frances Carpenter (ed.), *Carp's Washington* (New York, 1960), p. 305.

[16] White, *Republican Era*, pp. 23–24; E. B. Andrews, *The History of the Last Quarter-Century in the United States* (2 vols. New York, 1896), I, 323; G. F. Hoar, *Autobiography of Seventy Years* (2 vols., New York, 1903), II, 57; J. B. Foraker, *Notes of a Busy Life* (2 vols., Cincinnati, 1917), I, 424.

emergency of the Civil War were concerned. Hayes accepted this theory, and although in practice he often battled stubbornly with Congress, his position was largely defensive—he contested what he called Congress' "revolutionary and unconstitutional" efforts to cut down further on his authority, but he did not try to extend the sphere of presidential power.[17] None of Hayes's immediate successors behaved very differently; they resisted congressional bullying, and gradually won back control over appointments wrested from Johnson and Grant, yet seldom took the initiative in legislative matters. Even Cleveland, the one Democratic President of the period, took a narrow view of presidential power. "It don't look as though Congress was very well prepared to do anything, but maybe it will get into shape," he wrote a friend in December, 1885. "If a botch is made at the other end of the Avenue, I don't mean to be a party to it." And shortly thereafter he told reporters: "The most important benefit that I can confer on the country by my Presidency is to insist upon the entire independence of the executive and legislative branches of government."[18]

These Presidents all lacked personal qualities of leadership that an effective Chief Executive must have. Hayes was moody and cautious, Garfield too eager to please everyone, Arthur unaggressive, Cleveland stubborn and negative, Harrison so reserved as to win the nickname, "the human iceberg." However, in other times men equally colorless or meek have risen to the occasion and become powerful Presidents. While the personal element cannot be ignored, mere chance alone did not deprive the nation of strong executive leadership. At least as important were the close party divisions of the period; no President could command majorities in both houses for long enough to fashion and push through a

---

[17] David Donald, *Lincoln Reconsidered* (New York, 1961), pp. 187–208; White, *Republican Era*, p. 25; T. H. Williams (ed.), *Hayes: The Diary of a President, 1875–1881* (New York, 1964), p. 208. "While the administration of Hayes is something of a landmark in the history of the presidency, it is because of a successful defense and not because of any great constructive accomplishment in the character of the office." W. E. Binkley, *President and Congress* (New York, 1962), pp. 214–215.

[18] Allan Nevins (ed.), *The Letters of Grover Cleveland: 1850–1908* (Boston, 1933), p. 98; H. S. Merrill, *Bourbon Leader: Grover Cleveland and the Democratic Party* (Boston, 1957), p. 113. Harrison took an even narrower view of executive power vis à vis Congress. Binkley, *President and Congress*, pp. 221–223.

program. The party organizations lacked conherence; they could not discipline individual legislators. As Senator George F. Hoar wrote, referring to his colleagues in 1877, each important senator "kept his own orbit and shone in his sphere, within which he tolerated no intrusion from the President or from anybody else."[19]

Congress in this era was powerful, but not particularly distinguished, either in the opinion of contemporaries or in the perspective of history. "No high qualities of statesmanship are expected from a Congressman," Bryce noted, and many persons, including some of its members, commented on the decline of the Senate from the days of Webster, Clay, and Calhoun. Stories of congressional corruption were legion. Bryce estimated that 5 per cent of the members of Congress took bribes and that another 15 per cent were what today would be called influence peddlers. Henry Adams placed the number of the openly corrupt at 10 per cent. Collis P. Huntington, president of the Southern Pacific Railroad, divided the members of the Senate in 1876 into three groups: the "clean" (who would do what he wanted without asking for favors), the "commercial" (who would do the right thing if paid for it), and the "communists" (who resisted both his logic and his money).[20]

Although there were undoubtedly a number of legislators who were crooked by any standard and others, such as James G. Blaine, whose careers were injured by revelations of unethical, if not actually criminal, behavior, these estimates distort the state of congressional morality considerably. But so do such protestations of congressional purity as that offered in 1883 by Senator Henry W. Blair of New Hampshire, who said: "I have never known a single

[19] White, *Republican Era*, p. 42; Hoar, *Autobiography*, II, 46; D. J. Rothman, *Politics and Power: The United States Senate, 1869–1901* (Cambridge, Mass., 1966), p. 4. It is no mere coincidence that when the party deadlock was broken in the mid-nineties, Presidents began to appear much more powerful. Writing in 1898, Henry Jones Ford gave full recognition to the power of the office, describing it as "the organ of the will of the nation," a kind of "elective kingship." Ford called the President a "national boss." He was even able to discover examples of strong presidential leadership in the seventies and eighties, but he was of course unable to show that these Presidents had exercised their power consistently or with any sustained effect. Ford, *American Politits*, pp. 214, 282–283, 293, 302.

[20] Bryce, *American Commonwealth*, I, 190; II, 164; Wilson, *Congressional Government*, p. 149; Henry Adams, "The Session," *North American Review*, CVIII (1869), 617; Rothman, *Politics and Power*, pp. 195–196.

instance of bribery in the House of Representatives or in the Senate of the United States; never a single instance of the kind, and I have been there eight years."[21]

Actually, moral standards in Congress improved gradually after the retirement of President Grant, partly because his successors fought corruption vigilantly and partly because traditional conceptions of propriety gradually reasserted themselves. Yet the reputation of Congress for probity remained poor; even Senator Blair admitted that "there is a very general and wide-spread misconception as to the personal character of the legislators of this country." Although Congress contained few real rogues, the ethics of many members seem shady by modern standards. Washington teemed with lobbyists, many of them former congressmen, and what were known as "lobbyesses," a classification that covered sophisticated society matrons, the widows of army officers and government officials, and plain prostitutes. The tactics employed ranged from every kind of legitimate persuasion to outright bribery, and included such techniques as deliberately losing money to legislators at cards, beguiling them with elaborate dinners and entertainments, and, as one scandalized newspaperman explained, using "the lever of lust."[22]

The prevailing attitude toward conflicts of interest was somewhat more relaxed than that of the present day. Most congressmen, for example, openly accepted passes from railroads. Many would vote against the interests of a line that refused to give them one. But they took passes as their due, feeling no obligation to the companies that handed them out. When Senator John Sherman of Ohio delivered a speech favoring the protective tariff, he solicited (and received) the support of the American Iron and Steel Association in distributing copies without any sense of having compromised his independence. Many congressmen accepted favors from lobbyists and advantageous offers of stock and information from businessmen in the same spirit. They also retained business connections and law

---

21 U.S. Senate, *Report on . . . Labor and Capital*, I, 778, 782.

22 *Ibid.*, I, 782; White, *Republican Era*, pp. 379–380; B. P. Poore, *Perley's Reminiscences of Sixty Years in the National Metropolis* (2 vols., Philadelphia, 1886), I, 443; II, 513–515; E. W. Martin, *Behind the Scenes in Washington* (Washington, 1873), pp. 215–247; Bryce, *American Commonwealth*, I, 677–682; Carpenter, *Carp's Washington*, pp. 12, 269, 279–281; G. H. Haynes, *The Senate of the United States: Its History and Practice* (2 vols., New York, 1960), I, 496.

practices while dealing with legislation affecting these interests, arguing that they found no difficulty in keeping their private concerns separate from the public interest, and that participation in the economic affairs of the country improved their ability to determine public policy intelligently. Nevertheless, as the increasing complexity of the economy led Congress to deal more and more extensively with economic matters, public support for a narrower view of what constituted conflict of interest increased, and congressmen tended to adapt themselves to this demand.[23]

Both branches of Congress, despite their power, were also remarkably inefficient legislative bodies. In the seventies and eighties, the House of Representatives in particular presented an appearance of disorder bordering on chaos. Members seldom paid full attention to the business of the moment; instead they carried on private conversations, or spent their time hailing pages, writing letters, reading newspapers, and walking about the chamber noisily while colleagues attempted to carry on the debates. Such was the din and confusion that when members actually wished to hear what a speaker was saying, they left their seats and crowded close around him.[24]

This confusion was compounded by the cumbersome and archaic rules of the House, product of generations of haphazard, *ad hoc* accumulation, "calculated," one congressman said, "to disturb legislators and obstruct legislation," rather than to expedite business. These rules permitted the minority party to block bills through the device of the "disappearing quorum." No measure could be passed unless a quorum was present *and voting;* thus, in the closely divided chambers of the period, a minority could often delay legislation interminably merely by refusing to answer when the roll was called. Equally vexing was the fact that the rules did not allow the Speaker or any group of leaders to direct the flow of House business intelligently. Year by year, the number of bills introduced skyrocketed, partly because of the increasing tendency of the gov-

23 Rothman, *Politics and Power,* pp. 200–201, 206, 214–215, 217–219.

24 Carpenter, *Carp's Washington,* pp. 12–13; Ford, *American Politics,* p. 252; Bryce, *American Commonwealth,* I, 143–144; Wilson, *Congressional Government,* pp. 73–74; Martin, *Behind the Scenes,* pp. 190–191. Of course, the House had never been noted for orderliness and decorum. Tocqueville, for example, was "struck by the vulgar demeanor of that great assembly" in the 1830's. Alexis de Tocqueville, *Democracy in America* (2 vols., New York, 1945), I, 204.

ernment to legislate in social and economic areas and partly because of the desire of congressmen to attract attention and push projects dear to the hearts of their constituents. Only 613 bills were introduced in the House during the first Civil War Congress, but over 7,200 were introduced in the Congress of 1879–81 and over 11,200 in that of 1885–87. Most of these bills were first submitted to one of the forty-seven standing committees of the House. Theoretically, they were supposed to be considered and reshaped in committee and then presented to the whole House for discussion and decision. However, since no one controlled the order in which measures were debated, the chairmen of these committees scrimmaged constantly to get their favorites to the floor, meanwhile quietly burying any bill, no matter how important, that they did not like.

Even those bills reported from a committee seldom received mature consideration. Hundreds of measures were rushed through without debate, most members voting without any detailed understanding of what they were deciding. "The House is losing its freedom of debate, of amendment, even of knowledge," a congressman of long experience complained in 1879. "There is no man on the floor whose position gives him the right to lead; no man who is responsible that each measure receives its due share of attention." "House discussion," another legislator recalled, "had little deliberation in it. One had to watch his chance, be instantaneous on seizing it, and then, with eyes on the clock delivering what was possible within two given spaces."[25]

Woodrow Wilson penned the most convincing attack on this system in *Congressional Government*. "The House has as many leaders as there are subjects of legislation," he wrote; it is "a disintegrate mass of jarring elements." When a bill went to a committee room, he added, it crossed " a parliamentary bridge of sighs to dim dungeons of silence," doomed to expire unless the "petty baron" in charge of that committee was willing to exert himself in its behalf. In 1880 the House voted some slight revisions of its rules, but failed to improve the situation significantly. By the late eighties

25 W. A. Robinson, *Thomas B. Reed: Parliamentarian* (New York, 1930), p. 65; Bryce, *American Commonwealth*, I, 136; G. B. Galloway, *History of the House of Representatives* (New York, 1961), p. 120; G. F. Hoar, "The Conduct of Business in Congress," *North American Review*, CXXVIII (1879), 122, 133; Rothman, *Politics and Power*, p. 155.

the condition of the chamber had become a national scandal. Newspapers printed editorials under such headings as "Slowly Doing Nothing" and "Legislative Lunacy," while prominent members of the House itself were publishing articles demanding reform.[26]

In the Senate a different type of problem hampered action. Both Bryce and Wilson thought the Senate contained "the best men that the system calls into politics,"[27] and because of its relatively small size its proceedings were far more decorous and measures were debated more fully than in the House.[28] But Senators prided themselves on their independence; although a handful of leading members possessed great national prestige, no group or faction was able consistently to dominate or even to give much direction to the chamber's proceedings. Wilson called the Senate "merely a body of individual critics," and a recent student of the subject, David J. Rothman, has echoed and documented Wilson's judgment. No one controlled senatorial caucuses closely; most decisions were made on the floor, where the voting tended to cut across party lines. Senators formed alliances, but these shifted constantly according to each issue under discussion.[29]

[26] Wilson, *Congressional Government*, pp. 58, 63, 76, 145; Robinson, *Reed*, pp. 65–73, 175–194.

[27] Wilson, *Congressional Government*, p. 136; Bryce, *American Commonwealth*, I, 114. Critics, however, accused the Senate of being a citadel of wealth and privilege. In his anonymous *roman à clef, Democracy,* Henry Adams wrote that the United States had a "government of the people, by the people, for the benefit of Senators." Bryce remarked (I, 119) that "some . . . are senators because they are rich; a few are rich because they are senators," while Wilson admitted (p. 153) that senators were "almost altogether removed from [the] temptation to servile obedience to the whims of popular constituencies." There were certainly a large number of wealthy senators, but David J. Rothman has argued that as a group the Senate was not drawn from the ranks of the rich and well-born exclusively. Roughly 40 per cent of those serving between 1869 and 1901 came from relatively humble surroundings. Rothman also argues that service in the Senate was "economically unrewarding" for its wealthier members. *Politics and Power*, pp. 111–136 (especially 112, 125) and 250.

[28] Ford, *American Politics*, p. 271. There was, however, a good deal of letter writing and chatter during the sessions. "I find my seat . . . a very uncomfortable place to write to you in," Senator John P. Jones of Nevada wrote his wife in 1881, "especially as there is so much confusion and noise and interruption." Rothman, *Politics and Power*, pp. 140–141. See also Martin, *Behind the Scenes*, pp. 147–149.

[29] Wilson, *Congressional Government*, p. 147; Rothman, *Power and Politics*, pp. 31, 35, 76, 88.

Congressmen worked hard; most attended sessions regularly and were looked at askance by their colleagues when they did not. However, a large proportion of their time was devoted to trivia, much of the rest dissipated in unproductive wrangling. The system was not adjusting smoothly to the increased demands placed upon it by the rapidly growing, industrializing nation.[30]

The ineffectiveness of Congress and the Presidents made it more than ordinarily difficult for voters to affiliate with one party or the other on the basis of issues. Whether a man voted Democratic or Republican depended upon many variables, among which the official pronouncements of the parties on national affairs ranked low. While this has always been true in America to some extent, it was particularly true in the seventies and eighties. The great sectional cleavage which led to the Civil War remained the most significant single determinant of political loyalty. Southerners tended to be Democrats, Northerners Republicans. This, however, was only a tendency, one complicated by many other influences. In 1889, Senator Hoar of Massachusetts, giving an affirmative (and incorrect) answer to the self-posed question "Are the Republicans in to Stay?" in the *North American Review,* divided the voters as follows: The Republicans, he wrote, consisted of "the men who do the work of piety and charity in our churches . . . who administer our school systems . . . who own and till their own farms . . . who perform skilled labor . . . who went to the war and stayed all through . . . who paid the debt, and kept the currency sound, and saved the nation's honor." The Democrats, he added, were made up of "the old slave-owner and slave-driver, the saloon-keeper, the ballot-box-stuffer, the Kuklux, the criminal class of the great cities, and men who cannot read or write." Bryce, attempting a less partisan survey in his *American Commonwealth,* arrived at a not very different conclusion. He wrote that " 'the best people' " in most of the northern cities were Republicans, along with a substantial majority of the members of the professions, the businessmen, "the more solid part" of the wage-earning class, the Negroes, most farmers, and veterans of the Civil War. The Democrats, in Bryce's opinion, could claim "nearly all the talent, education, and

---

30 H. J. Sievers, *Benjamin Harrison: Hoosier Statesman* (New York, 1959), p. 213; White, *Republican Era,* pp. 68–73; Rothman, *Power and Politics,* pp. 147–151.

wealth of the South," as well as the overwhelming majority of southern farmers, a minority of "good men" in the Middle States, a "vast ignorant fluctuating mass of people" in the northern cities, many of them recent immigrants, and a small but influential handful of upper-class Northerners, Republican by tradition, who had left that party because of its "mal-administration" of the federal government after the Civil War.[31]

A case can be made for these generalizations on a number of grounds other than the authority and experience of Hoar and Bryce. The South was solidly Democratic after the end of Reconstruction, although the variety of local factional conflicts was almost infinite and the Republicans never gave up hope of building a strong following in the region.[32] In large sections of New England and the Middle West, Republican strength was so solid as to lend credence to the argument that most people, without regard for wealth or social status, supported the G.O.P. It was also true that in New York, Boston, and a number of other northern cities, the unsavory elements and a large majority of the immigrants were controlled by powerful Democratic machines. However, if the generalizations were correct, the Republicans would have swept the North and West in every election, which of course they did not.

If most of the farmers, businessmen, professional people, and substantial wage earners of New England and the Middle West were Republicans, how explain the results of the 1880 presidential election, when the G.O.P. carried New Hampshire by only 4,101 votes out of 86,399 cast, and Wisconsin by 30,056 votes out of 266,368? Or how account for the Democrats winning 235 seats in the House of Representatives in 1890 to the Republicans' 88? Irish-Americans *tended* to vote Democratic, but by majorities that fluctuated sharply from year to year and from city to city, depending upon local issues and personalities. Businessmen perhaps did prefer

[31] G. F. Hoar, "Are the Republicans in to Stay?" *North American Review,* CXLIX (1889), 621; Bryce, *American Commonwealth,* II, 31–34. Many later historians have accepted this analysis. See, for example, P. H. Buck, *The Road to Reunion* (New York, 1959), p. 274.

[32] C. V. Woodward, *Origins of the New South* (Baton Rouge, 1951), pp. 51–52, 76–89, 106; S. P. Hirshson, *Farewell to the Bloody Shirt: Northern Republicans and the Southern Negro, 1877–1893* (Bloomington, Ill., 1962), *passim;* V. P. De Santis, *Republicans Face the Southern Question—The New Departure Years, 1877–1897* (Baltimore, 1959), *passim.*

the Republican party in the main, but enough of them were Democratic so that the vice-chairman of the Republican National Committee felt compelled to warn presidential candidate Benjamin Harrison in 1888 that "the influence and money of the great corporation interest . . . cannot safely be calculated." Middlewestern rural devotion to the party of Lincoln was neither complete nor unswerving. When the Republican William D. Washburn ran for Congress in Minnesota in 1878 against Ignatius Donnelly, he won by carrying the cities of his district while Donnelly captured a majority of the farm vote. Jonathan P. Dolliver, a Republican congressman from Iowa, boasted that his rural state would vote Democratic only when Hell went Methodist, but the Democrats carried Iowa in 1889. Despite the supposed allegiance of the urban masses to the Democrats, in the three presidential elections of the 1880's the Republicans carried Philadelphia, Chicago, Cleveland, Cincinnati, and well over half the cities of 50,000 or more in the United States.[33]

The safest generalization that can be made about political alignments, aside from the obvious sectional division, is that party preferences were more influenced by family tradition, religion, and local issues of the moment than by the policies or pronouncements of statesmen and their organizations. Personalities were important. The Republican perennial, James G. Blaine, always attracted wide support in normally Democratic Irish districts. A colorful character like Benjamin F. Butler was able at one time or another to win elections while running as a Republican, as a Democrat, and as the candidate of the Greenback party. Studies of voting behavior in particular areas during these years suggest that local issues and ethnic or cultural differences usually affected the outcome more than the positions taken by the national parties. The Democratic congressional victories of 1890 in normally Republican districts of Iowa, Wisconsin, and Illinois appear to have resulted from the popularity of the party's local stands on prohibition and education. In turn, religious loyalties influenced elections repeatedly, cutting

[33] W. D. Burnham, *Presidential Ballots, 1836–1892* (Baltimore, 1955) , p. 247, 249; *Hist. Stat.*, p. 691; T. N. Brown, *Irish-American Nationalism: 1870–1890* (Philadelphia, 1966) , pp. 133–151, 187; Sievers, *Harrison*, p. 423; H. S. Merrill, *Bourbon Democracy in the Middle West: 1865–1896* (Baton Rouge, 1953) , pp. 130–131, 203; C. N. Degler, "American Political Parties and the Rise of the City: An Interpretation," *Journal of American History*, LI (1964) , 46.

across supposedly solid ethnic lines: German Methodists and Presbyterians tended to vote Republican; German Lutherans and Roman Catholics, Democratic. Among New York City's Jews, those of pre–Civil War origin were usually Democrats; the immigrants of the sixties and seventies, Republicans; later arrivals, Democrats; and the balance among them all was so tenuous and shifting that in the seven presidential elections between 1888 and 1912, neither party carried the heavily Jewish Eighth Assembly District of New York twice in succession.[34]

Factional conflicts within the parties, while frequently bitter, were also, more often than not, based on personal rivalries and emotional clashes rather than meaningful differences of opinion. The division of congressional Republicans into Stalwarts and Half-Breeds did not separate members according to principle, nor did it lead to the establishment of effective working coalitions capable of controlling and disciplining legislators. The Stalwarts were merely the personal friends of Senator Roscoe Conkling of New York, dedicated to the frustration of the ambitions of Conkling's enemy, James G. Blaine of Maine. The conflict between these two men, each talented and attractive but incapable of subordinating his dislike of the other to the interest of country or party, was entirely personal. These factions differed slightly in style, the Stalwarts being rather more blatant in their pursuit of the spoils of office, but they no more resembled organized political groups than did the "Jelly-fish," those Republicans who refused to take sides in the Conkling-Blaine war. Yet their battles determined more than once who would be President of the United States.[35]

The Democrats were both more disorganized and less faction-ridden than the Republicans. The party contained urban machine politicians, old-fashioned southern agrarians, men closely allied with northern industrial tycoons, and representatives of dissatisfied middlewestern farmers. Some historians, most notably Horace Samuel Merrill, have described a split between business-minded, conservative "Bourbon" Democrats and a liberal wing supporting

34 S. P. Hays, "The Social Analysis of American Political History," *Political Science Quarterly*, LXXX (1965), 386–387; Moses Rischin, *The Promised City: New York's Jews, 1870–1914* (Cambridge, Mass., 1962), 221–224.

35 Matthew Josephson, *The Politicos* (New York, 1938), pp. 90, 179; Rothman, *Politics and Power*, pp. 31–32; Andrews, *Last Quarter-Century*, I, 327.

the interests of workingmen and farmers, but a systematic review of the behavior of congressional Democrats reveals little evidence that they divided consistently over social and economic issues or worked together in any organized way to control party policy.[36]

Indeed, when men felt strongly about particular issues, they usually created new parties or formed nonpartisan organizations and called themselves "independents." The Greenbackers of the 1870's, who advocated currency inflation, drew supporters from both the Republicans and the Democrats. When numbers of eastern "Mugwump" Republicans interested in civil-service reform boggled at the nomination of James G. Blaine for President in 1884, they organized a vigorous campaign and voted with the Democrats. Disgruntled western and southern farmers created the Populist party of the early nineties.

Since the major parties seldom adopted unambiguous positions and could not discipline their members in any case, political debate in the seventies and eighties was particularly murky and unenlightening; it is difficult to describe a consistent Republican or Democratic position on most of the issues, whether one studies party platforms or congressional roll calls. And since political discussion focused on issues that were at best only tangentially related to the important questions of the time, it is no wonder that the politics of the era appear so remarkably vacuous and fruitless.

The closest thing to a subject that really separated Republican from Democrat was also the most meaningless. It involved refighting the Civil War—the Republican argument that the Democrats were "the party of treason," and thus unfit to govern the country. Until the mid-seventies this charge had some basis in fact: the Republican party did stand for defending the rights of southern Negroes and imposing harsh reconstruction policies on the seceded states. Many northern veterans and others who had suffered during the rebellion profoundly resented the Democrats because a large element in that party's northern wing had opposed resistance to secession. But by 1876 the Republican party had abandoned its radical reconstruction policies and the anger of Northerners was rapidly fading away.

---

[36] Merrill, *Bourbon Democracy, passim,* and *Bourbon Leader,* p. 45; Rothman, *Politics and Power,* pp. 35-39.

Nevertheless, Republican politicians continued to try to revive past animosities by "waving the bloody shirt."[37] This dead horse was beaten repeatedly to distract northern voters from the inadequacies of Republican candidates and to avoid waging campaigns on controversial questions that divided the electorate. In 1876, when James G. Blaine's campaign for the presidential nomination was threatened by revelations connecting him with congressional bribery, his supporter Robert G. Ingersoll defended him as "the man who has torn from the throat of treason the tongue of slander . . . who has snatched the mask of Democracy from the hideous face of rebellion." Blaine was not nominated, but the successful candidate, Rutherford B. Hayes, although on record as wishing to forget the past and restore friendly relations with the South, wrote Blaine during the heat of the contest: "Our strong ground is the dread of a solid south, rebel rule, etc., etc. I hope you will make these topics prominent in your speeches. It leads people away from 'hard times,' which is our deadliest foe."[38]

Spellbinders continued to employ this tactic, although after 1880 a drive to bury the bloody shirt, sparked by younger leaders, gradually gathered force. Paradoxically, however, Republicans repeatedly dealt in the most cynical manner possible with the only meaningful question related to sectional animosity: the treatment of Negroes in the southern states. In addition to the obvious moral argument that the Republicans could make against Negro disfranchisement, they had sound practical reasons for opposing the racial policies of southern Democrats. An overwhelming majority of the Negroes of the South were Republicans, yet, with increasing effectiveness, these potential voters were being kept from the polls by chicanery and intimidation. Negroes were counted, however, in determining the representation of their states in Congress, and in the Electoral College. Blaine described the situation clearly after his narrow defeat in the presidential election of 1884: "Not only is the

[37] This term referred to the action of Massachusetts congressman Benjamin F. Butler, who dramatically exhibited to his colleagues the bloodstained shirt of an Ohioan who had been flogged in Mississippi in 1866 to buttress his argument that Southerners were unwilling to accept the results of the war and should be treated harshly. R. S. Holzman, *Stormy Ben Butler* (New York, 1954), p. 180.

[38] C. H. Cramer, *Royal Bob: The Life of Robert G. Ingersoll* (Indianapolis, 1952), p. 80; Gail Hamilton, *Biography of James G. Blaine* (Norwich, 1895), p. 422.

negro population disfranchised, but the power which rightfully and Constitutionally belongs to them is transferred to the white population of the South, enabling them to exert an electoral influence far beyond that exerted by the same number of white people in the North." In that election (as Blaine pointed out), Louisiana, Mississippi, Alabama, Georgia, and North Carolina cast forty-eight electoral votes for Cleveland. Five northern and western states—Minnesota, Wisconsin, Iowa, Kansas, and California—cast forty-eight electoral votes for Blaine. The two groups of states had about equal populations; but in the Republican ones 1,349,000 voters went to the polls, in the Democratic only 795,000.

Abstract justice and party advantage would both have been served by a policy of inflexible opposition to Negro disfranchisement; instead, the Republicans made periodic efforts to entice dissident southern Democratic factions into their ranks, with little regard for the views of these groups on the race, or any other question. Garfield and Arthur, for example, stifled their dislike of the radical financial policies of William Mahone of Virginia when his Readjuster party rose to power. They supplied federal patronage liberally both to Mahone and to radical groups in several other southern states.[39]

At other times the Republicans tried to win over southern business interests by playing up such matters as the protective tariff and de-emphasizing the race issue. When these tactics failed, as they usually did, Republican leaders reverted to demanding federal protection of Negro rights and excoriating the Democrats. Hayes tried to build up the Republican party in the South by promising federal aid for southern railroads and other internal improvements, and by trusting to white leaders to protect Negro civil rights. The congressional elections of 1878 produced another solid Democratic delegation from the South, however, whereupon Hayes and his party reverted to attacking the section and posing as friends of the Negro. "The policy of the President has turned out to be a giveaway," James A. Garfield complained. "Everywhere in the South

39 J. G. Blaine, *Political Discussions: Legislative, Diplomatic, and Popular* (Norwich, 1887), pp. 468–469; Burnham, *Presidential Ballots*, pp. 249–257; Buck, *Road to Reunion*, pp. 75–118, 273–293; De Santis, *Southern Question*, pp. 142–147, 153–160, 167; Woodward, *Origins of the New South*, pp. 101–103; R. W. Logan, *The Negro in American Life and Thought: The Nadir, 1877–1901* (New York, 1954), pp. 44–47.

. . . they have spent their time in whetting their knives for any Republican they could find." Running for the Presidency in 1880, Garfield adopted the traditional Republican position on the Negro question.[40]

This pattern was repeated again and again throughout the eighties and early nineties. When Blaine, a famous shirt-waver, sought to break the solid South in 1884, he played down sectional animosities. The South needed "capital and occupation, not controversy," he asserted. When it became clear during the campaign that the South was not responding to this appeal, he reverted to the argument that a Democratic victory would put rebels in control of the government. "It would be as if the dead Stuarts were recalled to the throne of England, as if the Bourbons should be invited to administer the government of the French Republic," he said. Benjamin Harrison, seeking to win the votes of southern industrialists, stressed the protective tariff and de-emphasized the Negro question, urging (1889) that racial justice be sought through "kindness and education" rather than by federal force. But this policy led Negroes to defect from the Republican ranks without producing corresponding gains; by the end of 1889, Harrison was demanding congressional action to "secure to all people a free exercise of the right of suffrage and every other civil right." In 1888, Harrison had favored the Blair education bill, a measure providing federal funds to combat illiteracy which had received much white support in the Deep South. By 1890, however, the Republican congressional leadership had backed away from the bill, and it was defeated.[41]

At the same time, the Republicans tried to pass Congressman Henry Cabot Lodge's Force Bill, which would have placed federal supervisors in charge of congressional elections. This directly challenged white southern efforts to deprive Negroes of the vote. "The suppression of the suffrage . . . is an evil of the greatest and most menacing kind," Lodge charged, and Harrison and other party leaders joined him in an attack they knew would destroy any

---

[40] Barnard, *Hayes*, pp. 420–434, 439–440; Hirshson, *Farewell to the Bloody Shirt*, pp. 21–44, 79.

[41] Hirshson, *Farewell to the Bloody Shirt*, pp. 124–126, 171, 177, 194–200, 206–207; A. J. Going, "The South and the Blair Education Bill," *Mississippi Valley Historical Review*, XLIV (1957), 267–290.

possibility of attracting white southern converts to Republicanism. Lodge's Federal Elections Bill passed the House of Representatives handily, but went down to defeat in the Senate when it became entangled with the consideration of other measures that many Republicans considered more important. Senate Democrats undertook a filibuster to block it, and six Republicans interested in the free coinage of silver deserted their party when an effort was made to cut off debate. Both as an example of the failure of party discipline and of the subordination of a genuine issue to partisan advantage, the incident was typical of the politics of the period.[42]

On other questions party divisions had even less significance. One constant source of political argument was the protective tariff. Throughout the period the nation maintained high duties on manufactured goods. Although the domestic market absorbed more than American manufacturers could produce,[43] labor was convinced, probably correctly, that high duties acted to support American wage levels, and industrialists, of course, wished to keep the prices of competing foreign manufactures as high as possible. Almost no one other than economists of the classical school and a handful of doctrinaire Darwinists favored free trade. A number of "tariff reform" and "free trade" organizations existed, but they advocated more moderate protection, rather than no protection at all for American goods.

Nevertheless, the tariff was a hot political issue in the seventies and eighties. Tradition played a part; some Democrats, especially among the Southerners, were congenitally committed to tariff reduction even though they often favored high duties on the products of their own region. Tariff duties were also deeply entangled in the broader question of federal finance. Every year from 1866 to 1893, in bad times and in good, the Treasury took in more money than it spent, an average of over $100 million a year in the eighties. The government was thus locking up large amounts of cash needed by the expanding economy. It could use this surplus to reduce the

42 J. A. Garraty, *Henry Cabot Lodge: A Biography* (New York, 1953), p. 117; Hirshson, *Farewell to the Bloody Shirt,* pp. 205–211, 232–235; De Santis, *Southern Question,* pp. 198–214.

43 In 1870 the United States imported $230 million worth of manufactures and exported $70 million. The corresponding figures for 1890 were $348 million and $179 million. *Hist. Stat.,* pp. 544–545.

national debt, and it did so steadily—the debt fell from $2.8 billion in 1866 to $2 billion in 1881 and $1 billion in 1891.[44] But whenever the government began buying its unmatured bonds on the open market, the prices of these securities soared, providing a premium to investors at the expense of the mass of taxpayers that was politically unpalatable. Large sums were also squandered on pensions for Civil War veterans, and on "pork-barrel" projects. Pensions caused no serious political difficulties outside the South, but many public-works projects provoked controversy. Some persons feared that these projects would involve waste and corruption, and others, alarmed by the rate at which federal activities were expanding, opposed them as a matter of principle. Above all, every proposal to spend additional federal funds was assailed by the tariff reductionists as a nefarious scheme to justify maintaining high duties.

Much pressure therefore developed to cut tariffs and excise taxes. As early as 1871, the purely revenue-raising duties on tea and coffee were repealed. Removal of the steep federal excises on liquor and tobacco would have helped to reduce the surplus; but since this step would have aroused prohibitionists and persons opposed to smoking and tobacco chewing, both parties shied away from doing so. To many, tariff reduction seemed the only practical way to lower the surplus. Thus, despite the widespread sentiment in favor of protecting American industry against foreign competition, the tariff issue remained a constant source of political conflict.

Historically, the Republicans were "for" high duties, the Democrats "against," but an average of about forty Democrats in the House of Representatives, led by Samuel J. Randall of Pennsylvania, were rabid protectionists, while numbers of Republicans, chiefly Middlewesterners, favored some reduction of the rates. Actually, almost every congressman was both partisan and local-minded on the issue. In 1888, for example, the Democrats tried to push through a superficially moderate reduction. The proposed cuts averaged about 7 per cent. However, this bill, framed by Roger Q. Mills of Texas, the chairman of the House Ways and Means Committee, discriminated outrageously in favor of the South. Mills

[44] *Ibid.*, p. 711.

slashed the rates on iron and other metal products, and on glass, wool, and many other items made or grown in northern states. Duties on sugar and rice and on iron ore (mined in increasing amounts in Alabama) were lowered only slightly. Cheap foreign cotton goods, which competed with the products of new southern mills, remained subject to high duties; rates on high-quality cotton goods and on woolens were reduced sharply. The defeat of the Mills bill was, therefore, far from being a victory for protectionism as such, or for Republicans over Democrats.[45]

The politicians engaged continually in the rankest kind of obfuscation and manipulation when dealing with the tariff. A few examples must suffice. In 1882 the Indiana convention of the Democratic party came out for downward revision of "the present unjust tariff." But the next year Democratic Senator Daniel W. Voorhees of Indiana said during a clash with one of his southern party colleagues: "I am a protectionist for every interest which I am sent here by my constituents to protect." Republican congressman Henry Cabot Lodge, who represented the shoe manufacturing city of Lynn, told a Massachusetts newspaper editor in 1890: "To protect our own great industries . . . it is necessary to make some sacrifices." Massachusetts consumers must reconcile themselves to paying higher prices for goods manufactured in other states so that their own products could also be protected. But he quickly added: "By this of course you understand I do not mean hides." When Grover Cleveland committed the Democrats to tariff reduction in 1887, James G. Blaine immediately devised an ingenious counter-proposal to deal with the Treasury's surplus without reducing duties. By keeping tariffs high, America would continue to force foreigners to contribute to the national revenues, he claimed. The tax on tobacco should be eliminated instead, for that would reduce the cost of living for thousands of American smokers. He would not remove the excises on whisky, but he would devote all the money collected from this source to the construction of fortifications along the Atlantic coast. He did not say so, but everyone knew that the only nation with a navy even remotely capable of threatening this coast was Great Britain. Thus Blaine's suggestion appealed both to prohibitionists and to proverbially hard-drinking Irish-Americans,

[45] Nevins, *Cleveland*, pp. 389–393; Merrill, *Bourbon Leader*, pp. 123–125.

who hated and feared the English. That these Irishmen usually voted for the Democrats was a bonus benefit of the scheme—and a fine example of Blaine's political acuity.[46]

Party alignments throw almost no light on another important issue of the times, the currency question. No subject inspired more heated and continuous controversy; few caused so much confusion and misunderstanding. During the Civil War, the government had issued about $450 million in "greenbacks"—paper currency supported only by the credit of the United States, and not convertible into gold or silver. This inflation of the money supply contributed to the steep wartime rise in prices and shook the faith of the people in the stability of the government; when the war ended, public sentiment was almost unanimously in favor of retiring the greenbacks from circulation. However, a postwar depression marked by a decline of prices soon caused a split in public opinion. From the late sixties to the late seventies, the argument centered around what was known as the resumption of specie payments, that is, returning to a metallic standard under which all paper money would be exchangeable for specie. Resumptionists wished to withdraw all the greenbacks, or at least to make them convertible; "Greenbackers" demanded that the amount of inconvertible paper money in circulation be increased. The fortunes of these two camps (each composed of many, many elements motivated by a variety of considerations) fluctuated, but eventually the volume of greenback currency was reduced to $300 million, and in 1879 greenbacks were made convertible into gold on demand. Thereafter the greenback question faded from the political scene and attention shifted to the question of silver-backed money. Those favoring inflation (again a complex coalition) pressed for the unlimited coinage of silver along with gold; their opponents insisted that the single gold standard be maintained. This battle raged through the eighties and nineties and was settled only in 1900 with the victory of the gold forces.[47]

Public attitudes toward the money question were far more complicated than those on the tariff, although the two issues were not unrelated. In the first place, even in the highly materialistic society

[46] Sievers, *Harrison*, p. 212; Garraty, *Lodge*, p. 114; Nevins, *Cleveland*, pp. 383–384.

[47] Milton Friedman and A. J. Schwartz, *A Monetary History of the United States, 1867–1960* (Princeton, 1963), pp. 16–134; D. R. Dewey, *Financial History of the United States* (New York, 1909), pp. 360–468.

of the era, many persons saw the paper-money controversy in moral terms. Any government action that lowered the purchasing power of the dollar or reneged on a "contract" to pay an obligation in gold seemed to such persons sinful. As the New York *Christian Advocate* declared in 1878, "atheism is not worse in religion than an unstable or irredeemable currency in political economy." To pay off gold bonds in greenbacks, for example, would be to violate the government's obligation "to make its word good." Men who held such views were reluctant to support inflationary schemes even when they knew they would profit from them personally. Extremists of this type would not even countenance paper money that was convertible into gold if the banks did not have an actual dollar in metal in their vaults for every paper dollar they circulated.[48]

Second, the money issue was complicated by the inability of experts to agree on theoretical questions. Laissez-faire economists of the dominant classical school opposed all forms of currency control. They argued that deflation would not inhibit economic growth, reasoning that interest rates (which of course influenced economic activity) depended upon the amount of capital available as security for loans, not upon the currency supply. However, the older mercantilistic school of economists had not died out in the United States, chiefly because the mercantilistic defense of protective tariffs was congenial to so many Americans. The mercantilists insisted that high interest rates resulted from a scarcity of money, not of capital, and favored issuing more greenbacks.[49]

Bankers also failed to understand fully the mechanics of their own operations. Prices and interest rates are affected not merely by the amount of currency in circulation but also by the volume of bank deposits. These depend upon how much credit the banks create by making loans to businessmen, farmers, and other borrowers. Except for a brief period (1877-79), bank deposits rose steadily from 1868 to 1893, more than making up for the decline in the volume of currency[50] caused by the retirement of greenbacks.

[48] Irwin Unger, *The Greenback Era: A Social and Political History of American Finance, 1865-1879* (Princeton, 1964), pp. 26-28, 121-122.

[49] *Ibid.*, pp. 51-52, 57; Sidney Fine, *Laissez Faire and the General-Welfare State: A Study of Conflict in American Thought, 1865-1901* (Ann Arbor, 1956), pp. 69-70; D. A. Wells, *Recent Economic Changes* (New York, 1889), pp. 208-209.

[50] Modern economists call currency "high-powered" money because, when held by banks, it provides the basis for creating money in the form of commercial credit. Friedman and Schwartz, *Monetary History*, pp. 29-44, 50, 53-58.

Little wonder, under such conditions, that ordinary persons found the money question confusing. "In the great diversity of opinion existing amongst minds equally educated," one voter complained in 1878 to Senator John Sherman, a leading congressional financial expert, it was "difficult to know where the *right* is."[51]

For the pragmatic, untheoretically minded mass of the people, however, opinions on the money question usually depended upon practical considerations. But these, too, were not always clear. Workingmen might favor deflation when they thought of the cost of living, but not when it led to wage cuts or when they allowed themselves to be influenced by their prejudices against bankers and bondholders. Hatred of "the money power" combined with alarm at the steady decline of agricultural prices to make inflationists of many farmers, but other farmers distrusted all paper-money schemes. Bankers as a group opposed first the greenbacks and then the free coinage of silver, but numbers of western bankers and a few prominent Easterners interested in the financing of western railroads supported inflationary policies. Older, more established businessmen and most merchants engaged in foreign trade tended to favor deflation, but the aggressive new enterprisers interested in industrial expansion and western development usually preferred to see the money supply increased. Furthermore, in slack times inflationary pressures mounted; when the economy was booming, those favoring resumption of specie payments and the gold standard grew in influence.[52]

The politicians proved incapable of organizing these diverse groups. Eventually, the Republicans became the party of "sound money," but in most important votes on the greenback and silver questions before 1896, party lines in Congress disintegrated, despite the fact that all the Presidents were conservative and uncharacteristically firm when dealing with monetary policy. Grant had to veto a bill passed by a Republican Congress in 1874 that would have expanded the supply of greenbacks. The debates on the Bland-Allison Silver Purchase Act of 1878 were marked by "party chaos," one financial historian has written; the majority that pushed it through was "non-partisan and almost wholly sectional." President Hayes denounced this measure in his veto message, but although

---

[51] Unger, *Greenback Era*, p. 35.
[52] *Ibid.*, pp. 118–119, 142–144, 162, 222–224, 332–336, 403–404, *passim.*

the Republicans controlled the Senate and the Democratic majority in the House was only 13, the veto was overridden easily, 46–19 and 193–73. In February, 1885, President-elect Grover Cleveland urged Congress to suspend the purchase of silver under this act temporarily. A thin majority of the Republicans in the House of Representatives supported his request, but the Democrats rejected it, 118–54. He was "slapped in the face by his own party" his biographer, Allan Nevins, records.[53]

Unable to discipline their representatives in Congress, both parties responded by equivocating on the issue, and the financial legislation of the era took the form of compromises, satisfactory to almost no one and, in the perspective of history and modern economic knowledge, muddleheaded.

In their *Monetary History of the United States,* Milton Friedman and Anna Jacobson Schwartz offer a dispassionate but devastating analysis of the financial policies of the era:

1. The tremendous importance that both inflationists and deflationists placed on the silver issue in the eighties ignored the fact that money in the form of bank deposits was expanding rapidly— from less than $2 per dollar of currency in 1879 to almost $4 in 1892. During the eighties the amount of new currency created accounted for only about half of the increase in the total "money stock" of the country.

2. Conservatives wanted to stabilize the value of the dollar; but more than any other force, the Treasury, which they dominated throughout the period, was responsible for destabilizing the dollar. Its policy of buying up government bonds with surplus federal revenue led directly to a sharp contraction of the volume of national bank notes, which were secured by the banks' holdings of bonds.

3. The inflationists' pressure for increased silver coinage was actually deflationary, because it discouraged foreigners from investing in the United States and led American investors to ship capital abroad.

4. The Treasury's goal of preserving the gold standard in the face of its legal obligation to purchase silver could easily have been

[53] Friedman and Schwartz, *Monetary History,* p. 46; A. D. Noyes, *Thirty Years of American Finance* (New York, 1898), p. 40; Barnard, *Hayes,* p. 464; Nevins, *Cleveland,* p. 204.

achieved by stockpiling the silver; instead, it tried to force the silver into circulation, which caused the dollar to fall on international exchanges, creating an unfavorable balance of trade and thus leading to the export of gold.

5. Fears that the government's silver purchases threatened the gold standard and would cause serious inflation were groundless. On balance, the Treasury's operations between 1879 and 1890 increased the amount of currency in circulation by an average of only $14 million a year. Over the next three years, spurred by the requirements of the Sherman Silver Purchase Act of 1890, about $180 million in silver money was created, but even at this rate the silver "could almost surely have been absorbed indefinitely without seriously threatening the gold standard," had it not been for the effect of the purchases on public confidence. "The entire silver episode is a fascinating example of how important what people think about money can sometimes be," Friedman and Schwartz conclude. But wherever the final responsibility for the ineptness of government fiscal policy lies, the parties certainly failed to deal forthrightly with the issue.[54]

The parties also functioned ineffectively in their handling of another important issue of the period, civil service reform. The federal bureaucracy, according to Leonard D. White, its most careful historian, was "generally undistinguished" throughout the period, because the system of selecting officials and supervising their work was irrational. That system had evolved during the first half of the nineteenth century, when it had suited the needs of the country fairly well. Its underlying principles, unwritten but generally adhered to, were the "spoils system" and "rotation in office." After every turnover of party control, the victors proceeded to divide up "the spoils." They fired government employees who had supported their opponents to make room for persons who had helped achieve their victory. "Rotation" occurred when the same party remained in power for a protracted period. The normal term of service in most positions was considered to be four years. Anyone who had held a government job that long could be discharged (rotated) without other reason. These principles were thought to be both democratic and in the public interest. Supposedly they

would ensure that civil servants were loyal to the current administration, that the largest possible number of citizens would share
both the emoluments and responsibilities of public service, and that
no entrenched bureaucracy would develop. Andrew Jackson, who
perfected if he did not invent the system, defended it cogently in his
first annual message to Congress in 1829: "No one man has any
more intrinsic right to official station than another. . . . The
duties of all public officers are, or at least admit of being made, so
plain and simple that men of intelligence may readily qualify
themselves for their performance."[55]

Even in Jackson's day, this method of staffing government departments left something to be desired. Frequent turnover and appointments made without regard for the ability of job holders to carry
out the responsibilities of their positions produced inefficiency.
Moreover, winning office became for many persons almost a mental
disorder—they sought preferment for itself, with little regard for
the practical rewards of the positions, which were mostly ill-paid
and dull. Too many of them also developed a totally selfish attitude
toward government service, approaching their jobs the way a pirate
viewed a defenseless merchant ship. Still worse, every election
caused panic to run through the departments, each petty official
feeling, as Henry Clay said in 1829, "like the inhabitants of Cairo
when the plague breaks out; no one knows who is next to encounter
the stroke of death."

As the years passed, the flaws of the system became more serious.
On the one hand, political leaders forced appointees to contribute
both time and money to party affairs; on the other, high officials
found themselves besieged after each election by an army of importunate applicants for government jobs. Wrangling between the
executive and Congress over patronage became both chronic and
intense. By the eighties, Washington newspapers were sprinkled
with classified advertisements placed by prospective employees:

WANTED—A GOVERNMENT CLERKSHIP at salary of not less than $1,000 per
annum. Will give $100 to any one securing me such a position.

55 White, *Republican Era*, p. 1; L. D. White, *The Jacksonians: A Study in
Administrative History, 1829–1861* (New York, 1954), pp. 300–324; J. D. Richard-
son (ed.), *Messages and Papers of the Presidents* (10 vols., Washington, 1898),
II, 448–449.

WANTED—BY TWO YOUNG LADIES situations in Government office; will give first month's pay and $10 monthly as long as retained.[56]

The increasing size of the federal bureaucracy had, by the eighties, made the situation almost intolerable. In Jackson's time there had been about 20,000 persons on the federal payroll. By the end of the Civil War, there were 53,000; by 1884, 131,000; by 1891, 166,000. With offices and office-seekers multiplying so rapidly, the relatively fixed number of statesmen who had to dispense the appointments were deluged. Even Jackson had complained of the hordes of candidates seeking a "tit" to suck "Treasury pap" from. While Lincoln was struggling to solve the secession crisis, he had had to cope with what one congressman called "a swarm of miscellaneous people . . . as hungry and as fierce as wolves," all looking for jobs. In 1877, President Hayes found that even his wife was being harassed by job applicants, and when Garfield became President he discovered prospective civil servants "lying in wait" for him "like vultures for a wounded bison." "It has been a steeple chase, I fleeing and they pursuing," he wrote. A few years later, Cleveland was grumbling about "the damned, everlasting clatter for office," and Harrison, after his retirement, estimated that during the first eighteen months of his term he had spent on the average between four and six hours a day dealing with job-seekers. "At the end of one hundred days of this work," Harrison added, "the President should not be judged too harshly if he shows . . . a hunted expression in his eyes!"[57]

Moreover, far more government jobs required special skills than in earlier periods. To take the simplest example, the use of typewriters (twenty were clacking away in the Justice Department alone by the first Cleveland administration) meant that mere literacy and normal intelligence no longer qualified a person for an ordinary clerkship. As the government's need for scientists and other profes-

56 White, *Jacksonians*, p. 330, Carpenter, *Carp's Washington*, p. 123.

57 White, *Republican Era*, pp. 2, 6; Ari Hoogenboom, *Outlawing the Spoils: A History of the Civil Service Reform Movement, 1865–1883* (Urbana, 1961), pp. 1, 279; Marquis James, *The Life of Andrew Jackson* (Indianapolis, 1938), p. 502; B. P. Thomas, *Abraham Lincoln: A Biography* (New York, 1952), p. 252; Williams, *Hayes Diary*, p. 85; Nevins, *Cleveland*, p. 248; Benjamin Harrison, *This Country of Ours* (New York, 1901), pp. 168, 179–180.

sionals increased, the patronage system proved steadily less capable of supplying it. Such persons were, in general, hired on the basis of merit and were seldom discharged for political reasons, but the confusion and low morale engendered by the system hampered their work. No rational examination or promotion policy existed. The truly professional employees in each department devoted much of their energies to training the flood of ignorant recruits who descended upon their offices after each change of administration. "No one felt sure of holding his position," a fifty-year veteran in the Department of Agriculture recalled in 1930. "Personal congressional influence was sought for and relied upon. No one working under the government at the present time can begin to realize the unrest of those days and how it affected the efficiency of most employees. Nor, indeed, can one today realize how many utterly incompetent persons were given clerkships and other official positions."[58]

With the civil service so patently in need of reform, one might suppose that the question would have aroused little controversy. This was not the case, for the whole machinery of American politics rested upon the patronage system. Without the bait of jobs, party leaders believed, they could not attract the armies of workers who organized campaigns and supplied much of the money to wage them. Office was also the grease lubricating the lumbering legislative wheels of Congress; administration officials maintained good relations with legislators, in large measure, by appointing their friends and supporters to postmasterships, jobs in the customs and diplomatic services, clerical posts in the government departments, and other minor places. However burdensome the task of distributing these offices, practical politicians from the Presidents to the lowliest ward heelers found it very difficult to envisage life without it. Senator Conkling, pre-eminent among the realists on this question, expressed a widely held belief when he reminded a New York Republican convention that parties "are not built up by deportment, or by ladies' magazines, or by gush."

Practical men and those simply trying to preserve their selfish interests nearly always scoff at reformers who seek to do away with

---

[58] Hoogenboom, *Outlawing the Spoils*, pp. 2–3; L. O. Howard, "A History of Applied Entomology," Smithsonian Institution *Miscellaneous Publications*, LXXXIV (1930), 88–89.

established institutions. In ridiculing the civil-service reformers, however, the politicians tested the limits of their well-stocked vocabularies. These men, the Half-Breed James G. Blaine told Garfield in 1880, were "upstarts, conceited, foolish, vain, without knowledge of measures, ignorant of men, shouting a shibboleth. . . . They are noisy but not numerous, pharisaical but not practical, ambitious but not wise, pretentious but not powerful!" The Stalwart Conkling called them "oracular censors . . . the man-milliners, the dilettanti, and carpet knights of politics" whose "stock in trade is rancid, canting, self-righteousness." Another defender of the system called them "moral lepers," and "ulcers, warts, tumors, sties, and fistulas," and "a moving, crawling breathing pestilence."[59]

Sprinkled among such hyperbolic expressions of indignation were some justifiable criticisms of civil-service reformers. As a group the reformers showed little grasp of the practical implications of their proposal that the bureaucracy be divorced from politics. Far from being radicals, most held old-fashioned, laissez-faire views about the actual functions that government should perform. They favored the establishment of an aristocratic civil service modeled on the British system, and tended (like Theodore Roosevelt's friends) to consider politics a sordid business. Some were merely thwarted politicians, whose own ambitions for office had been frustrated and who responded by attacking the men who had rejected them.[60] Their vision was both limited and blurred, for they were reacting chiefly against the corruption of the Grant era, which was already fast disappearing by the time Hayes had become President, and had relatively little to do with the patronage system in the first place. But their indignation was in the main disinterested, their objectives pure, although rather old-fashioned. Most of the prominent reformers in the seventies and eighties were young men, comfortably

[59] Hamilton, *Blaine*, p. 491; A. R. Conkling, *The Life and Letters of Roscoe Conkling* (New York, 1889), pp. 538–549; Josephson, *Politicos*, pp. 246–247; White, *Republican Era*, p. 18.

[60] Hoogenboom, *Outlawing the Spoils*, pp. ix, 196–197. Hoogenboom also has written: "The civil service reform movement fits into a pattern of those out of power versus those in power. Reformers invariably wished to curtail the appointing power after . . . men of their social station or political faction were not appointed to office." H. W. Morgan (ed.), *The Gilded Age: A Reappraisal* (Syracuse, 1963), p. 79. This seems rather an overstatement, or at least an uncharitable view of the movement.

well off and well educated, genuinely idealistic if somewhat naïve in their belief that the antique virtues of the early days of the Republic could be restored merely by establishing a merit system among federal workers.[61]

The intemperance of the politicians when confronting civil-service reform probably resulted from their awareness that the patronage system would soon have to be drastically modified. They feared the effects of change upon their power. The insufferable priggishness of the leading reformers added enormously to the politicians' sense of frustration, but did not prevent them from yielding to necessity.

No significant reform sentiment developed until after the Civil War, and when it did, neither of the major parties took a strong or consistent position for or against it. If any generalization can be made, it is that the party out of power tended to support reform, the party in power to oppose it. The Republicans employed the idea to check the appointive power of Andrew Johnson in 1867. During the Grant era, however, when a reform-minded Republican introduced a bill limiting party patronage, most of its support came from Democrats, and the proposal failed. *After* Garfield was elected President in 1880, the defeated Democrats suddenly began demanding that the President's power of appointment be restricted; but when Cleveland became President four years later, most of the Democratic politicians, in Congress and out, denounced him for refusing to discharge every Republican officeholder in the country.[62]

The position of the politicians on civil service was further muddled by the conflict that patronage always stirred up between the President and Congress. Presidents tended to favor reform, because the office made them more likely to see the national interest and because the burdens of distributing patronage weighed so heavily upon them. Every President, beginning with Hayes, fought to restore the balance of executive-legislative power that had been upset by the congressional radicals during the Johnson administration. This led them, among other things, to resist congressional misuse of patronage. Presidents could afford (once elected) to deny at least the most blatant demands of spoils-minded politicians

[61] Blodgett, *Gentle Reformers*, pp. 19–31.
[62] Hoogenboom, *Outlawing the Spoils*, pp. 7, 33, 109–110, 199; Nevins, *Cleveland*, pp. 242–243.

because they were not so directly dependent upon office seekers for their power. Like generals, they had little direct contact with their troops; whereas congressmen, and especially senators, were more like colonels, the actual leaders of the regiments of party workers in each state whose clamor for spoils had to be regarded.

When Hayes ran for President in 1876, he committed himself to civil-service reform, partly out of conviction and partly to counter the bad reputation the Republican party had accumulated during the era of the Grant scandals. But when he tried to make good on his campaign promises, Republicans in the Senate rose up in arms. Senator George Edmunds of Vermont, supposedly a friend of reform, denounced his "defiance" and called him "a political dreamer." When the President reminded senators of the party platform pledges, Senator Henry Teller sneered: "He thinks he is George Washington!" Hayes nonetheless stuck to his guns. He issued an order forbidding officeholders to participate in the management of party affairs and abolishing the practice of levying monetary assessments upon them. He also ordered an investigation of the New York Customs House, and when the collector, Chester A. Arthur, and his principal assistant, Alonzo Cornell, refused to carry out his commands, he attempted to replace them as part of a general reorganization of the Customs House. This action precipitated a terrible wrangle in the Senate, where Conkling, trying to protect his henchmen, demanded that his colleagues refuse to confirm Hayes's appointees. In the showdown vote, only six of thirty-four Republican senators supported the President. Hayes, however, persisted. He summarily removed Arthur and Cornell, and eventually the Senate confirmed his nominees, although a majority of the Republicans voted against them to the end.[63] All the other Presidents of the period, whether predisposed toward civil-service reform or not, ran into similar, if less extreme, difficulties.

The assassination of President Garfield by Charles Guiteau, a demented admirer of Senator Conkling, produced a public clamor for civil-service reform that the politicians could not ignore. In 1883, both houses of Congress passed the Pendleton Act by large, nonpartisan majorities. This law "classified" certain government

[63] Barnard, *Hayes*, pp. 450–456; Hoogenboom, *Outlawing the Spoils*, pp. 155–171.

jobs and set up a Civil Service Commission to administer competitive examinations to applicants. It also outlawed political assessments and established an orderly, nonpartisan system for advancement in the service. Presidents were empowered to add new positions to the classified service from time to time, a procedure that proved extremely important over the next dozen years, when each presidential election brought defeat for the party in power. Rather than see their supporters turned out by their successors, each President "froze" increasing numbers of places by adding them to the classified list. In 1883, less than 15,000 jobs were classified; by 1897, when McKinley became President, 86,000—almost half of all federal employees—were under civil service. Thus the quality of the federal bureaucracy steadily improved, but neither party could claim much credit for what was accomplished.[64]

Such were the assumptions, strategies, tactics, and weapons of the politicians. Let us now descend into the arena and observe these sturdy gladiators as they grappled with one another.

[64] White, *Republican Era*, pp. 301, 317; Hoogenboom, *Outlawing the Spoils*, pp. 209–249, 260–264, 279.

CHAPTER 7

From Hayes to Harrison

O N March 5, 1877, in an atmosphere charged with tension born of uncertainty, Rutherford B. Hayes delivered his inaugural address as President of the United States. Although the election had taken place as scheduled the previous November, Hayes's title to the office had not been established until February 26, and many citizens were still not reconciled to the result. Dozens of Democratic congressmen and many other prominent figures had refused to attend the inaugural ceremonies; dark talk of revolution, of assassination threats, filled the air. Since March 4 was a Sunday, the inauguration had been postponed to the fifth, but so great was the apprehension surrounding the transfer of power that Hayes had reluctantly agreed to take the oath secretly on the evening of Saturday, March 3, in the Red Room of the White House.

This deplorable state of affairs had resulted not from the extreme closeness of the electoral vote, or from the fact that Hayes' opponent, Samuel J. Tilden, had received a plurality of 250,000 in the popular vote, but rather from the irregularities that had disgraced the electoral process. These had far exceeded the degree of fraud and corruption that the public had learned to tolerate. In Florida, South Carolina, and Louisiana particularly, Negro Republicans had been kept from the polls by force and intimidation. At the same time, Republican election officials in these states had systematically thrown out or invalidated thousands of Democratic ballots. Rival sets of returns had been submitted.

To unravel the tangle, which could not be decided by ordinary constitutional procedures, Congress, after protracted wrangling, created a special fifteen-man Electoral Commission and charged it with the task of evaluating the rival claims. If all the nineteen electors of Florida, South Carolina, and Louisiana were assigned to Hayes, he was entitled to the presidency; but if a single elector were credited to Tilden, he was the winner of the contest. In this supposedly impartial commission, each member voted consistently in favor of his own party. Deciding every question by identical eight-to-seven votes, the commission gave all the disputed places to the Republicans. This outrageous display of partisanship made Hayes President, and left the Democrats more convinced than ever that their candidate had been deprived of office by fraud.[1]

However, the inaugural ceremonies passed without incident, partly because Democratic leaders had obtained certain promises from Hayes, but also because thoughtful men realized that there was *no* truly just way to settle the dispute. How could anyone say who was entitled to the electoral votes of South Carolina, Louisiana, or Florida, when a fair election had not been held in those states?[2] Public-spirited persons regardless of party could take heart that a President had been legally installed, and without bloodshed.

Hayes offered promise of being a wise and humane leader, as well as a vigorous and decisive one. His inaugural address emphasized the importance of protecting the rights of Negroes in the South but also of restoring local autonomy to the region, and conveyed the impression that these apparently contradictory objectives could be reconciled. He also stressed the need for civil-service reform, insisting that "radical and complete" changes were actually possible; that the whole patronage system, not merely its worst abuses, could be eliminated. When he closed his address with an appeal for national unity—"a union depending not upon the constraint of force, but upon the loving devotion of a free people"—he made the words

1 Harry Barnard, *Rutherford B. Hayes and His America* (Indianapolis, 1954), pp. 314–404; Allan Nevins, *Abram S. Hewitt: With Some Account of Peter Cooper* (New York, 1935), pp. 320–385; C. V. Woodward, *Reunion and Reaction* (Boston, 1951), pp. 16–19, 150–165. The best account of the negotiations and of the motives of the leading figures is Woodward's.

2 In an honest election, Hayes would probably have carried Louisiana and South Carolina, but not Florida. Woodward, *Reunion and Reaction,* p. 19. However, it is impossible to be sure; the reasoning depends mainly on the fact that Negroes were in the majority in Louisiana and South Carolina, but not in Florida.

sound like something more than a stale political slogan. In constructing his cabinet, Hayes displayed good judgment and considerable independence: most of his appointees were men of intelligence and integrity but also politically experienced, and he refused to allow powerful, patronage-minded Republican leaders such as Conkling and Blaine to dictate his selections.[3]

Hayes might well, it seemed in 1877, preside over a peaceful and successful administration. Although the Democrats controlled the House of Representatives, the President's almost pathetic eagerness to conciliate the South and restore the reputation of the Democratic party appeared likely to reduce partisan opposition to a minimum. Besides appointing a southern Democrat, David M. Key, as Postmaster General, he swiftly withdrew the last remnants of federal troops from the South.[4] In September, he undertook a "good-will" tour of Kentucky, Tennessee, Alabama, Georgia, and Virginia. Before almost uniformly cordial audiences, he urged his "Confederate friends" to "obey the whole Constitution" and improve Negro educational opportunities. At the same time he assured southern Negroes that their "rights and interests" would be safer if the "great mass of intelligent white men were let alone by the general government." Hayes was convinced that his policy of conciliation would so enchant southern Democrats that they would allow the Republican minority to organize the House of Representatives in the new Congress. That he was able to persuade Congressman James A. Garfield of Ohio to turn down a chance of promotion to the Senate in order to be available for the Speakership, suggests that the possibility did not seem totally unrealistic.[5]

The President's determination to press for civil-service reform was bound to rouse opposition within his own party, but he approached this problem with a mixture of firmness and moderation that offered considerable hope of success. He did not entirely reject the claims of the spoilsmen, cheerfully rewarding politicians who had helped swing the disputed electoral votes his way, interpreting very

[3] Barnard, *Hayes*, pp. 414–416; J. D. Richardson (ed.), *Messages and Papers of the Presidents* (10 vols., Washington, 1898), VII, 442–447.

[4] In South Carolina, only 350 soldiers were involved; in Louisiana, 293. R. W. Logan, *The Negro in American Life and Thought: The Nadir, 1877–1901* (New York, 1954), p. 20.

[5] *Ibid.*, pp. 21–29; T. C. Smith, *The Life and Letters of James Abram Garfield* (New Haven, 1925), p. 653.

leniently his executive order requiring government workers who were concurrently holding party offices to relinquish one or the other, and devoting many hours to the distribution of petty political plums. While insisting upon first-rate men for major cabinet posts, he allowed influential Republican leaders considerable say in the selection process. He permitted Senator Oliver P. Morton of Indiana to name the Secretary of the Navy and to veto two other candidates for the cabinet, and he followed Blaine's advice in picking his Attorney General.

When Hayes fought with the politicians over spoils, he carefully rested his case on high ground—the right of the President to control the executive departments and the necessity to combat corruption. In his controversy with Senator Conkling over the removal of the top New York Customs House officials, for example, Hayes did not act until an investigating committee had revealed that about 200 placeholders were drawing salaries without performing significant work, that importers were systematically defrauding the government by bribing customs men, and that high officials were siphoning off some $1.5 million annually from the duties collected.[6]

The President also displayed consistently a firmness and fairness that seemed to mark him as an outstanding leader. His decision to employ federal troops during the riotous railroad strikes of 1877 was made promptly but on the basis of careful evaluation of the situation. He recognized that despite their violent behavior, most of the strikers were "good men, sober, intelligent and industrious." When he decided that the Bland-Allison Silver Purchase bill of 1878 threatened the financial stability of the nation, he vetoed it despite the warnings of many advisers that to do so would be both politically disastrous and, since Congress was certain to override his veto, futile.[7] Again, in 1879 he vetoed important appropriation

---

[6] Barnard, *Hayes*, pp. 416, 472–473, 451–452; L. D. White, *The Republican Era: 1869–1901* (New York, 1958), p. 96; D. S. Muzzey, *James G. Blaine: A Political Idol of Other Days* (New York, 1934), p. 134; 45 Cong. 1 sess., *House Executive Document* No. 8, pp. 15–16, 38–39.

[7] Barnard, *Hayes*, pp. 445–447; C. R. Williams, *The Life of Rutherford Birchard Hayes* (2 vols., Boston, 1914), II, 119–127. Even Secretary of the Treasury John Sherman, notably conservative on financial questions, urged Hayes to sign the bill because of the "strong public sentiment" in favor of silver inflation. Sherman employed a typical politician's argument—by limiting actual purchases to the minimum required by the bill, $2 million monthly, the purpose of the measure could be circumvented. John Sherman, *Recollections of Forty Years in the House, Senate, and Cabinet* (2 vols., Chicago, 1895), II, 623.

bills after the Democratic-controlled Congress had attached riders designed to prevent the use of troops "to keep the peace at the polls," and forced the Democrats to back down.[8]

In handling foreign relations, Hayes acted with equal firmness. When brigands based on Mexican soil attacked border settlements in Texas in 1877, he authorized American commanders to cross the Rio Grande in "hot pursuit" of invaders. The Mexican government (and many Americans) protested angrily, but Hayes did not relent until, with the co-operation of Mexican military units, the brigands had been destroyed or dispersed. News of the plan of a French company to cut a canal across Panama produced still another determined stand by the President, early in 1880. American policy, he insisted, was "a canal under American control, or no canal." Swiftly he dispatched two warships to Panamanian waters, and he sent a message to Congress stating his position in blunt language. If existing treaties "stand in the way of this policy" (he added without referring specifically to the Clayton-Bulwer Treaty of 1850 with Great Britain, which had guaranteed that neither power would control any future canal independently of the other), "suitable steps" ought to be taken to modify them.[9] Yet he was no mere saber-rattler. He dealt with the Mexican situation patiently. When anti-Chinese elements on the West Coast persuaded Congress to abrogate the Burlingame Treaty of 1868, which guaranteed the right of Chinese subjects to enter the United States, he vetoed the bill as a violation of a binding international agreement, although he personally favored keeping the Chinese out.[10]

Nevertheless, Hayes's administration was marked chiefly by bickering, confusion, and frustration. His effort to conciliate the Democrats ended in fiasco. The southern Democrats refused from the start to honor their pledge to treat southern Negroes fairly.

[8] Williams, *Hayes*, II, 174–199.

[9] Barnard, *Hayes*, pp. 443–444; T. H. Williams (ed.), *Hayes: The Diary of a President, 1875–1881* (New York, 1964), p. 265; D. M. Pletcher, *The Awkward Years: American Foreign Relations Under Garfield and Arthur* (Columbia, Mo., 1961), pp. 8, 28–29; Richardson, *Messages and Papers*, VII, 585–586. Americans without regard for party disliked the Clayton-Bulwer Treaty. Democratic Congressman S. S. Cox, for example, called it "the diplomatic blunder of the century." E. L. Godkin of the *Nation*, who consistently criticized expansionist diplomatic ventures, applauded Hayes's message. David Lindsey, *"Sunset" Cox: Irrepressible Democrat* (Detroit, 1959), p. 194; W. M. Armstrong, *E. L. Godkin and American Foreign Policy: 1865–1900* (New York, 1957), pp. 137–139.

[10] Barnard, *Hayes*, pp. 447–479.

Instead of allowing the Republicans to organize the House of Representatives, the Democratic congressmen quickly demonstrated that they would seize every opportunity to embarrass the President. In 1878 they launched an investigation of the 1876 election in the disputed states that was aimed only at embarrassing the administration. This investigation backfired, because it revealed that the Democrats had been as guilty of fraud as their opponents, but it infuriated the Republicans. When Hayes persisted in trying to placate the Southerners, his party turned its ire on him. Garfield, for example, had originally urged other Republican leaders to give the President's strategy "a fair trial." Soon, however, he was accusing Hayes of blindly ignoring the effects which the policy was having on their party, and when the Democrats undertook their investigation he began to denounce it as "a give-away." Garfield genuinely wished Hayes well; a less sympathetic man like Blaine— and he was typical of many Republican politicians—opposed the conciliation of the South with increasing vehemence and remained grumpily silent when the Democratic-controlled investigating committee sought to discredit Hayes's title to the presidency.[11]

Where civil service was concerned, Hayes was even more actively involved in his own failure. Again the behavior of Garfield is instructive. A sound practical politician, Garfield knew how important patronage was to the party system, but he was ready to give Hayes a "chance to test his policy," as outlined in the inaugural address. A real return to "the policy of the Fathers," when government jobs had not been considered "party rewards," might possibly succeed, Garfield thought. But halfway measures were sure to fail. "If nobody is to be appointed because he is your friend or my friend, then nobody should be appointed because he is any other man's friend. The President himself should exercise the same self-denial as other officials." In practice, however, Hayes did not eschew the use of patronage; rather, he denied it to some factions (notably the Conklingites) and doled it out freely to others: those who had helped win and hold the disputed electoral votes, various middle-western politicos, personal friends, no less than forty-seven members of the carpetbagger Louisiana legislature who had acquiesced in turning the state over to the Democrats in conformity with Hayes's

11 45 Cong. 3 sess., *House Exec. Doc.* No. 140; Williams, *Hayes*, II, 142–169; Smith, *Garfield*, pp. 652, 656–657, 664–665; Muzzey, *Blaine*, pp. 134, 142.

southern policy. Furthermore, when the party treasury began to suffer during the 1878 campaign, he modified his executive order forbidding assessments. Officeholders could make *voluntary* contributions, he announced, but would not be removed from their positions if they did not do so. Little wonder that an experienced politician like Garfield, although still eager to support Hayes, was soon complaining of the "outrageous and unjust" practices of his administration and telling him to his face that "he must abandon some of his notions of Civil Service." In private (like the President, Garfield kept a diary) he accused Hayes of being timid when confronted by "men of his own party who are larger than he." By 1880 he was denouncing Hayes's "absurd attempt to get on without the aid of Congressmen in making selections."

Hayes's ambivalent handling of civil-service questions also dismayed the reformers. George W. Curtis, later organizer of the National Civil Service Reform League, claimed in 1878 that the administration was being defeated "with weapons which its own inconsistency had furnished." Many other reformers voiced similar criticisms. Hayes tended toward smugness when evaluating his own achievements, yet he eventually admitted that he had perhaps erred in handling patronage, because of his "anxiety to complete the great work of pacification" in the South.[12]

The most curious aspect of Hayes's record was his almost total disregard of the economic and social problems of the period. He dealt forthrightly with the riotous railroad strike of 1877, but in his annual message the following December he discussed the disturbances only in a routine reference to the report of the Secretary of War on the activities of the Army. As for the economic slump of the seventies, he repeatedly insisted that the restoration of good times waited only upon returning to the gold standard. Once that was accomplished, he sat back and waited for time to prove his point. "I am persuaded," he told Congress in December, 1878, a month before the Resumption Act went into effect, "that the welfare of legitimate business and industry . . . will be best promoted by abstaining from all attempts to make radical changes. . . . Let it be understood that during the coming year the business of the

---

[12] Smith, *Garfield*, p. 654; E. P. Oberholtzer, *A History of the United States Since the Civil War* (5 vols., New York, 1931), IV, 342–346; Ari Hoogenboom, *Outlawing the Spoils: A History of the Civil Service Reform Movement, 1865–1883* (Urbana, 1961), pp. 163–166; Williams, *Hayes Diary*, p. 101.

country will be undisturbed by governmental interference with the laws affecting it." He spoke occasionally of the need to increase American exports, but chiefly because of "solicitude" caused by "the outward drain of the precious metals" that the nation's unfavorable trade balance was producing. And he suggested few means of expanding trade other than the "vigorous efforts" of "enterprising citizens."[13]

Hayes had announced at the start of his term that he would not seek re-election. This was fortunate for his peace of mind and self-esteem, for his chances even of being renominated would have been minuscule.[14] His administration was, in the opinion of most observers, a failure. Southern ingratitude, the selfish shortsightedness displayed by both Democratic and Republican politicians in all matters related to patronage, and Hayes's strange combination of stubborn integrity and whiggish executive passivity combined to produce this result.

Thus, as the 1880 Presidential election approached, the reigning Republicans had neither a record of successful legislation to rely on nor a candidate who could draw upon the power and prestige of the White House. Their position all through the North and West was strong, but, outside of New England, far from impregnable. The Democrats, on the other hand, now controlled the solid South—135 of the 185 electoral votes needed to win. A pattern had emerged that was to dominate presidential politics for more than a decade.

The Republicans had the more difficult problem. No northern or western state was beyond their grasp, but they must hold nearly all of them to elect a President. They were like an army defending a huge, densely populated city; any break in their widely extended lines might mean disaster. To relieve the pressure they could attempt sorties into enemy country, and, as we have seen, they tried repeatedly to invade the Democratic South. By doing so, however, they weakened their northern defenses with little hope of obtaining

13 Richardson, *Messages and Papers,* VII, 445, 461, 469, 472, 509, 570, 612–613, 615.

14 Although some contemporaries believed Hayes was hoping to be "drafted," there is no direct evidence that this was so. His most recent biographer suggests that he may have wanted to be asked to run again, but only for the satisfaction of being able to refuse. Barnard, *Hayes,* pp. 486–488. In any case, the delegates practically ignored him; he had no influence over the choice of his successor. *Ibid.,* pp. 492–493.

corresponding advantages. Electoral votes came in small bunches in the South, whereas in the big northern states, one or two key losses would cost them the presidency. This situation kept the G.O.P. primarily on the defensive.

The Democrats, secure in their sprawling southern base, could concentrate upon finding a few weak spots in the Republican lines and striking hard against them. New York, with its fractionated politics, its powerful Democratic New York City machine, and its tradition of sympathy for the South (product of the old alliance between its cotton merchants and the great planters), was the chief Democratic objective in every election. Although not large enough to exert a critical influence in most national elections, New York's neighbors, New Jersey and Connecticut, were also vulnerable. The three northern states bordering the Ohio River, Illinois, Indiana, and Ohio, offered the other major target for the Democrats. The political pattern established in these states during the sectional conflict over slavery in the 1850's persisted in the postwar decades to a remarkable degree. Their southern counties had been settled chiefly by people from the slave states who tended to vote Democratic. Their northern districts, inhabited mainly by migrants from New England opposed to the extension of slavery, were usually Republican. Lagrange County in northern Indiana was consistently Republican; Sullivan County, in the southwestern part of the state, consistently Democratic. Ashtabula County in northern Ohio gave Republican presidential candidates huge majorities throughout the period, while Pike County in southern Ohio was a Democratic stronghold. There were numerous exceptions to this geographic division, but in effect, to continue the military metaphor, the Democrats held a powerful salient within the Republican lines. If they could extend it even slightly, they could carry the day.

The thirty-five electoral votes of New York, plus those of either Ohio or Indiana or Illinois, would, with the South, mean victory. The Democrats could nominate a New Yorker for President and a citizen of one of these middlewestern states for Vice-President and hope that the local popularity of their candidates alone would win the election.[15]

[15] W. D. Burnham, *Presidential Ballots: 1836–1892* (Baltimore, 1955), pp. 400–401, 408–409, 678–679, 692–693. Ethnic and religious factors complicated matters, as did the existence of strong Democratic political machines in Chicago and other

Of course, the strategy of the parties was never quite so simple. Despite the assiduous and sometimes ingenious efforts of both organizations to straddle or obscure issues, the wording of party platforms and the utterances of stump speakers often affected elections in unexpected ways. The rival ambitions of dozens of hopeful candidates vexed the attempts of party organizations to marshal their forces efficiently. Chance events also influenced the results. But every election in this period was essentially a battle for New York and the Middle West, and in each the outcome was determined by a tiny fraction of the total vote cast.

In 1880, Republican disillusionment with Hayes's policies was so complete that party leaders had no difficulty agreeing over issues. All the prominent politicians took a dim view of civil-service reform and, abandoning hope of winning southern support, waved the bloody shirt lustily. The vacuum created by Hayes's failure, however, together with the venomous feelings stirred up by his policies, made the choice of a presidential candidate particularly difficult. The administration supported Secretary of the Treasury John Sherman, whose appeal stemmed from his record of having successfully managed the resumption of specie payments, his long political experience, and his residence in a key state, Ohio. But Sherman was too stiff and colorless to be genuinely popular; his main chance lay in the possibility of a deadlock between the Blaine and Conkling wings. Blaine wanted the nomination himself. Conkling and his followers, dead set against either Blaine or anyone connected with the Hayes administration, preferred ex-President Grant, who, despite his inadequacies as an executive, remained the great national hero of the age.

The Blaine and Conkling forces were so evenly balanced that, as events unfolded at the long Chicago convention in June, 1880, neither could obtain a majority. For thirty-three roll calls they remained deadlocked. Then the Shermanites made their move, but failed to break the impasse. Finally, on the thirty-sixth ballot, the exhausted delegates swung to James A. Garfield.[16]

---

cities, but the Ohio River states were always closely contested. Of the sixteen men nominated for President or Vice-President by the major parties between 1876 and 1892, all but two were residents of New York, Ohio, Indiana, or Illinois.

[16] Hoogenboom, *Outlawing the Spoils*, pp. 179–181; S. P. Hirshson, *Farewell to the Bloody Shirt: Northern Republicans and the Southern Negro, 1877–1893*

Few were enthusiastic about the Ohio congressman, but he had a good war record, came from an important state, and was a fine-looking man with a warm personality. Most significantly, he had not offended any of the major candidates. Although some of the shrewdest politicians at Chicago were convinced that he had been maneuvering steadily to win the nomination, he had not sought it openly and had repeatedly and conspicuously posed as the advocate of conciliation, fairness, and moderation. The election in November could not be won "by assailing our Republican brethren," he had reminded the delegates. In victory, Garfield achieved the remarkable feat of uniting not only Blaine and Conkling but also Sherman and even the civil-service reformers. The convention completed the job of bandaging party wounds by selecting Conkling's lieutenant, Chester A. Arthur, former head of the New York Customs House, as the vice-presidential candidate.[17]

The Democrats, meeting later in June at Cincinnati, also experienced difficulty in choosing a candidate. Except for his failing health, Samuel J. Tilden would have been the logical nominee, both because of the importance of his home state, New York, and because he could employ the emotionally persuasive argument that he had been cheated of election in 1876. As it was, Tilden vacillated, refusing either to seek the nomination actively or withdraw categorically. Senator Thomas F. Bayard of Delaware developed considerable strength, but in a leaderless, confused convention the delegates coalesced behind Winfield Scott Hancock of Pennsylvania, a war hero without political experience who was acceptable to the Southerners because of his mild administration of the Fifth Military District (Louisiana and Texas) during Reconstruction. The Republicans' rejection of Grant also raised the possibility that Hancock might win the votes of northern veterans and others whose memories of the Civil War remained fresh. The Democrats com-

---

(Bloomington, 1962), pp. 79, 86; V. P. De Santis, *Republicans Face the Southern Question—The New Departure Years, 1877–1897* (Baltimore, 1959), pp. 133–134; H. J. Clancy, *The Presidential Election of 1880* (Chicago, 1958), pp. 35, 82–121; Smith, *Garfield*, pp. 943–992; L. B. Richardson, *William E. Chandler: Republican* (New York, 1940), pp. 247–255.

[17] Smith, *Garfield*, p. 975; Sherman, *Recollections*, II, 775–778; Hoogenboom, *Outlawing the Spoils*, pp. 182–183; G. F. Howe, *Chester A. Arthur* (New York, 1934), pp. 108–110.

pleted their ticket by nominating William H. English of Indiana for Vice-President.[18]

The campaign itself was typical of the contests of the period. Garfield and Hancock were plagued as much by intrigues within their own parties as by the tactics of their opponents. Mighty efforts were made to rouse ethnic and religious prejudices. Each side worried constantly about the frauds and deceits practiced by the other and resolved to fight fire with fire. While devoting enormous amounts of energy and ingenuity to supervising the management of the armies of politicos on the stump, the candidates avoided participating openly in the struggle. Everywhere, but especially in the crucial northern states, the public was treated to torchlight parades, marching bands, and the windy oratory of countless local leaders and visiting luminaries.

Early in August, Garfield met with all the prominent Republican politicians in a great conclave in New York to ratify his peace with the Conkling machine. He insisted that he had emerged from these talks uncommitted—"no trades, no shackles," he wrote in his diary —but since Conkling and his henchmen then threw themselves and considerable New York money into the contest, he must at least have allowed them to misunderstand his intentions with regard to New York patronage. Hancock hastened to arrive at a political understanding with Senator Bayard and to try to reconcile the differences separating the warring Irving Hall and Tammany Hall factions of the Democracy in New York.[19]

Charges and countercharges filled the air. The Democrats, dredging up Garfield's connection with the Crédit Mobilier scandal, accused him of having sold his soul to the Union Pacific for $329. They also publicized a flagrant forgery in which Garfield purportedly came out against restricting Chinese immigration on the

18 Clancy, *Election of 1880*, pp. 68–69, 122–140; Oberholtzer, *History*, IV, 83–84. Garfield, of course, was also an ex-general, as were the two minor-party candidates, James B. Weaver of the Greenback party and Neal Dow of the Prohibition party.

19 Smith, *Garfield*, pp. 1007–1017; L. J. Lang (ed.), *The Autobiography of Thomas Collier Platt* (New York, 1910), pp. 126–134; Clancy, *Election of 1880*, pp. 209–210. Whatever promises Garfield actually made at the New York meeting, he was emotionally committed to the Blaine faction. He called Blaine "a prince of good fellows," forgetting that only a year earlier he had expressed "distrust" of this "brilliant, aggressive, calculating man." He corresponded with Blaine on the most intimate terms during the campaign. R. G. Caldwell, *James A. Garfield: Party Chieftain* (New York, 1931), p. 301; Gail Hamilton, *Biography of James G. Blaine* (Norwich, 1895), pp. 486–489.

ground that employers "have the right to buy labor where they can buy it cheapest." The Republicans described General Hancock as a pliant tool of unreconstructed rebels. Famous war heroes lashed out at one or another of their former comrades-in-arms viciously. General William Rosecrans, who was running for Congress on the Democratic ticket in California, denounced Garfield, his former chief of staff, as an "unmitigated fraud." General Grant characterized Hancock as a "weak, vain man." The wife of General William Tecumseh Sherman declared against Garfield on the theory that he "would do all he could to injure our holy Catholic Church," while various Republicans tried to play both sides of the religious issue, attacking Hancock for his role in the allegedly unfair conviction of the Catholic Mary Surratt for *her* alleged role in the assassination of the sainted Lincoln, and simultaneously charging that Hancock's Catholic wife was planning to make the White House "the headquarters of priests, nuns, monks and so on."[20]

Each side charged the other with bribery and the misuse of money. These accusations, although difficult to substantiate in detail at the time, still harder at this distance, were undoubtedly based on fact. Both parties poured money into crucial Indiana, where the October state elections were counted upon to produce a bandwagon effect. When Benjamin Harrison informed Garfield in September that ten thousand southern Democrats were ready to "pay their own expenses for the privilege of putting in a Dem. vote in Indiana," he was probably being carried away by his own heated emotions, but he obviously believed that such a possibility existed. The Democratic national chairman, alarmed by rumors that the Republicans were planning to run illegal voters into Indiana from Kentucky, urged Indiana leaders to "check this outrageous fraud, and if necessary to organize some plan to keep even with them." A little later in the campaign, a Republican orator reported to Garfield that there were thirty thousand "merchantable" votes in Indiana. "Which side will manage to buy most of them is the question," he added coolly.[21]

The Republicans carried Indiana in October and the country in

[20] Smith, *Garfield*, pp. 1027, 1030–1031; Caldwell, *Garfield*, pp. 306–307; Clancy, *Election of 1880*, pp. 172–180, 202, 213–214, 233.
[21] H. J. Sievers, *Benjamin Harrison: Hoosier Statesman* (New York, 1959), pp. 177 n., 179; A. V. House, "The Democratic State Central Committee of Indiana in 1880," *Indiana Magazine of History*, LVIII (1962), 202.

November. Outside the South, only New Jersey, California, and Nevada gave their electoral votes to Hancock. The outcome in the Electoral College, 214–155, would have been reversed if the Democrats had won New York's 35 votes; nevertheless, the new President's title to his office was clear.[22]

Garfield worked manfully to establish a successful administration. By nature prone to conciliation and compromise, he would have preferred to deal evenhandedly with both the Stalwarts and the Half-Breeds. However, the former, possessed of a sense of mission that would have been formidable if directed toward any rational public objective but which was merely vexing when aimed, as it was, only at the achievement of office for its own sake, were determined to dominate the new government. They forced Garfield to choose between themselves and the Blaine faction, which really gave him no choice at all. Whatever his inadequacies, Blaine was a public man; he had policies, some quite imaginative and farsighted, and was capable of subordinating himself to the elected head of the nation even though he was as interested as Conkling in patronage and was a diabolically clever political manipulator.

The Conklingites had contributed mightily to the Republican triumph, especially in their own New York and in Indiana. Now they claimed as their reward absolute control of New York patronage and their choice of the rest of the spoils of victory. They demanded first that Levi P. Morton, a New York banker, be made Secretary of the Treasury. Garfield had no personal objection to Morton, who had been his own first choice as his running mate in the campaign, but the banker's Wall Street connections and his extremely conservative views on the money question made him unacceptable to western Republicans. As the President-elect told a group of Morton's importunate supporters, "it would be most unwise in a party sense to give the place to N.Y. city." He offered to name Morton Secretary of the Navy and to consider alternative recommendations for the Treasury post. The Stalwarts' answer was simple: Morton must be Secretary of the Treasury. Desperately seeking a meeting of the minds, Garfield asked Conkling to come to

---

[22] Garfield received 4,453,211 votes, Hancock 4,445,843. The winner's margin in Connecticut was 2,660; in Indiana, 6,625; in New York, 21,033. Hancock carried California by twenty-two votes out of a total of over 164,000. James B. Weaver, running on a Greenback-Labor ticket, received over 300,000 votes nationally. Burnham, *Presidential Ballots*, pp. 130–131, 134, 889.

Ohio for a conference. The two met on February 16, 1881, and discussed the matter at length, but Conkling refused every counter-suggestion that Garfield proposed.

Garfield could not possibly yield to this senseless intransigence. Shortly before his inauguration he filled the "New York" post in the Cabinet by selecting Thomas L. James, nominally a member of the Conkling faction but not highly regarded by the senator, to be Postmaster General. Conkling thereupon descended upon Garfield in his rooms at the Riggs House in Washington with Vice-President-elect Arthur and Thomas C. Platt, the other New York senator, in tow, and denounced him to his face with unbridled ferocity. Such fanaticism merely propelled the President further into the embrace of Blaine, who not only became Secretary of State but exerted an increasing influence over presidential appointments. Still seeking to "go as far as I can to keep the peace," Garfield named a number of Conkling's henchmen to important offices (for example, he made Levi P. Morton minister to France), but he was now determined to establish once and for all his right to control major appointments. The climax came when he nominated William H. Robertson as collector of the Port of New York. Robertson was Conkling's deadly enemy, his nomination a declaration of war against the New York senator and also against the whole system of senatorial courtesy that had given senators a veto over presidential appointments in their own states.

Had Conkling not been so unreasonable, Garfield might not have been able to win this test of strength. However, even patronage-minded senators would not stand by their New York colleague under the circumstances. When the President's victory appeared certain, both Conkling and Platt resigned, hoping that the New York legislature would enable them to save face by re-electing them. The legislature would not do so; after a protracted struggle, in which Blaine figured importantly behind the scenes, two other men were chosen to fill the vacancies. Against his will, Garfield had been forced to take a stand that marked a milestone in the revival of the power and prestige of the White House.[23]

[23] Caldwell, *Garfield*, pp. 315–327, 341–343, 345–348; Clancy, *Election of 1880*, pp. 119, 190, 199, 253; Robert McElroy, *Levi Parsons Morton: Banker, Diplomat and Statesman* (New York, 1930), pp. 105–107, 119–130; E. B. Andrews, *History of the Last Quarter-Century in the United States* (2 vols., New York, 1896), I, 323; Smith, *Garfield*, pp. 1103–1142.

In this contest with Conkling, Garfield drew heavily (but by no means exclusively) on the advice and support of Blaine. The new Secretary of State, one of the most enigmatic political characters of the age, was eager to play a large role in the new administration and did nothing to discourage rumors that he would be its real head. Where matters of patronage and domestic policy were concerned, these rumors were exaggerated—Blaine had great influence, but Garfield was not his puppet.[24] In the field of foreign affairs, however, the President gave the Secretary remarkable freedom.

Blaine approached foreign affairs with energy and imagination, but, as was common with him, his performance was marred by a certain slapdash quality. In Latin America he sought to increase American influence and also to help the republics of the area achieve internal stability. He consistently opposed even the most harmless kind of European intervention, objecting, for example, to a treaty between Costa Rica and Colombia that provided for arbitration of their joint boundary by the King of Belgium. He took a very advanced position with regard to the projected Central American canal, going so far as to warn the European powers that the United States considered exclusive control of such a waterway as necessary to its security as control of its own transcontinental railroads. When Mexico threatened to seize disputed territory along its border with Guatemala, Blaine let the Mexican government know that the United States would treat an invasion as an unfriendly act, adding that America claimed "the right to use its friendly offices in discouragement of any movement on the part of neighboring states which may tend to disturb the balance of power between them." During the so-called War of the Pacific between Chile and Peru, which resulted in a decisive victory for the Chileans, Blaine labored to prevent Chile from annexing Peruvian territory, but resisted a French suggestion that the United States, Great Britain, and France offer to mediate the dispute jointly.

However, his warnings and pronouncements were mostly bluster. He tended to initiate bold policies and then fail to follow them up. Many of the representatives he sent to handle delicate negotiations in Latin America were inexperienced political hacks, some of them outright rogues. Thus, his basically sensible and intelligent policies

24 For example, the President exacted a pledge from Blaine that he would not be a candidate for President in 1884.

were often misunderstood in Latin America; they produced few results during his tenure as Secretary of State except tension and fear.[25]

To be sure, fate did not grant Blaine much time to mature his policies. On July 2, 1881, a deranged lawyer named Charles J. Guiteau shot President Garfield in the back in a Washington railroad station.[26] Although the President lingered until September 19 before expiring, little government business was transacted during that summer. Thus, when the Conklingite Chester A. Arthur took over the White House, Blaine naturally offered to resign; and although Arthur asked him to stay on temporarily, he knew that his tenure must of necessity be brief.[27] He therefore launched a kind of diplomatic *Blitzkrieg,* unprecedented in those days of leisurely foreign relations, that had few immediate results but which foreshadowed many later trends in American policy. Between the middle of November, 1881, and his surrender of the State Department to his successor, Frederick T. Frelinghuysen, a month later, he asked Great Britain to consent to major revisions of the Clayton Bulwer Treaty that would make the issue of an isthmian canal "solely . . . an American question, to be dealt with and decided by the American governments," and, in another note, warned the British not to meddle in the Hawaiian Islands, which, he said, "the United States regards . . . as essentially a part of the American system."[28] He also dispatched what was practically an ultimatum to

25 Pletcher, *Awkward Years,* pp. 22, 30–32, 36, 40–51, 58; Smith, *Garfield,* 1166; A. F. Tyler, *The Foreign Policy of James G. Blaine* (Minneapolis, 1927) , pp. 32–36, 52–58, 66–69, 110–114.

26 Smith, *Garfield,* 1146, 1179–1180. Although Guiteau was mentally unbalanced, he was not insane in the legal sense of not knowing what he was doing. He testified that he had killed (he used the word "removed") the President on command of "the Diety" in order to restore Republican harmony. The event that led to his inspiration, he said, was Conkling's resignation from the Senate. Although previous to that event he had plagued both Garfield and Secretary of State Blaine for a diplomatic appointment, he insisted that after Conkling's resignation he would not have accepted any office; therefore he was not, as the cliché has it, a "disappointed office seeker." Considering the state of public feeling—two separate attempts to murder him were made during his incarceration—his long trial was conducted fairly. *Report of Proceedings in the Case of Charles J. Guiteau* (Washington, 1882) , *passim.*

27 From Blaine's selfish point of view, resignation was also imperative if he hoped to reassert his position of leadership within the Republican party.

28 Pletcher, *Awkward Years,* pp. 65, 70; Tyler, *Foreign Policy of Blaine,* pp. 38–42, 195–199. Blaine favored annexing the Islands, which were already tied

Chile on the question of its occupation of Peruvian territory, and increased his pressure on Mexico with regard to the Mexican-Guatemalan border dispute. Finally, he invited all the Latin American nations to attend a conference on hemispheric problems, to be held in Washington late in 1882.

All this was both overly precipitous and unfair to the new Arthur administration, which, lacking any clear idea of what its foreign policy should be, backed away from as many of Blaine's ambitious schemes as it could. The invitations to the pan-American conference were withdrawn and Blaine's strong note on the Chilean-Peruvian controversy was repudiated. When the British responded coldly to Blaine's request for modification of the canal treaty, Arthur and Frelinghuysen continued the discussions, but without significant results. Adopting a less urgent tone toward Mexico's conflict with Guatemala, they merely offered the good offices of the United States. Eventually these two nations worked out an agreement of sorts without American assistance.[29]

The new President soon laid to rest the worst fears of those who had expected him to turn the White House into a larger version of the New York Customs House. Although he offered Conkling a seat on the Supreme Court (which Conkling refused), he did not make himself his former leader's puppet. He gave the bulk of the patronage at his disposal to Stalwarts, but refrained from open warfare against the Blaine wing. He left his enemy William H. Robertson in command of the New York customs and insisted on continuing an investigation of the Post Office frauds begun under Garfield, even though important Stalwart politicos were deeply implicated by the disclosures. In short, he showed a sound awareness of what was fitting, both in his personal life—he had the White House completely redecorated and installed a French chef in his kitchen—and in his public performance.[30]

economically to the United States by a reciprocity treaty, as a prelude to a major effort to stimulate American emigration to Hawaii. Merze Tate, *The United States and the Hawaiian Kingdom: A Political History* (New Haven, 1965), pp. 45–46.

[29] Pletcher, *Awkward Years*, pp. 74–80, 85, 89–111; Muzzey, *Blaine*, pp. 248–249; Tyler, *Foreign Policy of Blaine*, pp. 52–62, 165–168; R. H. Bastert, "Diplomatic Reversal: Frelinghuysen's Opposition to Blaine's Pan-American Policy in 1882," *Mississippi Valley Historical Review*, XLII (1956), 653–671.

[30] Oberholtzer, *History*, IV, 122, 127–128; Howe, *Arthur*, pp. 166–167.

However much the responsibilities and honor of his office had sobered Arthur, they had not changed his basic nature. He remained essentially an administrator, more reasonable, more intelligent, and more urbane than most, yet lacking in breadth of vision. He responded fairly well to the routine duties of his office—which were few enough—but seldom displayed statesmanlike qualities. In 1882, exasperated by the tendency of Congress to spend money ever more lavishly on the "improvement" of rivers and harbors, most of it for projects that served no national purpose, he vetoed the current appropriation, suggesting that the sum be cut in half and that he be authorized to implement only those projects that he deemed worth while.[31]

But on more important questions, Arthur seldom took a strong stand. His sound grasp of administration, together with the circumstances that had made him President, ought to have led him to fight hard for civil-service reform. Yet the mounting demand for reform, a demand all the more significant because most of the leading newspapers and a remarkably large number of the nation's most distinguished private citizens were active in the cause, apparently had little effect upon him. Although he informed Congress that he favored a civil-service law, he went out of his way to question many of the important practical proposals of the reformers. He opposed full reliance on competitive examinations, employing the specious reasoning that "wide knowledge of books, or . . . promptitude in answering questions" were not sound tests of a candidate's aptitude for most government posts. His argument that "the evils which are complained of can not be eradicated at once; the work must be gradual" was certainly defensible, but he gave very little direction or moral support to the reform movement.

Congress, therefore, debated the civil-service issue, thus providing unreconstructed spoilsmen with another opportnity to shock decent citizens by the coarseness of their attacks on reformers, but did not enact a civil-service law. Public irritation mounted when, as the 1882 congressional elections approached, stories of continued assessments levied against officeholders by hungry party leaders

---

[31] Richardson, *Messages and Papers*, VIII, 120–122. The rivers and harbors bill of 1870 had appropriated less than $4 million; that of 1880, almost $9 million; that of 1882, $18.7 million. Congress, however, passed the bill over Arthur's veto.

filled the papers. The overriding of Arthur's veto of the rivers and harbors bill was a further cause of national exasperation. As the party in power, the Republicans suffered most from this state of affairs. The elections produced dramatic Democratic gains; the party won sixty-two new seats in the House of Representatives, important local victories in key states like Ohio, Indiana, New York, Connecticut, and New Jersey, and even elected governors in the Republican strongholds of Pennsylvania and Massachusetts.[32]

This shattering setback sobered the Republicans. President Arthur, who naturally hoped to win election in his own right in 1884, at once attempted to play a more prominent role as head of the nation and leader of his party. In his second annual message, delivered a month after the election, he urged Congress to take "prompt and definite action" on the civil-service problem, to slash excise taxes, make "large reductions" in tariff duties, appropriate more money for building up the Navy, and pass laws regulating the railroads and conserving the "fast disappearing" forest resources of the country. The extent of his suggestions was indeed remarkable when compared with those in his first annual message, or with any of those of President Hayes.[33]

Arthur had not, however, really changed. Congress passed the Pendleton Civil Service bill without further presidential urging, but showed little inclination to adopt his other suggestions. He, in turn, displayed still less inclination to drive his program through the Congress.[34] Instead, he concentrated his energies on sordid political manipulation, seeking to strengthen his position in the Republican party by liberal dispensations of patronage. Before the 1882 elections he had tried to build up the party in the South by supporting the "Readjusters," discontented Democrats, chiefly the followers and imitators of General William Mahone of Virginia, who had emerged as a power in that state in 1879. Backing Mahone

32 *Ibid.*, VIII, 60-63; Hoogenboom, *Outlawing the Spoils*, pp. 215-235; Oberholtzer, *History*, IV, 148-151. The Democratic gains in the House included eleven seats in Ohio, eight in New York, five in Indiana, six in Michigan, three in Illinois, and five in Pennsylvania. The Democratic majority in the new House was 201 to 119.

33 Richardson, *Messages and Papers*, VIII, 126-148.

34 In discussing his plan for reducing excise taxes, for example, Arthur did so, he said, "with little hope that I can make [a] valuable contribution to this vexed question." *Ibid.*, VIII, 135.

involved the sacrifice of two cherished Republican principles—conservative finance and Negro rights. The Readjusters favored debt repudiation and soft-money schemes, and were, in the main, dedicated Negro-baiters. Most southern Negro leaders, lacking a practicable alternative, grumblingly went along with Arthur's strategy, and the Republican-Readjuster alliance achieved a few small victories in 1882. However, the bulk of the southern whites remained loyal to the Democrats, and after 1883 Arthur reverted to a pro-Negro position. His policy, C. Vann Woodward suggests, would have been "a test for the social conscience of a Machiavelli."[35]

Arthur's handling of the tariff issue after 1882 further illustrates his inadequacy. To the general argument that protective duties raised the cost of living, those who favored reductions, a group which included the President, could add telling references to the problem of the Treasury surplus. The boom of 1879–82 resulted in a huge increase in the volume of imports—from $466 million in 1879 to $767 million in 1882—and consequently of customs revenues, which soared from $137 million to $220 million.[36] In 1881, Arthur had recommended that Congress create a tariff commission to study the problem and suggest reductions. This was done, and, although dominated by protectionists, the commission recommended (December, 1882) cuts in tariff levels averaging about 20 or 25 per cent.

There followed one of the most disgraceful examples of shiftiness by "lame duck" legislators in the long history of Congress. The Senate maneuvered to usurp the House's constitutional right to initiate tariff bills. The House approved a special rule to circumvent the low-tariff interest which allowed the representatives to vote to reject the Senate tariff bill, but not to vote to accept it.[37] The

35 C. V. Woodward, *Origins of the New South* (Baton Rouge, 1951), pp. 98–103; Hirshson, *Farewell to the Bloody Shirt,* pp. 105–107; V. P. De Santis, "President Arthur and the Independent Movements in the South in 1882," *Journal of Southern History,* XIX (1953), 346–363, and "Negro Disaffection with Republican Policy in the South, 1882–1884," *Journal of Negro History,* XXXVI (1951), 148–159.

36 *Historical Statistics of the United States: Colonial Times to 1957* (Washington, 1960), pp. 537–538, 712.

37 "The proposition was wholly unprecedented. The rule provided for a suspension of the rules by a majority of members, instead of two thirds; it authorized a motion to non-concur, but not one to concur in the Senate amendment; and in case of the failure of the motion, it sent the bill back to the

conference committee of both houses was packed with high-tariff men in order to ensure that the proposals of the tariff commission would be sidetracked, and then the most outrageous dilatory tactics (including the reading of the entire conference committee report, which filled nearly ten pages of fine type in the *Congressional Record*) were employed by foes of the bill in a futile attempt to block it.

These shenanigans produced the "Mongrel Tariff," which was passed on March 3, 1883, last day of the lame-duck session, a measure which affected tariff schedules only slightly. Throughout the whole sordid contest, Arthur, who had said only three months earlier, "the present tariff system is in many respects unjust," did nothing. As his generally sympathetic biographer, George F. Howe, admitted, "he took no position upon the merits of the Commission's proposals." With "cynical resignation" he "abandoned leadership" and "let others seize the reins."[38]

Arthur's failure to fight for tariff reform, however, must be viewed in the context of the sterile congressional politicking of those years; as Henry Adams commented the day after the Mongrel Tariff was passed, "this last session is just foul; nothing was ever so rotten."[39] Even the President's desire to build up the Navy, a nonpartisan objective if one ever existed, foundered on the rocks of party politics.

Every expert agreed that the once-powerful American fleet was no longer a match even for the navies of many South American nations. It possessed no up-to-date warships at all, and most of the vessels in commission were in a state of dreadful disrepair. Arthur urged Congress to appropriate funds for new ships. His Secretary of the Navy, William E. Chandler, an energetic administrator although an unabashed spoilsman as well, worked hard to revitalize his department, to improve the morale of the service, and to

Speaker's table, from which it could not be taken save by a two thirds vote." Edward Stanwood, *American Tariff Controversies in the Nineteenth Century* (2 vols., Boston, 1903) , II, 212.

[38] Richardson, *Messages and Papers*, VIII, 135; Stanwood, *Tariff Controversies,* II, 202–219; Pletcher, *Awkward Years*, pp. 153–157; Howe, *Arthur*, pp. 218–226; J. A. Barnes, *John G. Carlisle: Financial Statesman* (New York, 1931) , pp. 45–63.

[39] W. C. Ford (ed.), *Letters of Henry Adams: 1858–1891* (Boston, 1930) , pp. 348–349.

persuade Congress to undertake a building program. The same Congress that passed the Mongrel Tariff authorized construction of three steel cruisers and a dispatch boat, but thereafter partisan squabbling blocked every effort at further expansion.

Chandler awarded the contracts for the four new ships to the firm of John Roach of Chester, Pennsylvania. Although Roach was the largest shipbuilder in the United States and his bids were the lowest submitted, he had been accused in the past of cheating the government on contract work. He was also a personal friend of Chandler's. The Democrats cried fraud. Ignoring or discounting the fact that Roach was the low bidder for the contracts, they denounced Chandler and made it clear that they *hoped* the ships would not live up to specifications. After Arthur's term had ended, the dispatch boat *Dolphin*, first of the new ships to be completed, became the cause of further political controversy when the new Democratic Secretary of the Navy, William C. Whitney, pronounced it unsatisfactory and voided all of the Roach contracts. Roach, who was not entirely innocent of blame for the *Dolphin's* inadequacies, was bankrupted, and the Republicans then unleashed a partisan assault on Whitney. The difficulties involved in designing and building warships in an age of swiftly changing naval technology were enormous, inadequacies and defects inevitable in the first of these "modern" vessels. Chandler and Whitney were both good secretaries, genuinely eager to strengthen the Navy. But few politicians in either party were willing to give an opponent credit for good intentions. The necessary revitalization of the Navy was thus delayed. Narrow partisanship had triumphed over national defense.[40]

As the 1884 election approached, nearly everyone agreed that Arthur had been a better President than might have been expected on the strength of his earlier record, but his positive accomplishments had been negligible. The Democratic trend, highlighted by

[40] Richardson, *Chandler*, pp. 291–304, 370–379; Harold and Margaret Sprout, *The Rise of American Naval Power: 1776–1918* (Princeton, 1939), pp. 187–189, 191; Pletcher, *Awkward Years*, pp. 116–125; L. A. Swann, Jr., *John Roach: Maritime Engineer* (Annapolis, 1965), pp. 125–134, 176–183, 209–234; M. D. Hirsch, *William C. Whitney: Modern Warwick* (New York, 1948), pp. 274–289. Actually, the *Dolphin* proved a sturdy if not brilliant performer. It remained in commission for thirty-six years, ending its days as a presidential yacht during the administrations of Theodore Roosevelt and Woodrow Wilson.

the 1882 elections, and the slackening of prosperity seemed to presage a Republican defeat. Within the ranks of his own party, the President had not been able to check the influence of Blaine or to develop a solid machine of his own. Frustrated in the area of domestic legislation by a recalcitrant Congress, he tried to build a record in the field of foreign relations, eventually adopting an expansionist policy similar to Blaine's. Secretary of State Frelinghuysen negotiated a reciprocity treaty with Mexico which was ratified by the Senate in March, 1884, but efforts to work out similar agreements with other Caribbean nations and to obtain the right to build a canal across Nicaragua hung fire until well after the Republicans had chosen their candidate. Like Blaine before them, Arthur and Frelinghuysen acted too hastily, employed too many incompetent subordinates, and failed to develop consistent, well-thought-out policies.[41] At the time of the Republican national

41 Howe, *Arthur*, pp. 254–255; Pletcher, *Awkward Years*, pp. 177–191, 270–278, 348–351. Recently, a number of historians have found in the foreign policies of the Presidents of the 1870's and 1880's a foreshadowing of the imperialism of the late 1890's. They suggest that American foreign policy during these years was heavily influenced by economic pressures, especially by rapid industrialization. Manufacturers, and farmers as well, they argue, obsessed by fears of overproduction, sought eagerly for new markets in Latin America and Asia, hence the government's concern with an isthmian canal, trade treaties, and the like. See Walter LaFeber, *The New Empire: An Interpretation of American Expansion, 1860–1890* (Ithaca, 1963), pp. vii–ix, 60–61, *passim;* Milton Plesur, "Rumblings Beneath the Surface: America's Outward Thrust, 1865–1890" in H. W. Morgan (ed.), *The Gilded Age: A Reappraisal* (Syracuse, 1963), pp. 140–168; Ray Ginger, *Age of Excess: The United States from 1877 to 1914* (New York, 1965), pp. 53–55, 183–185. While the evidence advanced by these historians is interesting, it does not justify the conclusion that economic motives dominated the thinking of American policy makers in these years. The inconsistency and the obviously opportunistic character of the behavior of the Presidents and their Secretaries of State, along with the partisan treatment afforded diplomatic questions by Congress, suggest that economic factors exerted at most a peripheral influence on the formulation of policy. Blaine, for example, certainly a leading expansionist, was of two minds on the subject. He spoke frequently of the importance of finding new markets for surplus production, but he also said: "It is vastly more important not to lose our own great market for our own people. . . . It is not our foreign trade that has caused the wonderful growth and expansion of the Republic." Cf. LaFeber, *New Empire*, pp. 105–106, and Muzzey, *Blaine*, p. 365. And many prominent political leaders feared that talk of foreign markets would lead to undesirable tariff reductions. Thomas B. Reed, opposing tariff cuts in 1888, compared the search for foreign markets to the dog in Aesop's fable who lost his "succulent shoulder of mutton" by plunging into the water after its reflection. W. A. Robinson, *Thomas B. Reed: Parliamentarian* (New York, 1930), p. 180. Few persons, of course, were opposed to increasing the nation's commerce

convention in June, 1884, Arthur had little to show for his nearly three years in office.

While Arthur struggled to win the nomination, his major rival, James G. Blaine, coolly refused to press his own claims. Blaine wanted the office, yet—it was his most attractive quality—he would not demean himself to get it. He had told his wife as early as December, 1882, that "the presidency came no more into his calculations"; if he had any political ambition, it was to serve again as Secretary of State. Possibly he was convinced that the Republicans would be defeated in 1884; possibly he sensed that his best hope lay in remaining aloof. Instead of scrambling to line up delegates, he busied himself with his memoirs. On the eve of the convention, he made an apparently sincere effort to persuade General William Tecumseh Sherman to seek the office. Yet he was clearly the most popular Republican in the country. More important, with Conkling now retired, most of the politicians felt that he would represent their interests and point of view better than anyone else. As Conkling's lieutenant Thomas C. Platt put it at the convention, "his turn has come . . . the Republican people of the Republican states that must give the Republican majorities want him."

Blaine's support at the convention was both wide and deep. On the first ballot he got well over 300 votes, drawn from every section of the country, whereas President Arthur's 278 votes, coming mainly from the South, counted for little as an indication of real strength. Furthermore, the minor candidates, who controlled about 200 votes, were split into two roughly equal groups: the civil-service reformers, who voted for Senator George Edmunds of Vermont, and the middlewestern professionals, chiefly the followers of Senators John Sherman of Ohio and John A. Logan of Illinois. The former group disliked Blaine and Arthur with equal vehemence and had little stomach for either Sherman or Logan. The latter, preferring Blaine to the President, quickly concluded that the candidate must be one

---

in principle. But not many appear to have given this objective a particularly high priority. Indeed, foreign relations seldom attracted much attention of any kind. Bryce even wrote in the *American Commonwealth:* "The President has rarely leisure to give close or continuous attention to foreign policy." James Bryce, *The American Commonwealth* (2 vols., New York, 1895), I, 54. For an excellent, balanced account of the subject, see M. B. Young, "American Expansion, 1870–1900: The Far East," in B. J. Bernstein (ed.), *Towards A New Past: Dissenting Essays in American History* (New York, 1968), pp. 176–201.

or the other, and on the fourth ballot swung decisively to Blaine. Logan was then nominated for Vice-President.[42]

The Democrats had no outstanding leader in 1884, but every prospect, after their 1882 gains, of winning the Presidency—a situation that might have been expected to produce a long-drawn-out contest for the nomination. Instead, Governor Grover Cleveland of New York won an easy second-ballot victory. Four years earlier, Cleveland had been an unknown Buffalo lawyer. In 1881 he had been elected mayor of Buffalo on a reform ticket, and success in that office won him the governorship in 1882. Although his achievements at Albany had been chiefly negative (he stressed economy, limited government, and opposition to machine politics, and was more praised for his vetoes than for positive actions), by 1884 he had earned a reputation for honesty and courage, for what would today be called moderation but which in those times was labeled "sound conservatism." He advocated civil-service reform, yet remained a party man, willing to co-operate with professional politicians. His control of the important New York delegation, based on the support of the Tilden faction, was of course a priceless asset at the Convention, while the opposition of Tammany Hall did nothing to lessen his attractiveness to the delegates of other states. Knowledge that many of the Republicans who disliked Blaine were ready to vote Democratic if Cleveland was nominated also contributed to his victory.[43]

The contest between Blaine and Cleveland was dramatic and close—in some respects the closest presidential election in American history. Both parties faced the same basic problems as in 1880: for the Republicans, to hold the North and West and, if possible, make inroads in the South; for the Democrats, to carry a few key northern states. But a number of special considerations complicated the race. The anti-Blaine Republicans, called Mugwumps, were strong in

---

[42] Hamilton, *Blaine*, pp. 618, 624; H. S. B. Beale (ed.), *Letters of Mrs. James G. Blaine* (2 vols., New York, 1908), II, 90; Muzzey, *Blaine*, pp. 252–254, 285–286; H. C. Thomas, *The Return of the Democratic Party to Power in 1884* (New York, 1919), pp. 162, 164–166.

[43] Allan Nevins, *Grover Cleveland: A Study in Courage* (New York, 1932), pp. 79–155; H. S. Merrill, *Bourbon Leader: Grover Cleveland and the Democratic Party* (Boston, 1957), pp. 14–55; Thomas, *Return of the Democratic Party*, pp. 169–194. The convention chose Thomas A. Hendricks of Indiana, Cleveland's most serious, though undeclared rival, as the vice-presidential candidate.

Massachusetts and New York, although only in the latter state did they stand much chance of affecting the result. On the other hand, many Irish-Americans in the big eastern cities, normally Democrats, were admirers of Blaine—in New York especially, this fact, together with Cleveland's difficulties with Tammany Hall, tended to compensate for the loss of Mugwump votes.[44]

During the early stages of the campaign, Blaine tried to make the protective tariff the main issue, arguing that high duties were essential for the maintenance of prosperity and American wage standards. This made political sense for several reasons—the Democrats were badly split over the tariff, Cleveland had already been accused of being antilabor, and Irish-born voters were emotionally committed to protection, mainly because the hated British were free-traders. Although he had criticized Arthur's catering to disaffected white Southerners in 1882, Blaine also hoped to win over conservative southern white voters by appealing to the growing industrial element in the section.[45]

As the campaign heated up, however, especially after Democratic victories in the October election in West Virginia revealed that the solid South was not being broken, more emotionally charged questions dominated the proceedings. The Democrats hit hard at Blaine's questionable ethical standards, bringing to light a new series of "Mulligan letters." The Republicans exposed the fact that Cleveland had fathered a child out of wedlock. On the eve of the election, a Republican clergyman, Samuel D. Burchard, caused a furor. During a political meeting in New York, he characterized the Democrats as the party of "Rum, Romanism, and Rebellion," a slur bound to offend Blaine's Irish-American backers. When Blaine,

[44] The Tammany Democrats had accused Cleveland of being anti-Irish and anti-Catholic. But radical Irish nationalists in America, who made up the bulk of the defectors, liked Blaine because of his anti-British position in foreign affairs. They desired to draw Irish-Americans away from their unswerving allegiance to the Democrats simply to increase their political influence and thus to win the support of the United States government for the Irish independence movement. T. N. Brown, *Irish-American Nationalism: 1870–1890* (New York, 1966), pp. 135–136, 140.

[45] Muzzey, *Blaine*, pp. 290–291; Hirshson, *Farewell to the Bloody Shirt*, pp. 124–125. In *The Two Parties and the Tariff in the 1880's* (Syracuse, 1966), S. W. Poulshock claims that the tariff issue had an important influence on the result. Although this work was withdrawn after publication because it was "based confessedly in part upon evidence which does not exist," its thesis cannot be entirely discounted. *American Historical Review*, LXXI (1966), 1536.

who was present in body during Burchard's speech but not, apparently, in mind, failed to repudiate this sentiment immediately, the Democrats pounced avidly upon his lapse.[46]

The individual effect of these developments, and a dozen others, cannot be measured accurately. What is certain is that Cleveland's electoral majority, achieved by carrying New York, Indiana, Connecticut, New Jersey, and the South, would have been reversed if New York had gone Republican, and that his margin in New York was under 1,200 votes.[47] Historians have studied the New York election exhaustively. The Burchard incident seems less significant than it did at the time because Blaine ran very well in the Irish-American wards of New York City and Boston.[48] Nevertheless, he might have run still better had he denounced Burchard on the spot. Mugwump opposition certainly hurt the Republicans in New York. The ticket of the Prohibition party also drained off more than enough votes from the Republicans to have elected Blaine.

While any of these factors and others that had nothing to do with personalities or issues, such as the rain which cut down the vote in certain Republican rural counties,[49] may have been decisive, the conclusion that Blaine was a weak candidate does not follow from them. Study of the vote in the context of earlier and later elections suggests rather that Blaine ran a very strong race. From 1880 to 1892, Republican strength in presidential elections declined steadily. The party got 48.3 per cent of the popular vote in 1880, 48.2 per cent in 1884, 47.8 per cent in 1888, and slightly less than 43 per cent in 1892. As these figures show, the decline was smallest in 1884, when Blaine headed the ticket. Actually, in comparison with the Democratic sweep of 1882, the Republicans made a remarkable

---

[46] Hirshson, *Farewell to the Bloody Shirt*, pp. 125–126; Nevins, *Cleveland*, pp. 160–182; Muzzey, *Blaine*, pp. 298–317; J. R. Lambert, *Arthur Pue Gorman* (Baton Rouge, 1953), pp. 108–109. Blaine naturally denounced Burchard once he realized what had happened. He later characterized him as "an ass in the shape of a preacher."

[47] He carried Connecticut by 1,108, New Jersey by 4,412, and Indiana by 6,530. Burnham, *Presidential Ballots*, pp. 246–249.

[48] Brown, *Irish-American Nationalism*, p. 187.

[49] Blaine is said to have remarked: "I should have carried New York by 10,000 if the weather had been clear on election day and Dr. Burchard had been doing missionary work in Asia Minor or Cochin China." G. H. Mayer, *The Republican Party: 1854–1964* (New York, 1964), p. 534.

recovery in 1884. Nationally, they gained twenty-two seats in the House of Representatives.

Blaine seems also to have helped his party in New York. Cleveland had carried New York while running for governor in 1882 by over 190,000 votes; with Blaine leading their ticket, the Republicans almost completely erased this comfortable majority. In New York City, the Democrats' percentage of the vote in 1884 was smaller than in any presidential election between the Civil War and 1896. Thus, while Blaine's personal defects and political errors surely cost him many votes, his virtues, personal and political, gained him others, and on balance the latter appear to have outnumbered the former.[50]

The Democrats, however, won the election, and this was of major significance. For Cleveland was the first Democratic President in a quarter of a century. His victory, viewed with alarm by some Northerners and with joy by many in the South, produced no drastic changes, but that was itself of great importance. Moderate men in every section hailed his election as heralding the true end of the conflicts generated by the Civil War. Cleveland spared no effort to prove them correct. As head of a party that drew most of its support from the South, he appointed many Southerners to high office, including two to posts in his cabinet. Southerners were entitled to a fair share of power in his administration, he insisted. He was careful, however, to select men who were not professional Southerners or unreconstructed rebels. For example, L. Q. C. Lamar of Mississippi, his Secretary of the Interior, had been for years a leader among southern politicians urging sectional reconciliation.

Once reasonable Republicans had a chance to observe that Democratic control of the White House was not going to mean the undoing of all the results of the Civil War, sectional animosities cooled down. No permanent moratorium on waving the bloody shirt was achieved, but the effectiveness of the device declined, and, with this, its employment. From every quarter came signs of increasing national harmony. In November, 1884, the *Century Magazine* began publishing a series of reminiscences by Union and Confeder-

[50] Lee Benson, "Research Problems in American Political Historiography," in Mirra Komarovsky (ed.), *Common Frontiers of the Social Sciences* (Glencoe, Ill., 1957), pp. 123–146, 168.

ate soldiers, "Battles and Leaders of the Civil War." Readers responded to these articles, which stressed "the skill and valor of both sides," with enthusiasm. Over the next three years, while the series continued, the *Century's* circulation soared to 250,000, almost three times its former level. The popularity of U. S. Grant's *Memoirs,* published in 1885, was also enormous, in no small part because the great Union commander adopted in his recollections a consistently magnanimous attitude toward former Confederate foes.[51]

The transition to Democratic leadership also offered the first test of the new federal policy toward the civil service laid down in the Pendleton Act. Cleveland's party associates clamored for government jobs, but his Mugwump supporters counted upon him to apply the principles of the new law not merely to the classified system but to all nonpolicy-making positions. The President, finding the dispensation of patronage as annoying and time-consuming as any of his predecessors, quickly announced a policy that satisfied most of the reformers. He would, of course, enforce the Pendleton Act. He would discharge workers outside the classified service only for cause, and insist that their replacements be properly qualified for the posts. To make sure that these principles were adhered to, he devoted an inordinate proportion of his time to appointments, even scrutinizing the applications of candidates for fourth-class postmasterships and other petty positions.

This approach yielded a number of outstanding appointments and won cheers for the President from reformers. An army of Democratic politicians, however, was soon up in arms against him. Vice-President Hendricks complained because his Indiana organization was slighted. The Irish boss of Boston, Patrick Collins, sulked because his candidate for collector of the port was rejected. Dozens of congressmen, together with many Democratic newspaper editors, assaulted the new regime. One party hack denounced the President's "treacherous conduct"; another called him "a cowardly knave and fraud."[52]

[51] P. H. Buck, *The Road to Reunion: 1865–1900* (New York, 1959), pp. 280–283, 256–258; Nevins, *Cleveland,* p. 197.

[52] Nevins, *Cleveland,* pp. 211, 235–243, 248; Geoffrey Blodgett, *The Gentle Reformers: Massachusetts Democrats in the Cleveland Era* (Cambridge, Mass., 1966), pp. 50–51, 57–60; Allan Nevins (ed.), *Letters of Grover Cleveland: 1850–1908* (Boston, 1933), pp. 52–53; Andrews, *Last Quarter-Century,* II, 108; Merrill, *Cleveland,* pp. 91–101.

Actually, despite the furor, Cleveland had not attacked the patronage system in any basic way, nor did his policy deal constructively with the fundamental weaknesses of the federal bureaucracy. He did not understand what had to be done to create a truly professional civil service. He held firmly to old-fashioned Jacksonian ideas. While insisting upon "merit and fitness" as proper standards of selection, he suggested in the next breath that "a reasonable intelligence and the education which is freely furnished . . . the youth of our land, are the credentials to office." He accepted the principle of rotation, seeing no harm in discharging any officeholder, Republican or Democratic, once his four-year "term" had ended. Apparently he did not see that this system, if generally applied by Presidents, would simply spread out over four years what ordinarily took place in a few hectic weeks after each inauguration.

Given these outmoded assumptions, no amount of attention to the selection of government employees could have had much effect upon the quality of the bureaucracy. But eventually Cleveland also yielded to the demands of party leaders eager to find places for their henchmen. From the start he had conceded that "offensive partisans" who "used their places for party purposes, in disregard of their duty to the people" might be fired immediately. Soon high Democratic officials were using this statement to justify the dismissal of men who had made speeches for Blaine during the campaign, or engaged in equally harmless political activity for the Republicans. Old-fashioned spoilsmen like Cleveland's Democratic rival in New York, Governor David B. Hill, who believed in removing Republican officeholders merely "because they are republicans," considered Cleveland a hypocrite.

Republican leaders, of course, agreed with Hill. Senator Benjamin Harrison of Indiana denounced the "hypocrisy of the Administration in its professions of Civil Service Reform" as early as December, 1885, and in the following months he accumulated a bulky file of letters from bitter constituents who had been dismissed for purely partisan reasons. By October, 1886, 70 per cent of the 110,000 nonclassified workers had been replaced; by the middle of 1888, about 42,000 postmasters had lost their jobs. Cleveland's collector of internal revenue for the Philadelphia district admitted to a Senate committee in April, 1888, that only four of the sixty-two workers in his office had been there since before March, 1885, and that every person currently under his command was a Democrat. Cleveland's record on appointments was good, considering the character of the times. Many first-rate men and relatively few rogues or incompetents held office under his administration. He did not, however, contribute notably to the expansion and improvement of the classified service.[53]

For all his courage and good intentions, Cleveland proved in other respects as well to be a President of limited vision. If his conception of the civil service was Jacksonian, he was no Jackson as a leader. He adhered to the prevailing philosophy that the Chief Executive should not attempt to shape legislation or meddle in the affairs of Congress. He was not, however, a rigid, states' rights Democrat in the southern mold. It is easy to overemphasize his veto of the Texas Seed bill of 1887, a minor measure appropriating $10,000 for seed for farmers in drought-stricken sections of Texas. Although Cleveland based this veto on a narrow interpretation of the Constitution and expressed the opinion that "the expectation of paternal care on the part of the Government . . . weakens the sturdiness of our national character," he was actually striking generally at wasteful "pork-barrel" bills, which Congress had been passing in wholesale lots, chiefly because the perennial Treasury surplus encouraged the legislators to satisfy the political needs of individual members recklessly.[54]

Where more important matters were concerned, Cleveland usually supported measures that required an expansion of federal authority. The Interstate Commerce Act received his cordial approval. During the labor troubles of 1886, he suggested that Congress create machinery for the voluntary arbitration of strikes. He

53 Nevins, *Cleveland Letters*, pp. 52, 75; H. J. Bass, *"I Am a Democrat": The Political Career of David Bennett Hill* (Syracuse, 1961), p. 78; Sievers, *Harrison*, pp. 278, 285; Nevins, *Cleveland*, pp. 249–251; White, *Republican Era*, p. 309; P. P. van Riper, *History of the United States Civil Service* (Evanston, 1958), pp. 119–120.

54 Richardson, *Messages and Papers*, VIII, 557–558. The seed-bill veto also criticized obliquely the Department of Agriculture's silly seed-distribution policy. The President pointed out that if 10 per cent of the money already appropriated for seeds were diverted to the drought area, the object of the bill could be achieved. Those who thus sacrificed their share "could well bear the temporary deprivation, and the donors would experience the satisfaction attending deeds of charity."

interested himself in efforts to improve the treatment of the Indians, which culminated in the passage of the Dawes Severalty Act. He signed the law raising the Department of Agriculture to cabinet rank despite the insistence of many of his advisers that it was unconstitutional so to dignify an organization serving the needs of a particular economic interest. He even (reluctantly, it is true) gave his approval to a federal tax on oleomargarine, which could easily have been construed as an improper interference with private enterprise.[55] Yet in all such instances he neither influenced the actual shape of legislation, nor exerted himself very much to see that it was passed, nor showed any particular grasp of the scope and nature of the social and economic problems of the times. He lacked some of the most essential characteristics of a popular leader: enjoyment of his job, enthusiasm for managing men, insight into the mysteries and paradoxes of practical democracy.

Nevertheless, Cleveland possessed great strength of character and considerable pride; in his unimaginative way, he wished to leave his mark on history. As the end of his term drew near, it was apparent that he had not done so. The 1886 congressional elections had not been reassuring; the Democrats lost fourteen seats in the House. The President therefore dropped his usual hands-off attitude toward legislation and, in a striking message, demanded that Congress cut tariff duties sharply.

Behind this action lay the complicated question of the Treasury surplus and its supposed relation to the sluggish condition of the economy and the gradual price deflation of the times. Unwilling to see federal revenues doled out to undeserving pensioners or invested in public-works projects he believed unnecessary, and appreciating the political risks involved in the prepayment of the national debt and the repeal of federal taxes on liquor, Cleveland decided that reducing the tariff offered the best solution to the surplus problem. Moreover, tariff cuts could be defended as helpful to consumers and as a means of preventing monopoly. Most intellectuals and professional economists of the classical school favored reductions, and so did Mugwump types, who by 1887 were becoming disillusioned

---

[55] Nevins, *Cleveland*, pp. 349–350, 355–359, 362–363. For a further defense of Cleveland as a postive, forward-looking President, see P. L. Robertson, "Cleveland's Constructive Use of the Pension Vetoes," *Mid-America*, XLIV (1962), 33–45.

with Cleveland's civil-service policies. Numbers of middlewestern farmers and powerful railroad and commercial interests in every section also approved.

On the other hand, with the Senate in Republican hands and the thin Democratic majority in the House divided on the question, Cleveland's chances of obtaining a satisfactory bill in an election year were not good. Recent experience with tariff bills suggested that significant reform would be hard to accomplish. The divisive effect of a fight and the discouragement that would result from defeat might weaken the Democratic party and thus cost Cleveland a second term as President. Historians have differed in estimating his motives and in evaluating the wisdom of his course, but one thing is clear: the tariff message of December, 1887, was a bold and dramatic attempt to exert presidential leadership in domestic affairs as it had not been exercised in a generation. When doubters reminded him of the danger of committing himself on such a controversial issue in an election year, he replied: "What is the use of being elected or reelected, unless you stand for something?"[56]

As an argument for reducing the tariff, Cleveland's message could scarcely have been improved upon. By devoting his entire annual message to the subject, an unprecedented step, he focused national attention on the subject and created a sense of urgency that was sure to aid his cause. Moreover, he explained the difficulties of the surplus problem in terms the voter could understand, and offered well-reasoned criticisms of other possible approaches, such as the elimination of excise taxes and the expenditure of additional federal funds on what he called "unnecessary and extravagant" projects. Anticipating the counterargument of the protectionists that cuts would hurt manufacturers and depress wage levels, he pointed out that only a small minority of workingmen (2.6 million of 17.3 million, according to his figures) were employed in protected industries, and that real wages would not be affected, even for these men, because the cost of living would go down at least enough to balance any loss of cash income. He appealed to the

56 Nevins, *Cleveland*, pp. 368–380; Merrill, *Cleveland*, pp. 118–121; Blodgett, *Gentle Reformers*, pp. 77–80; F. P. Summers, *William L. Wilson and Tariff Reform* (New Brunswick, 1953), pp. 67–71; Richardson, *Messages and Papers*, VIII, 580–591; R. M. McElroy, *Grover Cleveland: The Man and the Statesman* (2 vols., New York, 1923), I, 271.

popular fear of trusts by suggesting that the protective tariff fostered monopoly. Finally, he urged only *selective* reductions, stressing raw materials used in manufacturing and, in general, the necessities of life rather than luxuries—it was no "hardship" for the rich to pay taxes, he implied.

He insisted that he was not a free-trader; indeed, not a doctrinaire of any kind. "It is a *condition* which confronts us, not a theory," he said. Taxes were too high. The collection of revenues the government did not need was an "indefensible extortion and a culpable betrayal of American fairness and justice." The simplest, most effective, and most equitable way to solve this problem was to lower the tariff.

While the opposition to tariff reduction was formidable and Cleveland's attack rather late in the game if results were to be expected before the election, the President had made a strong case for reform and could rely on powerful allies in the forthcoming battle. Reformers agreed that protection aggravated the monopoly problem; conservatives liked the stress placed on economy in government; old-fashioned economists saw the proposal, despite Cleveland's express rejection of theoretical considerations, as a step toward classical free trade. The public at large could be counted upon to respond favorably to a tax cut that would simultaneously reduce the cost of living. With the business interests divided and the President so solidly on record as willing to tolerate reasonable protective duties where truly necessary, the chances for reform seemed good.[57]

Rational tariff legislation could only be obtained, however, if Congress would subordinate sectional interests to the general needs of the country. Since past experience indicated that this would not occur if the legislators were left to their own devices, Cleveland should have maintained constant pressure on the members of his own party and at the same time mobilized public opinion in order to prevent both the Democrats and the Republicans from turning the debates to purely selfish ends. He did not do so. The House delayed until April, 1888, before introducing a bill. This Mills bill,

[57] Nevins, *Cleveland*, pp. 379–381, 386–387; Blodgett, *Gentle Reformers*, pp. 79–80; Stanwood, *Tariff Controversies*, II, 229; F. B. Joyner, *David A. Wells: Champion of Free Trade* (Cedar Rapids, 1939), pp. 171–172; Barnes, *Carlisle*, pp. 126–128.

drafted by southern Democrats, flagrantly favored southern interests.[58] Cleveland neither urged Democratic leaders to consider the
total national interest nor pressed them to bring the bill to a vote
promptly. The debate, as the tariff historian Edward Stanwood put
it, was "inspired by and permeated with a political purpose." It
dragged on until July, long after the national conventions. When
the bill finally passed the House in a vote closely following party
lines, the politicos had long since determined to make the tariff an
issue in the election rather than try to work out a reasonable
compromise that would solve the surplus problem.[59]

At the same time, the President, despite his vaunted courage,
began to hedge. He sent his former campaign manager, Senator
Arthur P. Gorman of Maryland, a protectionist, to the Democratic
nominating convention at St. Louis with a tariff plank that merely
reaffirmed the vague Democratic platform of 1884; only a determined stand by low-tariff delegates, headed by Henry Watterson of
Kentucky, led the convention to endorse the President's own message in the platform.[60] Through inaction, Cleveland then permitted the convention to nominate the aged Senator Allen G.
Thurman of Ohio as his running mate, although Thurman was a
protectionist. He also acquiesced in the appointment of two high-
tariff men, William H. Barnum of Connecticut and Calvin S. Brice
of Ohio, to manage his campaign for re-election.

To make matters worse, Cleveland refused to campaign personally, even to issue pronouncements in support of his tariff position.
His single important statement, made in officially accepting the
nomination, hit far less hard at the protectionists than his message
of 1887. The Republicans, meanwhile, pushed the tariff issue hard.
At their national convention they declared uncompromisingly for
protection, suggesting that federal revenues be reduced by repeal-
ing the excises on tobacco and on alcoholic products not used as
beverages. In the Senate, which they controlled, they sidetracked
the Mills bill, bringing up instead, purely for campaign purposes, a
bill that slashed the tariff on sugar (which could cost them votes
only in solidly Democratic Louisiana), and embodying their plat-

[58] See Chapter 6, pp. 245–246.

[59] Stanwood, *Tariff Controversies*, II, 234–236; Summers, *Wilson*, pp. 82–83.

[60] A number of years later, after they had clashed over another issue, Cleveland admitted to Watterson that he had been "injured" by the Kentuckian's
behavior at the 1888 convention. Henry Watterson, *"Marse Henry": An Autobiography* (2 vols., New York, 1919), II, 140.

form proposals on excise taxes. The Senate adjourned two weeks before the election without voting on this bill.[61]

Cleveland's tariff message had forced Congress to debate the issue, and the parties had responded to the challenge by taking far clearer stands for and against protection than they had taken in two decades. But the President had failed utterly to control events or even to maintain the sense of urgency and public purpose that had led him to focus attention on tariff reform. He had allowed this important and highly technical subject to become once again a plaything of the politicians.

Like a great lethargic bear, Cleveland had bestirred himself in December, 1887, and shaken the political hive, but then he slumped back into querulous inactivity. Like disturbed bees, the Republicans, once roused, swarmed forth busily and efficiently to the attack. If Cleveland seemed as impervious as a bear to their barbs, he nevertheless suffered heavily as a result.

The Republicans managed the 1888 presidential campaign skillfully. There is little doubt that James G. Blaine could have obtained his party's nomination if he had wished it. A colossus among pygmies as a leader of men in his generation, he was vacationing in Europe when Cleveland released his tariff message. A Paris correspondent of the New York *Tribune* questioned him about the message the same day that the news was published in the Paris newspapers; he casually dashed off a statement that set the tone for the entire Republican counterattack. Most observers assumed that he would again be the Republican candidate. But he had no intention of running and soon made that fact abundantly clear. Although repeated pressures were brought to bear upon him, he held to this resolution, remaining abroad until August, 1888, long after the candidate had been selected.[62]

With Blaine removed from contention, the struggle at the Re-

[61] Lambert, *Gorman*, pp. 140–142; Nevins, *Cleveland*, pp. 415–416; Merrill, *Cleveland*, pp. 126–127; Stanwood, *Tariff Controversies*, II, 237–238, 240; L. L. Sage, *William Boyd Allison: A Study in Practical Politics* (Iowa City, 1956), pp. 231–233.

[62] Muzzey, *Blaine*, pp. 364–365, 368–372, 382. Blaine's reasons for refusing to run remain somewhat obscure. He was concerned about his health, but the "personal" reasons he advanced were not convincing. Apparently he had simply had his fill of political squabbling, although he continued to react to political events with instinctive speed and canniness. The incident may be but another example of his perversity. Perhaps in some unconscious way he sensed that effective political accomplishment was impossible in the 1880's.

publican convention centered around John Sherman of Ohio, Benjamin Harrison of Indiana, Governor Russell Alger of Michigan, Judge Walter Q. Gresham of Illinois, and Chauncey M. Depew of New York, president of the New York Central Railroad and one of the most famous after-dinner orators of the time. Sherman led on the early ballots, but Depew, who would have been an entirely unacceptable candidate in the West because of his railroad connections, and many of Blaine's close friends, soon concentrated behind Harrison, and on the seventh ballot the Indiana senator was nominated.[63]

Study of the Republican candidate, the campaign, and its results provides an effective way of summarizing post-Reconstruction politics. Harrison's solid qualities—intelligence, diligence, and honesty—have already been mentioned, along with his personal remoteness. Although eager to serve his country, he was, like Cleveland, an unimaginative man who sometimes failed to see the relationship between his acts and their consequences. Like so many politicians caught up in the hectic confusion of events, he tended to do what seemed expedient without examining all the implications of his behavior. He realized, for example, that the large Treasury surplus tempted political mischief-makers and made possible "all sorts of jobbery and official rascality." Yet he saw no harm in dispensing federal pensions lavishly to undeserving veterans; according to his biographer, he viewed the goings-on that took place in the office of the commissioner of pensions "with a simplicity almost childlike."

Harrison devoted his life to government service, but the importance of improving the efficiency of the federal bureaucracy escaped him. When one of his supporters who had secured a diplomatic post was accused of incompetence, he admitted that he might have "oversized the man or undersized the place," but argued that the poor fellow should not be deprived of his office. Discharging him would cause his family "needless hurt." He voted grudgingly for the Pendleton Civil Service Act in the Senate only after blocking an amendment designed to prevent government employees from contributing money to political parties. All persons, he claimed, had a

[63] Oberholtzer, *History*, V, 19–24; Sievers, *Harrison*, pp. 342–352. Levi P. Morton of New York received the vice-presidential nomination.

right to use their property as they wished. He often devoted his considerable intelligence and legal skill to the construction of such elaborate constitutional barriers to common-sense policies. He was willing to spend federal funds to improve the navigation of the Mississippi River, but not to build levees to prevent floods or reclaim land. He filled page after page in the *Congressional Record* with learned nonsense interpreting the Constitution in order to buttress his argument, when in reality his objection was partisan and sectional.[64]

Despite his frigid reserve, Harrison had a bombastic oratorical style, in which respect he was like most politicians of his generation. He appeared not to recognize the trite intellectual emptiness of much of what he said. "Cheaper coats," he explained in defending the wool tariff, would "necessarily" involve "a cheaper man and woman under the coat." He was an accomplished waver of the bloody shirt and twister of the British lion's tail; his speeches reverberate with references to battlefields "wet with the blood of loyal men," and to the "grasping avarice" of British diplomacy. When describing the nation and the Republican party, he favored weary nautical metaphors. "If there are any barnacles on the old ship," he said in 1887 while defending the G.O.P. against Mugwump attacks, "it is a poor policy to scuttle her."

We took the ship of state [he orated on another occasion] when there was treachery at the helm, when there was mutiny on the deck, when the ship was among the rocks, and we put loyalty at the helm. . . . We have brought the ship into the wide and open sea of prosperity.[65]

During the 1888 campaign, Harrison indulged this fondness for political clichés freely and with apparent good results. While Cleveland remained silent in deference to the idea that campaigning was beneath the dignity of a President, he delivered over eighty speeches to dozens of groups, large and small, that flocked to Indianapolis. His remarks, usually extemporaneous, contained such nuggets of mindless volubility as these:

To 300 Indianapolis Negroes: I have a sincere respect for, and a very deep interest in, the colored people. . . . I know nowhere in this country

[64] Sievers, *Harrison,* pp. 198 n., 209–210, 216–217.
[65] *Ibid.,* pp. 211, 307, 324; Charles Hedges (ed.), *Speeches of Benjamin Harrison* (New York, 1892), pp. 19–21.

of a monument . . . that touches my heart so deeply, as that monument at Washington representing the Proclamation of Emancipation by President Lincoln, the kneeling black man at the feet of the martyred President, with the shackles falling from his limbs.

To 1000 railroad workers: You have signalled the Republican train to go ahead. . . . The necessities and responsibilities of the business of transportation have demanded a body of picked men—inventive and skilful, faithful and courageous, sober and educated—and the call has been answered, as your presence here tonight demonstrates.

To 100 little girls: Children have always been attractive to me. I have found not only entertainment but instruction in their companionship. Little ones often say wise things. . . . Some of the best friends I have are under ten years of age.

To the Chicago German-American Republican Club: My German-American friends, you are a home-loving people; father, mother, wife, child are words that to you have a very full and a very tender meaning. . . . Out of this love of home there is naturally born a love of country . . . and so our fellow-citizens of German birth and descent did not fail to respond with alacrity and enthusiasm to the call of their adopted country when armies were mustered for the defence of the Union.

To a group of Civil War veterans: When you lifted your hands and swore to protect and defend the Constitution and the flag you didn't even know what your pay was to be. . . . And now peace has come; no hand is lifted against the flag; the Constitution is again supreme and the Nation one. My countrymen, it is no time now to use an apothecary's scale to weigh the rewards of the men who saved the country.[66]

If these remarks suggest that Harrison was an old-fashioned hack politician, the circumstances of their delivery reveal that he and his managers had evolved a new method of conducting a presidential campaign. The tradition that a candidate should not speak in his own behalf had been shaken four years earlier when Blaine had reluctantly undertaken a six-week speaking tour of the eastern and middlewestern states. The advantages of presenting the candidate and his opinions to the public firsthand proved to be considerable, but Blaine's trip had not been without its drawbacks. Unexpected situations arose that a travel-weary politician could not always handle smoothly. The "Burchard break" might not have occurred had Blaine not been tired out by his hectic tour.

[66] Sievers, *Harrison*, p. 371; Hedges, *Speeches of Harrison*, pp. 33–34, 47, 71, 107, 172–173.

Harrison, therefore, devised a different technique, the front-porch campaign. From near and far to Indianapolis came delegations representing regional and special-interest groups to meet and be addressed by the candidate, either from his doorstep or in a nearby park. A committee on arrangements co-ordinated these pilgrimages and checked over the speeches of the leaders of each delegation before delivery to make sure that they contained no politically inept sentiments. While Harrison replied off the cuff, his remarks, mostly conventional to begin with, were recorded by a stenographer and carefully checked before being released to the press. This system ensured that many thousands of voters would see and hear the candidate and that his opinions (such as they were) would receive steady publicity in the newspapers. Although Harrison found the business fatiguing, it put far less strain on him than an extended speaking tour, and greatly reduced the chance of an embarrassing blunder.[67]

The front-porch technique was only one of the new methods developed by the Republicans in 1888. The Democratic managers worked at cross purposes and with little enthusiasm; Harrison's organization, on the other hand, headed by Senator Matthew S. Quay of Pennsylvania and John C. New, an Indianapolis publisher, had been put together with the particular needs of the contest fully in mind. Aided by William W. Dudley, a one-legged veteran noted for his liberality as commissioner of pensions, New led the fight in Indiana. Quay concentrated on the eastern industrial states. The dry-goods merchant John Wanamaker headed a national "advisory board" of businessmen, whose chief function was to raise money among their fellows. Of course, wealthy men had been solicited for contributions in past elections, but the Wanamaker committee systematized the practice and raised unprecedentedly large sums by focusing attention on the protective-tariff issue.[68]

The Republicans recognized that the character of American politics was changing. Mass-circulation newspapers and press associations with their networks of reporters had become at once a boon

[67] Muzzey, *Blaine*, pp. 311–321; Sievers, *Harrison*, pp. 371–373.
[68] Nevins, *Cleveland*, pp. 415–417; Sievers, *Harrison*, pp. 366–368, 378–379; H. A. Gibbons, *John Wanamaker* (2 vols., New York, 1926), I, 257–259; Herbert Croly, *Marcus Alonzo Hanna* (New York, 1912), p. 149.

and a threat to party leaders. They provided massive new opportunities for influencing voters, but increased the need for organizing and integrating party efforts. Any local slip could now have national repercussions; and the old trick of saying one thing in one section, something different elsewhere, in order to cater to local prejudices, could no longer be relied upon. Furthermore, reform of the civil service was reducing the number of party hacks available for campaign work, making officeholders less willing to contribute money to party war chests, and encouraging the public to demand that government employees steer clear of politics and stick to their jobs. At the same time, campaigning was becoming far more expensive. As Wanamaker pointed out, the growth of the country required that thousands of speakers take the stump and that tons of literature be printed and distributed.

By calling upon wealthy businessmen outside the political system to supply what Wanamaker called the "sinews of war," and by using this money in an expanded effort to shape public opinion, the Republicans were adjusting to this new state of affairs intelligently. Since the purpose was to *persuade* voters, not to intimidate or corrupt them, it could be undertaken openly and with a clear conscience by respectable citizens.

Genuinely concerned about the protective tariff and no doubt flattered by the new role offered them by Wanamaker's advisory board, most of the businessmen who contributed did so apparently without thought of exercising much direct influence on party policies. But by relying so heavily upon men of wealth, the politicians would eventually discover that they were creating a new pressure group and thus endangering much of their power. In 1888, however, this lay still in the future. Wanamaker, for example, took on the job as head of the advisory board because of his emotional commitment to "the party of Lincoln," not for any economic reason. He was not even at the time a high-tariff man and, as his later career demonstrated, he believed wholeheartedly in the spoils system.[69]

The Republicans did not rely only upon men of wealth in their

[69] Gibbons, *Wanamaker*, I, 254, 259–260, 300–301; Matthew Josephson, *The Politicos: 1865–1896* (New York, 1938), pp. 327–329, 406–413, 423–426; D. J. Rothman, *Politics and Power: The United States Senate, 1869–1901* (Cambridge, Mass., 1966), pp. 219–220, 261–262.

effort to broaden the base of their operations. Local Republican clubs had been developing all over the North and West; by 1887, some 6,500 existed, a year later about 10,000. James M. Clarkson, vice-chairman of the national committee, organized these clubs into a League of Republican Voters and put them to work arranging meetings and rallies, distributing campaign literature, and getting out the vote on election day. The Democrats adopted this idea as well; their National Association of Democratic Clubs had about 3,000 member clubs in 1888.

The emphasis placed by both parties on the tariff question brought other, nominally nonpolitical organizations into the campaign. The American Iron and Steel Association; the Protective Tariff League, which boasted a thousand members willing to contribute $100 each to the cause; a group of Home Market Clubs; and various other organizations threw their weight behind Harrison. The American Free Trade League, the Massachusetts Tariff Reform League, and the Reform Club of New York were all active in Cleveland's behalf. Both camps printed reams of pamphlets, distributed "boiler plate" editorials and articles to small newspapers all over the country without charge, and spent money freely both in the presidential contest and in many congressional races.[70]

The volume of campaign literature probably exceeded that of any earlier election. Aside from the frankly partisan outpourings, a number of books and pamphlets by tariff experts appeared in response to the great public interest in the subject roused by the politicians. David A. Wells's *Relation of the Tariff to Wages* defended the free-trade position. Henry Varnum Poor's *Twenty-Two Years of Protection* argued for the other side. Albert Shaw edited a volume of papers of a theoretical nature by scholarly specialists, and several other tomes of no particular distinction appeared. Unfortunately, as an economist reviewing all these volumes in 1889 concluded, none attempted "to investigate carefully and without bias the practical working of protective duties."[71]

Whatever the quality of this flood of words, at least the electorate

[70] Andrews, *Last Quarter-Century*, II, 159; Mayer, *Republican Party*, pp. 218–219; Summers, *Wilson*, p. 89; Nevins, *Cleveland*, pp. 418–422; B. J. Hendrick, *The Training of an American* (New York, 1928) , pp. 198–199.

[71] "Tariff Literature of the Campaign," *Quarterly Journal of Economics*, III (1889) , 212–217; Summers, *Wilson*, p. 90.

was being asked to settle a significant question in 1888. Nevertheless, the usual number of trivial incidents and personal squabbles arose to confuse the issue, and, since the contest was extremely close, all or any one of these may have determined the outcome. The notorious "Murchison letter" incident, involving a ruse by which a Republican partisan tricked the British minister to Washington, Sir Lionel Sackville-West, into expressing a preference for Cleveland, was believed at the time to have cost the Democrats large numbers of Irish-American votes in New York and other crucial states. However, Cleveland ran well ahead of his 1884 performance in districts with large Irish populations. Attempts by certain Democrats to picture Harrison as antilabor by distorting the record of his activities during the 1877 railroad strike caused the candidate much concern, but were disproved with relative ease.

Another quarrel within the New York Democratic party, involving the supposed corruption of Governor David B. Hill, and his personal dislike of Cleveland, was also believed to have cost the Democrats dearly. Yet, as Hill's biographer has pointed out, Hill supported Cleveland in the campaign and won re-election as governor easily; the argument that substantial numbers of voters rejected Cleveland because they disliked Hill seems rather farfetched. A relatively mild disagreement with Canada and Great Britain over the rights of American fishermen in Newfoundland waters was blown up into a major controversy, as both Cleveland and the Republican-controlled Senate sought to make political capital by outdoing one another in their denunciations of the British.[72]

Nor did the fact that the parties were for once clearly divided over a matter of principle discourage either of them from using money unscrupulously. Contemporary observers agreed that the election set a new high for corruption. Especially in the doubtful states, large sums were spent in purchasing votes. It was charged, for example, that the Republicans paid $150,000 to a group of New York Democratic bosses, who delivered the ballots of their followers

---

[72] Nevins, *Cleveland*, pp. 406–413, 423–431; Sievers, *Harrison*, pp. 395–400, 409–411; Brown, *Irish-American Nationalism*, p. 187; Bass, *Hill*, pp. 121–125; F. R. Dulles, *Prelude to World Power: American Diplomatic History, 1860–1900* (New York, 1965), pp. 68–71; C. C. Tansill, *The Foreign Policy of Thomas F. Bayard: 1885–1896* (New York, 1940), pp. 298–320, 325–340; J. A. S. Grenville and G. B. Young, *Politics, Strategy, and American Diplomacy: Studies in Foreign Policy, 1873–1917* (New Haven, 1966), pp. 63–72.

by the tens of thousands in exchange, and that numbers of Pennsylvanians were transported to New York to vote illegally for Harrison on election day.[73]

Indiana witnessed the most flagrant election illegalities in its checkered history. No state was more hotly contested. Local Democrats were confident of victory, but eager to nail their triumph down at any cost. The Republican National Committee, sensing danger, poured in money from outside the state. Each side was sure the other would stop at nothing to win, and both were correct.

Much of the talk of fraud that circulated at the time was mere rumor, designed to shock respectable voters and encourage loyal supporters to work harder for their own side. But the confidential statements of the leaders themselves reveal that the threat was very real. Harrison reported to Whitelaw Reid, editor of the New York *Tribune*, in October that the Democrats were compiling lists of purchasable voters in Indiana and expected to carry the state by "the free use of money." The Republican state chairman, in an urgent plea to the national committee for additional funds, claimed that "the enemy are importing hundreds of illegal voters" into the state.[74]

Almost on the eve of the election, a Democratic paper in Indianapolis published a letter purportedly sent by Republican treasurer William W. Dudley to Indiana county leaders urging them to "divide the floaters into blocks of five and put a trusted man with necessary funds in charge of these five and made him responsible that none get away and that all vote our ticket." Publication of this letter created a sensation. Dudley denounced it as a forgery and sued a number of the newspapers which printed it for libel. He admitted that he had written a letter to the county leaders, but claimed he had not suggested any illegal actions. No one has ever proved that he was lying, although it is certainly significant that none of the ninety-odd Republican county chairmen came forward with a different version of the "blocks of five" letter. But the published version was perhaps too damning, too flagrantly immoral, to be believed. No sudden swing against the Republicans developed, in Indiana or elsewhere, partly because the Democrats failed

[73] Andrews, *Last Quarter-Century*, II, 167; Bryce, *American Commonwealth*, II, 148; Josephson, *Politicos*, pp. 430–431; Nevins, *Cleveland*, pp. 437–438.

[74] Nevins, *Cleveland Letters*, p. 190; Sievers, *Harrison*, pp. 415–416.

to exploit the incident effectively, partly because, amid the confusion of charge and countercharge, voters apparently had given up the hope that either party was honest.[75]

The result of this mad mixture of old- and new-style campaigning, of hullabaloo, trickery, and reasoned argument was as quixotic as that of any election of the era. The basic sectional balance remained unaffected. The Republicans, pressing the tariff issue hard, came close to breaking the Democratic monopoly in the industrializing sections of the South. Cleveland carried West Virginia by only 500 votes, Virginia by 1,600, North Carolina by 13,000. However, the Democrats increased their lead in most other southern states. The crucial battlegrounds in the North once again determined the victor. Cleveland won in Connecticut and New Jersey, his plurality in the former state being 344 votes out of 154,000 cast. But he lost New York and Indiana by narrow margins, and thus the Electoral College. In the national popular vote, however, he had a plurality of about 90,000, for his losses in the Middle Atlantic and North Central states were more than made up for by his useless gains in the Deep South.

None of these shifts was substantial; neither the tariff issue nor any of the "breaks" of the contest caused a major realignment in any state. Harrison got less than 1 per cent more of the vote in carrying New York and Indiana than Blaine had received in losing these states in 1884.[76] The experiment of campaigning on a real issue and the use of new political techniques had small or self-canceling effects upon the behavior of voters, although in such an extremely close contest any influence may have been decisive. What seems most likely is that the efficiency of Harrison's organization and the inefficiency of Cleveland's made the difference in the crucial states.

What happened thereafter is not the province of this volume.[77] Having won control of Congress as well as the White House, the Republicans pushed through a still higher tariff in 1890, dealing with the surplus problem by lavish expenditures on pensions and various "pork barrel" projects, and by removing the duty on sugar.

[75] Matilda Gresham, *Life of Walter Quinton Gresham* (Chicago, 1919), p. 604; Sievers, *Harrison*, pp. 418-421.

[76] Burnham, *Presidential Ballots*, pp. 141, 246-257; Hirshson, *Farewell to the Bloody Shirt*, p. 165; Benson, "Problems in Historiography," p. 134.

[77] See H. U. Faulkner, *Politics, Reform, and Expansion* (New York, 1959), Chaps. 5-7, 9.

Although this Congress also passed the Sherman Antitrust Act and expanded the coinage of silver in response to inflationist pressures, it proved to be one of the most unpopular on record; in 1890 the Democrats regained control of the House by a huge majority. President Harrison won a certain grudging respect in some quarters for his industry and his dignified supervision of the nation's affairs, but his icy personality detracted from his effectiveness. He quarreled with national chairman Quay and alienated other powerful Republicans, including Blaine, Speaker Reed, and the New York leader, Thomas C. Platt. However, his main inadequacy was his profoundly reactionary point of view, reactionary not in the sense that he favored entrenched wealth and privilege, but in the sense that his understanding of politics and of government was antediluvian. Cleveland had surrendered to the patronage system after a battle; Harrison embraced it from the start. Cleveland squabbled with Congress, and fumbled toward presidential leadership at least once; Harrison cheerfully submitted to being practically a figurehead. His four years demonstrated the ineffectiveness of the politics of the era convincingly. The presidential election of 1892 produced a Democratic victory that, by the standards of the times, amounted to a landslide. Cleveland carried all the doubtful states and also Illinois and Wisconsin, along with part of the electoral votes of California, Michigan, North Dakota, and Ohio. His Electoral College majority was 277–145, his popular plurality nearly 400,000.[78]

Neither party had yet learned how to deal with the changing country each sought to rule. The 1892 campaign was more sedate and marked by fewer appeals to emotion, but both the Republicans and the Democrats straddled or ignored meaningful national questions, slashing at each other with swords dulled by long use and wielded less forcefully only because the outcome appeared from the start to be in little doubt. Leaders of both parties observed apprehensively the rising strength of the new Populist party in the West— the Populist candidate, General James B. Weaver, polled over a million votes in 1892—but neither actually responded to the conditions that had produced the Populists. Cleveland's victory, it must be emphasized, was only a landslide by comparison with the fantastically close contests that had preceded it. He obtained 46 per

[78] *Ibid.*, pp. 112–114, 119–140.

cent of the popular vote.[79] Finally, Cleveland himself had learned very little, either from his Presidency or from the perspective offered by temporary retirement. Dimly, he sensed the need for new approaches, but even the pressure of a mammoth economic crisis failed to break the mold of his thought. When he moved, he blundered. When he fought, it was in a vain attempt to hold back the tide of history. Like Harrison's, his fate was to be repudiated.

Ineffective Presidents, narrow-minded legislators, parties that existed chiefly for the sake of winning and holding office, a Congress weighted down by antiquated procedures and paralyzed by narrow and shifting majorities, an inefficient, demoralized bureaucracy—little wonder that the political history of the era appears so sordid and insignificant. Yet great changes lay just ahead when Cleveland began his second term. The great depression ushered in by the panic of 1893 caught the Democrats in power: a massive shift of angry voters in the 1894 elections enabled the G.O.P. nearly to double its representation in the House and win seven new seats in the Senate, thus attaining solid control of Congress. The impact of this depression extended far beyond 1894; its political repercussions were enormous. President Cleveland alienated workingmen by his crushing of the Pullman strike and by his conservative approach to social and economic problems. When the Democrats then nominated the rural-oriented William Jennings Bryan for President in 1896 and fought the campaign mainly on the issue of free silver, they suffered still heavier losses among workers and other city voters. Since the industrial-urban element was the fastest growing segment of the population, the Republican party emerged, almost by default, as the party of the future. From 1897 to 1911, it dominated every branch of the government.[80]

The depression also forced political leaders to come to grips with the question of how to govern a complex, industrialized nation. The parties began to take clearer stands on social and economic issues. Both houses of Congress vastly improved their capacity for conducting public business. Within a decade, Theodore Roosevelt

[79] Burnham, *Presidential Ballots*, p. 247.

[80] C. N. Degler, "American Political Parties and the Rise of the City: An Interpretation," *Journal of American History*, LI (1964), 47–49; S. P. Hays, *The Response to Industrialism: 1885–1914* (Chicago, 1957), pp. 46–47; Benson, "Problems in Historiography," pp. 166–171.

had restored the prestige and power of the Presidency, and the administrative system of the national government had been greatly improved.

Most of these changes had roots in the late eighties and early nineties. Cleveland, in his second term, employed presidential power more vigorously (if not necessarily more wisely) than any President since Lincoln, forcing Congress to repeal the Sherman Silver Purchase Act in 1893, using federal troops to break the Pullman strike in 1894, and exerting American influence in Latin America dramatically in the Venezuela boundary crisis of 1895.[81] In 1890, Speaker Reed, in a confrontation with Democratic obstructionists in the House of Representatives, rammed through changes in the rules which won him the title "Czar" and enabled him and his successors to control the business of the House with machinelike precision.[82] Whereas Woodrow Wilson had written in 1885, "Power [in the House of Representatives] is nowhere concentrated," Henry Jones Ford wrote in 1898 of the "absolute, discretionary" power of the Speaker, and the ability of the House leadership "to compel obedience to its behests."[83]

The structure of the Senate also underwent significant alteration in these years. Party discipline, centered in the Republican and Democratic caucuses, became far more effective. Senate caucuses named the members of all committees; fixed the order of business; even, in critical instances, worked out the specific language of legislation. In votes on important bills, party lines held far more firmly than in the seventies and early eighties.[84]

Moreover (and this applied to the attitude of representatives as

[81] Nevins, *Cleveland*, pp. 523–548, 611–648.

[82] Reed solved the problem of the "disappearing quorum" (see above, p. 233) by ordering the clerk to record the names of silent Democrats as "present and refusing to vote." After days of angry debate, during which the protesters were handicapped by the fact that when they complained they merely confirmed Reed's assertion that they were present, the House finally altered its rules. This, besides solving the problem of the disappearing quorum, outlawed dilatory motions and streamlined the entire order of legislative business. Robinson, *Reed*, pp. 204–234; G. B. Galloway, *History of the House of Representatives* (New York, 1961), pp. 134–136.

[83] Woodrow Wilson, *Congressional Government* (New York, 1956), p. 76; H. J. Ford, *The Rise and Growth of American Politics: A Sketch of Constitutional Development* (New York, 1911), pp. 250–251, 254.

[84] Rothman, *Power and Politics*, pp. 43–74, 88–90. Rothman argues that party regularity in the Senate also increased because more senators were "full-time politicians" who had "painstakingly mounted the political ladder" and were therefore predisposed to go along with caucus decisions. Pp. 112, 128.

well as senators), as the business of government became both more extensive and more technical, individual members had to concentrate more on particular kinds of issues; therefore, they had to depend upon other experts in order to know how to vote on many highly complex bills. In this respect, legislative bodies became organizations of specialists that dealt with a multiplicity of problems in a manner similar to that evolved by the great corporations. Party leaders, like the great tycoons, became the heads of enormous organizations. "It is because organization has come to be so very important," Professor Anson Morse of Amherst College wrote in 1896, "that the man who can organize has risen to . . . high position in party management."[85] Organization implied close control; parties became machines, not in the pejorative sense of cliques of corruptionists and manipulators, but as institutions for the management of large numbers of individuals occupied with the multiform tasks of framing legislation and directing the ever-growing government bureaucracy of an industrial society. As patronage, the old cement of party, began to crumble, the new adhesive of mutual interdependence rapidly replaced it. When the parties found that they could no longer raise significant sums by assessing officeholders, they turned to other sources, first, as in 1888, to wealthy businessmen, eventually to the large corporations these men of wealth controlled.

In sum, although the American political system failed to respond smoothly to the changes that were convulsing the country, the delay in adjustment was, in the perspective of history, brief. By the end of the century, the system had changed enormously. It was not better in any moral sense, although the politicians of the Progressive Era were in the main a highly moralistic group. But it was better adapted to dealing with current conditions, and therefore a far more effective instrument of government.

[85] Quoted *ibid.*, p. 235.

CHAPTER 8

Social Thought

THE Americans who lived through the great changes of the post-Reconstruction years were hard pressed when they attempted to evaluate their experiences. Their achievements had been remarkable. They increased their material wealth, lived at peace with the rest of the world, developed their social institutions, made large advances in science and technology, in education and the arts, and maintained a degree of internal harmony and a sense of common purpose far greater than that of any other country of comparable size and diversity. On the other hand, the era was marked by grave social and economic injustices, by disorder, confusion, error, and ineptitude of monumental proportions. The Founding Fathers had sought to establish a just and tranquil society where men could live happy and free, but in some respects their descendants a hundred-odd years later appeared not so much to have failed to reach these noble goals as to have rejected them.

Any large nation with a dynamic, diversified economy inhabited by persons of widely different social and ethnic backgrounds is certain to exhibit such paradoxes. But since the United States was rapidly creating a highly organized and integrated civilization, the contrasts and conflicts became both more noticeable and, to many persons, more alarming. Individuals responded with different degrees of understanding and ignorance, approval and dislike. The times produced eager crusaders and cautious critics and standpat conservatives, and each type its full share both of wise men and of fools.

Nevertheless, the contemporary record suggests that Americans shared as large a stock of common values in the early nineties as they had in the seventies, and that, in the main, these had not changed much in the interval. Flexible and mobile though they were, the people held firm to their basic social and ethical assumptions.

Clinton Rossiter has described the process (he calls it "the great train robbery of American intellectual history") by which the conservatives of the post-Civil War years adopted the vocabulary of Jeffersonian liberalism. Words like "progress," "opportunity," "equality," and "individualism" became as much a part of the intellectual baggage of the right as of the left. At the same time, nearly all the reformers of the era accepted established institutions like private property and the capitalist system as unquestioningly as the most blatant reactionaries. Conservatives extolled the virtues of an open society in the language of Horatio Alger, liberals in the words of the Declaration of Independence. Both assumed that progress was inevitable and desirable, reformers counting on it to solve social problems, conservatives glorifying it as the means by which the best of all possible worlds had been created. "Real" radicalism was as rare as "true" conservatism: few poor men believed that rich and poor had antithetical interests; few rich men urged those less fortunate than themselves to endure the trials of this world patiently and accept their reward in the next.[1]

Most Americans also agreed about what was wrong with their society. The hardening of class distinctions and the "maldistribution" of wealth, status, and opportunity excited the indignation of both liberals and conservatives. In 1879, the reformer Henry George denounced these evils eloquently in *Progress and Poverty*. "Where the conditions to which material progress everywhere tends are most fully realized," he wrote, "we find the deepest poverty. . . . It is as though an immense wedge were being forced, not underneath society, but through society." In 1890, ex-President Rutherford B. Hayes, no radical, complained in his diary about "the wrong and evils of the money-piling tendency of our country" which were

[1] Clinton Rossiter, *Conservatism in America: The Thankless Persuasion* (New York, 1962), pp. 128–129, 145; Arthur Mann, *Yankee Reformers in the Urban Age* (Cambridge, Mass., 1954), p. 238.

"giving all power to the rich and bringing in pauperism and its attendant crimes and wretchedness like a flood."[2]

The American tendency to worship material values was similarly criticized from every side: by reformers like Henry George and Edward Bellamy; by conservative men with inherited wealth, such as the historian Francis Parkman; even by many of the new-rich tycoons themselves. So, of course, was the corruption so prevalent in the government—as vigorously denounced by conservative businessmen as by radical reformers.[3]

Nor did many persons deny that poverty was a serious problem in the United States, especially in the cities. Individuals might differ as to whether vice sprang from poverty or poverty from vice, whether bad economic and social institutions made men poor or whether their own stupidity, improvidence, and bad character were responsible for their destitution. Among urban clergymen, for example, Henry Ward Beecher claimed that in America poverty was presumptive evidence of sinfulness, but Washington Gladden blamed it and its related evils upon "the social conditions produced by the herding together of so many people . . . in our large industrial communities." Other religious leaders exhibited every possible shade of opinion between these extremes, but nearly all agreed that too much poverty existed and that something could and should be done about it.[4]

Probably the development that Americans most widely and diversely criticized in these years was the growth of large corporations and their combination into "trusts." At the time of the 1877 rail-

[2] Henry George, *Progress and Poverty* (New York, 1887), pp. 6, 8; C. R. Williams (ed.), *Diary and Letters of Rutherford Birchard Hayes* (5 vols., Columbus, 1926), IV, 556.

[3] In the concluding pages of his *Montcalm and Wolfe* (1884), Parkman denounced the contemporary "race for gold and the delirium of prosperity" and urged the nation to "turn some fair proportion of her vast mental forces to other objects than material progress and the game of party politics." Francis Parkman, *Montcalm and Wolfe* (2 vols., Boston, 1892), II, 413–414. In his famous essay on the "Gospel of Wealth," Andrew Carnegie wrote disparagingly of the type of rich family "chiefly known for display, for extravagance in home, table, or equipage, for enormous sums ostentatiously spent." E. C. Kirkland (ed.), *The Gospel of Wealth and Other Timely Essays* (Cambridge, Mass., 1962), p. 26.

[4] R. H. Bremner, *From the Depths: The Discovery of Poverty in the United States* (New York, 1964), pp. 80–81; H. F. May, *Protestant Churches and Industrial America* (New York, 1949), pp. 69, 120; Washington Gladden, *Applied Christianity: Moral Aspects of Social Questions* (Boston, 1894), p. 30.

road riots, strikers in Pittsburgh justified their resort to violence by saying that they were entitled to employ "any means to break down the power of corporations." Ten years later, a Senate committee headed by Republican Shelby M. Cullom reported after holding extensive hearings that "the steady growth and extending influence of corporate power" was the most important problem occupying the public mind. In 1888, a religious periodical in Nashville, Tennessee, described the trusts as the "worst publicans the world ever saw." These illustrations might be multiplied endlessly. Foes of corporate concentration could not agree about what should be done to solve the problem. Some wished to break up the big corporations; others hoped to inhibit their growth by lowering tariffs or changing the patent laws; still others favored government regulation of the giants; a few urged that they be nationalized. That *something* should be done, few articulate persons denied.[5]

Similarity of assumptions and agreement about the problems of the times did not, however, produce uniform social attitudes. Those who, on balance, found American civilization satisfactory emphasized the universally admitted achievements of the United States. They naturally made much of the productivity of the economy, which they attributed more to the "American system" than to the natural resources of the country, but they also stressed the nonmaterial virtues of American civilization—the idea of the melting pot; the opportunity the nation offered to "the huddled masses yearning to breathe free" of Emma Lazarus' poem, engraved upon the Statue of Liberty; civil and political liberties, which were indeed far more extensive in the United States than in other nations. Reverence for these aspects of the American experience lay behind the oft-quoted statement of the stockbroker Henry Clews, himself an immigrant, written during the labor disturbances of 1886. "The Almighty has made this country for the oppressed of other nations," Clews said, "and the hand of the laboring man should not be raised against it. The laboring man in this bounteous and hospitable country has no

[5] R. V. Bruce, *1877: Year of Violence* (Indianapolis, 1959), p. 183; U.S. Senate, *Report of the Select Committee on Interstate Commerce* (Washington, 1886), Part 1, pp. 2–3; C. V. Woodward, *Origins of the New South: 1877–1913* (Baton Rouge, 1951), p. 173; Sidney Fine, *Laissez Faire and the General-Welfare State: A Study of Conflict in American Thought, 1865–1901* (Ann Arbor, 1956), pp. 335–340.

ground for complaint. His vote is potential and he is elevated thereby to the position of man. Elsewhere he is a creature of circumstance, which is that of abject depression. Under the government of this nation the effort is to elevate the standard of the human race and not to degrade it. In all other nations it is the reverse."[6]

Many persons discounted the need for reform in the United States because of their optimistic faith in the generosity and good intentions of their countrymen. Americans were, indeed, hopeful and philanthropic. It was, Bryce noted in his *American Commonwealth*, "natural for them to believe in their star," and to be "tolerant of evils which they regard as transitory, removable as soon as time can be found to root them up." This attitude of mind, product of the richness and rapid growth of the country and of its relative youth, infected Bryce himself. "A hundred times in writing this book," he admitted, "I have been disheartened by the facts I was stating: a hundred times has the recollection of the abounding strength and vitality of the nation chased away these tremors."[7]

Pride in national achievements and confidence that solutions for social problems lay just over the horizon led Americans of conservative temper to react strongly against social criticism of almost any type. Memories of the horrors of the Paris Commune of 1871 apparently lingered as long in the United States as they did in Europe, and the epithets "un-American" and "communist" were employed nearly as frequently in the 1870's and 1880's as in the decades following the Russian Revolution of 1917. Every minor outburst of labor violence stirred fears of communist terrorism in many quarters. The mildest suggestion that government should extend its activities into new areas was met with the argument that such laws "play into the hands of the communists." Proposals for limiting the hours of labor or for regulating railroads were repeatedly denounced in these terms. When the Democrats in Congress launched their investigation of irregularities in the 1876 presidential election, Republican newspapers charged that only communists and revolutionaries would benefit therefrom.[8]

---

[6] Henry Clews, "The Labor Question," *North American Review*, CXLII (1886), 601.

[7] James Bryce, *The American Commonwealth* (2 vols., New York, 1895), I, 11; II, 283.

[8] Massachusetts Bureau of Labor Statistics, *11th Report*, 1879 (Boston, 1880), p. 162; Fine, *Laissez Faire*, p. 60; Harry Barnard, *Rutherford B. Hayes and His*

Persons opposed to social reform could find additional support in vulgarized versions of the teachings of the classical economists. However outdated the laissez-faire philosophy was becoming, it retained its appeal to traditionalists, no doubt in part because it harkened back to an earlier time. The emphasis that classical theorists placed on natural law (the idea, as a banker put it, that "all material values are governed by influences far beyond the reach of human vision and legislation") [9] served to protect the successful against invasion of their rights by the state, and incidentally to reassure them in the face of their actual ignorance of how the economy functioned.

The Jeffersonian concepts of individual liberty, equality, and limited government, deeply ingrained in the national character, were also deftly adapted by conservatives. These beliefs, a reflection both of colonial experience with the arbitrary power of Crown and Parliament and of the simplicity of society in the sparsely settled agrarian communities of eighteenth-century America, were transferred by defenders of the *status quo* without any sense of their inappropriateness to a democratic system in a complex industrial nation. During the seventies and eighties, conservative jurists marked out a "new constitutionalism" which hampered both the federal government and the states in their efforts to deal with contemporary problems through legislation. Beginning with his dissenting opinion in the Slaughter-House Cases, Supreme Court Justice Stephen J. Field argued that the injunction in the Fourteenth Amendment forbidding a state to deprive persons of property without due process of law, and the natural right of every man "to pursue his own calling," made much state social and economic regulation illegal. "It should never be forgotten that protection to property and to persons cannot be separated," Field said in 1890. By thus identifying economic freedom with personal liberty, he could use the Declaration of Independence to justify laissez faire. In *Limitations of Police Power* (1886), Professor Christopher G. Tiedeman insisted that although the state could restrict individual liberty in order to protect the public interest, every exercise of its

---

America (Indianapolis, 1954), p. 468; R. C. Cotner, *James Stephen Hogg: A Biography* (Austin, 1959), pp. 172, 205.

[9] Fine, *Laissez Faire*, p. 103.

police power should be "jealously watched and scrutinized" by the courts. Universal suffrage, according to Tiedeman, represented a threat to liberty, majority rule "an absolutism more tyrannical and more unreasoning than any before experienced by man." These were minority views in the eighties, but by the early nineties a majority of the Supreme Court was finding them persuasive and using them to strike down both state and federal laws in the name of laissez faire.[10]

Charles Darwin's theory of evolution, applied to human society by the Englishman Herbert Spencer and espoused in the United States by William Graham Sumner, John Fiske, and a number of lesser writers, also supplied intellectual ammunition for the fight against reform, or rather, as these Spencerians put it, against human efforts to alter the rate and direction of change. By focusing upon the Darwinian idea that species evolved by adapting to a relentless environment, that progress resulted from the elimination of the weak and the "survival of the fittest" (Spencer's term) in the struggle for life, conservatives could argue, on the one hand, that men were powerless to alter the direction, or speed the glacial pace of evolution, and, on the other, that by tampering with the intricate balance of nature, men would only slow or reverse evolutionary progress by enabling the unfit to survive and reproduce themselves.[11]

These economic, political, and social theories were all under attack in the late nineteenth century, but they had by no means been exploded; their defenders could muster much practical evidence to support them. Prosperity and growth *were* characteristic of the United States; the country had flourished in an environment remarkably free of controls of all kinds. The frontier experience appeared to demonstrate the truth of social Darwinist arguments about the importance of adaptability and struggle in advancing civilization. Both laissez-faire economics and social Darwinism made considerable sense even in a society crying for orderly and intelligent direction because of the paucity of accurate social and eco-

[10] *Ibid.*, pp. 47–125; A. M. Paul, *Conservative Crisis and the Rule of Law: Attitudes of Bar and Bench, 1887–1895* (Ithaca, 1960), pp. 13–17, 64; R. G. McCloskey, *American Conservatism in the Age of Enterprise* (Cambridge, Mass., 1951), pp. 1–21, 104–126.

[11] Richard Hofstadter, *Social Darwinism in American Thought: 1860–1915* (Philadelphia, 1945), pp. 1–51.

nomic data available to planners. The complexity and dynamism of the nation made detailed information essential if regulation was to be effective; without this information, would it not be better to leave well enough alone? Critics of the regulatory state could point to the admitted failure of American democracy to produce either an efficient bureaucracy or political institutions capable of coping with the highly technical problems of modern life. Conservatives could also plausibly maintain that with an electorate wedded to the Jacksonian dogma that one man was as good as another, and with many political leaders claiming that truth could be discovered by counting noses, *less* government was what the times required rather than more government. The ubiquity of contemporary complaints about the low state of politics suggests that those who opposed expanding the authority and functions of government were not conjuring up their arguments entirely out of thin air.[12]

Foes of change, of course, were fighting a hopeless battle, however powerful the weapons they brought to the fray. Yet the most striking thing about the radicals of the era was the extent to which they shared the values of admitted conservatives. They praised the same virtues of American civilization—its economic abundance, political freedom, and relatively classless society. They were confirmed optimists, and fundamentally middle-class in point of view. Their approach to reform was religious and moral, rather than social.

In *Progress and Poverty,* Henry George proposed that the government confiscate all rent. Labor was the only true source of wealth, he argued, rent the unearned increment exacted by landlords for the right of workers to produce. "When non-producers can claim as rent a portion of the wealth created by producers," he wrote, "the right of the producers to the fruits of their labor is to that extent denied." George packed *Progress and Poverty* with savage attacks upon current conditions. "Amid the greatest accumulations of wealth, men die of starvation, and puny infants suckle dry breasts. . . . As liveried carriages appear, so do barefooted children." The power of landlords to collect rent, which by right and justice belonged to the community, was a "usurpation, a creation of force

---

[12] For a powerful indictment of the working of American democracy in the late nineteenth century, see E. L. Godkin, *Unforeseen Tendencies of Democracy* (Boston, 1898), esp. pp. 29–47, 115–144.

and fraud." Rent, he wrote in one of his most famous passages, "is a toll levied upon labor constantly and continuously."

Every blow of the hammer, every stroke of the pick, every thrust of the shuttle, every throb of the steam engine, pay it tribute. . . . It takes little children from play and from school and compels them to work before their bones are hard or their muscles firm; it robs the shivering of warmth; the hungry, of food; the sick, of medicine; the anxious, of peace. It debases, and embrutes, and embitters. . . . It sends greed and all evil passions prowling through society as a hard winter drives the wolves to the abodes of men.

The imposition of what came to be known as the "single tax" on rent, George claimed, would eliminate the need for all other taxes and make possible "a great co-operative society" whence poverty, greed, crime, and every other evil had been banished.[13]

Beneath his impassioned rhetoric, however, George was far from being a radical. As an economist he was essentially a member of the classical school, his point of departure being John Stuart Mill's *Principles of Political Economy*. He believed that the single tax would lead to a simpler, not to a more complicated government, a closer approach to "the ideal of Jeffersonian democracy." While favoring government ownership of railroads and municipal utilities, his basic assumption was that once the unearned profits of the landlords had been fairly distributed, such an era of prosperity would result that the repressive and regulatory functions of government would no longer be necessary. The state, he later wrote, should "clear the ways, and then let things alone."[14] George's naïvely optimistic view of human nature was typical of middle-class America. "Short-sighted is the philosophy which counts on selfishness as the master motive of human action," he wrote. He had no quarrel with capitalism, and saw no conflict of interest in the relationship of employer and worker. He opposed income taxes on the ground that they destroyed incentive, and thought that unions (while necessary under current conditions) were ineffective instru-

13 George, *Progress and Poverty*, pp. 8, 302, 327–328, 345, 353, 410.
14 C. A. Barker, *Henry George* (New York, 1955), pp. 122, 540–541. George believed that, aside from operating public utilities, government might serve as an agency for investing social surpluses in facilities for public instruction and amusement. Among the projects he suggested, in addition to museums, libraries, and universities, were public baths, dance halls, and shooting galleries!

ments for raising the income of workers, and basically undesirable because they compelled the individual member to "give up his personal freedom and become a mere part in a great machine." George specifically rejected socialism, considering Karl Marx "the prince of muddleheads."[15]

Edward Bellamy, who totally rejected classical economics and the free-enterprise system, was also only superficially a radical. In the utopia he described in *Looking Backward*, the government owned all the means of production and material rewards were shared equally by all citizens. With great gusto he attacked rampant individualism, private monopoly, and competition—all, he claimed, characteristic of the America of the eighties. He compared the position of unskilled factory workers with that of medieval serfs. Small businessmen struggling to survive in a world of big corporations, he said, were like "rats and mice, living in holes and corners, and counting on evading notice for the enjoyment of existence." He characterized competition as "sheer madness, a scene from bedlam," the price system as "an education in self-seeking at the expense of others." He denounced "the imbecility of the system of private enterprise," the "demagoguery and corruption" of the political leaders of the nation, and the callousness of industrialists, who "maim and slaughter [their] workers by thousands."[16]

Yet, like Henry George, Bellamy saw no *necessary* conflict between social groups. An incurable optimist, he believed that everyone could have everything he needed or desired, if only wasteful and irrational competition were eliminated, and that economic sufficiency would wipe out crime, greed, and all other varieties of human wickedness. Society could be completely reorganized without violence, for people were reasonable, their instincts fundamentally decent. Bellamy's socialism did not make him any less an individualist. Indeed, the ideal future state would require *less*

[15] George, *Progress and Poverty*, pp. 284, 367, 376–377, 415; Barker, *George*, p. 564. Marx, in turn, while appreciating the importance of *Progress and Poverty* as an attack on traditional economics, saw the work as a "last attempt to save the capitalist regime," an example of "bourgeois political economy." George, he wrote, was "utterly backward" as a theorist, full of "the repulsive presumption and arrogance which is displayed by all panacea mongers." Joseph Dorfman, *The Economic Mind in American Civilization* (New York, 1949), III, 148; Barker, *George*, p. 356.

[16] Edward Bellamy, *Looking Backward: 2000–1887* (Cleveland, 1945), pp. 59, 65, 72, 90, 119, 223, 231.

government rather than more, "most of the purposes for which governments formerly existed no longer remain[ing] to be subserved." There would be "far less interference of any sort with personal liberty." Congress (its members drawn from the ranks of the retired) would meet infrequently, pass few laws.

Although Bellamy assaulted the capitalist system, the citizens of his ideal society were as concerned with material things and creature comforts, as interested in gadgets and as worshipful of technology, as any American capitalist of his own day. Bellamy also rejected Marxian socialism, despite his hyperbolic criticisms of current conditions and the enormity of the changes that he advocated. He claimed that American Marxists were actually in the pay of the "great monopolists," employed by them "to wave the red flag and talk about burning, sacking, and blowing people up, in order, by alarming the timid, to head off any real reforms." He called the movement his book inspired "Nationalism," not socialism. The word socialist, he once told the novelist William Dean Howells, "suggest the red flag with all manner of sexual novelties, and an abusive tone about God and religion."[17] Bellamy's attitude toward mankind was somewhat like that of a minister of the Gospel: he appealed to the better nature of the masses, hoped to improve their character, yet was essentially paternalistic. In his ideal world of 2000, for example, ordinary citizens could not vote. Public officials were selected by men past retirement age, who in the wisdom of their years could be expected to choose dispassionately. To permit members of the "industrial army" to vote "would be perilous to its discipline."[18]

An even more striking illustration of the influence of traditional American values on reform thought in the eighties is provided by Laurence Gronlund's *The Cooperative Commonwealth*, published in 1884. Gronlund was the first writer to attempt to persuade American readers to adopt the ideas of Marxian (he called them

17 *Ibid.*, pp. 62, 117, 201–203, 242; Daniel Aaron, *Men of Good Hope: A Story of American Progressives* (New York, 1951), p. 112. Shortly after the publication of *Looking Backward*, Bellamy and Henry George met at a dinner. "Mr. George, why are you not a Nationalist?" Bellamy asked. "Because I am an individualist," George replied. Whereupon Bellamy said: "I am a Nationalist because I am an individualist." A. E. Morgan, *Edward Bellamy* (New York, 1944), pp. 392–393, 379–384.

18 Bellamy, *Looking Backward*, p. 185.

"German") socialists.[19] Capitalism, Gronlund insisted, contained the seeds of its own destruction. The wage system should be abolished; the state must take over the ownership of all means of production. He assaulted laissez-faire economics, competition, monopolists, middlemen, and speculators in heavily italicized phrases, his tone even more unbridled than that of George and Bellamy. "The *Wage-System, the* Profit-System, the Fleecing-System, *is utterly unfit for a higher civilization."* Under laissez faire, "capitalists monopolize all the instruments of production . . . and therefore, *exercise an automatic control of all industries and over the whole working class."* The American system was "nothing but Established Anarchy," middlemen were "parasites," bankers and speculators "vampires." Gronlund emphasized the "incapacity, imbecility, and ignorance" of the "money-bags, prominent politicians, prominent lawyers, who now lord it over us." Those who argued that the interests of capital and labor were identical were frauds, he said, for in truth, "Capital and Labor are just as harmonious as roast beef and a hungry stomach." Once socialism is established, however, a new era of co-operation will follow. "Capital will no longer be the *master* of Labor, but, as true National Wealth, the invaluable *hand-maid* of Labor."[20]

Yet, although he had been born and educated in Denmark, Gronlund's approach to social problems was distinctly American. His mind, he claimed, was "Anglo-Saxon in its dislike of all extravagancies, and in its freedom from any vindictive feeling against *persons."* While excoriating the capitalists, he insisted that men were inherently reasonable and good, that under socialism all could prosper, and that the co-operative commonwealth could be achieved peaceably by persuasion. The revolution was inevitable, but its coming would be *"most orderly."* The red flag of socialism, he said, "has no relation to blood, or if it has, certainly not to cold clotted

[19] In 1882, the economist Richard T. Ely had delivered a series of lectures on the subject, published the following year as *French and German Socialism in Modern Times.* Ely presented a fair picture of socialist ideas, but his work was descriptive rather than hortatory in purpose. B. G. Rader, *The Academic Mind and Reform: The Influence of Richard T. Ely in American Life* (Lexington, 1966), pp. 56–57. Gronlund actually referred to Marx only once in his book, and then indirectly. Stow Persons (ed.), Laurence Gronlund, *The Cooperative Commonwealth* (Cambridge, Mass., 1965), p. 44.

[20] Gronlund, *Cooperative Commonwealth*, pp. 27, 29, 35, 39, 45, 48, 65, 236.

blood but the blood that courses warm and throbbing through the veins of every youth and maiden." It was, of course, extremely difficult to describe Marx's ideas faithfully without reference to class conflict, but Gronlund played down the conflict skillfully. Socialists included "representatives of all classes," and they were, above all, "respectable." He invited members of the professions, even "the thoughtful among our small middle-men," to join in fashioning the new order.

Gronlund's Marxism, as Stow Persons has said, was "sugar-coated" even in 1884; by the end of the decade he was specifically denying that capitalism inevitably caused class conflicts. In the United States there were "noble hearts both among the rich and comfortable classes who had a true sympathy with the toilers and some even who were willing to sacrifice all to right their wrongs." He even stated in 1890 "that Karl Marx's doctrine, that the bread-and-butter question is the motive force of progress, is not tenable." To solve social problems, he believed, "we must grasp the very highest moral and religious truths."[21]

If the radicals of the eighties accepted most of the traditional values of the middle class, those who considered themselves mere reformers naturally accepted them too. Liberal clergymen, ex-pounders of the Social Gospel, resembled the radicals both in their rhetoric and in their essential conservatism. In 1886, Washington Gladden, the most influential of these ministers, described the "present industrial system" as "inequitable," a "social solecism," a "state of war." Monopolists, he said, were "outrageous." Speculators were vampires "sucking the life-blood of our commerce." Unre-stricted competition, "poisoning the very sources of the national life," was "fundamentally wrong." Yet Gladden admitted that "private enterprise has filled the world with blessings," he believed that the interests of capital and labor were not antithetical, and he rejected socialism as a threat to the freedom of the individual. Although he advanced no single simple cure for the ills of the day, he assumed, like the panacea merchants, that society could be regenerated if only men would adopt a truly Christian point of view. He called his most important analysis of social and economic

21 *Ibid.*, pp. xxii, 7, 234–235, 238–239; H. H. Quint, *The Forging of American Socialism: Origins of the Modern Movement* (Indianapolis, 1964), p. 87; May, *Protestant Churches,* p. 259.

problems *Applied Christianity*. Once Americans learned to treat one another like brothers, he believed, an era of harmony and plenty would surely follow.[22]

Gladden considered the new social sciences the natural allies of religion in the campaign to reform society. Rejecting the argument of Herbert Spencer that sociology and economics were cold, impersonal disciplines unconcerned with moral questions, he insisted that "Social Science is the child of Christianity." His logic was rather shaky, for nearly all the important sociologists, political scientists, and economists of the era, trained in German universities, were deeply imbued with the rational spirit of scientific analysis. Empirical research and inductive reasoning were their tools, absolute objectivity their ideal. Gladden's statement, however, was not really incorrect, because most of these German-trained social scientists were also ardent reformers who approached their work with moral and ethical objectives. Analysis, they believed, must be followed by action. "The last phase of social science is the transmuting of valuations into life," the sociologist Albion W. Small, who had studied at the Universities of Berlin and Leipzig before taking his doctorate at Johns Hopkins, explained. And the framework in which these scientists operated was the applied Christianity of Gladden.[23]

Their attachment to Christian ethics, especially the idea of the brotherhood of man, encouraged these social scientists to play down class conflict, reject the solutions proposed by socialists, and take an optimistic view of human nature. Economist Richard T. Ely could wax indignant about powerful industrialists corrupting legislatures and exploiting their workers. He attacked the injustice of unre-

---

22 Gladden, *Applied Christianity*, 15, 18–19, 31–32, 90–101, 125, 130–131; Washington Gladden, "Socialism and Unsocialism," *Forum* III (1887), 129. See also Gladden's *Recollections* (Boston, 1909), pp. 294–305.

23 Gladden, *Applied Christianity*, pp. 214–222; Jurgen Herbst, *The German Historical School in American Scholarship: A Study in the Transfer of Culture* (Ithaca, 1965), pp. 3, 37, 56–58, 71, 156; Fine, *Laissez Faire*, pp. 200–201, 253. "Small's sociological viewpoint was primarily ethical," Fine writes (p. 265). "He looked on Christian ideals and precise social science as complementary and sought to combine knowledge with love." Richard T. Ely (a graduate of Heidelberg) put it this way in his *Introduction to Political Economy* (1889): "There is within man an ethical feeling . . . which has been clarified by religion, telling us that in our economic life as well as elsewhere we must seek to promote the welfare of our neighbor and brother." Quoted in Rader, *Ely*, p. 48.

stricted competition, and said of the railroads: "They drag their slimy length over our country, and every turn in their progress is marked by a progeny of evils." But he proposed no drastic social changes. He insisted that the number of "hot-headed and vicious capitalists" was small. He opposed Marxian socialism, militant unionism, and all forms of violence. Labor unions could best benefit their members, he believed, by instructing them in the intricacies of practical politics and the social graces, and by discouraging intemperance. In his book *The Labor Movement* (1886), he called for the moral regeneration of the industrial system, "the union of capital and labor in the same hands, in grand, wide-reaching, co-operative enterprises."[24]

Henry Carter Adams, a more profound and original economist than Ely, wrote scathingly of corporations "gorged with profit" that "menace the stability of society." He criticized free competition for its tendency to depress the moral standards of businessmen to the level of the most ruthless and antisocial producer in each field, and commented harshly on the low state of political morality in the land. Although he generally eschewed their rhetorical flourishes and oversimplifications, Adams accepted most of the premises of the moralistic reformers. He disapproved of both unrestricted competition and socialism, believed the average American to be of good character, and saw the state as "an agency for the realization of the higher ideals of men" rather than as a force for coercion or control. While he realized that human behavior could be modified by altering social institutions, and argued persuasively against the philosophy of laissez faire, he made the preservation of American individualism his chief objective. His important monograph "Relation of the State to Industrial Action" was, he said, "a plea for the old principle of personal responsibility as adequate to the solution of all social, political, and industrial questions."[25]

Of the new social scientists, Lester Frank Ward was probably least concerned with moral and religious justifications of change, or with specific reforms. "All religions are based upon a fundamental error," he claimed, all "supernatural beliefs . . . have demon-

24 Rader, *Ely,* pp. 55, 58–60, 68, 75, 80–81, 83, 87.
25 H. C. Adams, "Relation of the State to Industrial Action," American Economic Association, *Publications,* I (1887), 507, 510, 527, 532, 535–539, 548; Fine, *Laissez Faire,* pp. 200–201.

strably impeded [man's] upward course." Although his pathbreaking work, *Dynamic Sociology* (1883), offered the fullest and most finely reasoned critique of laissez faire and Spencerian social Darwinism advanced in the late nineteenth century, he was more interested in theoretical analysis than in practical problems, and was convinced of "the utter powerlessness of the hortatory method" to effect social change.[26] Ward was atypical also in that, although immensely learned, he was largely self-taught and, until relatively late in life, had little contact with other leading social scientists. He wrote his most important books and articles while working as a civil servant in various departments of the federal government.[27]

Nevertheless, Ward's assumptions were in the main the same as those of most other Americans. He saw no need for class conflict in American society; believed in expanding the functions of government but not in socialism; had an exaggerated faith in the rationality and good intentions of men, in the value of education, and in the perfectability of institutions. The chief function of sociology, he insisted, was "the organization of happiness." He professed to value individual liberty as highly as any of the defenders of the laissez faire he so forcefully attacked, and referred to himself as "an apostle of human progress." He even wrote (although admittedly the sentence is here taken slightly out of context), "nearly all objects of human desire can be obtained for money."[28]

This description of the common assumptions of conservatives and social critics could be extended almost indefinitely. What separated

[26] L. F. Ward, *Dynamic Sociology* (2 vols., New York, 1897), II, 266, 287; Fine, *Laissez Faire*, p. 263; H. S. Commager, *The American Mind: An Interpretation of American Thought and Character Since the 1880's* (New Haven, 1950), p. 213. Upon occasion, Ward did speak out in general terms against social injustice. See, for example, his "False Notions of Government," *Forum* III (1887), 372, and *Psychic Factors in Civilization* (Boston, 1906), pp. 320–322.

[27] Only 500 copies of *Dynamic Sociology* were sold in the first decade after its publication. The work first attracted extensive attention in the United States in 1891, when news that 1,200 copies of the Russian translation had been seized and destroyed by the censor. At that time Albion W. Small wrote Ward: "At last Americans will discover . . . that an epoch-making book has been before their eyes since 1883, and only a handful of them have had the wit to discover it." *Dynamic Sociology*, I, xii–xiv.

[28] *Ibid.*, II, 341; Fine, *Laissez Faire*, p. 254; Hofstadter, *Social Darwinism*, pp. 60, 66; "Lester Frank Ward," *Encyclopedia of the Social Sciences*, XV, 353–354; Commager, *American Mind*, pp. 210–215.

conservative from reformer was chiefly a matter of temperament—
the former's complacency in contrast with the latter's sense of
urgency. The oft-told story of Henry George's conversation with
Spencer's disciple Edward L. Youmans reveals the difference in
extreme form. The two agreed readily about what was wrong with
America; but whereas George believed that the imposition of his
single tax would eliminate the evils practically overnight, Youmans
insisted that only time—four or five thousand years of it—could
correct the situation.[29]

Post–Civil War economic growth made conservatives complacent
and those who were unwilling to wait for evolution to solve the
world's ills still more impatient. Henry George prefaced his argument for the single tax with an impassioned account of how the
"prodigious increase in wealth-producing power" in America had
roused popular expectations that "the golden age of which mankind
have always dreamed" would soon materialize. The failure of
progress to eliminate poverty was the inspiration of George's work,
and of that of most other reformers. Bryce captured the psychology
of the reformers in a paragraph. "Men," he wrote, "are impatient of
the slow working of natural laws."

The triumphs of physical science have enlarged their desires for comfort,
and shown them how many things may be accomplished by the application
of collective skill and large funds. . . . The sight of preventable evil is
painful, and is felt as a reproach. He who preaches patience and reliance
upon natural progress is thought callous. . . . There is a warmer recognition of the responsibility of each man for his neighbour, and a more
earnest zeal in works of moral reform.[30]

The reformers of the period, in other words, were frustrated but
not alienated critics. Their radical rhetoric reflected their loyalty to
traditional values and their indignation that the promise of American life was not being fulfilled. And they felt a strong emotional
commitment to action. Thus, the theorists among them, with few
exceptions, directed their minds to the task of discrediting laissez-
faire ideas. As we have seen, the individualistic approach to life was

29 Hofstadter, *Social Darwinism*, pp. 33–34. It is interesting that Youmans,
despite his attachment to Spencer, was influential in facilitating the publication
of Ward's *Dynamic Sociology*. See Ward, *Dynamic Sociology*, I, xxxii.

30 George, *Progress and Poverty*, pp. 3–4; Bryce, *American Commonwealth*, II,
539.

already being tacitly abandoned by practical men grappling with the complexities of an industrialized civilization. The theorists provided plausible explanations and justifications of this behavior.

Although laissez faire continued to find intellectual defenders, in every branch of social science new thinkers were at war with the "let alone" philosophy. Beginning in the seventies, American economists trained in the "historical school" then dominant in the German universities assaulted the ideas of the classical political economists from several angles. All so-called laws of economics applied only to specific historical situations, they argued; each generation must formulate new economic principles suited to its particular circumstances. Classical laissez faire made both political and economic sense in the world of Adam Smith, when tyrannical governments had stifled economic freedom beneath a blanket of mercantilistic laws. But in a democratic society grappling with monopolistic corporations and other powerful vested interests, government regulation of the economy was both safe and essential. "Smith called upon private enterprise to check and circumscribe government activity," Professor Edmund James of the Wharton School, a graduate of the University of Halle, wrote in 1886. "We are forced to call upon government to circumscribe and regulate private enterprise."[31]

James, Richard T. Ely of Johns Hopkins, Henry Carter Adams of Michigan and Cornell, E. Benjamin Andrews of Brown, E. R. A. Seligman of Columbia, and numerous other German-trained Amer-

[31] Joseph Dorfman, "The Role of the German Historical School in American Economic Thought," *American Economic Review*, XLV, No. 2 (1955), 17–28; E. J. James, "The Relation of the Modern Municipality to the Gas Supply," American Economic Association, *Publications*, I (1886), 54. This line of argument had the practical advantage of allowing the younger economists to criticize the prestigious figures of the past without saying they had been wrong. "This is not a rebellion against Adam Smith, Malthus, Ricardo and Mill," Alexander Johnston, one of the founders of the American Economic Association, pointed out in 1885, "only a struggle for freedom of development of their work." R. T. Ely, "Report of the Organization of the American Economic Association," *ibid.*, I, 22. However, the historical school also claimed that the classical economists' veneration of free competition was based on faulty logic and a misunderstanding of human psychology. Economic principles could be discovered only by study of actual conditions, not by deduction from abstractions. When this approach was followed, the assumption that material self-interest always governed the behavior of men was quickly disproved. Fine, *Laissez Faire*, pp. 198–199; Herbst, *Historical School*, pp. 129–137; Rader, *Ely*, pp. 12–13.

ican economists contributed to the critique of laissez faire. The most persuasive arguments advanced during the 1880's were those of Adams. Applying the method of historical analysis with great subtlety, Adams admitted that legislation was not a cure-all for economic and social problems, and that, for large segments of the economy, free competition worked admirably. He pointed out that the great classical economists had never claimed that *all* government regulation was wrong, and he challenged only "the universality of the rule of noninterference." The major flaw in the laissez-faire argument, he said, was the assumption that every individual, by working to advance his own interests, necessarily advanced the interests of society. The state should and must intervene in cases where this assumption proved to be unfounded.[32]

Of course, all but the most fanatical protagonists of laissez faire admitted the right of government to check clearly antisocial economic behavior. Adams' contribution was to define the proper scope of government in economic rather than personal or moral terms. The key, he wrote, was "the relationship that exists between the increment of product which results from a given increment of capital or labor." In some businesses, such as retail merchandising, output tends to increase in direct proportion to increases of capital and labor. In others, such as farming, output increases at a declining rate when additional capital and labor are invested. In such fields, regulation is necessary only to the extent of establishing rules raising the ethical plane of fair competition (such as the prohibition of child labor). Competition itself remains desirable. Since competing entrepreneurs can succeed only by reducing costs, self-interest and community interest are identical.

In some industries, however, increases in the amount of capital and labor produce proportionally greater returns, Adams declared. These (he used the railroads as his chief example) are natural monopolies; large companies in these industries have inherent advantages over small ones, new competitors are disadvantaged. "We . . . deceive ourselves in believing that competition can secure for the public fair treatment in such cases." Since competition could not work in these industries, "the only question at issue is, whether society shall support an irresponsible, extra-legal monop-

---

[32] Fine, *Laissez Faire*, pp. 199–251; Dorfman, *Economic Mind*, III, 160–188; Adams, "Relation of the State to Industrial Action," pp. 475, 479–482.

oly, or a monopoly established by law and managed in the interest of the public." To say that American governments were too corrupt and inefficient to be trusted with such tasks, Adams claimed, was to confuse cause and effect. A do-nothing government was naturally corrupt and inefficient. The state had suffered the fate of sick men in the days when every illness was treated with "the leech and the lance"—by bleeding it of all power, the laissez-faire philosophy had reduced it to "feebleness and disintegration." Give government something useful to do and honest and talented men will enter government service. Then the commonwealth will quickly regain its health and strength.[33]

Not every "new" economist was prepared to go as far as Adams in regulating economic affairs. Some felt, as E. R. A. Seligman of Columbia put it, that their discipline had "not yet attained that certainty in results which would authorize us to invoke increased governmental action as a check to various abuses of free competition." When the members of the new school met in 1885 to found the American Economic Association, they refused to approve the prospectus prepared by Richard T. Ely, which included the flat statement: "The doctrine of *laissez-faire* is unsafe in politics and unsound in morals." But they wrote into the constitution of the association the sentence: "We regard the state as an agency whose positive assistance is one of the indispensable conditions of human progress." Social problems existed, they added, "whose solution requires the united efforts, each in its own sphere, of the church, of the state, and of science."[34]

The economists were attacking laissez faire by analyzing its practical effects; the sociologist Lester Frank Ward attacked it more fundamentally by questioning the biological and psychological

---

33 *Ibid.*, pp. 507–508, 519–540.

34 Ely, "Report," pp. 6–7, 27, 35–36; Rader, *Ely*, pp. 33–38. A highly esteemed older American economist, Francis A. Walker, was elected president of the association. Walker believed that government regulation of social and economic matters should be attempted only cautiously, and by the states, where untested legislation could not have nationally disastrous results. "I believe in general that that government is best which governs least," he said in 1883. "Yet I recognize the fact that evils may and do exist which require correction by the force of law. . . . Social science, or sociology, is at present in a very primitive condition. . . . We have yet much to learn." He called for "direct experiment" at the state level as a means of discovering how best to deal with contemporary problems. U.S. Senate, *Report on . . . Labor and Capital* (Washington, 1885), III, 325–326. See also Fine, *Laissez Faire*, pp. 73–79.

bases of noninterference. Whereas Herbert Spencer had insisted that competition in nature led to the survival of the fittest, Ward (a far more knowledgeable biologist) argued that the struggle for existence inhibited the full development of species. He stressed the waste and mindlessness of evolution. In nature, "the whole struggling mass is held by the relentless laws of competition in a condition far below its possibilities." By interfering with the evolutionary process, human beings had repeatedly shown that competitive forces could be constructively manipulated. Aside from the obvious biological examples, such as the improvement of plants and animals by selective breeding, "every implement or utensil, every mechanical device, every object of design, skill, and labor, every artificial thing that serves a human purpose, is a triumph of mind over the physical forces of nature in ceaseless and aimless competition."[35]

Civilization, Ward insisted, was the result of men *not* leaving things alone. The laissez-faire economists were correct in saying that social phenomena are governed by laws, he wrote in 1881, but "they have accompanied this by the false declaration and *non sequitur* that neither physical nor social phenomena are capable of human control." Society, he reasoned, had evolved blindly out of man's gregarious nature, but government was "an invention of the human mind, the result of an extraordinary exercise of the rational, or thinking, faculty." Government was not necessarily good; indeed, so far as it functioned to restrain men, it diminished men's happiness by limiting their freedom to gratify their desires. Yet government could also be made to help mankind, to aid as well as hamper the individual in his search for happiness. The task was to discover how to make men happy and to teach them to recognize their true interests as members of society. Knowledge was the key to good government, social science the key to this knowledge. Once men understood the workings of their society, they could devise "attractive legislation" to replace the "prohibitive legislation" of the current day. Society could then undertake "the systematic realization of its own interests, in the same manner that an intelligent and keen-sighted individual pursues his life-purposes."[36]

35 L. F. Ward, "Broadening the Way to Success," *Forum*, II (1886), 349; Ward, *Psychic Factors*, pp. 260–261.

36 Hofstadter, *Social Darwinism*, p. 57; Ward, *Dynamic Sociology*, II, 224, 235, 249.

Ward did not deny that the American government, as then constituted, was a feeble instrument. Even so, it was clearly better than no government at all, and in those areas where its functions were universally recognized as desirable, and where, therefore, it had been intelligently developed (such as education, and the post office system), it worked reasonably well. If only Americans would cast off the fetters of laissez faire and devote themselves to the scientific study of their society, both the weakness of their government and the inadequacies of their society would soon disappear.

Those who claimed that intelligent economic and social regulation was impossible Ward called "croakers" and *"retardataires."* Most were eagerly seeking special favors from the state while denouncing the state's efforts to help others. "Why cry *'Laissez faire!'* " he asked. "People are no longer in any danger from governmental oppression. What they really need is more government in its primary sense, greater protection from the rapacity of the favored few."[37]

That Ward may have overstated both the ability of planners to devise rational social institutions and the ability of men in general to conduct their affairs intelligently in no way reduced the persuasiveness of his argument against laissez faire and in favor of social planning. While his seminal work, *Dynamic Sociology,* was not widely read, he reached a substantial public throughout the late eighties with a series of magazine articles, and by the early nineties many of the new social scientists were reading him carefully.[38]

Influence, however, is always difficult to isolate and examine. As Ward himself wrote modestly in 1896, "my own contribution was simply a product of the *Zeitgeist.*" The thinking of creative men in all the social sciences was running against the let-alone philosophy. In the early 1870's, Oliver Wendell Holmes, Jr., had begun to argue in legal periodicals that "law is not a science, but is essentially empirical." Like Spencer, Holmes tried to apply Darwin's insights to society, but like Ward he assumed that the course of social

---

37 Ward, *Dynamic Sociology,* I, 53–54, and "False Notions," p. 370.

38 Hofstadter, *Social Darwinism,* p. 55; Samuel Chugarman, *Lester Frank Ward: The American Aristotle* (New York, 1965), pp. 51–52; Ward, *Dynamic Sociology,* I, xiv. In 1894, Albion W. Small and George G. Vincent presented Ward's ideas to college students in their text, *An Introduction to the Study of Society.* Fine, *Laissez Faire,* p. 265 n.

evolution had been shaped by human intelligence. As a jurist he had no patience with scholars who saw the law as a set of logical principles. "The life of the law has not been logic: it has been experience," he stated in 1880 while criticizing the work of a colleague of that persuasion. "The law finds its philosophy not in self-consistency . . . but in history and the nature of human needs." Holmes developed this argument in a series of lectures at Harvard, published in 1881 as *The Common Law*. Although he was even less concerned with practical reform than Ward, and did not discuss laissez faire directly in his studies, the implication of his thought was clear. If law reflected "the felt necessities of the time," these needs, rather than *any* theory, should determine public policy.[39]

A similar point of view pervaded the work of the young political scientist Woodrow Wilson. Although personally conservative in his social attitudes and an admirer of the classical English economists, Wilson rejected laissez faire as a political dogma. "The government of a country so vast and various must be strong, prompt, wieldy, and efficient," he wrote in his doctoral dissertation, *Congressional Government*. Wilson had been trained at Johns Hopkins. Although he did not accept all the proposals of the new economists for specific reforms, he was much influenced by their historical, inductive approach. In *The State* (1889), he traced the "evolution" of governments "from the dim morning hours of history" to his own day. His conception of the speed of social evolution was Spencerian. "Institutions," he wrote, "have to wait upon the slow, the almost imperceptible formation of habit. . . . Nothing may be done by leaps." His concept of the role of government, however, was anything but Spencerian. Besides what he called the "constituent functions" of government, such as the protection of property, the punishment of crime, and the conduct of foreign relations, those acceptable "even in the eyes of strictest *laissez faire*," the state could legitimately perform "ministrant functions," which included the regulation of trade, industry, and labor, the management of railroads, the care of the poor, the education of youth, and even the operation of public utilities.

[39] Ward, *Dynamic Sociology*, I, vii; M. deW. Howe, *Justice Holmes: The Proving Years, 1870–1882* (Cambridge, Mass., 1963), pp. 47, 63, 156–157; O. W. Holmes, Jr., *The Common Law* (Boston, 1881), p. 1.

Society existed to benefit the individual, government *"to accomplish the objects of organized society."* Intelligent adjustment of the functions of government "to the needs of a changing social and industrial organization" was imperative in order to assure the individual "the best means, the best and fullest opportunities, for complete self-development." Wilson sharply criticized "extremists who cry constantly to government, *'Hands off,' 'laissez faire,' 'laissez passer'!"* While admitting that too much state interference would threaten individual liberty, he denied that government was "in itself and by nature a necessary evil."

If the name had not been restricted to a single, narrow, extreme, and radically mistaken class of thinkers, we ought all to regard ourselves and to act as *socialists,* believers in the wholesomeness and beneficence of the body politic. . . . Every means, therefore, by which society may be perfected through the instrumentality of government . . . ought certainly to be diligently sought, and, when found, sedulously fostered by every friend of society.[40]

Men like Wilson, Holmes, Ward, and the new economists were still in the minority in their respective professions at the beginning of the nineties. But they practically monopolized the creative social thinking of the times in America. This is not simply the judgment of hindsight, a reflection of the historical truth that theirs were the ideas that most influenced later developments; in the eighties, except for the judicial advocates of the "new constitutionalism," laissez faire found few defenders capable of original thought. Even William Graham Sumner, the most lucid and persuasive expositor of the let-alone philosophy in the United States, had little to say that was new. Sumner was not a mere rationalizer of the *status quo,* or a slave to the intellectually lax optimism that so many of his contemporaries employed to justify inactivity. He disapproved of protective tariffs, subsidies, and other forms of state aid that businessmen desired, as vigorously as the restrictive legislation they opposed. Yet despite his intellectual courage and consistency, in most essentials Sumner only parroted the language of Spencer and the classical economists, at least in his writings on social and economic questions. As he himself admitted, most of his ideas in

---

[40] Woodrow Wilson, *Congressional Government* (New York, 1956), p. 206, and *The State* (Boston, 1889), pp. 575, 638–640, 656–661, 667.

these fields were based on books he had read as a youth before the Civil War, and on Spencer's *Study of Sociology*. His claim to a place among important American social scientists rests chiefly on his work as a founder of the science of anthropology, culminating in his book *Folkways* (1907), work which he did not even begin until the 1890's.[41]

By the end of the eighties, industrialization and its many interrelated influences had significantly changed the social and economic structure of the United States and was fast altering the thinking of the American people. Farmers and workers, businessmen, political leaders, and intellectuals were reshaping their behavior to conform to the demands of a new way of life in which each individual affected his fellows in numberless, if often obscure, ways. American civilization was becoming so complex that it was submerging the individual and forcing him to seek expression and self-realization through combining with others.

Most Americans clung to the old ideal of the self-reliant, independent individual, and saw co-operation as a means of preserving this ideal. Their attitudes changed very slowly because, more than at any earlier time, their world confronted them with many baffling paradoxes. The United States was becoming a more unified country, but also a more diverse one. Improvements in transportation and communication were shrinking distances and easing intercourse, but the population was growing ethnically more dissimilar and the people were living under a far wider variety of conditions than ever before. New technologies eased the burdens and improved the material welfare of the average citizen, but undermined his inde-

---

41 Hofstadter, *Social Darwinism*, pp. 37–51; McCloskey, *American Conservatism*, pp. 22–41. In 1885, a committee of scientists recommended to Congress a plan for establishing a Department of Science. During the hearings held on this proposal, the biologist Alexander Agassiz opposed the expansion of government scientific activity, stressing the dangers of paternalism and centralization. "The government should limit its support of science to such work as is within neither the province nor the capacity of the individual or of the universities, or of associations of scientific societies." The geologist John Wesley Powell, however, reflected the more modern view. The government, he said, "should promote the welfare of the people" by conducting "investigations in those fields most vitally affecting the great industries in which the people engage. . . . All government research stimulates, promotes, and guides private research." A. H. Dupree, *Science in the Federal Government: A History of Policies and Activities to 1940* (Cambridge, Mass., 1951), pp. 220–227.

pendence, and some said were beginning to enslave him. The burgeoning cities of the land expanded the opportunities and fired the imagination of their inhabitants, yet seemed at the same time to narrow their horizons and reduce them to ciphers.

In addition to presenting a formidable challenge to individualism, the new order seemed to threaten the moral purity and the peace of mind of the American people. Wealth could be a corrupting influence, machine production a stifling one. Many found the anonymity and hectic pace of urban life a temptation to immorality and an unbearable strain, both upon the body and upon the mind. In *Recent Economic Changes,* which he wrote in the late eighties, David A. Wells noted certain aspects of contemporary life that vastly disturbed him. Industrialization had provided the populace with unprecedented bounty. Americans were eating more and varying their diets. (The consumption of bananas had multiplied forty times between 1880 and 1887.) They were growing literally larger (as seen in the production statistics of ready-made-clothing manufacturers). They were enjoying more luxuries, and at the same time saving more money. On the other hand, the "continuous mental and nervous activity which modern high-tension methods of business have necessitated" was producing new "diseases of civilization"—heart trouble, "nervous exhaustion," divorce. Crime, Wells noted, was rapidly increasing. He speculated as to whether or not mankind was actually improving its lot.[42]

There are men in every generation who find change alarming and who attribute to each new fad and casual shift of taste a revolutionary significance. The changes that were taking place in the eighties, however, were destined to give a special character to at least a century of the nation's history. Modern America was being born.[43] After reading some of Wells's observations, a prominent journalist of the day penned a critique that many a mid-twentieth-century social commentator might have written:

I get up from the reading of what you have written scared, and more satisfied than ever before that the true and wise course of every man is . . . to get out of the crushing process. It seems to me that what we call

[42] D. A. Wells, *Recent Economic Changes* (New York, 1889), pp. 324, 337–348, 350.

[43] H. S. Commager discusses this point brilliantly in his *American Mind,* pp. 41–54. He places the "watershed" between the old and the new in the nineties, but admits that the shift was in full swing by the mid-eighties.

civilization is to degrade and incapacitate the mass of men and women.
. . . [It is] a preposterous fraud. It does not give us leisure; it does not
enable us to be clean except at a monstrous cost; it affects us with horrible
diseases . . . poisoning our water and the air we breathe; it fosters the
vicious classes . . . and it compels mankind to a strife for bread, which
makes us all meaner than God intended us to be.[44]

Of course, other persons, equally observant, found the new tendencies less disturbing, or, like the Harvard art historian Charles
Eliot Norton, were alarmed by relatively minor results of industrialization, such as the deleterious effect of machine production on
standards of craftsmanship.[45] That society was exerting enormous
new pressures on the individual, few, however, denied.

The frightening impact of the great depression of the nineties
speeded the development of new social concepts, although, by
rousing conservatives to the defense of vested interests, it delayed
the application of many of these concepts for a decade or more. But
before 1890 the basic ideas that flowered in the Progressive Era had
all been formulated. The civil-service reformers had laid the foundations for rationalizing the machinery of democratic government
and attacking the boss system. Every important suggestion for
dealing with the power of large corporations advanced in the early
twentieth century had been made in the 1880's. Nothing that
Herbert Croly said about applying Hamiltonian means to achieve
Jeffersonian ends in *The Promise of American Life* (1909) had not
already been said by the new economists as early as 1886. The
essence of Woodrow Wilson's New Freedom can be found in the
concluding chapters of his treatise on *The State*.

The rhetoric of the old order continued to be heard; indeed, it
rose in pitch and volume. But the insistent pressures of the new
order could not long be resisted. Americans, as Wilson said, had to
become socialists in order to live in an industrial society. Laissez
faire was dead as an intellectual issue, moribund as a practical
guide to statecraft. It was even beginning to lose its vitality as a
shibboleth.

44 Wells, *Recent Economic Changes,* p. 325.

45 Norton characterized the eighties as a "degenerate and unlovely age." While
recognizing the importance of the material benefits of industrialization, he
blamed it for "the ascendant power of mediocrity" and the "predominance of the
taste and standards of judgment of the uneducated and unrefined masses." Mann,
Yankee Reformers, p. 8; Kermit Vanderbilt, *Charles Eliot Norton: Apostle of
Culture in a Democracy* (Cambridge, Mass., 1959) , pp. 128, 207–208.

Bibliography

General Works

Only a relative handful of scholars have sought to deal comprehensively with the history of the United States between the end of Reconstruction and the 1890's, and most of these have treated the period as part of a larger survey. E. B. Andrews, *The Last Quarter-Century in the United States: 1870–1895* (New York, 1896), lacks both perspective and depth of research, but remains valuable. J. F. Rhodes, *History of the United States from Hayes to McKinley: 1877–1896* (New York, 1919), is thin and shallow, far below the quality of the preceding seven volumes of his *History of the United States from the Compromise of 1850*. E. P. Oberholtzer covers the period in Volumes 4 and 5 of his *History of the United States since the Civil War* (5 vols., New York, 1917–37), but, while based on sound scholarship, this work is uninspired and, like Rhodes's book, primarily a political narrative. Two volumes in the *History of American Life* series—A. M. Schlesinger, *The Rise of the City* (New York, 1933), and I. M. Tarbell, *The Nationalizing of Business* (New York, 1936)—stress social, cultural, and economic developments at the expense of politics. Taken together, two volumes by Matthew Josephson, *The Robber Barons: The Great American Capitalists, 1860–1901* (New York, 1934), and *The Politicos: 1865–1896* (New York, 1938), provide a sharply critical, somewhat slanted, yet useful and stimulating analysis of the political and economic history of the period.

Of more recent general studies, the most important is S. P. Hays, *The Response to Industrialism: 1885–1914* (Chicago, 1957), which more than any other volume has established the connection between the post-Reconstruction era and the main trends of the twentieth century. Ray Ginger, *The Age of Excess: The United States from 1877 to 1914* (New York, 1965), is less closely reasoned and at times is too opinionated, but it contains a wealth of information and a number of challenging interpretations. R. H. Wiebe, *The Search for Order: 1877–1920* (New York, 1967), attempts to explain the era in terms of a shift from a society of autonomous "island" communities to one characterized by a centralized nation organized around highly specialized interest groups. Although the work of many authors and thus somewhat lacking in unity and comprehensiveness, H. W. Morgan (ed.), *The Gilded Age: An Age in Need of Reinterpretation* (Syracuse, 1963), is important as a summary of much of the most recent historical thinking about the era, reflecting the tendency of most scholars to treat it more sympathetically. On the other hand, F. A. Shannon's posthumously published *The Centennial Years: A Political and Economic History of America from the Late 1870s to the Early 1890s* (Garden City, 1967), edited by R. H. Jones, adopts a much darker view of the period.

Agriculture

The best general account of agricultural developments is F. A. Shannon, *The Farmer's Last Frontier: Agriculture, 1860–1897* (New York, 1945). The 1899 *Yearbook* of the Department of Agriculture (Washington, 1900) contains many valuable articles by experts summarizing agricultural developments down to that time, while the 1940 *Yearbook*, published separately as *Farmers in a Changing World* (Washington, [1940]), contains two invaluable long essays, E. E. Edwards, "American Agriculture—The First 300 Years," and P. H. Johnstone, "Old Ideals versus New Ideas in Farm Life," which place the post-Reconstruction era in proper perspective. The annual *Reports* of the Department of Agriculture for 1877–91 (and beyond) are full of valuable information, including a wealth of statistics. Leo Rogin, *The Introduction of Farm Machinery . . . During the Nineteenth Century* (Berkeley, 1931), is full of useful detail.

Important regional studies of farming include J. C. Ballaugh (ed.), *Economic History: 1865–1909* (Richmond, 1909), a volume in the *South in the Building of the Nation* series; A. G. Bogue, *From Prairie to Corn Belt: Farming on the Illinois and Iowa Prairies in the Nineteenth Century* (Chicago, 1963); H. M. Drache, *The Day of the Bonanza: A History of Bonanza Farming in the Red River Valley of the North* (Fargo, 1964); E. N. Dick, *The Sod-House Frontier: 1854–1890* (New York, 1937); J. C. Malin, *Winter Wheat in the Golden Belt of Kansas* (Lawrence, 1944); and the contemporary account of the land reformer W. G. Moody, *Land and Labor in the United States* (New York, 1883). C. V. Woodward, *Origins of the New South: 1877–1913* (Baton Rouge, 1951), contains an excellent discussion of southern agriculture, while V. L. Wharton, *The Negro in Mississippi: 1865–1890* (Chapel Hill, 1947), and G. B. Tindall, *South Carolina Negroes: 1877–1900* (Columbia, S.C., 1952), two outstanding studies of the fate of the southern Negro after Reconstruction, treat agricultural conditions at length. Many memoirs and fictional accounts of rural life in this era provide invaluable insights. Outstanding among these are Hamlin Garland, *A Son of the Middle Border* (New York, 1917); A. S. Johnson, *Pioneer's Progress* (New York, 1952); Mari Sandoz, *Old Jules* (Boston, 1935); and Willa Cather, *My Ántonia* (Boston, 1913), and *O Pioneers!* (Boston, 1915).

The standard work on the Patrons of Husbandry is S. J. Buck, *The Granger Movement* (Cambridge, Mass., 1913); on the protest movements of the 1880's and 1890's, J. D. Hicks, *The Populist Revolt* (Minneapolis, 1931), Theodore Saloutos, *Farmer Movements in the South* (Berkeley, 1960), and R. V. Scott, *The Agrarian Movement in Illinois: 1880–1896* (Urbana, 1962), are important regional studies of agricultural protest. The debate over the character of populism precipitated by Richard Hofstadter, *The Age of Reform: From Bryan to F.D.R.* (New York, 1961), which stresses the reactionary character of the movement and of the late-nineteenth-century rural mind, has produced, among other works, W. T. K. Nugent, *The Tolerant Populists* (Chicago, 1963), and Norman Pollack, *The Populist Response to Industrial America* (Cambridge, Mass., 1962), the latter an interesting but, in my opinion, misguided attempt to portray the Populists as profound critics of modern industrial society. R. F. Durden, *The Climax of Populism* (Lexington, 1965), defends the leaders of the movement in more moderate terms. A. G. Bogue, *Money at Interest* (Ithaca, 1955), shows that the Populists' dislike of money-gouging eastern bankers was not based on real grievances.

For the role of government in agricultural developments, see the chapter on the Department of Agriculture in L. D. White, *The Republican Era: 1869–1901* (New York, 1958); A. C. True, *A History of Agricultural Experimentation and Research in the United States: 1607–1925* (Washington, 1937); F. W. Powell, *The Bureau of Animal Industry* (Baltimore, 1927); and many of the articles in the 1899 *Yearbook* of the Department. On the land-grant colleges and other government activities related to farming, see E. D. Ross, *Democracy's College* (Ames, Iowa, 1942), and A. C. True, *A History of Agricultural Education in the United States: 1785–1925* (Washington, 1929). Two biographies of heads of the Department of Agriculture in these years are useful: G. F. Lemmer, *Norman J. Colman and Colman's Rural World* (Columbia, Mo., 1953), and Henry Casson, *"Uncle Jerry": Life of General Jeremiah M. Rusk* (Madison, 1895).

Industrialization

Any understanding of the growth of industry must begin with the basic facts of production, which, so far as they are known, can be conveniently consulted in *Historical Statistics of the United States: Colonial Times to 1957* (Washington, 1965). The censuses of 1870, 1880, and 1890 are also full of useful data. A number of economic historians, working with these and other materials, provide insights into the significance of the statistics. See especially Edwin Frickey, *Production in the United States: 1860–1914* (Cambridge, Mass., 1947); Simon Kuznets, *National Income: A Summary of Findings* (New York, 1946); Harold Barger, *Distribution's Place in the American Economy* (Princeton, 1955); A. H. Hansen, *Business Cycles and National Income* (New York, 1964); Rendigs Fels, *American Business Cycles: 1865–1897* (Chapel Hill, 1959); Milton Friedman and A. J. Schwartz, *A Monetary History of the United States, 1867–1960* (Princeton, 1963); and G. H. Evans, Jr., *Business Incorporations in the United States: 1800–1943* (New York, 1948).

The most useful contemporary analysis of industrialization is D. A. Wells, *Recent Economic Changes* (New York, 1889), but C. D. Wright, *The Industrial Evolution of the United States* (New York, 1897), is also important. The best modern study is E. C. Kirkland, *Industry Comes of Age: Business, Labor, and Public Policy, 1860–1897* (New York, 1961). T. C. Cochran and William Miller, *The Age of Enterprise* (New York, 1942), provides another overview, and, for the beginning of the period, Allan Nevins, *The Emergence of Modern America* (New York, 1928), is also excellent. V. S. Clark, *History of Manufactures* (Washington, 1929), offers a wealth of detail, while D. C. North, *Growth and Welfare in the American Economy* (Englewood Cliffs, N.J., 1966), places the developments of the era in larger perspective and summarizes the new concepts and theories of recent economic historians.

Technological changes are summarized in H. J. Habakkuk, *American and British Technology in the Nineteenth Century* (Cambridge, Eng., 1962), while W. P. Strassmann, *Risk and Technological Innovation: American Manufacturing Methods during the Nineteenth Century* (Ithaca, 1959), provides a detailed analysis of how technological changes were adopted in selected industries, challenging the assumption that American manufacturers were bold and daring innovators. See also F. B. Copley, *Frederick W. Taylor* (New York, 1923). Changes in the organization of business are discussed in many of the histories of particular industries mentioned below. On advertising, see R. M. Hower, *The History of an Advertising Agency: N. W. Ayer & Son at Work, 1869–1949* (Cambridge, Mass., 1949); Frank Presbrey, *The History and Development of*

Advertising (New York, 1929); and J. P. Wood, *The Story of Advertising* (New York, 1958). On merchandising, see R. M. Hower, *History of Macy's of New York, 1858–1919: Chapters in the Evolution of the Department Store* (Cambridge, Mass., 1943); T. D. Clark, *Pills, Petticoats, and Plows: The Southern Country Store* (Indianapolis, 1944); and Boris Emmet and J. E. Jeuck, *Catalogues and Customers: A History of Sears, Roebuck and Company* (Chicago, 1950). On the financial and securities market, see A. D. Chandler, Jr., *Henry Varnum Poor, Business Editor, Analyst, and Reformer* (Cambridge, Mass., 1956); Henry Clews, *Fifty Years in Wall Street* (New York, 1908); and Fritz Redlich, *The Molding of American Banking: Men and Ideas, Part II, 1840–1910* (Ann Arbor, 1940–51).

Important contemporary studies of the railroad industry include C. F. Adams, Jr., *Railroads: Their Origin and Problems* (New York, 1879); A. T. Hadley, *Railroad Transportation* (New York, 1885); and J. S. Jeans, *Railway Problems* (London, 1887). G. R. Taylor and I. D. Neu, *The American Railroad Network: 1861–1890* (Cambridge, Mass., 1956), describes the changes in the character of the system, whereas R. E. Riegel, *The Story of Western Railroads* (New York, 1926), is chiefly descriptive. Good regional studies include E. C. Kirkland, *Men, Cities, and Transportation: A Study in New England History, 1820–1900* (Cambridge, Mass., 1948); J. F. Stover, *Railroads of the South, 1865–1900: A Study in Finance and Control* (Chapel Hill, 1955); and Oscar Lewis, *The Big Four* (New York, 1938), on the Central Pacific Railroad. J. F. Stover, *American Railroads* (Chicago, 1961), is a good brief history.

Other volumes dealing with the organization and operation of railroads include Julius Grodinsky, *The Iowa Pool: A Study in Railroad Competition, 1870–84* (Chicago, 1950), and *Transcontinental Railway Strategy, 1869–1893: A Study of Businessmen* (Philadelphia, 1962); T. C. Cochran, *Railroad Leaders, 1845–1890: The Business Mind in Action* (Cambridge, Mass., 1953), which contains a wealth of comment by railroad executives on every aspect of the business, and extensive selections from their correspondence; and L. E. Decker, *Railroads, Lands, and Politics: The Taxation of the Railroad Land Grants, 1864–1897* (Providence, 1964). A. D. Chandler (ed.), *Railroads: The Nation's First Big Business* (New York, 1965), is an excellent introduction to the study of railroad organizational problems. W. Z. Ripley, *Railroads: Finance and Organization* (New York, 1915), is still worth consulting.

A book of special interest, difficult and also controversial in method, is R. W. Fogel, *Railroads and Economic Growth: Essays in Econometric History* (Baltimore, 1964), which attempts to assess the importance of railroads by estimating what would have happened to the economy if they had not existed!

The best modern study of the steel industry is Peter Temin, *Iron and*

Steel in Nineteenth Century America: An Economic Inquiry (Cambridge, Mass., 1964). D. L. Burn, *Economic History of Steelmaking* (Cambridge, Eng., 1940), takes a world view of the subject. T. A. Wertime, *The Coming of the Age of Steel* (Chicago, 1962), is detailed on the evolution of steel technology. The favorable view of the subject taken by B. J. Hendrick, *The Life of Andrew Carnegie* (New York, 1922), is balanced by J. H. Bridge, *The Inside History of the Carnegie Steel Company* (New York, 1903). See also Ethel Armes, *The Story of Coal and Iron in Alabama* (Birmingham, 1910).

For the petroleum industry, see H. F. Williamson and A. R. Daum, *The American Petroleum Industry: The Age of Illumination, 1859–1899* (Evanston, 1959); R. W. and M. E. Hidy, *Pioneering in Big Business* (New York, 1955); Allan Nevins, *John D. Rockefeller: The Heroic Age of American Industry* (New York, 1940), revised as *Study in Power: John D. Rockefeller, Industrialist and Philanthropist* (New York, 1953); and A. M. Johnson, *The Development of American Petroleum Pipelines: A Study in Private Enterprise and Public Policy, 1862–1906* (Ithaca, 1956). H. C. Passer, *The Electrical Manufacturers, 1875–1900: A Study in Competition, Entrepreneurship, Technical Change and Economic Growth* (Cambridge, Mass., 1953), and Matthew Josephson, *Edison: A Biography* (New York, 1959), provide together an admirable picture of the early development of the electrical industry.

Of many studies of other industries, the following are among the best, without particular regard for the importance of the industries: T. R. Navin, *The Whitin Machine Works Since 1831: A Textile Machinery Company in an Industrial Village* (Cambridge, Mass., 1950); G. S. Gibb, *The Saco-Lowell Shops: Textile Machinery Building in New England, 1813–1949* (Cambridge, Mass., 1950); Broadus Mitchell, *The Rise of Cotton Mills in the South* (Baltimore, 1921); T. C. Cochran, *The Pabst Brewing Company* (New York, 1948); A. H. Cole, *The American Wool Manufacture* (Cambridge, Mass., 1926); and J. S. Ewing and N. P. Norton, *Broadlooms and Businessmen: A History of the Bigelow-Sanford Carpet Company* (Cambridge, Mass., 1955).

The industrialists of the era were not very articulate. J. D. Rockefeller, *Random Reminiscences of Men and Events* (New York, 1909), and Andrew Carnegie, *Autobiography* (Boston, 1920), stand almost alone. Carnegie's *Triumphant Democracy: Or Fifty Years' March of the Republic* (New York, 1886), shows the American booster spirit in extreme form, while his many articles and speeches reveal his point of view fully. Some of these are readily available in E. C. Kirkland (ed.), *Andrew Carnegie's Gospel of Wealth and Other Timely Essays* (Cambridge, Mass., 1962), but see also Andrew Carnegie, *The Empire of Business* (New York, 1902).

Cochran's *Railroad Leaders,* already noted, is important. E. C. Kirkland, *Dream and Thought in the Business Community* (Ithaca, 1956), and Sigmund Diamond, *The Reputation of American Businessmen* (Cambridge, Mass., 1955), are both suggestive, the first illustrating how the businessman viewed himself, the second seeking to analyze the changing public image of the businessman as revealed in obituaries. C. F. Adams, Jr., *Autobiography* (Boston, 1916), is mainly concerned with nonbusiness affairs, but contains some trenchant observations. Adams' point of view is further elucidated in E. C. Kirkland, *Charles Francis Adams, Jr., 1835–1915: The Patrician at Bay* (Cambridge, Mass., 1965).

State and national regulation of industry is considered broadly in J. W. Hurst, *Law and the Condition of Freedom in the Nineteenth-Century United States* (Madison, 1956), and *Law and Economic Growth: The Legal History of the Lumber Industry in Wisconsin* (Cambridge, Mass., 1964), and in Carter Goodrich, *Government Regulation of American Canals and Railroads: 1800–1890* (New York, 1960). These books are invaluable for an understanding of the changing character of regulation: from policies aimed chiefly at support and stimulation to ones restricting and controlling business. On the conditions leading to stiffer regulation of railroads, see Buck, *Granger Movement;* Adams, *Railroads: Their Origin and Problems;* Hadley, *Railroad Transportation;* Cochran, *Railroad Leaders;* and most of the other volumes on the railroads already mentioned. Two important government investigations, State of New York, *Proceedings of the Special [Hepburn] Committee on Railroads* (New York, 1879), and U. S. Senate, *Select [Cullom] Committee on Interstate Commerce,* Report No. 46 (Washington, 1886), are loaded with important material. The movement for railroad regulation is traced in L. H. Haney, *A Congressional History of Railways in the United States: 1850–1887* (Madison, 1910); Lee Benson, *Merchants, Farmers, and Railroads: Railroad Regulation and New York Politics, 1850–1887* (Cambridge, Mass., 1955); S. M. Cullom, *Fifty Years of Public Service* (Chicago, 1911); and J. W. Neilson, *Shelby M. Cullom: Prairie State Republican* (Urbana, 1962). Gabriel Kolko, *Railroads and Regulation: 1877–1916* (Princeton, 1965), takes a jaundiced view both of the motives of the advocates of regulation and of the effectiveness of the Interstate Commerce Commission. The early reports of the commission, especially the *First Annual Report* (Washington, 1887), provide valuable insights into the difficulty of regulating this complex business and the approaches of the early commissioners. See also W. Z. Ripley, *Railroads, Rates and Regulations* (New York, 1912). The standard work on the origins of the Sherman Antitrust Act is H. B. Thorelli, *Federal Antitrust Policy: The Origination of an American Tradition* (Baltimore, 1955).

Labor

A great deal has been written about organized labor and about strikes in this period; very little about workingmen, the conditions of labor, and the ideas and attitudes of employers and employees. By far the most valuable source for understanding these subjects is the four volumes of testimony taken by the Senate Committee on Education and Labor in 1883, *Report on the Relations Between Labor and Capital* (Washington, 1885). The committee questioned many important business leaders and union executives, but also dozens of ordinary workingmen. Selections from this mass of testimony are conveniently reprinted in J. A. Garraty (ed.), *Labor and Capital in the Gilded Age* (Boston, 1968). Although taken at a somewhat later date, much of the testimony in Volumes VII and XIV of U.S. Industrial Commission on Capital and Labor, *Report* (Washington, 1901), is similarly valuable. There is also a wealth of evidence· in the reports of the state bureaus of labor statistics. The bureaus of Massachusetts, Illinois, Ohio, and Wisconsin were especially active; the reports which I found most useful are referred to in the footnotes of Chapter 4. The best guide to the reports of the bureaus and to the materials in U.S. Commissioner of Labor, *Reports of the Bureau of Labor Statistics* (Washington, 1886–1901), is C. D. Wright (ed.), *Index to all the Reports of the Bureaus of Labor Statistics of the United States Prior to March 1, 1902* (Washington, 1902).

Of the secondary literature on workingmen, David Brody, *Steelworkers in America: The Nonunion Era* (Cambridge, Mass., 1960), is outstanding. R. H. Bremner, *From the Depths: The Discovery of Poverty in the United States* (New York, 1956), is useful, and Stephan Thernstrom, *Poverty and Progress: Social Mobility in a Nineteenth-Century City* (Cambridge, Mass., 1964), is a valuable study of the standard of living of unskilled workers, based on manuscript census materials. Businessmen's attitudes are discussed in Cochran, *Railroad Leaders*; Kirkland, *Dream and Thought in the Business Community;* and in many of the business histories referred to above. Gerd Korman, *Industrialization, Immigrants, and Americanization: The View from Milwaukee, 1866–1921* (Madison, 1967), discusses the welfare policies of firms in Milwaukee, and Robert Ozanne, *A Century of Labor-Management Relations at McCormick and International Harvester* (Madison, 1967), treats the labor policies of one of the most enlightened corporations of the era. C. D. Long, *Wages and Earnings in the United States: 1860–1890* (Princeton, 1960), summarizes the available material on real and money wages. The most useful studies of the role of the immigrant as a worker and of the attitudes of organized labor toward immigrants are R. T. Berthoff, *British Immigrants in Industrial America:*

1790–1950 (Cambridge, Mass., 1953); C. K. Yearley, Jr., *Britons in American Labor: A History of the Influence of United Kingdom Immigrants in American Labor, 1820–1914* (Baltimore, 1957), which focuses on the ideas of labor leaders; Charlotte Erickson, *American Industry and European Immigration: 1860–1885* (Cambridge, Mass., 1957); Oscar Handlin, *The Uprooted: The Epic Story of the Great Migrations That Made the American People* (Boston, 1951); and John Higham, *Strangers in the Land: Patterns of American Nativism, 1860–1925* (New Brunswick, 1955).

On the major strikes of the period, see R. V. Bruce, *1877: Year of Violence* (Indianapolis, 1959); Henry David, *The History of the Haymarket Affair* (New York, 1936); and D. L. McMurry, *The Great Burlington Strike of 1888* (Cambridge, Mass., 1956). Leon Wolff, *Lockout: The Story of the Homestead Strike of 1892* (New York, 1965); Almont Lindsey, *The Pullman Strike* (Chicago, 1942); and Stanley Buder, *Pullman: An Experiment in Industrial Order and Community Planning, 1880–1930* (Chicago, 1967), deal with strikes of the early 1890's, but contain material helpful in understanding earlier developments.

For the history of organized labor, the second volume of J. R. Commons et al., *History of Labour in the United States* (New York, 1918), is still indispensable. Philip Taft, *Organized Labor in American History* (New York, 1964), and Henry Pelling, *American Labor* (Chicago, 1960), are useful summaries, as is Taft's, *The AFL in the Time of Gompers* (New York, 1957). More specialized studies include Lloyd Ulman, *The Rise of the National Trade Union* (Cambridge, Mass., 1955), R. A. Christie, *Empire in Wood: A History of the Carpenters' Union* (Ithaca, 1956); and G. N. Grob, *Workers and Utopia* (Evanston, 1961). N. J. Ware, *The Labor Movement in the United States: 1860–1895* (New York, 1929), the best history of the Knights of Labor, adopts a generally critical view of that organization; the attitude of leaders of the Knights is clearly revealed in T. V. Powderly, *Thirty Years of Labor: 1859 to 1889* (Columbus, 1889), and G. E. McNeill (ed.), *The Labor Movement: The Problem of Today* (Boston, 1887). Samuel Gompers, *Seventy Years of Life and Labor* (New York, 1925), surveys the scene from the perspective of a founder of the A. F. of L.

On the activities of the state and federal governments with regard to labor, see the reports of the state bureaus of labor statistics and of the U.S. commissioner of labor already mentioned. James Leiby, *Carroll Wright and Labor Reform* (Cambridge, Mass., 1960), is a biography of the foremost labor commissioner of the era. G. G. Eggert, *Railroad Labor Disputes: The Beginnings of Federal Strike Policy* (Ann Arbor, 1967), stresses the antilabor policy of the federal government in dealing with railroad strikes during this period.

Urbanization

The idea of urban history as a special subject and of urbanization as a key to understanding American development dates from A. M. Schlesinger's *The Rise of the City* (New York, 1933). However, the book is somewhat disappointing as a synthesis. The most detailed general urban history is Blake McKelvey, *The Urbanization of America* (New York, 1963). C. N. Glaab and A. T. Brown, *A History of Urban America* (New York, 1967), is briefer but more interpretive. See also C. M. Green, *American Cities and the Growth of the Nation* (New York, 1957), and *The Rise of Urban America* (New York, 1965). C. N. Glaab (ed.), *The American City: A Documentary History* (Homewood, Ill., 1963), contains interesting contemporary materials dealing with this period, and Glaab's essay, "The History of the American City: A Bibliographical Survey," in P. M. Hauser and L. F. Schnore (eds.), *The Study of Urbanization* (New York, 1965), is an excellent guide to the literature. Willard Glazier, *Peculiarities of American Cities* (Philadelphia, 1883), provides reportorial descriptions of most of the major cities in the early eighties. A. F. Weber, *The Growth of Cities in the Nineteenth Century: A Study in Statistics* (New York, 1899), is still important. Other volumes worth consulting include W. Z. Hirsch (ed.), *Urban Life and Form* (New York, 1967); J. W. Reps, *The Making of Urban America* (Princeton, 1965); C. N. Glaab, *Kansas City and the Railroads* (Madison, 1962); and D. A. Smith, *Rocky Mountain Mining Camps: The Urban Frontier* (Bloomington, 1967).

Among the many histories of individual cities containing material for this period are the following: B. L. Pierce, *A History of Chicago* (New York, 1957), III, which can be supplemented with Pierce's anthology, *As Others Saw Chicago* (Chicago, 1933); H. C. Syrett, *The City of Brooklyn: 1865–1898* (New York, 1944); C. M. Green, *Washington: Capital City, 1879–1950* (Princeton, 1963); Blake McKelvey, *Rochester: The Flower City, 1855–1890* (Cambridge, Mass., 1949); Bayard Still, *Milwaukee: The History of a City* (Madison, 1948); R. M. Fogelson, *The Fragmented Metropolis: Los Angeles, 1850–1930* (Cambridge, Mass., 1967); D. B. Cole, *Immigrant City: Lawrence, Massachusetts, 1845–1921* (Chapel Hill, 1963); R. G. Osterweis, *Three Centuries of New Haven* (New Haven, 1953); W. G. Rose, *Cleveland: The Making of a City* (Cleveland, 1950). Bayard Still (ed.), *Mirror for Gotham: New York as Seen by Contemporaries from Dutch Days to the Present* (New York, 1956), covers this period, and Francis Carpenter (ed.), *Carp's Washington* (New York, 1960), contains valuable comments by a sharp-eyed newspaperman on Washington in the eighties.

Books dealing with the physical growth and development of cities include S. B. Warner, Jr., *Streetcar Suburbs: The Process of Growth in Boston, 1870–1900* (Cambridge, Mass., 1962), which is superficially a narrow monograph, but which is actually one of the most wide-ranging and enlightening studies of urban life so far written; John Buchard and Albert Bush-Brown, *The Architecture of America: A Social and Cultural History* (Boston, 1961), which does not entirely live up to its ambitious title, but which is very useful; N. M. Blake, *Water for the Cities: A History of Urban Water Supply Problems in the United States* (Syracuse, 1956); and J. H. Cassedy, *Charles V. Chapin and the Public Health Movement* (Cambridge, Mass., 1962). See also C. M. Robinson, *The Improvement of Towns and Cities* (New York, 1901); C. V. Chapin, *Municipal Sanitation in the United States* (Providence, 1901); and E. W. Bemis (ed.), *Municipal Monopolies* (New York, 1899).

The interaction of immigration and urbanization is discussed in many of the books dealing with immigration in the section on labor. See also Moses Rischin, *The Promised City: New York's Jews, 1870–1914* (Cambridge, Mass., 1962); T. N. Brown, *Irish-American Nationalism: 1870–1890* (Philadelphia, 1966); B. M. Solomon, *Ancestors and Immigrants: A Changing New England Tradition* (Cambridge, Mass., 1956); and Grace Abbott, *The Immigrant and the Community* (New York, 1917).

The literature on urban housing and the slum is large. Jacob Riis, *How the Other Half Lives* (New York, 1890), is a classic; Jane Addams, *Twenty Years at Hull-House* (New York, 1910), is almost equally well known. Other contemporary studies of importance include A. T. White, *Better Homes for Working People* (New York, 1885), and Hutchins Hapgood, *The Spirit of the Ghetto* (New York, 1965). See also two books by Roy Lubove, *The Progressives and the Slums* (Pittsburgh, 1962), and *The Professional Altruist: The Emergence of Social Work as a Profession* (Cambridge, Mass., 1965), and Gordon Atkins, *Health, Housing, and Poverty in New York City: 1865–1898* (New York, 1947).

The reformers' views on urban problems can be traced in S. L. Loomis, *Modern Cities and Their Religious Problems* (New York, 1887); A. I. Abell, *The Urban Impact on American Protestantism: 1865–1900* (Cambridge, Mass., 1943), and *American Catholicism and Social Action* (Garden City, 1960); C. D. Hopkins, *The Rise of the Social Gospel in American Protestantism* (New Haven, 1940); and H. F. May, *Protestant Churches and Industrial America* (New York, 1949). R. D. Cross (ed.), *The Church and the City: 1865–1910* (Indianapolis, 1967), contains a convenient selection of contemporary commentary, as well as a brilliant introductory essay by the editor. For a jaundiced view of urban life, see Josiah Strong, *Our Country* (New York, 1885), a best-seller in its day.

The problems of urban government are treated in James Bryce, *The American Commonwealth* (New York, 1888) which contains important essays by Seth Low and F. J. Goodnow as well as Bryce's classic observations. Scholarly studies include F. W. Patton, *The Battle for Municipal Reform: Mobilization and Attack, 1875–1900* (Washington, 1940), and A. B. Callow, Jr., *The Tweed Ring* (New York, 1966).

Political History

Of the contemporary political commentaries, James Bryce, *The American Commonwealth* (New York, 1888), stands without a peer. Although perhaps less dramatically insightful than de Tocqueville's commentary on the United States in the 1830's, *Democracy in America,* it is far more systematic and scholarly. Woodrow Wilson, *Congressional Government* (New York, 1885), is also a classic, as are two somewhat later studies, M. Y. Ostrogorski, *Democracy and the Organization of Political Parties* (New York, 1902), and H. J. Ford, *The Rise and Growth of American Politics: A Sketch of Constitutional Development* (New York, 1898). There is also a wealth of material in the periodical press, especially the *Nation,* the *North American Review,* and the *Forum.*

Of later studies, in addition to the works of Oberholtzer, Rhodes, Andrews, and Josephson mentioned under general works, above, see L. D. White, *The Republican Era: A Study in Administrative History* (New York, 1958), which is outstanding as a discussion of the structure and functions of the federal government. On the Presidency, see W. E. Binkley, *The President and Congress* (New York, 1962); on the Senate, G. H. Haynes, *The Senate of the United States: Its History and Practice* (New York, 1960), a conventional survey, and D. J. Rothman, *Politics and Power: The United States Senate, 1869–1901* (Cambridge, Mass., 1966), which is more analytical. G. B. Galloway, *History of the House of Representatives* (New York, 1961), and Neil McNeill, *Forge of Democracy: The House of Representatives* (New York, 1963), discuss the lower house. On the Supreme Court, in addition to the standard Charles Warren, *The Supreme Court in United States History* (Boston, 1926), and R. G. McCloskey, *The American Supreme Court* (Chicago, 1960), a briefer but more up-to-date account, see A. M. Paul, *Conservative Crisis and the Rule of Law: Attitudes of Bar and Bench, 1887–1895* (Ithaca, 1960). Other useful books on political history include H. S. Merrill, *Bourbon Democracy in the Middle West: 1865–1896* (Baton Rouge, 1953); Geoffrey Blodgett, *The Gentle Reformers: Massachusetts Democracy in the Cleveland Era* (Cambridge, Mass., 1966); T. N. Brown, *Irish-American Nationalism: 1870–1890* (Philadelphia, 1966); C. V. Woodward, *Origins of the New South: 1877–1913* (Baton Rouge, 1951); and J. R. Hollingsworth, *The Whirligig of Politics: The Democracy of Cleveland and Bryan* (Chicago, 1963), which deals with a slightly later period, but which is helpful for understanding the 1880's.

Among the most important volumes by contemporary politicians and other observers are Henry Adams, *The Education of Henry Adams* (Boston, 1918), and his novel, *Democracy* (New York, 1880); W. C. Ford (ed.), *Letters of Henry Adams, 1858–1891* (Boston, 1930); J. G. Blaine, *Political Discussions* (Norwich, 1887); Frances Carpenter (ed.), *Carp's Washington* (New York, 1960); S. M. Cullom, *Fifty Years of Public Service* (Chicago, 1911); J. B. Foraker, *Notes of a Busy Life* (Cincinnati, 1917); Benjamin Harrison, *This Country of Ours* (New York, 1901); G. F. Hoar, *Autobiography of Seventy Years* (New York, 1903); E. W. Martin, *Behind the Scenes in Washington* (Washington, 1873); L. J. Lang (ed.), *Autobiography of Thomas Collier Platt* (New York, 1910); B. P. Poore, *Perley's Reminiscences of Sixty Years in the National Metropolis* (Philadelphia, 1886); and John Sherman, *Recollections of Forty Years in the House, Senate, and Cabinet* (Chicago, 1895).

On civil-service reform, see White's *Republican Era* and also Ari Hoogenboom, *Outlawing the Spoils: A History of the Civil Service Reform Movement, 1865–1883* (Urbana, 1961), which is somewhat critical of the reformers; Blodgett's *Gentle Reformers*, which treats them as his title indicates; and P. P. Van Riper, *History of the United States Civil Service* (Evanston, 1958). On the Negro and politics, and the bloody-shirt question, see P. H. Buck, *The Road to Reunion: 1865–1900* (New York, 1937); R. W. Logan, *The Negro in American Life and Thought: The Nadir, 1877–1901* (New York, 1954); S. P. Hirshson, *Farewell to the Bloody Shirt: Northern Republicans and the Southern Negro, 1877–1897* (Bloomington, 1962); and V. P. DeSantis, *Republicans Face the Southern Question: The New Departure Years, 1877–1897* (Baltimore, 1959).

Monetary policy is covered in Milton Friedman and A. J. Schwartz, *A Monetary History of the United States, 1867–1960* (Princeton, 1963), which, in treating this period, stresses the irrationality of policy; Irwin Unger, *The Greenback Era: A Social and Political History of American Finance, 1865–1879* (Princeton, 1964), an excellent study which, because of its concern with the relationship between policy and ideas, throws light on every aspect of late-nineteenth-century financial history; and two older works that are still useful, D. R. Dewey, *Financial History of the United States* (New York, 1909), and A. D. Noyes, *Thirty Years of American Finance* (New York, 1898). The closely related tariff question is covered by F. W. Taussig, *Tariff History of the United States* (New York, 1892), and Edward Stanwood, *American Tariff Controversies in the Nineteenth Century* (Boston, 1903). For the free-trade point of view, see Henry George, *Protection or Free Trade* (New York, 1886), and F. B. Joyner, *David A. Wells: Champion of Free Trade* (Cedar Rapids, 1939).

For the Presidents of the period, J. D. Richardson (ed.), *Messages and Papers of the Presidents* (Washington, 1898), Volumes 7 and 8, is indispensible. On Hayes, consult Harry Barnard, *Rutherford B. Hayes and His*

America (Indianapolis, 1954) ; C. R. Williams, *The Life of Rutherford Birchard Hayes* (Boston, 1914) ; C. R. Williams, *Diary and Letters of Rutherford Birchard Hayes* (Cincinnati, 1922–26) ; and T. H. Williams, *Hayes: Diary of a President, 1875–1881* (New York, 1964). On Garfield, see T. C. Smith, *Life and Letters of James Abram Garfield* (New Haven, 1925) ; R. G. Caldwell, *James A. Garfield: Party Chieftain* (New York, 1931) ; and H. J. Brown and F. D. Williams, *Diary of James A. Garfield* (East Lansing, 1967–). The standard biography of Arthur is G. F. Howe, *Chester A. Arthur* (New York, 1934).

The fullest life of Cleveland is Allan Nevins, *Grover Cleveland: A Study in Courage* (New York, 1932). H. S. Merrill, *Bourbon Leader: Grover Cleveland and the Democratic Party* (Boston, 1957), is briefer and less friendly. See also Robert McElroy, *Grover Cleveland: The Man and the Statesman* (New York, 1923), and Allan Nevins (ed.), *Letters of Grover Cleveland: 1850–1908* (Boston, 1933). The best biography of Benjamin Harrison is H. J. Sievers, *Benjamin Harrison* (Chicago and New York, 1952–68). Charles Hedges (ed.), *Speeches of Benjamin Harrison* (New York, 1892), records the man's political mentality and provides summaries of his position on major questions of the day.

Other useful biographies include N. W. Stephenson, *Nelson W. Aldrich: A Leader in American Politics* (New York, 1930) ; L. L. Sage, *William Boyd Allison: A Leader in Practical Politics* (Iowa City, 1956) ; D. S. Muzzey, *James G. Blaine: A Political Idol of Other Days* (New York, 1934) ; Gail Hamilton, *Biography of James G. Blaine* (Norwich, 1895) ; H. S. B. Beale (ed.), *Letters of Mrs. James G. Blaine* (New York, 1908) ; J. A. Barnes, *John G. Carlisle: Financial Statesman* (New York, 1931) ; L. B. Richardson, *William E. Chandler: Republican* (New York, 1940) ; A. R. Conkling, *The Life and Letters of Roscoe Conkling* (New York, 1889) ; David Lindsey, *"Sunset" Cox: Irrepressible Democrat* (Detroit, 1959) ; J. W. Neilson, *Shelby M. Cullom: Prairie State Republican* (Urbana, 1962) ; J. R. Lambert, *Arthur Pue Gorman* (Baton Rouge, 1953) ; Matilda Gresham, *The Life of Walter Quinton Gresham* (Chicago, 1919) ; Herbert Croly, *Marcus Alonzo Hanna* (New York, 1912) ; H. J. Bass, *"I Am a Democrat": The Political Career of David Bennett Hill* (Syracuse, 1961) ; Allan Nevins, *Abram S. Hewitt: With Some Account of Peter Cooper* (New York, 1935) ; C. R. Cramer, *Royal Bob: The Life of Robert G. Ingersoll* (Indianapolis, 1952) ; J. A. Garraty, *Henry Cabot Lodge: A Biography* (New York, 1953) ; Robert McElroy, *Levi P. Morton: Banker, Diplomat, and Statesman* (New York, 1930) ; W. A. Robinson, *Thomas B. Reed: Parliamentarian* (New York, 1930) ; A. C. Flick, *Samuel Jones Tilden: A Study in Political Sagacity* (New York, 1939) ; H. A. Gibbons, *John Wanamaker* (New York, 1926) ; M. D. Hirsch, *William C. Whitney: Modern Warwick* (New York, 1948) ; F. P. Summers, *William L. Wilson and Tariff Reform* (New Brunswick, 1953).

Most of the above books deal with elections and general politics, but there are additional special volumes of importance for these subjects. W. D. Burnham, *Presidential Ballots: 1836–1892* (Baltimore, 1955), is an invaluable compendium of election statistics. E. H. Roseboom, *A History of Presidential Elections* (New York, 1957), is a general survey, as is G. H. Mayer, *The Republican Party: 1854–1964* (New York, 1964). C. V. Woodward, *Reunion and Reaction* (Boston, 1951), is the best analysis of the election of 1876, and Woodward's *Origins of the New South* is on politics, as on the other topics it covers, superb. H. J. Clancy, *The Presidential Election of 1880* (Chicago, 1958), and H. C. Thomas, *The Return of the Democratic Party to Power in 1884* (New York, 1919), are routine but useful monographs. On the 1884 contest, Lee Benson, "Research Problems in American Political Historiography," in Mirra Komorovsky, (ed.), *Common Frontiers in the Social Sciences* (Glencoe, 1957), provides valuable new perspectives relative to the forces controlling the outcome.

The foreign policy of these years has received much recent attention. F. R. Dulles, *Prelude to World Power: American Diplomatic History, 1860–1900* (New York, 1965), is a good brief summary of the conventional view of the period. D. M. Pletcher, *The Awkward Years: American Foreign Relations Under Garfield and Arthur* (Columbia, Mo., 1961), is a solid monograph. Walter La Feber, *The New Empire: An Interpretation of American Expansion, 1860–1890* (Ithaca, 1963), traces the roots of American imperialism farther back into the past than earlier historians, while J. A. S. Grenville and G. B. Young, *Politics, Strategy, and American Diplomacy: Studies in Foreign Policy, 1873–1919* (New Haven, 1966), provides a series of essays throwing new light on a variety of questions. See also Merze Tate, *The United States and the Hawaiian Kingdom: A Political History* (New Haven, 1965); W. A. Armstrong, *E. L. Godkin and American Foreign Policy: 1865–1900* (New York, 1951); C. C. Tansill, *The Foreign Policy of Thomas F. Bayard: 1885–1897* (New York, 1940); and A. F. Tyler, *The Foreign Policy of James G. Blaine* (Minneapolis, 1927).

Social Thought

General works dealing with this subject include Merle Curti, *The Growth of American Thought* (New York, 1943); Louis Hartz, *The Liberal Tradition in America: An Interpretation of American Political Thought since the Revolution* (New York, 1955); and Clinton Rossiter, *Conservatism in America: The Thankless Persuasion* (New York, 1962). Sidney Fine, *Laissez Faire and the General-Welfare State: A Study of Conflict in American Thought, 1865–1901* (Ann Arbor, 1956), is both encyclopedic and perceptive, while H. S. Commager, *The American Mind: An Interpretation of American Thought and Character since the 1880's*

(New Haven, 1950), is less encyclopedic but equally perceptive and more stimulating. Other volumes of general relevance include Richard Hofstadter, *Social Darwinism in American Thought: 1860–1915* (Philadelphia, 1945); Arthur Mann, *Yankee Reformers in the Urban Age* (Cambridge, Mass., 1954); and R. G. McCloskey, *American Conservatism in the Age of Enterprise* (Cambridge, Mass., 1951).

For George, Bellamy, and Gronlund, see Henry George, *Progress and Poverty* (New York, 1879); C. A. Barker, *Henry George* (New York, 1955); Edward Bellamy, *Looking Backward: 2000–1887* (Cleveland, 1945); A. E. Morgan, *Edward Bellamy* (New York, 1944); Stow Persons (ed.), Laurence Gronlund, *The Cooperative Commonwealth* (Cambridge, Mass., 1965); and the appropriate chapters of Daniel Aaron, *Men of Good Hope: A Story of American Progressives* (New York, 1951). H. H. Quint, *The Forging of American Socialism: Origins of the Modern Movement* (Indianapolis, 1964), is also helpful. For the social-gospel movement, consult the volumes on the urban reformers in the section on urbanization, above.

The new economics is discussed in Fine's *Laissez Faire and the General-Welfare State*, but see also Volume 3 of Joseph Dorfman, *The Economic Mind in American Civilization* (New York, 1949); Jurgen Herbst, *The German Historical School in American Scholarship: A Study in the Transfer of Culture* (Ithaca, 1965); B. G. Rader, *The Academic Mind and Reform: The Influence of Richard T. Ely in American Life* (Lexington, 1967); and Joseph Dorfman's introduction to his edition of H. C. Adams, *Relation of the State to Industrial Action* (New York, 1954). On the founding of the American Economic Association, see Volume I (1887) of the *Publications* of the Association.

Lester Frank Ward's ideas can be studied in his *Dynamic Sociology* (New York, 1897) and his *Psychic Factors in Civilization* (Boston, 1906), but see also Samuel Chugarman, *Lester Frank Ward: The American Aristotle* (New York, 1965), and H. S. Commager's introduction to *Lester Frank Ward and the Welfare State* (New York, 1967). On Woodrow Wilson, see H. W. Bragdon, *Woodrow Wilson: The Academic Years* (Cambridge, Mass., 1967); William Diamond, *The Economic Thought of Woodrow Wilson* (Baltimore, 1943); Wilson's *The State* (Boston, 1889); and the early volumes of A. S. Link (ed.), *The Papers of Woodrow Wilson* (Princeton, 1966—). For trends in legal thought, see, besides O. W. Holmes, Jr., *The Common Law* (Boston, 1881), M. deW. Howe, *Justice Holmes: The Proving Years, 1870–1892* (Cambridge, Mass., 1963); A. M. Paul, *Conservative Crisis and the Rule of Law: Attitudes of Bar and Bench, 1887–1895* (Ithaca, 1960); and McCloskey's *American Conservatism*, mentioned above.

Index

Revised January, 1970

harper ✚ torchbooks

American Studies: General

HENRY STEELE COMMAGER, Ed.: The Struggle for Racial Equality   TB/1300
CARL N. DEGLER: Out of Our Past: *The Forces that Shaped Modern America*   CN/2
CARL N. DEGLER, Ed.: Pivotal Interpretations of American History
    Vol. I TB/1240;   Vol. II TB/1241
A. S. EISENSTADT, Ed.: The Craft of American History: *Selected Essays*
    Vol. I TB/1255;   Vol. II TB/1256
ROBERT L. HEILBRONER: The Limits of American Capitalism   TB/1305
JOHN HIGHAM, Ed.: The Reconstruction of American History   TB/1068
ROBERT H. JACKSON: The Supreme Court in the American System of Government   TB/1106
JOHN F. KENNEDY: A Nation of Immigrants. *Illus. Revised and Enlarged. Introduction by Robert F. Kennedy*   TB/1118
RICHARD B. MORRIS: Fair Trial: *Fourteen Who Stood Accused, from Anne Hutchinson to Alger Hiss*   TB/1335
GUNNAR MYRDAL: An American Dilemma: *The Negro Problem and Modern Democracy. Introduction by the Author.*
    Vol. I TB/1443;   Vol. II TB/1444
GILBERT OSOFSKY, Ed.: The Burden of Race: *A Documentary History of Negro-White Relations in America*   TB/1405
ARNOLD ROSE: The Negro in America: *The Condensed Version of Gunnar Myrdal's* An American Dilemma. *Second Edition* TB/3048
JOHN E. SMITH: Themes in American Philosophy: *Purpose, Experience and Community*   TB/1466
WILLIAM R. TAYLOR: Cavalier and Yankee: *The Old South and American National Character*   TB/1474

American Studies: Colonial

BERNARD BAILYN: The New England Merchants in the Seventeenth Century   TB/1149
ROBERT E. BROWN: Middle-Class Democracy and Revolution in Massachusetts, 1691–1780. *New Introduction by Author*   TB/1413
JOSEPH CHARLES: The Origins of the American Party System   TB/1049
WESLEY FRANK CRAVEN: The Colonies in Transition: 1660-1712†   TB/3084

CHARLES GIBSON: Spain in America †   TB/3077
CHARLES GIBSON, Ed.: The Spanish Tradition in America +   HR/1351
LAWRENCE HENRY GIPSON: The Coming of the Revolution: 1763-1775. † *Illus.*   TB/3007
PERRY MILLER: Errand Into the Wilderness   TB/1139
PERRY MILLER & T. H. JOHNSON, Eds.: The Puritans: *A Sourcebook of Their Writings*
    Vol. I TB/1093;   Vol. II TB/1094
EDMUND S. MORGAN: The Puritan Family: *Religion and Domestic Relations in Seventeenth Century New England*   TB/1227
WALLACE NOTESTEIN: The English People on the Eve of Colonization: 1603-1630. † *Illus.*   TB/3006
LOUIS B. WRIGHT: The Cultural Life of the American Colonies: 1607-1763. † *Illus.*   TB/3005

American Studies: The Revolution to 1860

JOHN R. ALDEN: The American Revolution: 1775-1783. † *Illus.*   TB/3011
RAY A. BILLINGTON: The Far Western Frontier: 1830-1860. † *Illus.*   TB/3012
GEORGE DANGERFIELD: The Awakening of American Nationalism, 1815-1828. † *Illus.* TB/3061
CLEMENT EATON: The Growth of Southern Civilization, 1790-1860. † *Illus.*   TB/3040
LOUIS FILLER: The Crusade against Slavery: 1830-1860. † *Illus.*   TB/3029
WILLIM W. FREEHLING: Prelude to Civil War: *The Nullification Controversy in South Carolina, 1816-1836*   TB/1359
THOMAS JEFFERSON: Notes on the State of Virginia. ‡ *Edited by Thomas P. Abernethy*   TB/3052
JOHN C. MILLER: The Federalist Era: 1789-1801. † *Illus.*   TB/3027
RICHARD B. MORRIS: The American Revolution Reconsidered   TB/1363
GILBERT OSOFSKY, Ed.: Puttin' On Ole Massa: *The Slave Narratives of Henry Bibb, William Wells Brown, and Solomon Northup* ‡   TB/1432
FRANCIS S. PHILBRICK: The Rise of the West, 1754-1830. † *Illus.*   TB/3067
MARSHALL SMELSER: The Democratic Republic, 1801-1815 †   TB/1406

---

†   The New American Nation Series, edited by Henry Steele Commager and Richard B. Morris.
‡   American Perspectives series, edited by Bernard Wishy and William E. Leuchtenburg.
a   History of Europe series, edited by J. H. Plumb.
§   The Library of Religion and Culture, edited by Benjamin Nelson.
‖   Researches in the Social, Cultural, and Behavioral Sciences, edited by Benjamin Nelson.
⅀   Harper Modern Science Series, edited by James A. Newman.
°   Not for sale in Canada.
+   Documentary History of the United States series, edited by Richard B. Morris.
#   Documentary History of Western Civilization series, edited by Eugene C. Black and Leonard W. Levy.
ʌ   The Economic History of the United States series, edited by Henry David et al.
¶   European Perspectives series, edited by Eugene C. Black.
**   Contemporary Essays series, edited by Leonard W. Levy.
*   The Stratum Series, edited by John Hale.

LOUIS B. WRIGHT: Culture on the Moving Frontier TB/1053

American Studies: The Civil War to 1900

T. C. COCHRAN & WILLIAM MILLER: The Age of Enterprise: *A Social History of Industrial America* TB/1054

W. A. DUNNING: Reconstruction, Political and Economic: 1865-1877 TB/1073

HAROLD U. FAULKNER: Politics, Reform and Expansion: 1890-1900. † *Illus.* TB/3020

GEORGE M. FREDRICKSON: The Inner Civil War: *Northern Intellectuals and the Crisis of the Union* TB/1358

JOHN A. GARRATY: The New Commonwealth, 1877-1890 † TB/1410

HELEN HUNT JACKSON: A Century of Dishonor: *The Early Crusade for Indian Reform.* † *Edited by Andrew F. Rolle* TB/3063

WILLIAM G. MCLOUGHLIN, Ed.: The American Evangelicals, 1800-1900: An Anthology ‡ TB/1382

JAMES S. PIKE: The Prostrate State: *South Carolina under Negro Government.* ‡ *Intro. by Robert F. Durden* TB/3085

VERNON LANE WHARTON: The Negro in Mississippi, 1865-1890 TB/1178

American Studies: The Twentieth Century

RAY STANNARD BAKER: Following the Color Line: *American Negro Citizenship in Progressive Era.* ‡ *Edited by Dewey W. Grantham, Jr. Illus.* TB/3053

RANDOLPH S. BOURNE: War and the Intellectuals: *Collected Essays, 1915-1919.* ‡ *Edited by Carl Resek* TB/3043

A. RUSSELL BUCHANAN: The United States and World War II. † *Illus.*
Vol. I TB/3044; Vol. II TB/3045

THOMAS C. COCHRAN: The American Business System: *A Historical Perspective, 1900-1955* TB/1080

FOSTER RHEA DULLES: America's Rise to World Power: 1898-1954. † *Illus.* TB/3021

HAROLD U. FAULKNER: The Decline of Laissez Faire, 1897-1917 TB/1397

JOHN D. HICKS: Republican Ascendancy: 1921-1933. † *Illus.* TB/3041

WILLIAM E. LEUCHTENBURG: Franklin D. Roosevelt and the New Deal: 1932-1940. † *Illus.* TB/3025

WILLIAM E. LEUCHTENBURG, Ed.: The New Deal: *A Documentary History* + HR/1354

ARTHUR S. LINK: Woodrow Wilson and the Progressive Era: 1910-1917. † *Illus.* TB/3023

BROADUS MITCHELL: Depression Decade: *From New Era through New Deal, 1929-1941* ∧ TB/1439

GEORGE E. MOWRY: The Era of Theodore Roosevelt and the Birth of Modern America: 1900-1912. † *Illus.* TB/3022

WILLIAM PRESTON, JR.: Aliens and Dissenters: TWELVE SOUTHERNERS: I'll Take My Stand: *The South and the Agrarian Tradition. Intro. by Louis D. Rubin, Jr.; Biographical Essays by Virginia Rock* TB/1072

Art, Art History, Aesthetics

ERWIN PANOFSKY: Renaissance and Renascences in Western Art. *Illus.* TB/1447

ERWIN PANOFSKY: Studies in Iconology: *Humanistic Themes in the Art of the Renaissance. 180 illus.* TB/1077

HEINRICH ZIMMER: Myths and Symbols in Indian Art and Civilization. *70 illus.* TB/2005

Asian Studies

WOLFGANG FRANKE: China and the West: *The Cultural Encounter, 13th to 20th Centuries. Trans. by R. A. Wilson* TB/1326

L. CARRINGTON GOODRICH: A Short History of the Chinese People. *Illus.* TB/3015

Economics & Economic History

C. E. BLACK: The Dynamics of Modernization: *A Study in Comparative History* TB/1321

GILBERT BURCK & EDITORS OF *Fortune:* The Computer Age: *And its Potential for Management* TB/1179

ROBERT L. HEILBRONER: The Future as History: *The Historic Currents of Our Time and the Direction in Which They Are Taking America* TB/1386

ROBERT L. HEILBRONER: The Great Ascent: *The Struggle for Economic Development in Our Time* TB/3030

FRANK H. KNIGHT: The Economic Organization TB/1214

DAVID S. LANDES: Bankers and Pashas: *International Finance and Economic Imperialism in Egypt. New Preface by the Author* TB/1412

ROBERT LATOUCHE: The Birth of Western Economy: *Economic Aspects of the Dark Ages* TB/1290

W. ARTHUR LEWIS: The Principles of Economic Planning. *New Introduction by the Author°* TB/1436

WILLIAM MILLER, Ed.: Men in Business: *Essays on the Historical Role of the Entrepreneur* TB/1081

HERBERT A. SIMON: The Shape of Automation: *For Men and Management* TB/1245

Historiography and History of Ideas

J. BRONOWSKI & BRUCE MAZLISH: The Western Intellectual Tradition: *From Leonardo to Hegel* TB/3001

WILHELM DILTHEY: Pattern and Meaning in History: *Thoughts on History and Society.° Edited with an Intro. by H. P. Rickman* TB/1075

J. H. HEXTER: More's Utopia: *The Biography of an Idea. Epilogue by the Author* TB/1195

H. STUART HUGHES: History as Art and as Science: *Twin Vistas on the Past* TB/1207

ARTHUR O. LOVEJOY: The Great Chain of Being: *A Study of the History of an Idea* TB/1009

RICHARD H. POPKIN: The History of Scepticism from Erasmus to Descartes. *Revised Edition* TB/1391

BRUNO SNELL: The Discovery of the Mind: *The Greek Origins of European Thought* TB/1018

History: General

HANS KOHN: The Age of Nationalism: *The First Era of Global History* TB/1380

BERNARD LEWIS: The Arabs in History TB/1029

BERNARD LEWIS: The Middle East and the West ° TB/1274

History: Ancient

A. ANDREWS: The Greek Tyrants TB/1103

THEODOR H. GASTER: Thespis: *Ritual Myth and Drama in the Ancient Near East* TB/1281

Vol. II: Renaissance, Enlightenment, Modern

LUDWIG WITTGENSTEIN: The Blue and Brown Books ° TB/1211
LUDWIG WITTGENSTEIN: Notebooks, 1914-1916 TB/1441

Political Science & Government

C. E. BLACK: The Dynamics of Modernization: A Study in Comparative History TB/1321
DENIS W. BROGAN: Politics in America. New Introduction by the Author TB/1469
ROBERT CONQUEST: Power and Policy in the USSR: The Study of Soviet Dynastics ° TB/1307
JOHN B. MORRALL: Political Thought in Medieval Times TB/1076
KARL R. POPPER: The Open Society and Its Enemies Vol. I: The Spell of Plato TB/1101
Vol. II: The High Tide of Prophecy: Hegel, Marx, and the Aftermath TB/1102
HENRI DE SAINT-SIMON: Social Organization, The Science of Man, and Other Writings. || Edited and Translated with an Introduction by Felix Markham TB/1152
CHARLES SCHOTTLAND, Ed.: The Welfare State ** TB/1323
JOSEPH A. SCHUMPETER: Capitalism, Socialism and Democracy TB/3008

Psychology

LUDWIG BINSWANGER: Being-in-the-World: Selected Papers. || Trans. with Intro. by Jacob Needleman TB/1365
MIRCEA ELIADE: Cosmos and History: The Myth of the Eternal Return § TB/2050
MIRCEA ELIADE: Myth and Reality TB/1369
SIGMUND FREUD: On Creativity and the Unconscious: Papers on the Psychology of Art, Literature, Love, Religion. § Intro. by Benjamin Nelson TB/45
J. GLENN GRAY: The Warriors: Reflections on Men in Battle. Introduction by Hannah Arendt TB/1294
WILLIAM JAMES: Psychology: The Briefer Course. Edited with an Intro. by Gordon Allport TB/1034

Religion: Ancient and Classical, Biblical and Judaic Traditions

MARTIN BUBER: Eclipse of God: Studies in the Relation Between Religion and Philosophy TB/12
MARTIN BUBER: Hasidism and Modern Man. Edited and Translated by Maurice Friedman TB/839
MARTIN BUBER: The Knowledge of Man. Edited with an Introduction by Maurice Friedman. Translated by Maurice Friedman and Ronald Gregor Smith TB/135
MARTIN BUBER: Moses. The Revelation and the Covenant TB/837
MARTIN BUBER: The Origin and Meaning of Hasidism. Edited and Translated by Maurice Friedman TB/835
MARTIN BUBER: The Prophetic Faith TB/73
MARTIN BUBER: Two Types of Faith: Interpenetration of Judaism and Christianity ° TB/75
M. S. ENSLIN: Christian Beginnings TB/5
M. S. ENSLIN: The Literature of the Christian Movement TB/6
HENRI FRANKFORT: Ancient Egyptian Religion: An Interpretation TB/77

Religion: Early Christianity Through Reformation

ANSELM OF CANTERBURY: Truth, Freedom, and Evil: Three Philosophical Dialogues. Edited and Translated by Jasper Hopkins and Herbert Richardson TB/317
EDGAR J. GOODSPEED: A Life of Jesus TB/1
ROBERT M. GRANT: Gnosticism and Early Christianity TB/136

Religion: Oriental Religions

TOR ANDRAE: Mohammed: The Man and His Faith § TB/62
EDWARD CONZE: Buddhism: Its Essence and Development. ° Foreword by Arthur Waley TB/58
H. G. CREEL: Confucius and the Chinese Way TB/63
FRANKLIN EDGERTON, Trans. & Ed.: The Bhagavad Gita TB/115
SWAMI NIKHILANANDA, Trans. & Ed.: The Upanishads TB/114
D. T. SUZUKI: On Indian Mahayana Buddhism. ° Ed. with Intro. by Edward Conze. TB/1403

Science and Mathematics

W. E. LE GROS CLARK: The Antecedents of Man: An Introduction to the Evolution of the Primates. ° Illus. TB/559
ROBERT E. COKER: Streams, Lakes, Ponds. Illus. TB/586
ROBERT E. COKER: This Great and Wide Sea: An Introduction to Oceanography and Marine Biology. Illus. TB/551
WILLARD VAN ORMAN QUINE: Mathematical Logic TB/558

Sociology and Anthropology

REINHARD BENDIX: Work and Authority in Industry: Ideologies of Management in the Course of Industrialization TB/3035
KENNETH B. CLARK: Dark Ghetto: Dilemmas of Social Power. Foreword by Gunnar Myrdal TB/1317
KENNETH CLARK & JEANNETTE HOPKINS: A Relevant War Against Poverty: A Study of Community Action Programs and Observable Social Change TB/1480
LEWIS COSER, Ed.: Political Sociology TB/1293
GARY T. MARX: Protest and Prejudice: A Study of Belief in the Black Community TB/1435
ROBERT K. MERTON, LEONARD BROOM, LEONARD S. COTTRELL, JR., Editors: Sociology Today: Problems and Prospects ||
Vol. I TB/1173; Vol. II TB/1174
GILBERT OSOFSKY, Ed.: The Burden of Race: A Documentary History of Negro-White Relations in America TB/1405
GILBERT OSOFSKY: Harlem: The Making of a Ghetto: Negro New York 1890-1930 ° TB/1381
PHILIP RIEFF: The Triumph of the Therapeutic: Uses of Faith After Freud TB/1360
ARNOLD ROSE: The Negro in America: The Condensed Version of Gunnar Myrdal's An American Dilemma. Second Edition TB/3048
GEORGE ROSEN: Madness in Society: Chapters in the Historical Sociology of Mental Illness. || Preface by Benjamin Nelson TB/1337
PITIRIM A. SOROKIN: Contemporary Sociological Theories: Through the First Quarter of the Twentieth Century TB/3046
FLORIAN ZNANIECKI: The Social Role of the Man of Knowledge. Introduction by Lewis A. Coser TB/1372